THE COMMUNISTIC SOCIETIES

OF

THE UNITED STATES;

OLD CHURCH.

THE MILL.

BAUMELER'S RESIDENCE.

LOG HUTS.

STREET VIEW.

VIEWS IN ZOAR.

THE COMMUNISTIC SOCIETIES

OF

THE UNITED STATES;

FROM PERSONAL VISIT AND OBSERVATION:

INCLUDING DETAILED ACCOUNTS OF THE

ECONOMISTS, ZOARITES, SHAKERS, THE AMANA, ONEIDA, BETHEL,
AURORA, ICARIAN, AND OTHER EXISTING SOCIETIES, THEIR
RELIGIOUS CREEDS, SOCIAL PRACTICES, NUMBERS,
INDUSTRIES, AND PRESENT CONDITION.

By CHARLES NORDHOFF,

AUTHOR OF

"NORTHERN CALIFORNIA, OREGON, AND THE SANDWICH ISLANDS," "CALIFORNIA:
FOR HEALTH, PLEASURE, AND RESIDENCE," ETC.

With Illustrations.

HILLARY HOUSE PUBLISHERS, Ltd.
New York

First Published 1875

Reprinted 1960
by
Hillary House Publ. Ltd.

Second impression 1961

Third impression 1962

Printed in the U.S.A.

Noble Offset Printers, Inc.
New York 3, N.Y.

TO MY FRIENDS,

DOCTOR AND MRS. JOHN DAVIS,

OF CINCINNATI.

TABLE OF CONTENTS.

LIST OF ILLUSTRATIONS.

INTRODUCTION.

THOUGH it is probable that for a long time to come the mass of mankind in civilized countries will find it both necessary and advantageous to labor for wages, and to accept the condition of hired laborers (or, as it has absurdly become the fashion to say, employés), every thoughtful and kind-hearted person must regard with interest any device or plan which promises to enable at least the more intelligent, enterprising, and determined part of those who are not capitalists to become such, and to cease to labor for hire.

Nor can any one doubt the great importance, both to the security of the capitalists, and to the intelligence and happiness of the non-capitalists (if I may use so awkward a word), of increasing the number of avenues to independence for the latter. For the character and conduct of our own population in the United States show conclusively that nothing so stimulates intelligence in the poor, and at the same time nothing so well enables them to bear the inconveniences of their lot, as a reasonable prospect that with industry and economy they may raise themselves out of the condition of hired laborers into that of independent employers of their own labor. Take away entirely the grounds of such a hope, and a great mass of our poorer people would gradually sink into stupidity, and a blind discontent which education would only increase, until they became a danger to the state; for the greater their intelligence, the greater would be the dissatisfaction with their situation— just as we see that the dissemination of education among the

English agricultural laborers (by whom, of all classes in Christendom, independence is least to be hoped for), has lately aroused these sluggish beings to strikes and a struggle for a change in their condition.

Hitherto, in the United States, our cheap and fertile lands have acted as an important safety-valve for the enterprise and discontent of our non-capitalist population. Every hired workman knows that if he chooses to use economy and industry in his calling, he may without great or insurmountable difficulty establish himself in independence on the public lands; and, in fact, a large proportion of our most energetic and intelligent mechanics do constantly seek these lands, where with patient toil they master nature and adverse circumstances, often make fortunate and honorable careers, and at the worst leave their children in an improved condition of life. I do not doubt that the eagerness of some of our wisest public men for the acquisition of new territory has arisen from their conviction that this opening for the independence of laboring men was essential to the security of our future as a free and peaceful state. For, though not one in a hundred, or even one in a thousand of our poorer and so-called laboring class may choose to actually achieve independence by taking up and tilling a portion of the public lands, it is plain that the knowledge that any one may do so makes those who do not more contented with their lot, which they thus feel to be one of choice and not of compulsion.

Any circumstance, as the exhaustion of these lands, which should materially impair this opportunity for independence, would be, I believe, a serious calamity to our country; and the spirit of the Trades-Unions and International Societies appears to me peculiarly mischievous and hateful, because they seek to eliminate from the thoughts of their adherents the hope or expectation of independence. The member of a Trades-Union is taught to regard himself, and to act toward society, as a hireling for life; and these societies are united, not as men seeking a way to exchange dependence for independence, but as hirelings, determined to remain such, and only demanding better conditions of their masters. If it were possible to infuse with this spirit all or the greater part of the non-capitalist class in the United States, this would, I believe, be one of the gravest calamities which could befall us as a nation; for it would degrade the mass of our voters, and make free government here very difficult, if it did not entirely change the form of our government, and expose us to lasting disorders and attacks upon property.

We see already that in whatever part of our country the Trades-Union leaders have succeeded in imposing themselves upon mining or manufacturing operatives, the results are—the corruption of our politics, a lowering of the standard of intelligence and independence among the laborers, and an unreasoning and unreasonable discontent, which, in its extreme development, despises right, and seeks only changes degrading to its own class, at the cost of injury and loss to the general public.

The Trades-Unions and International Clubs have become a formidable power in the United States and Great Britain, but so far it is a power almost entirely for evil. They have been able to disorganize labor, and to alarm capital. They have succeeded, in a comparatively few cases, in temporarily increasing the wages and in diminishing the hours of labor in certain branches of industry—a benefit so limited, both as to duration and amount, that it can not justly be said to have inured to the general advantage of the non-capitalist class. On the other hand, they have debased the character and lowered the moral tone of their membership by the narrow and cold-blooded selfishness of their spirit and doctrines, and have thus done an incalculable harm to society; and, moreover, they have, by alarming capital, lessened the wages fund, seriously checked enterprise, and thus decreased the general prosperity of their own class. For it is plain that to no one in society is the abundance of capital and its free and secure use in all kinds of enterprises so vitally important as to the laborer for wages —to the Trades-Unionist.

To assert necessary and eternal enmity between labor and capital would seem to be the extreme of folly in men who have predetermined to remain laborers for wages all their lives, and who therefore mean to be peculiarly dependent on capital. Nor are the Unions wiser or more reasonable toward their fellow-laborers; for each Union aims, by limiting the number of apprentices a master may take, and by other equally selfish regulations, to protect its own members against competition, forgetting apparently that if you prevent men from becoming bricklayers, a greater number must seek to become carpenters; and that thus, by its exclusive policy, a Union only plays what Western gamblers call a " cut-throat game " with the general laboring population. For if the system of Unions were perfect, and each were able to enforce its policy of exclusion, a great mass of poor creatures, driven from every desirable employment, would be forced to crowd into the lowest and least paid. I do not know where one could find so much ignorance, contempt for established principles, and cold-blooded selfishness, as among the Trades-Unions and International Societies of the United States and Great Britain—unless one should go to France. While they retain their present spirit, they might well take as their motto the brutal and stupid saying of a French writer, that " Mankind are engaged in a war for bread, in which every man's hand is at his brother's throat." Directly, they offer a prize to incapacity and robbery, compelling their ablest members to do no more than the least able, and spoiling the aggregate wealth of society by burdensome regulations restricting labor. Logically, to the Trades-Union leaders the Chicago or Boston fire seemed a more beneficial

event than the invention of the steam-engine; for plenty seems
to them a curse, and scarcity the greatest blessing.*

---

* Lest I should to some readers appear to use too strong language, I
append here a few passages from a recent English work, Mr. Thornton's
book " On Labor," where he gives an account of some of the regulations
of English Trades-Unions:

" A journeyman is not permitted to teach his own son his own trade,
nor, if the lad managed to learn the trade by stealth, would he be permitted to practice it. A master, desiring out of charity to take as ap-
prentice one of the eight destitute orphans of a widowed mother, has been
told by his men that if he did they would strike. A bricklayer's assistant who by looking on has learned to lay bricks as well as his principal,
is generally doomed, nevertheless, to continue a laborer for life. He will
never rise to the rank of a bricklayer, if those who have already attained
that dignity can help it."

" Some Unions divide the country round them into districts, and will
not permit the products of the trades controlled by them to be used except within the district in which they have been fabricated. . . . At Manchester this combination is particularly effective, preventing any bricks
made beyond a radius of four miles from entering the city. To enforce
the exclusion, paid agents are employed; every cart of bricks coming toward Manchester is watched, and if the contents be found to have come
from without the prescribed boundary the bricklayers at once refuse to
work. . . . The vagaries of the Lancashire brickmakers are fairly paral-
leled by the masons of the same county. Stone, when freshly quarried, is
softer, and can be more easily cut than later: men habitually employed
about any particular quarry better understand the working of its particular stone than men from a distance; there is great economy, too, in trans-
porting stone dressed instead of in rough blocks. The Yorkshire masons,
however, will not allow Yorkshire stone to be brought into their district
if worked on more than one side. All the rest of the working, the edg-
ing and jointing, they insist on doing themselves, though they thereby
add thirty-five per cent. to its price. . . . A Bradford contractor, requiring
for a staircase some steps of hard delf-stone, a material which Bradford
masons so much dislike that they often refuse employment rather than
undertake it, got the steps worked at the quarry. But when they arrived
ready for setting, his masons insisted on their being worked over again,
at an expense of from 5s. to 10s. per step. A master-mason at Ashton obtained some stone ready polished from a quarry near Macclesfield. His
men, however, in obedience to the rules of their club, refused to fix it until the polished part had been defaced and they had polished it again by
hand, though not so well as at first. . . . In one or two of the northern
counties, the associated plasterers and associated plasterers' laborers have
come to an understanding, according to which the latter are to abstain
from all plasterers' work except simple whitewashing; and the plasterers
in return are to do nothing except pure plasterers' work, that the laborers would like to do for them, insomuch that if a plasterer wants laths or
plaster to go on with, he must not go and fetch them himself, but must
send a laborer for them. In consequence of this agreement, a Mr. Booth,
of Bolton, having sent one of his plasterers to bed and point a dozen windows, had to place a laborer with him during the whole of the four days
he was engaged on the job, though any body could have brought him all

Any organization which teaches its adherents to accept as inevitable for themselves and for the mass of a nation the condition of hirelings, and to conduct their lives on that premise, is not only wrong, but an injury to the community. Mr. Mill wisely says on this point, in his chapter on " The Future of the Laboring Classes:" " There can be little doubt that the *status* of hired laborers will gradually tend to confine itself to the description of work-people whose low moral qualities render them unfit for any thing more independent; and that the relation of masters and work-people will be gradually superseded by partnership in one of two forms: in some cases, association of the laborers with the capitalist; in others, and perhaps finally in all, association of laborers among themselves." I imagine that the change he speaks of will be very slow and gradual; but it is important that all doors shall be left open for it, and Trades-Unions would close every door.

Professor Cairnes, in his recent contribution to Political Economy, goes further even than Mr. Mill, and argues that a change of this nature is inevitable. He remarks: " The modifications which occur in the distribution of capital among its several departments, as nations advance, are by no means fortuitous, but follow on the whole a well-defined course, and move toward a determinate goal. In effect, what we find is a constant growth of the national capital, accompanied with a nearly equally constant decline in the proportion of this capital which goes to support productive labor. . . . Though the fund for the remuneration of mere labor, whether skilled or unskilled, must, so long as industry is progressive, ever bear a

---

he required in half a day. . . . At Liverpool, a bricklayer's laborer may legally carry as many as twelve bricks at a time. Elsewhere ten is the greatest number allowed. But at Leeds 'any brother in the Union professing to carry more than the common number, which is eight bricks, shall be fined 1*s.*;' and any brother 'knowing the same without giving the earliest information thereof to the committee of management shall be fined the same.' . . . During the building of the Manchester Law Courts, the bricklayers' laborers struck because they were desired to wheel bricks instead of carrying them on their shoulders."

constantly diminishing proportion alike to the growing wealth and growing capital, there is nothing in the nature of things which restricts the laboring population to this fund for their support. In return, indeed, for their mere labor, it is to this that they must look for their sole reward; but *they may help production otherwise than by their labor : they may save, and thus become themselves the owners of capital;* and profits may thus be brought to aid the wages-fund."*

Aside from systematized emigration to unsettled or thinly peopled regions, which the Trades-Unions of Europe ought to organize on a great scale, but which they have entirely neglected, the other outlets for the mass of dissatisfied hand-laborers lie through co-operative or communistic efforts. Co-operative societies flourish in England and Germany. We have had a number of them in this country also, but their success has not been marked; and I have found it impossible to get statistical returns even of their numbers. If the Trades-Unions had used a tenth of the money they have wasted in futile efforts to shorten hours of labor and excite their members to hatred, indolence, and waste, in making public the statistics and the possibilities of co-operation, they would have achieved some positive good.

But while co-operative efforts have generally failed in the United States, we have here a number of successful Communistic Societies, pursuing agriculture and different branches of manufacturing, and I have thought it useful to examine these, to see if their experience offers any useful hints toward the solution of the labor question. Hitherto very little, indeed almost nothing definite and precise, has been made known concerning these societies; and Communism remains loudly but very vaguely spoken of, by friends as well as enemies, and is commonly a word either of terror or of contempt in the public prints.

* "Some Leading Principles of Political Economy newly expounded." By J. E. Cairnes, M.A. New York, Harper & Brothers.

In the following pages will be found, accordingly, an account of the COMMUNISTIC SOCIETIES now existing in the United States, made from personal visit and careful examination; and including for each its social customs and expedients; its practical and business methods; its system of government; the industries it pursues; its religious creed and practices; as well as its present numbers and condition, and its history.

It appears to me an important fact that these societies, composed for the most part of men originally farmers or mechanics—people of very limited means and education—have yet succeeded in accumulating considerable wealth, and at any rate a satisfactory provision for their own old age and disability, and for the education of their children or successors. In every case they have developed among their membership very remarkable business ability, considering their original station in life; they have found among themselves leaders wise enough to rule, and skill sufficient to enable them to establish and carry on, not merely agricultural operations, but also manufactures, and to conduct successfully complicated business affairs.

Some of these societies have existed fifty, some twenty-five, and some for nearly eighty years. All began with small means; and some are now very wealthy.

Moreover, while some of these communes are still living under the guidance of their founders, others, equally successful, have continued to prosper for many years after the death of their original leaders. Some are celibate; but others inculcate, or at least permit marriage. Some gather their members into a common or "unitary" dwelling; but others, with no less success, maintain the family relation and the separate household.

It seemed to me that the conditions of success vary sufficiently among these societies to make their histories at least interesting, and perhaps important. I was curious, too, to ascertain if their success depended upon obscure conditions, not gener-

ally attainable, as extraordinary ability in a leader ; or unde-
sirable, as religious fanaticism or an unnatural relation of the
sexes ; or whether it might not appear that the conditions absolutely necessary to success were only such as any company
of carefully selected and reasonably determined men and
women might hope to command.

I desired also to discover how the successful Communists
had met and overcome the difficulties of idleness, selfishness,
and unthrift in individuals, which are commonly believed to
make Communism impossible, and which are well summed
up in the following passage in Mr. Mill's chapter on Communism :

" The objection ordinarily made to a system of community of property
and equal distribution of the produce, that each person would be incessantly occupied in evading his fair share of the work, points, undoubtedly, to a real difficulty. But those who urge this objection forget to
how great an extent the same difficulty exists under the system on which
nine tenths of the business of society is now conducted. The objection
supposes that honest and efficient labor is only to be had from those who
are themselves individually to reap the benefit of their own exertions.
But how small a part of all the labor performed in England, from the
lowest paid to the highest, is done by persons working for their own
benefit. From the Irish reaper or hodman to the chief justice or the
minister of state, nearly all the work of society is remunerated by day
wages or fixed salaries. A factory operative has less personal interest in
his work than a member of a Communist association, since he is not, like
him, working for a partnership of which he is himself a member. It will
no doubt be said that, though the laborers themselves have not, in most
cases, a personal interest in their work, they are watched and superintended, and their labor directed, and the mental part of the labor performed, by persons who have. Even this, however, is far from being universally the fact. In all public, and many of the largest and most successful private undertakings, not only the labors of detail, but the control
and superintendence are intrusted to salaried officers. And though the
' master's eye,' when the master is vigilant and intelligent, is of proverbial
value, it must be remembered that in a Socialist farm or manufactory,
each laborer would be under the eye, not of one master, but of the whole

community. In the extreme case of obstinate perseverance in not performing the due share of work, the community would have the same resources which society now has for compelling conformity to the necessary conditions of the association. Dismissal, the only remedy at present, is no remedy when any other laborer who may be engaged does no better than his predecessor: the power of dismissal only enables an employer to obtain from his workmen the customary amount of labor, but that customary labor may be of any degree of inefficiency. Even the laborer who loses his employment by idleness or negligence has nothing worse to suffer, in the most unfavorable case, than the discipline of a workhouse, and if the desire to avoid this be a sufficient motive in the one system, it would be sufficient in the other. I am not undervaluing the strength of the incitement given to labor when the whole or a large share of the benefit of extra exertion belongs to the laborer. But under the present system of industry this incitement, in the great majority of cases, does not exist. If communistic labor might be less vigorous than that of a peasant proprietor, or a workman laboring on his own account, it would probably be more energetic than that of a laborer for hire, who has no personal interest in the matter at all. The neglect by the uneducated classes of laborers for hire of the duties which they engage to perform is in the present state of society most flagrant. Now it is an admitted condition of the communist scheme that all shall be educated; and this being supposed, the duties of the members of the association would doubtless be as diligently performed as those of the generality of salaried officers in the middle or higher classes; who are not supposed to be necessarily unfaithful to their trust, because so long as they are not dismissed their pay is the same in however lax a manner their duty is fulfilled. Undoubtedly, as a general rule, remuneration by fixed salaries does not in any class of functionaries produce the maximum of zeal; and this is as much as can be reasonably alleged against communistic labor.

"That even this inferiority would necessarily exist is by no means so certain as is assumed by those who are little used to carry their minds beyond the state of things with which they are familiar. . . .

"Another of the objections to Communism is similar to that so often urged against poor-laws: that if every member of the community were assured of subsistence for himself and any number of children, on the sole condition of willingness to work, prudential restraint on the multiplication of mankind would be at an end, and population would start forward at a rate which would reduce the community through successive stages of increasing discomfort to actual starvation. There would certainly be much ground for this apprehension if Communism provided no motives to restraint, equivalent to those which it would take away. But Communism is precisely the state of things in which opinion might be expected to declare itself with greatest intensity against this kind of selfish intemperance. Any augmentation of numbers which diminished the comfort or increased the toil of the mass would then cause (which now it does not) immediate and unmistakable inconvenience to every individual in the association—inconvenience which could not then be imputed to the avarice of employers or the unjust privileges of the rich. In such altered circumstances opinion could not fail to reprobate, and if reprobation did not suffice, to repress by penalties of some description, this or any other culpable self-indulgence at the expense of the community. The communistic scheme, instead of being peculiarly open to the objection drawn from danger of over-population, has the recommendation of tending in an especial degree to the prevention of that evil."

It will be seen in the following pages that means have been found to meet these and other difficulties; in one society even the prudential restraint upon marriage has been adopted.

Finally, I wished to see what the successful Communists had made of their lives; what was the effect of communal living upon the character of the individual man and woman; whether the life had broadened or narrowed them; and whether assured fortune and pecuniary independence had brought to them a desire for beauty of surroundings and broader intelligence: whether, in brief, the Communist had any where become something more than a comfortable and independent day-laborer, and aspired to something higher than a mere bread-and-butter existence.

To make my observations I was obliged to travel from Maine in the northeast to Kentucky in the south, and Oregon in the west. I have thought it best to give at first an impartial and not unfriendly account of each commune, or organized system of communes; and in several concluding chapters I have analyzed and compared their different customs and practices, and attempted to state what, upon the facts presented, seem to be the conditions absolutely requisite to the successful conduct of a communistic society, and also what appear to be the influences, for good and evil, of such bodies upon their members and upon their neighbors.

I have added some particulars of the Swedish Commune which lately existed at Bishop Hill, in Illinois, but which, after a flourishing career of seven years, has now become extinct; and I did this to show, in a single example, what are the causes which work against harmony and success in such a society.

Also I have given some particulars concerning three examples of colonization, which, though they do not properly belong to my subject, are yet important, as showing what may be accomplished by co-operative efforts in agriculture, under prudent management.

It is, I suppose, hardly necessary to say that, while I have given an impartial and respectful account of the religious faith of each commune, I am not therefore to be supposed to hold with any of them. For instance, I thought it interesting to give some space to the very singular phenomena called "spiritual manifestations" among the Shakers; but I am not what is commonly called a " Spiritualist."

MAP SHOWING LOCATION OF COMMUNISTIC SOCIETIES.

Fisk & See, N.Y.

EXPLANATION

SHAKERS, locations
represented thus .... *
PERFECTIONISTS .... ☀
HARMONISTS .... ⚭
SEPARATISTS .... ▣
INSPIRATIONISTS .... ☀
OTHER COMMUNES .... ☩
STATE CAPITAL .... ◉

WASHINGTON
OREGON
IDAHO
PACIFIC OCEAN
Columbia R.
Willamette R.
Umpqua R.
Malheur R.
Snake or Lewis R.
PORTLAND
SALEM
Aurora Commune
Roseburg

MINNESOTA
IOWA
MISSOURI
ILLINOIS
WISCONSIN
JEFFERSON CY.
Icaria Commune
Des Moines Commune
Bethel Commune
Amana Inspirationists
Des Moines R.
Missouri R.
Mississippi R.
St. Louis
SPRINGFIELD
CHICAGO
Illinois R.
Wabash R.

INDIANA
OHIO
KENTUCKY
WEST VIRGINIA
VIRGINIA
MICHIGAN
Pleasant Hill
South Union
Watervliet
White Water
Union Village
INDIANAPOLIS
White R.
Ohio R.
FRANKFORT
CINCINNATI
COLUMBUS
Zoar Separatists
North Union
CLEVELAND
TOLEDO
DETROIT
LANSING

PENNSYLVANIA
Economy Harmonists
Williamsport
HARRISBURG
PITTSBURGH
PHILADELPHIA
BALTIMORE
WASHINGTON
RICHMOND
NORFOLK
MARYLAND
DEL.
N. JERSEY
Potomac R.
James R.

ONTARIO
NEW YORK
TORONTO
BUFFALO
Groveland
Oneida Perfectionists
Wallingford
New Lebanon
ALBANY
Hudson R.
Waterville
OTTAWA
Ottawa R.
St. Lawrence R.
MONTREAL

VERMONT
N. HAMPSHIRE
MASS.
MAINE
CONN.
R.I.
HARTFORD
Enfield
Shirley
Tyringham
Harvard
New Gloucester
Alfred
Canterbury
CONCORD
Connecticut R.
Merrimac R.

LAKE ERIE
LAKE ONTARIO
LAKE HURON
LAKE MICHIGAN
Brocton

ATLANTIC OCEAN

THE INSPIRATIONISTS,

AT

AMANA, IOWA.

THE AMANA COMMUNITY.

I.

THE "True Inspiration Congregations," as they call themselves (" *Wahre Inspiration's Gemeinden* "), form a communistic society in Iowa, seventy-four miles west of Davenport.

The society has at this time 1450 members; owns about 25,000 acres of land; lives on this land in seven different small towns; carries on agriculture and manufactures of several kinds, and is highly prosperous.

Its members are all Germans.

The base of its organization is religion; they are pietists; and their religious head, at present a woman, is supposed by them to speak by direct inspiration of God. Hence they call themselves "Inspirationists."

They came from Germany in the year 1842, and settled at first near Buffalo, on a large tract of land which they called Eben-Ezer. Here they prospered greatly; but feeling the need of more land, in 1855 they began to remove to their present home in Iowa.

They have printed a great number of books—more than one hundred volumes; and in some of these the history of their peculiar religious belief is carried back to the beginning of the last century. They continue to receive from Germany accessions to their numbers, and often pay out of their common treasury the expenses of poor families who recommend themselves to the society by letters, and whom their inspired leader declares to be worthy.

They seem to have conducted their pecuniary affairs with eminent prudence and success.

II.—HISTORICAL.

The "Work of Inspiration" is said to have begun far back in the eighteenth century. I have a volume, printed in 1785, which is called the "Thirty-sixth Collection of the Inspirational Records," and gives an account of "Brother John Frederick Rock's journeys and visits in the year 1719, wherein are recorded numerous utterances of the Spirit by his word of mouth to the faithful in Constance, Schaffhausen, Zurich, and other places."

They admit, I believe, that the "Inspiration" died out from time to time, but was revived as the congregations became more godly. In 1749, in 1772, and in 1776 there were especial demonstrations. Finally, in the year 1816, Michael Krausert, a tailor of Strasburg, became what they call an "instrument" (*werkzeug*), and to him were added several others: Philip Mörschel, a stocking-weaver, and a German; Christian Metz, a carpenter; and finally, in 1818, Barbara Heynemann, a "poor and illiterate servant-maid," an Alsacian ("*eine arme ganz ungelehrte Dienstmagd*").

Metz, who was for many years, and until his death in 1867, the spiritual head of the society, wrote an account of the society from the time he became an "instrument" until the removal to Iowa. From this, and from a volume of Barbara Heynemann's inspired utterances, I gather that the congregations did not hesitate to criticise, and very sharply, the conduct of their spiritual leaders; and to depose them, and even expel them for cause. Moreover, they recount in their books, without disguise, all their misunderstandings. Thus it is recorded of Barbara Heynemann that in 1820 she was con-

demned to expulsion from the society, and her earnest entreat-
ies only sufficed to obtain consent that she should serve as a
maid in the family of one of the congregation; but even then
it was forbidden her to come to the meetings. Her exclusion
seems, however, to have lasted but a few months. Metz, in his
"Historical Description," relates that this trouble fell upon
Barbara because she had too friendly an eye upon the young
men; and there are several notices of her desire to marry, as,
for instance, under date of August, 1822, where it is related
that "the Enemy" tempted her again with a desire to marry
George Landmann; but "the Lord showed through Brother
Rath, and also to her own conscience, that this step was
against his holy will, and accordingly they did not marry,
but did repent concerning it, and the Lord's grace was once
more given her." But, like Jacob, she seems to have wrestled
with the Lord, for later she did marry George Landmann,
and, though they were for a while under censure, she regained
her old standing as an "inspired instrument," came over to
the United States with her husband, was for many years the
assistant of Metz, and since his death has been the inspired
oracle of Amana.

In the year 1822 the congregations appear to have attracted
the attention of the English Quakers, for I find a notice that
in December of that year they were visited by William Allen,
a Quaker minister from London, who seems to have been a
man of wealth. He inquired concerning their religious faith,
and told them that he and his brethren at home were also subject to inspiration. He persuaded them to hold a meeting, at
which by his desire they read the 14th chapter of John; and
he told them that it was probable he would be moved of the
Lord to speak to them. But when they had read the chapter,
and while they waited for the Quaker's inspiration, Barbara
Heynemann was moved to speak. At this Allen became im-
patient and left the meeting; and in the evening he told the

brethren that the Quaker inspiration was as real as their own,
but that they did not write down what was spoken by their
preachers; whereto he received for reply that it was not necessary, for it was evident that the Quakers had not the real inspiration, nor the proper and consecrated "instruments" to declare the will of the Lord; and so the Quaker went away on
his journey home, apparently not much edified.

The congregations were much scattered in Germany, and
it appears to have been the habit of the "inspired instruments" to travel from one to the other, deliver messages from
on high, and inquire into the spiritual condition of the faithful. Under the leadership of Christian Metz and several others,
between 1825 and 1839 a considerable number of their followers were brought together at a place called Armenburg,
where manufactures gave them employment, and here they
prospered, but fell into trouble with the government because
they refused to take oaths and to send their children to the
public schools, which were under the rule of the clergy.

In 1842 it was revealed to Christian Metz that all the congregations should be gathered together, and be led far away
out of their own country. Later, America was pointed out as
their future home. To a meeting of the elders it was revealed who should go to seek out a place for settlement; and Metz
relates in his brief history that one Peter Mook wanted to be
among these pioneers, and was dissatisfied because he was not
among those named; and as Mook insisted on going, a message
came the next day from God, in which he told them they
might go or stay as they pleased, but if they remained in Germany it would be "at their own risk;" and as Mook was not
even named in this message, he concluded to remain at home.

Metz and four others sailed in September, 1842, for New
York. They found their way to Buffalo; and there, on the advice of the late Mr. Dorsheimer, from whom they received
much kindness, bought five thousand acres of the old Seneca

GRACE BEFORE MEAT—AMANA.

SCHOOL-HOUSE—AMANA.

Indian reservation at ten dollars per acre. To this they added later nearly as much more. Parts of this estate now lie within the corporate limits of Buffalo; and though they sold out and removed to the West before the land attained its present value, the purchase was a most fortunate one for them. Metz records that they had much trouble at first with the Indians; but they overcame this and other difficulties, and by industry and ingenuity soon built up comfortable homes. Three hundred and fifty persons were brought out in the first year, two hundred and seventeen in 1844; and their numbers were increased rapidly, until they had over one thousand people in their different villages.

Between 1843 and 1855, when they began to remove to Iowa, they turned their purchase at Eben-Ezer (as they called the place) into a garden. I visited the locality last year, and found there still the large, substantial houses, the factories, churches, and shops which they built. Street cars now run where they found only a dense forest; and the eight thousand acres which they cleared are now fertile fields and market-gardens. Another population of Germans has succeeded the Amana Society; their churches now have steeples, and there is an occasional dram-shop; but the present residents speak of their predecessors with esteem and even affection, and in one of the large stores I found the products of the Iowa society regularly sold. A few of the former members still live on the old purchase.

They appear to have had considerable means from the first. Among the members were several persons of wealth, who contributed large sums to the common stock. I was told that one person gave between fifty and sixty thousand dollars; and others gave sums of from two to twenty thousand dollars.

They were not Communists in Germany; and did not, I was told, when they first emigrated, intend to live in community. Among those who came over in the first year were some families who had been accustomed to labor in factories. To these the agricultural life was unpleasant, and it was thought advisable to set up a woolen factory to give them employment. This was the first difficulty which stared them in the face. They had intended to live simply as a Christian congregation or church, but the necessity which lay upon them of looking to the temporal welfare of all the members forced them presently to think of putting all their means into a common stock.

Seeing that some of the brethren did not take kindly to agricultural labor, and that if they insisted upon a purely agricultural settlement they would lose many of their people, they determined that each should, as far as possible, have employment at the work to which he was accustomed. They began to build workshops, but, to carry these on successfully, they had business tact enough to see that it was necessary to do so by a general contribution of means.

"We were commanded at this time, by inspiration, to put all our means together and live in community," said one to me; "and we soon saw that we could not have got on or kept together on any other plan."

Eben-Ezer is a wide plain; and there, as now in Iowa, they settled their people in villages, which they called "Upper," "Lower," and "Middle" Eben-Ezer. From the large size of many of the houses, I imagine they had there, commonly, several families in one dwelling. At Amana each family has its own house; otherwise their customs were similar to those still retained in Iowa, which I shall describe in their proper place.

In 1854 they were "commanded by inspiration" to remove to the West. They selected Iowa as their new home, because land was cheap there; and in 1855, having made a purchase, they sent out a detachment to prepare the way.

It is a remarkable evidence of the prudence and ability with which they conduct their business affairs, that they were able to sell out the whole of their eight-thousand-acre tract near Buffalo, with all their improvements, without loss. Usually such a sale is extremely difficult, because the buildings of a

communistic society have peculiarities which detract from
their value for individual uses. The Rappists, who sold out
twice, were forced to submit to heavy loss each time. I do not
doubt that several of the northern Shaker societies would have
removed before this to a better soil and climate but for the
difficulty of selling their possessions at a fair price.

The removal from Eben-Ezer to Amana, however, required
ten years. As they found purchasers in one place they sent
families to the other; meantime they do not appear to have
found it difficult to maintain their organization in both.

III.—AMANA—1874.

" The name we took out of the Bible," said one of the officers
of the society to me. They put the accent on the first syllable.
The name occurs in the Song of Solomon, the fourth chapter
and eighth verse : " Come with me from Lebanon, my spouse,
with me from Lebanon : look from the top of Amana, from
the top of Shenir and Hermon, from the lions' dens, from the
mountains of the leopards."

Amana in Iowa, however, is not a mountain, but an extensive plain, upon which they have built seven villages, conveniently placed so as to command the cultivated land, and to
form an irregular circle within their possessions. In these
villages all the people live, and they are thus divided :

Name.	Popula-tion.	Business.
Amana....	450	Woolen-mill, saw and grist mill, and farming.
East Amana...........	125	Farming.
Middle Amana...	350	Woolen-mill and farming.
Amana near the Hill....	125	Farming, saw-mill, and tannery.
West Amana..........	150	Grist-mill and farming.
South Amana.........	150	Saw-mill and farming.
Homestead............	135	Railroad station, a saw-mill, farm-ing, and general dépôt.

The villages lie about a mile and a half apart, and each has a store at which the neighboring farmers trade, and a tavern or inn for the accommodation of the general public. Each village has also its shoemakers', carpenters', tailors', and other shops, for they aim to produce and make, as far as possible, all that they use. In Middle Amana there is a printing-office, where their books are made.

The villages consist usually of one straggling street, outside of which lie the barns, and the mills, factories, and work-shops. The houses are well built, of brick, stone, or wood, very plain; each with a sufficient garden, but mostly stand-ing immediately on the street. They use no paint, believing that the wood lasts as well without. There is usually a nar-row sidewalk of boards or brick; and the school-house and church are notable buildings only because of their greater size. Like the Quakers, they abhor "steeple-houses;" and their church architecture is of the plainest. The barns and other farm buildings are roomy and convenient. On the boundaries of a village are usually a few houses inhabited by hired laborers.

Each family has a house for itself; though when a young couple marry, they commonly go to live with the parents of one or the other for some years.

As you walk through a village, you notice that at irregular intervals are houses somewhat larger than the rest. These are either cook-houses or prayer-houses. The people eat in common, but for convenience' sake they are divided, so that a certain number eat together. For Amana, which has 450 people, there are fifteen such cooking and eating houses. In these the young women are employed to work under the super-vision of matrons; and hither when the bell rings come those who are appointed to eat at each—the sexes sitting at separate tables, and the children also by themselves.

"Why do you separate men from women at table?" I asked.

" To prevent silly conversation and trifling conduct," was the answer.

Food is distributed to the houses according to the number of persons eating in each. Meal and milk are brought to the doors; and each cooking-house is required to make its own butter and cheese. For those whom illness or the care of small children keeps at home, the food is placed in neat baskets; and it was a curious sight to see, when the dinner-bell rang, a number of women walking rapidly about the streets with these baskets, each nicely packed with food.

When the bell ceases ringing and all are assembled, they stand up in their places in silence for half a minute, then one says grace, and when he ends, all say, " God bless and keep us safely," and then sit down. There is but little conversation at table; the meal is eaten rapidly, but with decorum; and at its close, all stand up again, some one gives thanks, and thereupon they file out with quiet order and precision.

They live well, after the hearty German fashion, and bake excellent bread. The table is clean, but it has no cloth. The dishes are coarse but neat; and the houses, while well built, and possessing all that is absolutely essential to comfort according to the German peasants' idea, have not always carpets, and have often a bed in what New-Englanders would call the parlor; and in general are for use and not ornament.

They breakfast between six and half-past six, according to the season, have supper between six and seven, and dinner at half-past eleven. They have besides an afternoon lunch of bread and butter and coffee, and in summer a forenoon lunch of bread, to which they add beer or wine, both home-made.

They do not forbid tobacco.

Each business has its foreman; and these leaders in each village meet together every evening, to concert and arrange the labors of the following day. Thus if any department needs for an emergency an extra force, it is known, and the proper persons are warned. The trustees select the temporal foremen, and give to each from time to time his proper charge, appointing him also his helpers. Thus a member showed me his "ticket," by which he was appointed to the care of the cows, with the names of those who were to assist him. In the summer, and when the work requires it, a large force is turned into the fields; and the women labor with the men in the harvest. The workmen in the factories are, of course, not often changed.

The children are kept at school between the ages of six and thirteen; the sexes do not sit in separate rooms. The school opens at seven o'clock, and the children study and recite until half-past nine. From that hour until eleven, when they are dismissed for dinner, they knit gloves, wristlets, or stockings. At one o'clock school reopens, and they once more attend to lessons until three, from which hour till half-past four they knit again. The teachers are men, but they are relieved by women when the labor-school begins. Boys as well as girls are required to knit. One of the teachers said to me that this work kept them quiet, gave them habits of industry, and kept them off the streets and from rude plays.

They instruct the children in musical notation, but do not allow musical instruments. They give only the most elementary instruction, the "three Rs," but give also constant drill in the Bible and in the Catechism. "Why should we let our youth study? We need no lawyers or preachers; we have already three doctors. What they need is to live holy lives, to learn God's commandments out of the Bible, to learn submission to his will, and to love him."

The dress of the people is plain. The men wear in the winter a vest which buttons close up to the throat, coat and trousers being of the common cut.

The women and young girls wear dingy colored stuffs, mostly of the society's own make, cut in the plainest style, and often short gowns, in the German peasant way. All, even to the very small girls, wear their hair in a kind of black cowl or cap, which covers only the back of the head, and is tied under the chin by a black ribbon. Also all, young as well as old, wear a small dark-colored shawl or handkerchief over the shoulders, and pinned very plainly across the breast. This peculiar uniform adroitly conceals the marks of sex, and gives a singularly monotonous appearance to the women.

The sex, I believe, is not highly esteemed by these people, who think it dangerous to the Christian's peace of mind. One of their most esteemed writers advises men to " fly from intercourse with women, as a very highly dangerous magnet and magical fire." Their women work hard and dress soberly; all ornaments are forbidden. To wear the hair loose is prohibited. Great care is used to keep the sexes apart. In their evening and other meetings, women not only sit apart from men, but they leave the room before the men break ranks. Boys are allowed to play only with boys, and girls with girls. There are no places or occasions for evening amusements, where the sexes might meet. On Sunday afternoons the boys are permitted to walk in the fields; and so are the girls, but these must go in another direction. " Perhaps they meet in the course of the walk," said a member to me, " but it is not allowed." At meals and in their labors they are also separated. With all this care to hide the charms of the young women, to make them, as far as dress can do so, look old and ugly, and to keep the young men away from them, love, courtship, and marriage go on at Amana as elsewhere in the world. The young man " falls in love," and finds ways to make his passion known to its object; he no doubt enjoys all the delights of courtship, intensified by the difficulties which his prudent brethren put in his way; and he marries the object of his affection, in spite of her black hood and her sad-colored little shawl, whenever he has reached the age of twenty-four.

For before that age he may not marry, even if his parents consent. This is a merely prudential rule. " They have few cares in life, and would marry too early for their own good —food and lodging being secured them—if there were not a rule upon the subject;" so said one of their wise men to me. Therefore, no matter how early the young people agree to marry, the wedding is deferred until the man reaches the proper age.

And when at last the wedding-day comes, it is treated with a degree of solemnity which is calculated to make it a day of terror rather than of unmitigated delight. The parents of the bride and groom meet, with two or three of the elders, at the house of the bride's father. Here, after singing and prayer, that chapter of Paul's writings is read wherein, with great plainness of speech, he describes to the Ephesians and the Christian world in general the duties of husband and wife. On this chapter the elders comment " with great thoroughness " to the young people, and " for a long time," as I was told ; and after this lecture, and more singing and prayer, there is a modest supper, whereupon all retire quietly to their homes.

The strictly pious hold that marriages should be made only by consent of God, signified through the " inspired instrument."

While the married state has thus the countenance and sanction of the society and its elders, matrimony is not regarded as a meritorious act. It has in it, they say, a certain large degree of worldliness ; it is not calculated to make them more, but rather less spiritually minded—so think they at Amana— and accordingly the religious standing of the young couple suffers and is lowered. In the Amana church there are three " classes," orders or grades, the highest consisting of those members who have manifested in their lives the greatest spirituality and piety. Now, if the new-married couple should have belonged for years to this highest class, their wedding would put them down into the lowest, or the " children's order," for a year or two, until they had won their slow way back by deepening piety.

The civil or temporal government of the Amana communists consists of thirteen trustees, chosen annually by the male members of the society. The president of the society is chosen by the trustees.

This body manages the finances, and carries on the temporalities generally, but it acts only with the unanimous consent of its members. The trustees live in different villages, but exercise no special authority, as I understand, as individuals. The foremen and elders in each village carry on the work and keep the accounts. Each village keeps its own books and manages its own affairs; but all accounts are finally sent to the head-quarters at Amana, where they are inspected, and the balance of profit or loss is discovered. It is supposed that the labor of each village produces a profit; but whether it does or not makes no difference in the supplies of the people, who receive every thing alike, as all property is held in common. All accounts are balanced once a year, and thus the productiveness of every industry is ascertained.

The elders are a numerous body, not necessarily old men, but presumably men of deep piety and spirituality. They are named or appointed by inspiration, and preside at religious assemblies.

In every village four or five of the older and more experienced elders meet each morning to advise together on business. This council acts, as I understand, upon reports of those younger elders who are foremen and have charge of different affairs. These in turn meet for a few minutes every evening, and arrange for the next day's work.

Women are never members of these councils, nor do they hold, as far as I could discover, any temporal or spiritual authority, with the single exception of their present spiritual head, who is a woman of eighty years. Moreover, if a young man should marry out of the society, and his wife should desire to become a member, the husband is expelled for a year —at the end of which time both may make application to come in, if they wish.

They have contrived a very simple and ingenious plan for supplying their members with clothing and other articles aside from food. To each adult male an annual allowance is made of from forty to one hundred dollars, according as his position and labor necessitates more or less clothing. For each adult female the allowance is from twenty-five to thirty dollars, and from five to ten dollars for each child.

All that they need is kept in store in each village, and is sold to the members at cost and expenses. When any one requires an article of clothing, he goes to the store and selects the cloth, for which he is charged in a book he brings with him; he then goes to the tailor, who makes the garment, and charges him on the book an established price. If he needs shoes, or a hat, or tobacco, or a watch, every thing is in the same way charged. As I sat in one of the shops, I noticed women coming in to make purchases, often bringing children with them, and each had her little book in which due entry was made. "Whatever we do not use, is so much saved against next year; or we may give it away if we like," one explained to me; and added that during the war, when the society contributed between eighteen and twenty thousand dollars to various benevolent purposes, much of this was given by individual members out of the savings on their year's account.

Almost every man has a watch, but they keep a strict rule over vanities of apparel, and do not allow the young girls to buy or wear ear-rings or breastpins.

The young and unmarried people, if they have no parents, are divided around among the families.

They have not many labor-saving contrivances; though of course the eating in common is both economical and labor-

saving. There is in each village a general wash-house, where
the clothing of the unmarried people is washed, but each family does its own washing.

They have no libraries; and most of their reading is in the
Bible, and in their own "inspired" records, which, as I shall
show further on, are quite voluminous. A few newspapers
are taken, and each calling among them receives the journal
which treats of its own specialty. In general they aim to withdraw themselves as much as possible from the world, and
take little interest in public affairs. During the war they
voted; "but we do not now, for we do not like the turn politics have taken"—which seemed to me a curious reason for
refusing to vote.

Their members came originally from many parts of Germany and Switzerland; they have also a few "Pennsylvania
Dutch." They have much trouble with applicants who desire
to join the society; and receive, the secretary told me, sometimes dozens of letters in a month from persons of whom they
know nothing; and not a few of whom, it seems, write, not to
ask permission to join, but to say that they are coming on at
once. There have been cases where a man wrote to say that
he had sold all his possessions, and was then on the way, with
his family, to join the association. As they claim to be not
an industrial, but a religious community, they receive new
members with great care, and only after thorough investigation of motives and religious faith; and these random applications are very annoying to them. Most of their new members they receive from Germany, accepting them after proper
correspondence, and under the instructions of "inspiration."
Where they believe them worthy they do not inquire about
their means; and a fund is annually set apart by the trustees
to pay the passage of poor families whom they have determined to take in.

Usually a neophyte enters on probation for two years, signing an obligation to labor faithfully, to conduct himself according to the society's regulations, and to demand no wages. If at the close of his probation he appears to be a proper person, he is admitted to full membership; and if he has property, he is then expected to put this into the common stock; signing also the constitution, which provides that on leaving he shall have his contribution returned, but without interest.

There are cases, however, where a new-comer is at once admitted to full membership. This is where "inspiration" directs such breach of the general rule, on the ground that the applicant is already a fit person.

Most of their members came from the Lutheran Church; but they have also Catholics, and I believe several Jews.

They employ about two hundred hired hands, mostly in agricultural labors; and these are all Germans, many of whom have families. For these they supply houses, and give them sometimes the privilege of raising a few cattle on their land.

They are excellent farmers, and keep fine stock, which they care for with German thoroughness; stall-feeding in the winter.

The members do not work hard. One of the foremen told me that three hired hands would do as much as five or six of the members. Partly this comes no doubt from the interruption to steady labor caused by their frequent religious meetings; but I have found it generally true that the members of communistic societies take life easy.

The people are of varying degrees of intelligence; but most of them belong to the peasant class of Germany, and were originally farmers, weavers, or mechanics. They are quiet, a little stolid, and very well satisfied with their life. Here, as in other communistic societies, the brains seem to come easily to the top. The leading men with whom I conversed appeared to me to be thoroughly trained business men in the German fashion; men of education, too, and a good deal of intelli-

AMANA, A GENERAL VIEW.

gence. The present secretary told me that he had been during all his early life a merchant in Germany; and he had the grave and somewhat precise air of an honest German merchant of the old style—prudent, with a heavy sense of responsibility, a little rigid, and yet kindly.

At the little inn I talked with a number of the rank and file, and noticed in them great satisfaction with their method of life. They were, on the surface, the commoner kind of German laborers; but they had evidently thought pretty thoroughly upon the subject of communal living; and knew how to display to me what appeared to them its advantages in their society: the absolute equality of all men—" as God made us;" the security for their families; the abundance of food; and the independence of a master.

It seems to me that these advantages are dearer to the Germans than to almost any other nation, and hence they work more harmoniously in communistic experiments. I think I noticed at Amana, and elsewhere among the German communistic societies, a satisfaction in their lives, a pride in the equality which the communal system secures, and also in the conscious surrender of the individual will to the general good, which is not so clearly and satisfactorily felt among other nationalities. Moreover, the German peasant is fortunate in his tastes, which are frugal and well fitted for community living. He has not a great sense of or desire for beauty of surroundings; he likes substantial living, but cares nothing for elegance. His comforts are not, like the American's, of a costly kind.

I think, too, that his lower passions are more easily regulated or controlled, and certainly he is more easily contented to remain in one place. The innkeeper, a little to my surprise, when by chance I told him that I had spent a winter on the Sandwich Islands, asked me with the keenest delight and curiosity about the trees, the climate, and the life there; and wanted to know if I had seen the place where Captain Cook,

"the great circumnavigator of the world," was slain. He returned to the subject again and again, and evidently looked
upon me as a prodigiously interesting person, because I had
been fortunate enough to see what to him was classic ground.
An American would not have felt one half this man's interest; but he would probably have dreamed of making the
same journey some day. My kindly host sat serenely in his
place, and was not moved by a single wandering thought.

They forbid all amusements—all cards and games whatever, and all musical instruments; "one might have a flute,
but nothing more." Also they regard photographs and pictures of all kinds as tending to idol-worship, and therefore not
to be allowed.

They have made very substantial improvements upon their
property; among other things, in order to secure a sufficient
water-power, they dug a canal six miles long, and from five
to ten feet deep, leading a large body of water through Amana.
On this canal they keep a steam-scow to dredge it out annually.

As a precaution against fire, in Amana there is a little tower
upon a house in the middle of the village, where two men keep
watch all night.

They buy much wool from the neighboring farmers; and
have a high reputation for integrity and simple plain-dealing
among their neighbors. A farmer told me that it was not
easy to cheat them; and that they never dealt the second time
with a man who had in any way wronged them; but that they
paid a fair price for all they bought, and always paid cash.

In their woolen factories they make cloth enough for their
own wants and to supply the demand of the country about
them. Flannels and yarn, as well as woolen gloves and stockings, they export, sending some of these products as far as
New York. The gloves and stockings are made not only by
the children, but by the women during the winter months,
when they are otherwise unemployed.

At present they own about 3000 sheep, 1500 head of cattle, 200 horses, and 2500 hogs.

The society has no debt, and has a considerable fund at interest.

They lose very few of their young people. Some who leave them return after a few years in the world. Plain and dull as the life is, it appears to satisfy the youth they train up; and no doubt it has its rewards in its regularity, peacefulness, security against want, and freedom from dependence on a master.

It struck me as odd that in cases of illness they use chiefly homeopathic treatment. The people live to a hale old age. They had among the members, in March, 1874, a woman aged ninety-seven, and a number of persons over eighty.

They are non-resistants; but during the late war paid for substitutes in the army. "But we did wrongly there," said one to me; "it is not right to take part in wars even in this way."

To sum up: the people of Amana appeared to me a remarkably quiet, industrious, and contented population; honest, of good repute among their neighbors, very kindly, and with religion so thoroughly and largely made a part of their lives that they may be called a religious people.

IV.—Religion and Literature.

"If one gives himself entirely, and in all his life, to the will of God, he will presently be possessed by the Spirit of God."

"The Bible is the Word of God; each prophet or sacred writer wrote only what he received from God."

"In the New Testament we read that the disciples were 'filled with the Holy Ghost.' But the same God lives now, and it is reasonable to believe that he inspires his followers now as then; and that he will lead his people, in these days as in those, by the words of his inspiration."

"He leads us in spiritual matters, and in those temporal concerns which affect our spiritual life; but we do not look to him for inspired directions in all the minute affairs of our daily lives. Inspiration directed us to come to America, and to leave Eben-Ezer for Iowa. Inspiration sometimes directs us to admit a new-comer to full membership, and sometimes to expel an unworthy member. Inspiration discovers hidden sins in the congregation."

"We have no creed except the Bible."

"We ought to live retired and spiritual lives; to keep ourselves separate from the world; to cultivate humility, obedience to God's will, faithfulness, and love to Christ."

"Christ is our head."

Such are some of the expressions of their religious belief which the pious and well-instructed at Amana gave me.

They have published two Catechisms—one for the instruction of children, the other for the use of older persons. From these it appears that they are Trinitarians, believe in "justification by faith," hold to the resurrection of the dead, the final judgment, but not to eternal punishment, believing rather that fire will purify the wicked in the course of time, longer or shorter according to their wickedness.

They do not practice baptism, either infant or adult, holding it to be a useless ceremony not commanded in the New Testament. They celebrate the Lord's Supper, not at regular periods, but only when by the words of "inspiration" God orders them to do so; and then with peculiar ceremonies, which I shall describe further on.

As to this word "Inspiration," I quote here from the Catechism their definition of it:

"*Question.* Is it therefore the Spirit or the witness of Jesus which speaks and bears witness through the truly inspired persons?

"*Answer.* Yes; the Holy Ghost is the Spirit of Jesus, which brings to light the hidden secrets of the heart, and gives witness to our spirits that it is the Spirit of truth.

" *Q.* When did the work of inspiration begin in the later times ?

"*A.* About the end of the seventeenth and beginning of the eighteenth century. About this time the Lord began the gracious work of inspiration in several countries (France, England, and, at last, in Germany), gathered a people by these new messengers of peace, and declared a divine sentence of punishment against the fallen Christian world.

" *Q.* How were these ' instruments' or messengers called ?

"*A.* Inspired or new prophets. They were living trumpets of God, which shook the whole of Christendom, and awakened many out of their sleep of security.

*   *   *   *   *   *   *

" *Q.* What is the word of inspiration ?

"*A.* It is the prophetic word of the New Testament, or the Spirit of prophecy in the new dispensation.

" *Q.* What properties and marks of divine origin has this inspiration ?

"*A.* It is accompanied by a divine power, and reveals the secrets of the heart and conscience in a way which only the all-knowing and soul-penetrating Spirit of Jesus has power to do ; it opens the ways of love and grace, of the holiness and justice of God ; and these revelations and declarations are in their proper time accurately fulfilled.

" *Q.* Through whom is the Spirit thus poured out ?

" *A.* Through the vessels of grace, or ' instruments' chosen and fitted by the Lord.

" *Q.* How must these ' instruments' be constituted ?

" *A.* They must conform themselves in humility and childlike obedience to all the motions and directions of God within them ; without care for self or fear of men, they must walk in the fear of God, and with attentive watchfulness for the inner signs of his leading; and they must subject themselves in every way to the discipline of the Spirit."

Concerning the Constitution of the Inspiration Congregations or communities, the same Catechism asserts that it "is founded upon the divine revelation in the Old and New Testament, connected with the divine directions, instructions, and determinations, general and special, given through the words of the true inspiration."

"*Question.* Through or by whom are the divine ordinances carried out in the congregations?

"*Answer.* By the elders and leaders, who have been chosen and nominated to this purpose by God.

"*Q.* What are their duties?

"*A.* Every leader or elder of the congregation is in duty bound, by reason of his divine call, to advance, in the measure of the grace and power given him, the spiritual and temporal welfare of the congregation; but in important and difficult circumstances the Spirit of prophecy will give the right and correct decision.

"*Q.* Is the divine authority to bind and loose, intrusted, according to Matt. xvi., 19, to the apostle Peter, also given to the elders of the Inspiration Congregations?

"*A.* It belongs to all elders and teachers of the congregation of the faithful, who were called by the Lord Jesus through the power of his Holy Spirit, and who, by the authority of their divine call, and of the divine power within them, rule without abuse the congregations or flocks intrusted to them.

"*Q.* What are the duties of the members of the Inspiration Congregations?

"*A.* A pure and upright walk in the fear of God; heartfelt love and devotion toward their brethren, and childlike obedience toward God and the elders."

These are the chief articles of faith of the Amana Community.

They regard the utterances, while in the trance state, of their spiritual head as given from God; and believe—as is asserted in the Catechism—that evils and wrongs in the congregation will be thus revealed by the influence, or, as they say, the inspiration or breath of God; that in important affairs they will thus receive the divine direction; and that it is their duty to obey the commands thus delivered to them.

There were "inspired instruments" before Christian Metz. Indeed, the present "instrument," Barbara Landmann, was accepted before him, but by reason of her marriage fell from grace for a while. It would seem that Metz also was married; for I was told at Amana that at his death in 1867, at the age of sixty-seven, he left a daughter in the community.

The words of "inspiration" are usually delivered in the public meetings, and at funerals and other solemn occasions. They have always been carefully written down by persons specially appointed to that office; and this appears to have been done so long ago as 1719, when "Brother John Frederick Rock" made his journey through Constance, Schaffhausen, Zurich, etc., with "Brother J. J. Schulthes as writer, who wrote down every thing correctly, from day to day, and in weal or woe."

When the "instrument" "falls into inspiration," he is often severely shaken—Metz, they say, sometimes shook for an hour—and thereupon follow the utterances which are believed to proceed from God. The "instrument" sits or kneels, or walks about among the congregation. "Brother Metz used to walk about in the meeting with his eyes closed; but he always knew to whom he was speaking, or where to turn with words of reproof, admonition, or encouragement"—so I was told.

The "inspired" words are not always addressed to the general congregation, but often to individual members; and their feelings are not spared. Thus in one case Barbara Landmann, being "inspired," turned upon a sister with the words,

" But you, wretched creature, follow the true counsel of obedience ;" and to another : " And you, contrary spirit, how much
pain do you give to our hearts.   You will fall into everlasting
pain, torture, and unrest if you do not break your will and repent, so that you may be accepted and forgiven by those you
have offended, and who have done so much for you."

The warnings, prophecies, reproofs, and admonitions, thus
delivered by the " inspired instrument," are all, as I have said,
carefully written down, and in convenient time printed in
yearly volumes, entitled " Year-Books of the True Inspiration
Congregations : Witnesses of the Spirit of God, which happened and were spoken in the Meetings of the Society, through
the Instruments, Brother Christian Metz and Sister B. Landmann," with the year in which they were delivered.   In this
country they early established a printing-press at Eben-Ezer,
and after their removal also in Iowa, and have issued a considerable number of volumes of these records.   They are read
as of equal authority and almost equal importance with the
Bible.   Every family possesses some volumes ; and in their
meetings extracts are read aloud after the reading of the
Scriptures.

There is commonly a brief preface to each revelation, recounting the circumstances under which it was delivered ; as
for instance :

" No. 10. *Lower Eben-Ezer*, November 7, 1853. — Monday
morning the examination of the congregation was made here
according to the command of the Lord.   For the opening
service five verses were sung of the hymn, ' Lord, give thyself
to me ;' the remainder of the hymn was read.   After the
prayer, and a brief silence, Sister Barbara Landmann fell into
inspiration, and was forced to bear witness in the following
gracious and impressive revival words of love."

The phrase varies with the contents of the message, as, on
another occasion, it is written that " both ' instruments' fell into

inspiration, and there followed this earnest admonition to repentance, and words of warning;" or, again, the words are described as "important," or "severe," or "gentle and gracious and hope inspiring."

During his wanderings in Germany among the congregations, Metz appears to have fallen into inspiration almost daily, not only in meetings, but during conversations, and even occasionally at dinner—whereupon the dinner waited. Thus it is recorded that "at the Rehmühle, near Hambach, June 1, 1839 —this afternoon the traveling brethren with Brother Peter came hither and visited friend Matthias Bieber. After conversation, as they were about to sit down to eat something, Brother Christian Metz fell into inspiration, and delivered the following words to his friend, and Brother Philip Peter."

The inspired utterances are for the most part admonitory to a holier life; warnings, often in the severest language, against selfishness, stubbornness, coldness of heart, pride, hatred toward God, grieving the Spirit; with threats of the wrath of God, of punishment, etc. Humility and obedience are continually inculcated. "Lukewarmness" appears to be one of the prevailing sins of the community. It is needless to say that to a stranger these homilies are dull reading. Concerning violations of the Ten Commandments or of the moral law, I have not found any mention here; and I do not doubt that the members of the society live, on the whole, uncommonly blameless lives. I asked, for instance, what punishment their rules provided for drunkenness, but was told that this vice is not found among them; though, as at Economy and in other German communities, they habitually use both wine and beer.

When any member offends against the rules or order of life of the society, he is admonished (*ermahnt*) by the elders; and if he does not amend his ways, expulsion follows; and here as elsewhere in the communities I have visited, they seem vigilantly to purge the society of improper persons.

The following twenty-one " Rules for Daily Life," printed in one of their collections, and written by one of their older leaders, E. L. Gruber, give, I think, a tolerably accurate notion of their views of the conduct of life:

" I. To obey, without reasoning, God, and through God our superiors.

" II. To study quiet, or serenity, within and without.

" III. Within, to rule and master your thoughts.

" IV. Without, to avoid all unnecessary words, and still to study silence and quiet.

" V. To abandon self, with all its desires, knowledge, and power.

" VI. Do not criticise others, either for good or evil, neither to judge nor to imitate them ; therefore contain yourself, remain at home, in the house and in your heart.

" VII. Do not disturb your serenity or peace of mind—hence neither desire nor grieve.

" VIII. Live in love and pity toward your neighbor, and indulge neither anger nor impatience in your spirit.

" IX. Be honest, sincere, and avoid all deceit and even secretiveness.

" X. Count every word, thought, and work as done in the immediate presence of God, in sleeping and waking, eating, drinking, etc., and give him at once an account of it, to see if all is done in his fear and love.

" XI. Be in all things sober, without levity or laughter ; and without vain and idle words, works, or thoughts ; much less heedless or idle.

" XII. Never think or speak of God without the deepest reverence, fear, and love, and therefore deal reverently with all spiritual things.

" XIII. Bear all inner and outward sufferings in silence,

complaining only to God; and accept all from him in deepest reverence and obedience.

" XIV. Notice carefully all that God permits to happen to you in your inner and outward life, in order that you may not fail to comprehend his will and to be led by it.

" XV. Have nothing to do with unholy, and particularly with needless business affairs.

" XVI. Have no intercourse with worldly-minded men; never seek their society; speak little with them, and never without need; and then not without fear and trembling.

" XVII. Therefore, what you have to do with such men, do in haste; do not waste time in public places and worldly society, that you be not tempted and led away.

XVIII. Fly from the society of women-kind as much as possible, as a very highly dangerous magnet and magical fire.

" XIX. Avoid obeisance and the fear of men; these are dangerous ways.

" XX. Dinners, weddings, feasts, avoid entirely; at the best there is sin.

" XXI. Constantly practice abstinence and temperance, so that you may be as wakeful after eating as before."

These rules may, I suppose, be regarded as the ideal standard toward which a pious Inspirationist looks and works. Is it not remarkable that they should have originated and found their chief adherents among peasants and poor weavers?

Their usual religious meetings are held on Wednesday, Saturday, and Sunday mornings, and every evening. On Saturday, all the people of a village assemble together in the church or meeting-house; on other days they meet in smaller rooms, and by classes or orders.

The society consists of three of these orders—the highest, the middle, and the lower, or children's order. In the latter fall naturally the youth of both sexes, but also those older and married persons whose religious life and experience are not deep enough to make them worthy of membership in the higher orders.

The evening meeting opens a little after seven o'clock. It is held in a large room specially maintained for this purpose. I accompanied one of the brethren, by permission, to these meetings during my stay at Amana. I found a large, low-ceiled room, dimly lighted by a single lamp placed on a small table at the head of the room, and comfortably warmed with stoves. Benches without backs were placed on each side of this chamber; the floor was bare, but clean; and hither entered, singly, or by twos or threes, the members, male and female, each going to the proper place without noise. The men sat on one side, the women on the other. At the table sat an elderly man, of intelligent face and a look of some authority. Near him were two or three others.

When all had entered and were seated, the old man at the table gave out a hymn, reading out one line at a time; and after two verses were sung in this way, he read the remaining ones. Then, after a moment of decorous and not unimpressive silent meditation, all at a signal rose and kneeled down at their places. Hereupon the presiding officer uttered a short prayer in verse, and after him each man in his turn, beginning with the elders, uttered a similar verse of prayer, usually four, and sometimes six lines long. When all the men and boys had thus prayed—and their little verses were very pleasant to listen to, the effect being of childlike simplicity— the presiding elder closed with a brief extemporary prayer, whereupon all arose.

Then he read some verses from one of their inspired books, admonishing to a good life; and also a brief homily from one of Christian Metz's inspired utterances. Thereupon all arose, and stood in their places in silence for a moment; and then, in perfect order and silence, and with a kind of military precision, benchful after benchful of people walked softly out of the room. The women departed first; and each went home, I judge, without delay or tarrying in the hall, for when I got out the hall was already empty.

The next night the women prayed instead of the men, the presiding officer conducting the meeting as before. I noticed that the boys and younger men had their places on the front seats; and the whole meeting was conducted with the utmost reverence and decorum.

On Wednesday and Sunday mornings the different orders meet at the same hour, each in its proper assembly-room. These are larger than those devoted to the evening meetings. The Wednesday-morning meeting began at half-past seven, and lasted until nine. There was, as in the evening meetings, a very plain deal table at the head, and benches, this time with backs, were ranged in order, the sexes sitting by themselves as before; each person coming in with a ponderous hymn-book, and a Bible in a case. The meeting opened with the singing of six verses of a hymn, the leader reading the remaining verses. Many of their hymns have from ten to fourteen verses. Next he read some passages from one of the inspirational utterances of Metz; after which followed prayer, each man, as in the evening meetings, repeating a little supplicatory verse. The women did not join in this exercise.

Then the congregation got out their Bibles, the leader gave out the fifth chapter of Ephesians, and each man read a verse in his turn; then followed a psalm; and the women read those verses which remained after all the men had read. After this the leader read some further passages from Metz. After the reading of the New Testament chapter and the psalm, three of the leaders, who sat near the table at the head of the room, briefly spoke upon the necessity of living according to the words of God, doing good works and avoiding evil. Their exhortations were very simple, and without any attempt at eloquence, in a conversational tone.

Finally another hymn was sung; the leader pronounced a blessing, and we all returned home, the men and women going about the duties of the day.

On Saturday morning the general meeting is held in the church. The congregation being then more numerous, the brethren do not all pray, but only the elders; as in the other meetings, a chapter from the New Testament is read and commented upon by the elders; also passages are read from the inspired utterances of Metz or some other of their prophets; and at this time, too, the "instrument," if moved, falls into a trance, and delivers the will of the Holy Spirit.

They keep New-Year's as a holiday, and Christmas, Easter, and the Holy-week are their great religious festivals. Christmas is a three days' celebration, when they make a feast in the church; there are no Christmas-trees for the children, but they receive small gifts. Most of the feast days are kept double—that is to say, during two days. During the Passion-week they have a general meeting in the church every day at noon, and on each day the chapter appropriate to it is read, and followed by prayer and appropriate hymns. The week ends, of course, on Sunday with the ascension; but on Easter Monday, which is also kept, the children receive colored eggs.

At least once in every year there is a general and minute "Untersuchung," or inquisition of the whole community, including even the children—an examination of its spiritual condition. This is done by classes or orders, beginning with the elders themselves; and I judge from the relations of this ceremony in their printed books that it lasts long, and is intended to be very thorough. Each member is expected to make confession of his sins, faults, and shortcomings; and if any thing is hidden, they believe that it will be brought to light by the inspired person, who assumes on this occasion an important part, admonishing individuals very freely, and denouncing the sins and evils which exist in the congregation. At this time,

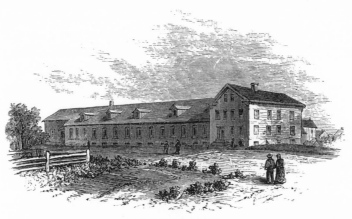

CHURCH AT AMANA.

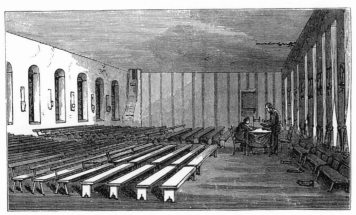

INTERIOR VIEW OF CHURCH.

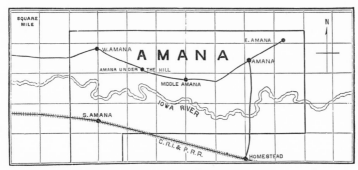

PLAN OF THE INSPIRATIONIST VILLAGES.

too, any disputes which may have occurred are brought up and healed, and an effort is made to revive religious fervor in the hearts of all. Not unfrequently the examination of a class is adjourned from day to day, because they are found to be cold and unimpressible; and I notice that on these occasions the young people in particular are a cause of much grief and trouble on account of their perverse hardness of heart.

The celebration of the Lord's Supper is their greatest religious event. It is held only when the "inspired instrument" directs it, which may not happen once in two years; and it is thought so solemn and important an occasion that a full account of it is sometimes printed in a book. I have one such volume: "*Das Liebes- und Gedächtniszmahl des Leidens und Sterbens unsers Herrn und Heilandes Jesu Christi, wie solches von dem Herrn durch Sein Wort und zeugnisz angekündigt, angeordnet und gehalten worden, in Vier Abtheilungen, zu Mittel und Nieder Eben-Ezer, im Jahr* 1855" ("The Supper of Love and Remembrance of the suffering and death of our Lord and Saviour Jesus Christ: How it was announced, ordered, and held by his word and witness, in four parts, in Middle and Lower Eben-Ezer, in the year 1855"). It is a neatly printed volume of 284 pages.

The account begins with the announcement of the Lord's command: "Middle Eben-Ezer, April 21st, 1855, Saturday, in the general meeting, in the beginning, when the congregation was assembled, came the following gracious word and determination of the Lord, through Brother Chr. Metz." Thereupon, after some words of preface, the "instrument" kneeled down, the congregation also kneeling, and said: "I am commanded humbly to reveal, according to the sacred and loving conclusion, that you are to celebrate the supper of love and remembrance in the presence of your God. The beginning and the course of it shall be as before. There will be on this occasion humiliations and revelations, if in any the true Worker of righteousness and repentance has not been allowed to do his work. The Lord will make a representation of the lack of his understanding in many of you; his great love will come to light, and will light up every one." After more of this kind of address, the "instrument" said: "You are to begin the Lord's Supper on Ascension-day, make ready then all your hearts, clean out all filth, all that is rotten and stinks, all sins and every thing idle and useless; and cherish pious thoughts, so that you shall put down the flesh, as you are commanded to," and so on.

On a following Sunday, the "instrument" recurred to the subject, and in the course of his remarks reproved one of the elders for disobedience to the Lord and resistance to grace, and displaced him in the assembly, calling another by name to his place. At the close, he spoke thus, evidently in the name and with the voice of God: "And I leave it to you, my servants, to take out of the middle order here and there some into the first, and out of the third into the second, but not according to favor and prejudice, but according to their grace and conduct, of which you are to take notice."

A day was given to admonitions and preparation; the "instrument" speaking not only to the congregation in general, in the morning and afternoon meetings, but to a great many in particular—admonishing, exhorting, blaming, encouraging them by name. The next morning there was a renewal of such hortatory remarks, with singing and prayer; and in the afternoon, all being prepared, the elders washed the feet of the brethren. This is done only in the higher orders.

Thereupon tables are brought in, and bread and wine are placed. After singing, the "inspired" person blesses these, and they are then received by the brethren and sisters from the hands of the elders, who pronounce the customary words of Scripture.

This being accomplished, the assembly temporarily adjourns, and persons previously appointed for this office spread on the tables a modest supper of bread and cake, coffee, chocolate, and a few other articles of food, and to this all sit down with solemn joy. At the conclusion of this meal, a hymn is sung, and the assembly retire to their homes.

When the three regular orders have gone through this celebration, there is a fourth, consisting of children under sixteen years, and of certain adult members who for various reasons have been thought unworthy to partake with the rest; and these also go through a thorough examination.

I asked one of their leading elders whether they believed in a "prayer-cure," explaining what the Oneida communists understand by this phrase. He replied, "No, we do not use prayer in this way, to cure disease. But it is possible. But if God has determined death, ten doctors can not help a man."

The present inspired instrument being very aged, I asked whether another was ready to take her place. They said No, no one had yet appeared; but they had no doubt God would call some one to the necessary office. They were willing to trust him, and gave themselves no trouble about it.

It remains to speak of their literature.

They have a somewhat ponderous hymnology, in two great volumes, one called "The Voice from Zion: to the Praise of the Almighty," by "John William Petersen (A.D. 1698)," printed at Eben-Ezer, N. Y., in 1851, and containing 958 pages. The hymns are called Psalms, and are not in rhyme. They are to be sung in a kind of chant, as I judge from the music prefixed to them; and are a kind of commentary on the Scripture, one part being taken up with the book of Revelation.

The other volume is the hymn-book in regular use. It contains 1285 pages, of which 111 are music—airs to which the different hymns may be sung. The copy I have is of the third edition, and bears the imprint, " Amana, Iowa, 1871." Its title is " Psalms after the manner of David, for the children of Zion." It has one peculiarity which might with advantage be introduced in other hymn-books. Occasional verses are marked with a *, and it is recommended to the reader that these be taught to the children as little prayers. In practice, I found that in their evening meetings the grown persons as well as the children recited these simple and devotional little verses as their prayers: surely a more satisfactory delivery to them and the congregation than rude and halting attempts at extemporary utterance.

Many of the hymns are very long, having from twelve to twenty-four verses; and it is usual at their meetings to sing three or four verses and then read the remainder. They do not sing well; and their tunes—those at least which I heard —are slow, and apparently in a style of music now disused in our churches. The hymns are printed as prose, only the verses being separated. I was told that they were " all given by the Spirit of God," and that Christian Metz had a great gift of hymn-writing, very often, at home or elsewhere, writing down an entire hymn at one sitting. They are all deeply devotional in spirit, and have not unfrequently the merit of great simplicity and a pleasing quaintness of expression, of which I think the German language is more capable than our ruder and more stubborn English.

Their writers are greatly given to rhyming. Even in the inspirational utterances I find frequently short admonitory paragraphs where rude rhymes are introduced. Among their books is one, very singular, called " Innocent Amusement " (" *Unschuldiges Zeitvertreib* "), in a number of volumes (I saw the fifth). It is a collection of verses, making pious applications of many odd subjects. Among the headings I found Cooking, Rain, Milk, The Ocean, Temperance, Salve, Dinner, A Mast, Fog, A Net, Pitch, A Rainbow, A Kitchen, etc., etc.

It is a mass of pious doggerel, founded on Scripture and with fanciful additions.

Another is called "Jesus's A B C, for his scholars," and is also in rhyme. Another is entitled "Rhymes on the sufferings, death, burial, and resurrection of Christ." There are about twelve hundred pages of the A B C book.

They have printed also a miniature Thomas à Kempis, "for the edification of children;" two catechisms; a little work entitled "Treasure for those who desire God," and other works of similar character. A list, not complete, but containing all the books I have been able to collect, will be found in the Bibliography at the end of this volume.

At the end of the Catechism are some pages of rules for the conduct of children, at home, in church, at school, during play hours, at meals, and in all the relations of their lives. Many of these rules are excellent, and the whole of them might well be added to the children's catechisms in use in the churches. Piety, orderly habits, obedience, politeness, cleanliness, kindness to others, truthfulness, cheerfulness, etc., are all inculcated in considerable detail, with great plainness of speech, and in sixty-six short paragraphs, easily comprehended by the youngest children. The fifty-fourth rule shows the care with which they guard the intercourse of the sexes: "Have no pleasure in violent games or plays; do not wait on the road to look at quarrels or fights; do not keep company with bad children, for there you will learn only wickedness. Also, *do not play with children of the other sex.*"

THE HARMONY SOCIETY,

AT

ECONOMY, PA.

THE HARMONY SOCIETY.

I.—Economy in 1874.

Traveling from Cleveland to Pittsburgh by rail, you strike the Ohio River at Wellsville; and the railroad runs thence, for forty-eight miles, to Pittsburgh, along the river bank, and through the edge of a country rich in coal, oil, potters' clay, limestone, and iron, and supporting a number of important manufactures.

To a traveler in search of the Rappist or Harmony settlement at Economy, the names of the towns along here seem to tell of the overshadowing influence of these communists; for, passing Liverpool, you come to Freedom, Jethro (whose houses are both heated and lighted with gas from a natural spring near by), Industry, and Beaver; you smile at the sign of the "Golden Rule Distillery;" and you wonder at the broken fences, unpainted houses, and tangled and weed-covered grounds, and that general air of dilapidation which curses a country producing petroleum and bituminous coal.

Presently, however, you strike into what is evidently a large and well-kept estate: high and solid fences; fields without weeds, and with clean culture or smooth and rich grass; and if you ask the conductor, he will tell you that for some miles here the land is owned by the "Economites;" and that the town or village of Economy lies among these neatly kept fields, but out of sight of the railroad on the top of the steep bluff.

Economy has, in truth, one of the loveliest situations on the Ohio River. It stands in the midst of a rich plain, with swelling hills behind, protecting it from cold winds in winter; a magnificent reach of the river in view below; and tall hills on the opposite shore to give a picturesque outlook. The town begins on the edge of the bluff; and under the shade-trees planted there benches are arranged, where doubtless the Harmonists take their comfort on summer evenings, in view of the river below them and of the village on the opposite shore. Streets proceed at right-angles with the river's course; and each street is lined with neat frame or brick houses, surrounding a square in such a manner that within each household has a sufficient garden. The broad streets have neat foot-pavements of brick; the houses, substantially built but unpretentious, are beautified by a singular arrangement of grape-vines, which are trained to espaliers fixed to cover the space between the top of the lower and the bottom of the upper windows. This manner of training vines gives the town quite a peculiar look, as though the houses had been crowned with green.

As you walk through the silent streets, and pass the large Assembly Hall, the church, and the hotel, it will occur to you that these people had, when they founded their place, the advantage of a sensible architect, for, while there is not the least pretense, all the building is singularly solid and honest; and in the larger houses the roof-lines have been broken and managed with considerable skill, so as to produce a very pleasing and satisfactory effect. Moreover, the color of the bricks used in building has chanced to be deep and good, which is no slight advantage to the place.

Neatness and a Sunday quiet are the prevailing characteristics of Economy. Once it was a busy place, for it had cotton, silk, and woolen factories, a brewery, and other industries; but the most important of these have now ceased; and as you walk along the quiet, shady streets, you meet only occasionally some stout, little old man, in a short light-blue jacket and a tall and very broad-brimmed hat, looking amazingly

ASSEMBLY HALL—ECONOMY.

CHURCH AT ECONOMY.

like Hendrick Hudson's men in the play of Rip Van Winkle;
or some comfortable-looking dame, in Norman cap and stuff
gown; whose polite "good-day" to you, in German or English as it may happen, is not unmixed with surprise at sight
of a strange face; for, as you will presently discover at the
hotel, visitors are not nowadays frequent in Economy.

The hotel is one of the largest houses in the place; it is of
two stories, with spacious bed-chambers, high ceilings, roomy
fire-places, large halls, and a really fine dining-room, all scrupulously clean. It was once, before the days of railroads, a favorite stopping-place on one of the main stage routes out of
Pittsburgh; in the well-built stable and barns opposite there
was room for twenty or thirty horses; the dining-room would
seat a hundred people; and here during many years was a
favorite winter as well as summer resort for Pittsburghers,
and an important source of income to the Economists.

When I for the first time entered the sitting-room on a
chilly December morning, the venerable but active landlord
was dusting chairs and tables, and looked up in some amazement at the intrusion of a traveler. "I can stay here, I suppose," said I, by way of introduction; and was answered:
"That depends upon how long you want to stay. We don't
take people to board here." My assurance that I meant to remain but two or three days, and that I had been recommended
by Mr. Henrici, the head of the society, secured me a room;
and the warning, as I went out for a walk, that I must be in
by half-past eleven, promptly, to dine; and by half-past four
for supper, because other people had to eat after me, and
ought not to be kept waiting by reason of my carelessness.
"For which reason," added the landlord, "it would be well
for you to come in and be at hand a quarter of an hour before
the times I have mentioned." When I had dined and supped
and slept, I saw what a loss to Pittsburghers was the closing
of the Economy hotel; for the Harmonists live well, and are

substantial eaters in their German fashion. Nor was any ceremony omitted because of the fewness of guests; and old Joseph, the butler and head-waiter, who, as he told me, came to serve here fifty years ago, and is now seventy-eight years old, attended upon my meals arrayed in a scrupulously white apron, ordered the lass who was his subordinate, and occasionally condescended to laugh at my jokes, as befitted his place, with as much precision and dignity as when, thirty or forty years ago, he used to serve a houseful of hungry travelers.

Later in the afternoon I discovered the meaning of my landlord's warnings as to punctuality, as well as the real use of the "Economy Hotel." As I sat before the fire in my own room after supper, I heard the door-bell ring with a frequency as though an uncommon number of travelers were applying for lodgings; and going down into the sitting-room about seven o'clock, I discovered there an extraordinary collection of persons ranged around the fire, and toasting their more or less dilapidated boots. These were men in all degrees of raggedness; men with one eye, or lame, or crippled—tramps, in fact, beggars for supper and a night's lodging. They sat there to the number of twenty, half naked many of them, and not a bit ashamed; with carpet-bags or without; with clean or dirty faces and clothes as it might happen; but all hungry, as I presently saw, when a table was drawn out, about which they gathered, giving their names to be taken down on a register, while to them came a Harmonist brother with a huge tray full of tins filled with coffee, and another with a still bigger tray of bread.

Thereupon these wanderers fell to, and having eaten as much bread and coffee as they could hold, they were consigned to a house a few doors away, peeping in at whose windows by and by, I saw a large, cheerful coal fire, and beds for the whole company.

"You see, after you have eaten, the table must be cleared, and then *we* eat; and then come these people, who have also to be fed, so that, unless we hurry, the women are belated with their work," explained the landlord of this curious inn to me.

"Is this, then, a constant occurrence?" I asked in some amazement; and was told that they feed here daily from fifteen to twenty-five such tramps, asking no questions, except that the person shall not have been a regular beggar from the society. A constant provision of coffee and bread is made for them, and the house set apart for their lodging has bed accommodations for twenty men. They are expected to wash at the stable next morning, and thereupon receive a breakfast of bread, meat, and coffee, and are suffered to go on their way. Occasionally the very destitute, if they seem to be deserving, receive also clothing.

"But are you not often imposed upon?" I asked.

"Yes, probably; but it is better to give to a dozen worthless ones than to refuse one deserving man the cup and loaf which we give," was the reply.

The tramps themselves took this benevolence apparently as a matter of course. They were quiet enough; some of them looked like decent men out of work, as indeed all professed to be going somewhere in search of employment. But many of them had the air of confirmed loafers, and some I should not have liked to meet alone on the road after dark.

Economy is the home of the "Harmony Society," better known to the outside world as the followers of Rapp. It is a town of about one hundred and twenty houses, very regularly built, well-drained, and paved; it has water led from a reservoir in the hills, and flowing into troughs conveniently placed in every street; abundant shade-trees; a church, an assembly hall, a store which supplies also to some extent the neighboring country; different factories, and a number of conveniences which villages of its size are too often without. Moreover, it contains a pleasant pleasure-garden, and is surrounded by fine, productive orchards and by well-tilled fields.

At present Economy is inhabited by all that remain of the society which was founded by George Rapp in 1805. These number one hundred and ten persons, most of whom are aged, and none, I think, under forty. Besides these, who are the owners of the place and of much property elsewhere, there are twenty-five or thirty children of various ages, adopted by the society and apprenticed to it, and an equal number living there with parents who are hired laborers; of these hired laborers, men and women, there are about one hundred. The whole population is German; and German is the language one commonly hears, and in which on Sunday worship is carried on. Nevertheless all the people speak English also.

The Harmonists themselves are sturdy, healthy-looking men and women, most of them gray haired; with an air of vigorous independence; conspicuously kind and polite; well-fed and well-preserved. As I examined their faces on Sunday in church, they struck me as a remarkably healthy and well-satisfied collection of old men and women; by no means dull, and very decidedly masters of their lives. Their working dress has for its peculiarity the roundabout or jacket I have before mentioned; on Sunday they wear long coats. The women look very well indeed in their Norman caps; and their dress, wholesome and sensible, is not in any way odd or inappropriate. Indeed, when Miss Rapp, the granddaughter of the founder of the society, walked briskly into church on Sunday, her bright, kindly face was so well set off by the cap she wore that she seemed quite an admirable object to me; and I thought no head-dress in the world could so well become an elderly lady.

II.—HISTORICAL.

George Rapp, founder and until his death in 1847 head of the "Harmony Society," was born in October, 1757, at Iptingen in Würtemberg. He was the son of a small farmer and vine-dresser, and received such a moderate common-school education as the child of parents in such circumstances would naturally receive at that time in South Germany. When he had been taught reading, writing, arithmetic, and geography, he left school and assisted his father on the farm, working as a weaver during the winter months. At the age of twenty-six he married a farmer's daughter, who bore him a son, John, and a daughter, Rosina, both of whom later became with him members of the society.

Rapp appears to have been from his early youth fond of reading, and of a reflective turn of mind. Books were probably not plentiful in his father's house, and he became a student of the Bible, and began presently to compare the condition of the people among whom he lived with the social order laid down and described in the New Testament. He became dissatisfied especially with the lifeless condition of the churches; and in the year 1787, when he was thirty, he had evidently found others who held with him, for he began to preach to a small congregation of friends in his own house on Sundays. The clergy resented this interference with their office, and persecuted Rapp and his adherents; they were fined and imprisoned; and this proved to be, as usual, the best way to increase their numbers and to confirm their dislike of the prevailing order of things. They were denounced as "Separatists," and had the courage to accept the name.

Rapp taught his followers, I am told, that they were in all things to obey the laws, to be peaceable and quiet subjects, and to pay all their taxes, those to the Church as well as to the

State. But he insisted on their right to believe what they pleased and to go to church where they thought it best. This was a tolerably impregnable platform.

In the course of six years, with the help of the persecutions of the clergy, Rapp had gathered around him not less than three hundred families; and had hearers and believers at a distance of twenty miles from his own house. He appears to have labored so industriously on the farm as to accumulate a little property, and in 1803 his adherents determined upon emigrating in a body to America, where they were sure of freedom to worship God after their own desires.

Rapp sailed in that year for Baltimore, accompanied by his son John and two other persons. After looking about in Maryland, Pennsylvania, and Ohio, they concluded to buy five thousand acres of wild land about twenty-five miles north of Pittsburgh, in the valley of the Connoquenessing. Frederick (Reichert) Rapp, an adopted son of George Rapp, evidently a man of uncommon ability and administrative talent, had been left in charge in Germany; and had so far perfected the necessary arrangements for emigration that no time was lost in moving, as soon as Rapp gave notice that he had found a proper locality for settlement. On the 4th of July, 1804, the ship *Aurora* from Amsterdam landed three hundred of Rapp's people in Baltimore; and six weeks later three hundred more were landed in Philadelphia. The remainder, coming in another ship, were drawn off by Haller, one of Rapp's traveling companions, to settle in Lycoming County, Pennsylvania.

The six hundred souls who thus remained to Rapp appear to have been mainly, and indeed with few exceptions, of the peasant and mechanic class. There were among them, I have been told, a few of moderately good education, and presumably of somewhat higher social standing than the great body; there were a few who had considerable property, for emigrants in those days. All were thrifty, and few were destitute. It is probable that they had determined in Germany to establish a community of goods, in accordance with their understanding of the social theory of Jesus; but for the present each family retained its property.

Rapp met them on their arrival, and settled them in different parts of Maryland and Pennsylvania; withdrawing a certain number of the ablest mechanics and laborers to proceed with him to the newly purchased land, where he and they spent a toilsome fall and winter in preparing habitations for the remainder; and on the 15th of February, 1805, these, and such as they could so early in the season gather with them, formally and solemnly organized themselves into the "Harmony Society," agreeing to throw all their possessions into a common fund, to adopt a uniform and simple dress and style of house; to keep thenceforth all things in common; and to labor for the common good of the whole body. Later in the spring they were joined by fifty additional families; and thus they finally began with about one hundred and twenty-five families, or, as I am told, less than seven hundred and fifty men, women, and children.

Rapp was then forty-eight years of age. He was, according to the best accounts I have been able to gather, a man of robust frame and sound health, with great perseverance, enterprise, and executive ability, and remarkable common-sense. It was fortunate for the community that its members were all laboring men. In the first year they erected between forty and fifty log-houses, a church and school-house, grist-mill, barn, and some workshops, and cleared one hundred and fifty acres of land. In the following year they cleared four hundred acres more, and built a saw-mill, tannery, and storehouse, and planted a small vineyard. A distillery was also a part of this year's building; and it is odd to read that the Harmonists, who have aimed to do all things well, were famous among Western men for many years for the excellence of the whisky they made; of which, however, they always used very sparingly themselves. Among their crops in succeeding years were corn, wheat, rye, hemp, and flax; wool from merino sheep, which they were the first in that part of Pennsylvania to own; and poppies, from which they made sweet-oil. They did not rest until they had established also a woolen-mill. It was a principle with Rapp that the society should, as far as possible, produce and make every thing it used; and in the early days, I am told, they bought very little indeed of provisions or clothing, having then but small means.

Rapp was, with the help of his adopted son, the organizer of the community's labor, appointing foremen in each department; he planned their enterprises—but he was also their preacher and teacher; and he taught them that their main duty was to live a sincerely and rigidly religious life; that they were not to labor for wealth, or look forward anxiously for prosperity; that the coming of the Lord was near, and for this they were waiting, as his chosen ones separated from the world.

At this time they still lived in families, and encouraged, or at any rate did not discourage, marriage. Among the members who married between 1805 and 1807 was John Rapp, the founder's son, and the father of Miss Gertrude Rapp, who still lives at Economy; and there is no doubt that the elder Rapp performed the marriage ceremony. During the year 1807, however, a deep religious fervor pervaded the society; and a remarkable result of this "revival of religion" was the determination of most of the members to conform themselves more closely in several ways to what they believed to be the spirit and commands of Jesus. Among other matters, they were persuaded in their own minds that it was best to cease to live in the married state. I have been assured by older members of the society, who have, as they say, often heard the whole of this period described by those who were actors in it, that this determination to refrain from marriage and from married life originated among the younger members; and that, though "Father Rapp" was not averse to this growth of asceticism, he did not eagerly encourage it, but warned his people not to act rashly in so serious and difficult a matter, but to proceed with great caution, and determine nothing without careful counsel together. At the same time he, I am told, gave it as his own conviction that the unmarried is the higher and holier estate. In short, there is reason to believe that he managed in this matter, as he appears to have done in others, with great prudence and judgment. He himself, and his son, John Rapp, set an example which the remainder of the society quickly followed; thenceforth no more marriages were contracted in Harmony, and no more children were born.

A certain number of the younger people, feeling no vocation for a celibate life, at this time withdrew from the society. The remainder faithfully ceased from conjugal intercourse. "Husbands and wives were not required to live in different houses, but occupied, as before, the same dwelling, with their children, only treating each other as brother and sister in Christ, and remembering the precept of the apostle: "This I say, brethren, the time is short; it remaineth that both they that have wives be as though they had none," etc. These are the words of one of the older members to the Reverend Dr. Aaron Williams, from whose interesting account of the Harmony Society I have taken a number of facts, being referred to it by Mr. Henrici, the present head of Economy. The same person added: "The burden was easier to bear, because it became general throughout the whole community, and all bore their share alike." Another member wrote in 1862: "Convinced of the truth and holiness of our purpose, we voluntarily and unanimously adopted celibacy, altogether from religious motives, in order to withdraw our love entirely from the lusts of the flesh, which, with the help of God and much prayer and spiritual warfare, we have succeeded well in doing now for fifty years."

Surely so extraordinary a resolve was never before carried out with so simple and determined a spirit. Among most people it would have been thought necessary, or at least prudent, to separate families, and to adopt other safeguards against temptation; but the good Harmonists did and do nothing of the kind. "What kind of watch or safeguard did or do you keep over the intercourse of the sexes," I asked in Economy, and received for reply, "None at all; it would be of no use. If you have to watch people, you had better give them up. We have always depended upon the strength of our religious convictions, and upon prayer and a Christian spirit."

"Do you believe the celibate life to be healthful?" I asked; and the reply was, "Decidedly so; almost all our people have lived to a hale old age. Father Rapp himself died at ninety; and no doubt many of our members would have lived longer than they did, had it not been for the hardships they suffered in Indiana, where we lived in a malarious region." I must add my own testimony that the Harmonists now living are almost without exception stout, well-built, hearty people, the women as well as the men.

At the same time that the celibate life was adopted, the community agreed to cease using tobacco in every form—a deprivation which these Germans must have felt almost as severely as the abandonment of conjugal joys.

The site of the Pennsylvania settlement proved to have been badly chosen in two respects. It had no water communication with the outer world; and it was unfavorable to the growth of the vine. In 1814, after proper discussion, the society determined to seek a more desirable spot; and purchased thirty thousand acres of land in Posey County, Indiana, in the Wabash valley. Thither one hundred persons proceeded in June, 1814, to prepare a place for the remainder; and by the summer of 1815 the whole colony was in its new home, having sold six thousand acres of land, with all their valuable improvements, in their old home, for one hundred thousand dollars.

The price they received is said to have been, and no doubt was, very much below the real value of the property. It is impossible to sell off a large and expensively improved estate like theirs all at once. It is probably true that the machinery and buildings were worth all they received for the whole property; and it would not be an overestimate to give the real value of what they sold at one hundred and fifty thousand dollars. They had begun, ten years before, with one hundred and twenty-five families; as after the second year they had bred no children, and as they then lost some members who left on account of their aversion to a celibate life, it is probable that they had not increased in numbers. If they had property worth one hundred and fifty thousand dollars, they would then have been able to divide, at the end of ten years, at the rate of twelve hundred dollars to each head of a family— a considerable sum, if we remember that they began with probably less than five hundred dollars for each family; and had not only lived comfortably for the greater part of ten years, but enjoyed society, had a good school for their children, a church, and all the moral and civil safeguards created by and incident to a well-settled community or town. Setting aside these safeguards and enjoyments of a thoroughly organized society, it seems to me doubtful if the same number of families, settling with narrow means at random in the wilderness, each independently of the others, could at that period, before railroads were built, have made as good a showing in mere pecuniary return in the same time. So far, then, the Harmony Society would seem to have made a pecuniary success—a fact of which they may have made but little account, but which is important to a general and independent consideration of communistic experiments.

On the Wabash they rapidly built up a town; but, possessing now both experience and some capital, they erected larger factories, and rapidly extended their business in every department. " Harmony," as they called the new town, became an important business centre for a considerable region. They sold their products and manufactured goods in branch stores as well as at Harmony ; they increased in wealth; and, what was of greater importance to them, they received some large accessions of members from Germany—friends and relatives of the founders of the colony. In 1817 one hundred and thirty persons came over at one time from Würtemberg. I was told that before they left Indiana they had increased to between seven and eight hundred members.

"Father Rapp" appears to have guided his people wisely. He continued to exhort them not to care overmuch for riches, but to use their wealth as having it not; and in 1818, " for the purpose of promoting greater harmony and equality between the original members and those who had come in recently," a notable thing was done at Rapp's suggestion. Originally a book had been kept, in which was written down what each member of the society had contributed to the common stock. This book was now brought out and by unanimous consent burned, so that no record should thenceforward show what any one had contributed.

In 1824 they removed once more. They sold the town of Harmony and twenty thousand acres of land to Robert Owen, who settled upon it his New Lanark colony when he took possession. Owen paid one hundred and fifty thousand dollars— not nearly the value of the property, it is said; but the Harmonists had suffered from fever and ague and unpleasant neighbors, and were determined to remove. They then bought the property they still hold at Economy, and in 1825 removed to this their new and final home. One of the older members told me that the first detachment which came up from Indiana

consisted of ninety men, mechanics and farmers; and these
"made the work fly." They laid out the town, cleared the timber from the streets and house places; and during some time
completed a log-house every day. Many of these log-cabins
are still standing, but are no longer used as residences. The
first church, now used as a storehouse, was a log-house of uncommonly large dimensions.

I think it probable, from what I have heard from the older
members, that when they were comfortably settled at Economy,
the Harmony Society was for some years in its most flourishing condition. All had come on together from Indiana; and
all were satisfied with the beauty of the new home. Those
who had suffered from malarious fevers here rapidly recovered.
The vicinity to Pittsburgh, and cheap water communication,
encouraged them in manufacturing. Economy lay upon the
main stage-road, and was thus an important and presently a
favorite stopping-place; the colonists found kindly neighbors; there was sufficient young blood in the community to
give enterprise and strength; and "we sang songs every day,
and had music every evening," said old Mr. Keppler to me,
recounting the glories of those days. They erected woolen
and cotton mills, a grist-mill and saw-mill; they planted orchards and vineyards; they began the culture of silk, and with
such success that soon the Sunday dress of men as well as
women was of silk, grown, reeled, spun, and woven by themselves.

In building the new town of Economy they displayed—
thanks, I believe, to the knowledge and skill of Frederick
Rapp—a good deal of taste, though adhering to their ancient
plainness; and their two removals had taught them valuable
lessons in the convenient arrangement of machinery; so that
Economy is even now a model of a well-built, well-arranged
country village. As soon as they began to substitute brick for
log houses, they insisted upon erecting for "Father Rapp" a

house somewhat larger and more spacious than the common dwelling-houses, though not in any other way different. This was advisable, because he was obliged to entertain many visitors and strangers of distinction. The house stands opposite the church; and has behind it a spacious garden, arranged in a somewhat formal style, with box-edgings to the walks, and summer-houses and other ornaments in the old geometrical style of gardening. This was open to the people, of course; and here the band played on summer evenings, or more frequently on Sunday afternoons; and here, too, flowers were cultivated, I am told, with great success.

How rapidly they made themselves at home in Economy appears from the following account of the Duke of Saxe-Weimar, who visited the place in 1826, only a year after it was founded:

"At the inn, a fine, large, frame house, we were received by Mr. Rapp, the principal, at the head of the community. He is a gray-headed and venerable old man; most of the members immigrated twenty-one years ago from Würtemberg along with him.

"The warehouse was shown to us, where the articles made here for sale or use are preserved, and I admired the excellence of all. The articles for the use of the society are kept by themselves; as the members have no private possessions, and every thing is in common, so must they, in relation to all their wants, be supplied from the common stock. The clothing and food they make use of is of the best quality. Of the latter, flour, salt meat, and all long-keeping articles, are served out monthly; fresh meat, on the contrary, is distributed as soon as it is killed, according to the size of the family, etc. As every house has a garden, each family raises its own vegetables and some poultry, and each family has its own bake-oven. For such things as are not raised in Economy, there is a store provided, from which the members, with the knowledge of the directors, may purchase what is necessary, and the people of the vicinity may do the same.

"Mr. Rapp finally conducted us into the factory again, and said that the girls had especially requested this visit that I might hear them sing. When their work is done, they collect in one of the factory rooms, to the number of sixty or seventy, to sing spiritual and other songs. They have a peculiar hymn-book, containing hymns from the old Würtemberg collection, and others written by the elder Rapp. A chair was placed for the old patriarch, who sat amid the girls, and they commenced a hymn in a very delightful manner. It was naturally symphonious, and exceedingly well arranged. The girls sang four pieces, at first sacred, but afterward, by Mr. Rapp's desire, of a gay character. With real emotion did I witness this interesting scene.

"Their factories and workshops are warmed during the winter by means of pipes connected with the steam-engine. All the workmen, and especially the females, had very healthy complexions, and moved me deeply by the warm-hearted friendliness with which they saluted the elder Rapp. I was also much gratified to see vessels containing fresh sweet-scented flowers standing on all the machines. The neatness which universally reigns is in every respect worthy of praise."*

This account shows the remarkable rapidity with which they had built up the new town.

But perfect happiness is not for this world. In 1831 came to Economy a German adventurer, Bernhard Müller by right name, who had assumed the title *Graf* or Count Maximilian de Leon, and had gathered a following of visionary Germans, whom he imposed, with himself, upon the Harmonists, on the pretense that he was a believer with them in religious matters. He proved to be a wretched intriguer, who brought ruin on all who connected themselves with him; and who began at once to make trouble in Economy. Having secured a lodgment, he began to announce strange doctrines, marriage, a livelier life, and other temptations to worldliness; and he finally succeeded in effecting a serious division, which, if it had not been prudently managed, might have destroyed the community. After bitter disputes, in which at last affairs came to such a pass that a vote had to be taken, in order to decide who were faithful to the old order and to Rapp, and who were for Count Leon,

---

* "Travels through North America, during the years 1825–26, by His Highness, Bernhard, Duke of Saxe-Weimar Eisenach." Philadelphia, 1828.

an agreement was come to. "We knew not even who was for and who against us," said Mr. Henrici to me; "and I was in the utmost anxiety as I made out the two lists; at last they were complete; all the names had been called; we counted, and found that five hundred were for Father Rapp, and two hundred and fifty for Count Leon. Father Rapp, when I told him the numbers, with his usual ready wit, quoted from the book of Revelation, 'And the tail of the serpent drew the third part of the stars of heaven, and did cast them to the earth.'"

The end of the dispute was an agreement, under which the society bound itself to pay to those who adhered to Count Leon one hundred and five thousand dollars, in three installments, all payable within twelve months; the other side agreeing, on their part, to leave Economy within three months, taking with them only their clothing and household furniture, and relinquishing all claims upon the property of the society. This agreement was made in March, 1832; and Leon and his followers withdrew to Phillipsburg, a village ten miles below Economy, on the other side of the river, which they bought, with eight hundred acres of land.

Here they set up a society on communistic principles, but permitting marriage; and here they very quickly wasted the large sum of money they received from the Harmonists; and after a desperate and lawless attempt to extort more money from the Economy people, which was happily defeated, Count Leon absconded with a few of his people in a boat to Alexandria on the Red River, where this singular adventurer perished of cholera in 1833. Those he had deluded meantime divided the Phillipsburg property among themselves, and set up each for himself, and a number afterward joined Keil in forming the Bethel Community in Missouri, of which an account will be found in another place.

In 1832, seven years only after the removal to Economy, the society was able, it thus appears, to pay out in a single year one hundred and five thousand dollars in cash—a very great sum of money in those days. This shows that they had largely increased their capital by their thrift and industry at New Harmony in Indiana, and at Economy. They had then existed as a community twenty-seven years; had built three towns; and had during the whole time lived a life of comfort and social order, such as few individual settlers in our Western States at that time could command.

III.—Doctrines and Practical Life in Economy; with some Particulars of "Father Rapp."

The Agreement or Articles of Association under which the " Harmony Society " was formed in 1805, and which was signed by all the members thenceforward, read as follows:

"ARTICLES OF ASSOCIATION.

" *Whereas*, by the favor of divine Providence, an association or community has been formed by George Rapp and many others upon the basis of Christian fellowship, the principles of which, being faithfully derived from the sacred Scriptures, include the government of the patriarchal age, united to the community of property adopted in the days of the apostles, and wherein the simple object sought is to approximate, so far as human imperfections may allow, to the fulfillment of the will of God, by the exercise of those affections and the practice of those virtues which are essential to the happiness of man in time and throughout eternity:

" *And whereas* it is necessary to the good order and well-being of the said association that the conditions of membership should be clearly understood, and that the rights, privileges, and duties of every individual therein should be so defined as to prevent mistake or disappointment, on the one hand, and contention or disagreement on the other;

" *Therefore* be it known to all whom it may concern that we, the undersigned, citizens of the County of Beaver, in the Commonwealth of Pennsylvania, do severally and distinctly, each for himself, covenant, grant, and agree, to and with the said George Rapp and his associates, as follows, viz. :

"ARTICLE I. We, the undersigned, for ourselves, our heirs, executors, and administrators, do hereby give, grant, and forever convey to the said George Rapp and his associates, and to their heirs and assigns, all our property, real, personal, and mixed, whether it be lands and tenements, goods and chattels, money or debts due to us, jointly or severally, in possession, in remainder, or in reversion or expectancy, whatsoever and wheresoever, without evasion, qualification, or reserve, as a free gift or donation, for the benefit and use of the said association or community; and we do hereby bind ourselves, our heirs, executors, and administrators, to do all such other acts as may be necessary to vest a perfect title to the same in the said association, and to place the said property at the full disposal of the superintendent of the said community without delay.

"ARTICLE II. We do further covenant and agree to and with the said George Rapp and his associates, that we will severally submit faithfully to the laws and regulations of said community, and will at all times manifest a ready and cheerful obedience toward those who are or may be appointed as superintendents thereof, holding ourselves bound to promote the interest and welfare of the said community, not only by the labor of our own hands, but also by that of our children, our families, and all others who now are or hereafter may be under our control.

"ARTICLE III. If contrary to our expectation it should so happen that we could not render the faithful obedience aforesaid, and should be induced from that or any other cause to withdraw from the said association, then and in such case we do expressly covenant and agree to and with the said George Rapp and his associates that we never will claim or demand, either for ourselves, our children, or for any one belonging to us, directly or indirectly, any compensation, wages, or reward whatever for our or their labor or services rendered to the said community, or to any member thereof; but whatever we or our families jointly or severally shall or may do, all shall be held and considered as a voluntary service for our brethren.

"ARTICLE IV. In consideration of the premises, the said George Rapp and his associates do, by these presents, adopt the undersigned jointly and severally as members of the said community, whereby each of them obtains the privilege of being present at every religious meeting, and of receiving not only for themselves, but also for their children and families, all such instructions in church and school as may be reasonably required, both for their temporal good and for their eternal felicity.

"ARTICLE V. The said George Rapp and his associates further agree to supply the undersigned severally with all the necessaries of life, as clothing, meat, drink, lodging, etc., for themselves and their families. And this provision is not limited to their days of health and strength; but when any of them shall become sick, infirm, or otherwise unfit for labor, the same support and maintenance shall be allowed as before, together with such medicine, care, attendance, and consolation as their situation may reasonably demand. And if at any time after they have become members of the association, the father or mother of a family should die or be otherwise separated from the community, and should leave their family behind, such family shall not be left orphans or destitute, but shall partake of the same rights and maintenance as before, so long as they remain in the association, as well in sickness as in health, and to such extent as their circumstances may require.

" Article VI. And if it should so happen as above mentioned that any of the undersigned should violate his or their agreement, and would or could not submit to the laws and regulations of the church or the community, and for that or any other cause should withdraw from the association, then the said George Rapp and his associates agree to refund to him or them the value of all such property as he or they may have brought into the community, in compliance with the first article of this agreement, the said value to be refunded without interest, in one, two, or three annual installments, as the said George Rapp and his associates shall determine. And if the person or persons so withdrawing themselves were poor, and brought nothing into the community, notwithstanding they depart openly and regularly, they shall receive a donation in money, according to the length of their stay and to their conduct, and to such amount as their necessities may require, in the judgment of the superintendents of the association."

In 1818, as before mentioned, a book in which was recorded the amount of property contributed by each member to the general fund was destroyed. In 1836 a change was made in the formal constitution or agreement above quoted, in the following words:

" 1st. The sixth article [in regard to refunding] is entirely annulled and made void, as if it had never existed, all others to remain in full force as heretofore. 2d. All the property of the society, real, personal, and mixed, in law or equity, and howsoever contributed or acquired, shall be deemed, now and forever, joint and indivisible stock. Each individual is to be considered to have finally and irrevocably parted with all his former contributions, whether in lands, goods, money, or labor, and the same rule shall apply to all future contributions, whatever they may be. 3d. Should any individual withdraw from the society or depart this life, neither he, in the one case, nor his representatives in the other, shall be entitled to demand an account of said contributions, or to claim any thing from the society as a matter of right. But it shall be left altogether to the discretion of the superintendent to decide whether any, and, if any, what allowance shall be made to such member or his representatives as a donation."

These amendments were signed by three hundred and nine-ty-one members, being all who then constituted the society. No other changes have been made; but on the death of Father Rapp, on the 7th of August, 1847, the whole society signed the constitution again, and put in office two trustees and seven elders, to perform all the duties and assume all the authority which Father Rapp had relinquished with his life.

Under this simple constitution the Harmony Society has flourished for sixty-nine years; nor has its life been threatened by disagreements, except in the case of the Count de Leon's in-trigue. It has suffered three or four lawsuits from members who had left it; but in every case the courts have decided for the society, after elaborate, and in some cases long-continued trials. It has always lived in peace and friendship with its neighbors.

Its real estate and other property was, from the foundation until his death in 1834, held in the name of Frederick (Reich-ert) Rapp, who was an excellent business man, and conducted all its dealings with the outside world, and had charge of its temporalities generally; the elder Rapp avoiding for himself all general business. Upon Frederick's death the society form-ally and unanimously imposed upon Father Rapp the care of the temporal as well as the spiritual affairs of the little com-monwealth, placing in his name the title to all their property.

But, as he did not wish to let temporal concerns interfere with his spiritual functions, and as besides he was then growing old, being in 1834 seventy-seven years of age, he appointed as his helpers and subagents two members, R. L. Bäker and J. Henrici, the latter of whom is still, with Mr. Jonathan Lenz, the head of the society, Mr. Bäker having died some years ago.

The theological belief of the Harmony Society naturally crystallized under the preaching and during the life of Father Rapp. It has some features of German mysticism, grafted upon a practical application of the Christian doctrine and theory.

At the foundation of all lies a strong determination to make the preparation of their souls or spirits for the future life the pre-eminent business of life, and to obey in the strictest and most literal manner what they believe to be the will of God as revealed and declared by Jesus Christ. In the following paragraphs I give a brief summary of what may be called their creed:

I. They hold that Adam was created "in the likeness of God;" that he was a dual being, containing within his own person both the sexual elements, reading literally, in confirmation of this, the text (Gen. i. 26, 27): "And God said, Let us make man in *our* image, after *our* likeness, and let *them* have dominion;" and, "So God created man in his own image, in the image of God created he him; male and female created he them;" which they hold to denote that both the Creator and the first created were of this dual nature. They believe that had Adam been content to remain in his original state, he would have increased without the help of a female, bringing forth new beings like himself to replenish the earth.

II. But Adam fell into discontent; and God separated from his body the female part, and gave it him according to his desire; and therein they believe consisted the fall of man.

III. From this they deduce that the celibate state is more

pleasing to God; that in the renewed world man will be restored to the dual Godlike and Adamic condition; and,

IV. They hold that the coming of Christ and the renovation of the world are near at hand. This nearness of the millennium is a cardinal point of doctrine with them; and Father Rapp firmly believed that he would live to see the wished-for reappearance of Christ in the heavens, and that he would be permitted to present his company of believers to the Saviour whom they endeavored to please with their lives. So vivid was this belief in him, that it lead some of his followers to fondly fancy that Father Rapp would not die before Christ's coming; and there is a touching story of the old man, that when he felt death upon him, at the age of ninety, he said, " If I did not know that the dear Lord meant I should present you all to him, I should think my last moments come." These were indeed his last words. To be in constant readiness for the reappearance of Christ is one of the aims of the society; nor have its members ever faltered in the faith that this great event is near at hand.

V. Jesus they hold to have been born " in the likeness of the Father"—that is to say, a dual being, as Adam before the fall.

VI. They hold that Jesus taught and commanded a community of goods; and refer to the example of the early Christians as proof.

VII. They believe in the ultimate redemption and salvation of all mankind; but hold that only those who follow the celibate life, and otherwise conform to what they understand to be the commandments of Jesus, will come at once into the bright and glorious company of Christ and his companions; that offenders will undergo a probation for purification.

VIII. They reject and detest what is commonly called " Spiritualism."

As the practical application to their daily lives of the religious faith which I have concisely stated, Father Rapp taught humility, simplicity in living, self-sacrifice, love to your neighbor, regular and persevering industry, prayer and self-examination.

In the admission of new members, they exact a complete confession of sins to one of the elders of the society, as being a wholesome and necessary part of true repentance, requisite to secure the forgiveness of God.

On Sunday two services are held, besides a Sunday-school for the children; and the preacher, who is the head of the society, does not stand up when delivering his discourse, but sits at a table on a platform. The church has two doors, and the men enter at one, the women at the other, each sex occupying one end of the building by itself; the pulpit being in the middle, and opposite a raised and inclosed space wherein sit the elders and the choir.

They observe as holy days Christmas, Good Friday and Easter, and Pentecost; and three great festivals of their own —the 15th of February, which is the anniversary of their foundation; Harvest-Home, in the autumn; and an annual Lord's Supper in October. On these festival occasions they assemble in a great hall; and there, after singing and addresses, a feast is served, there being an elaborate kitchen adjacent to the hall on purpose for the preparation of these feasts, while in the cellars of the same building are stores of wine of different ages and kinds.

They live well; all of them eat meat, and but a few abstain from pork. They rise between five and six, according to the season of the year; eat a light breakfast between six and seven; have a lunch at nine; dinner at twelve; an afternoon lunch, called "*vesper brodt*," at three; to which, when they have labored hard in the fields, they add wine or cider; supper between six and seven; and they go to bed by nine o'clock.

Father Rapp taught that every one ought to labor with his hands, and at agricultural labor where this was possible. He was himself fond of out-door employments, and liked to be in the fields, helping the plowmen or harvesters. The women attend to the housekeeping; and as this is simple and quickly done, they are fond of working in the gardens attached to the houses. In the old times, women as well as men labored in the fields in harvest time, or at other times when work was pressing; and the younger women still follow this habit, which was probably brought over from Germany.

Each household consists of men and women to the number of from four to eight, and usually in equal numbers. The houses have but one entrance door from the street. They carpet their floors, and generally deny themselves no comforts compatible with simplicity of life.

Father Rapp taught them to love music and flowers; almost all the people can read music, and there are but few who have not learned to play upon some instrument. In their worship they use instrumental music; and it forms an important part in their feasts. They do not practice dancing, to which they have always felt opposed. As they study plainness of dress, they use no jewelry.

They once had a museum, which has been sold. Father Rapp's house contains a number of pictures, among them a fine copy of Benjamin West's "Christ Healing the Sick;" the church and assembly hall have no works of art. The people read the newspapers; and those who wish for books have them, there being a library; but "the Bible is the book chiefly read among us," I was told.

Father Rapp taught that it was advisable for the society to make all it could for itself; and he had an intelligent appreciation of the value of labor-saving machinery. Economy has therefore complete and well-furnished shops of various kinds. Its steam-laundry is admirably contrived; and its slaughter-house, with piggery and soap-boiling house near by; its machine shop, with a cider-boiler annexed; its saw-mill, wagon

A STREET VIEW IN ECONOMY.

FATHER RAPP'S HOUSE—ECONOMY.

shop, blacksmith shop, tannery, carpenter's shop, bakery, vinegar factory (where much cider is utilized), hattery, tailor's and shoemaker's shops, tin shop, saddlery shop, and weaver's shop, show how various were and are the industries followed here, and how completely furnished the society was, from within, for all the wants of daily life. I saw even a shop for the repair of clocks and watches, and a barber's shop; the barber serving the aged and sick, and being otherwise foreman of the tailor's shop.

In this long list I have not specified the brewery, grist-mill, a large granary, a cotton and a woolen mill; nor the two great cellars full of fine wine casks, which would make a Californian envious, so well-built are they.

There is also a school, and the Harmony people have always kept up a good school for the children in their charge. They aim to give each child an elementary education, and afterwards a trade; and as the boys learn also agricultural labors of different kinds, they are generally self-helpful when they pass into the world. The instruction is in German and English; and the small girls and boys whom I examined wrote very well.

Each family cooks for itself. There were formerly bake-ovens in every block, one being used by several families; but there is now a general bakery, whence all carry bread in indefinite and unlimited supplies. Milk, too, is brought to the houses, and from what each household receives, it saves the cream for butter. When the butcher kills a beef, a little boy is sent around the village, who knocks at each window and cries out "*Sollt fleisch holen*"—"Come and get meat"—and the butcher serves to each household sufficient for its wants. Other supplies for the household are dealt out from the general storehouse at stated periods; but if any one needs more, he has only to apply. Tea is not generally used.

Clothing is given out as it is needed by each person; and I was told that the tailor usually keeps his eye upon the people's coats and trousers, the shoemaker upon their shoes, and so on; each counting it a matter of honor or pride that the brethren shall be decently and comfortably clad.

"As each labors for all, and as the interest of one is the interest of all, there is no occasion for selfishness, and no room for waste. We were brought up to be economical; to waste is a sin; we live simply; and each has enough, all that he can eat and wear, and no man can use more than that." This was the simple explanation I received from a Harmonist, when I wondered whether some family or person would not be wasteful or greedy.

In the season, all the people who are not too old labor more or less in the fields and orchards. This is their habit, and is thought healthful to body and soul.

The Harmonists have usually attained a hale and happy old age. I had access to no mortuary records, and there are no monuments in the cemetery, but a great part of the people have lived to be seventy and over; and they die without fear, trusting that they are the chosen people of the Lord.

Such is Economy at this time. Its large factories are closed, for its people are too few to man them; and the members think it wiser and more comfortable for themselves to employ labor at a distance from their own town. They are pecuniarily interested in coal-mines, in saw-mills, and oil-wells; and they control manufactories at Beaver Falls—notably a cutlery shop, the largest in the United States, and one of the largest in the world, where of late they have begun to employ two hundred Chinese; and it is creditable to the Harmony people that they look after the intellectual and spiritual welfare of these strangers as but too few employers do.

"Is there any monument to Father Rapp?" I asked; and the old man to whom I put the question said, quietly, "Yes, all that you see here, around us."

His body lies in a grave undistinguishable from others

surrounding it. There is no portrait of him—for he always refused to sit for one. But his memory is most tenderly and reverently cherished by his followers and survivors. From a number of persons I gathered the following personal details, which give a picture of the man : He was nearly if not quite six feet high; well-built, with blue eyes, a somewhat stately walk, and a full beard, which he was the first in the society to wear. He was extremely industrious, and never wasted even a minute; knew admirably how to use every spare moment. He was cheerful, kindly, talkative ; plain-spoken when he had to find fault; not very enthusiastic, but somewhat dry and very practical. In his earlier years, in Germany, he was witty; and to the last he was ready and apt in speech. His conversation centred always upon religion and the conduct of life; and no matter with whom he was speaking, or what was the character of the person, Rapp knew very well how to lead the talk to these topics.

The young people were very fond of him. " He was a man before whom no evil could stand." " When I met him in the street, if I had a bad thought in my head, it flew away." He was constantly in the fields or in the factories, cheering, encouraging, or advising the people. " He knew every thing— how to do it, what was the best way." " Ah, he was a *man;* he told us what to do, and how to be good." In his spare moments he studied botany, geology, astronomy, mechanics. " He was never idle, not even a quarter of an hour." He believed much in work; thought hard field-work a good cure for spiritual as well as bodily diseases. He was an " extraordinarily eloquent preacher;" and it is a singular fact that, dying at the great age of ninety, he preached in the church twice but two Sundays before his death; and on the Sunday before he died addressed his people from the window of his sick-room. He was " a good man, with true, honest eyes." He " always labored against selfishness, and to serve the brethren and the

Lord." He appears to have abhorred ostentation and needless forms and ceremonies, for he sat while preaching; never prescribed any uniform dress or peculiar form of speech; and neither in their worship nor in their daily lives taught the people to make merely formal differences between themselves and the world at large. That he did not feel the necessity of such outward protests against "the world," and relied for the bond of union in the community so entirely upon the effect of his teachings, seems to me one of the surest and most significant proofs of his real power.

Such is the report of their founder and guide from the older men now living, who knew him well. That he was a man of great force and high character it seems to be impossible to doubt. It has often been reported that he was tyrannical and self-seeking; and that he chose his people from among the most ignorant, in order to rule them. But the present members of the Harmony Society can not be called ignorant: they are a simple and pious people, but not incapable of taking care of their own interests; and their opinion of their founder is probably the correct one. Their love and reverence for him, their recital of his goodness, of his abilities, and of his intercourse with them, are the best testimony as to his character; and their continuance in the course he laid out for them, for more than a quarter of a century since his death, shows that not only did his teaching and life inspire confidence, but also that his training bore wholesome fruit in them.

He made religion the most important interest in the lives of his followers. Not only did he preach on Sundays, but he admonished, encouraged, reproved, and advised constantly during the week; he divided the people into companies or classes, who met on week-day evenings for mutual counsel in religious matters, and with these he constantly met; he visited the sick; he buried the dead—with great plainness and lack of ceremony. He taught that they ought to purify the body, and he was himself a model of plain and somewhat rigid and practical living, and of self-abnegation; and I think no thoughtful man can hear his story from the older members of the society who were brought up under his rule, and consider the history of Economy, and the present daily life of its people, without conceiving a great respect for Father Rapp's powers and for the use he made of them.

Pecuniarily Rapp's experiment has been an extraordinary success. The society is now reported to be worth from two to three millions of dollars. By an investigation into all its affairs and interests, made in the Pennsylvania courts in 1854, by reason of a suit brought by a seceding member, it was shown to be worth at that time over a million. In these days of defaulting bank officers and numerous breaches of trust, it is a singular commentary upon the communal system to know that the society has never required from its chiefs any report upon their administration of the finances. The investigation in the courts was the first insight they had since their foundation into the management of their affairs by Rapp and his successors; and there the utmost efforts of opposing lawyers, among whom, by the way, was Edwin M. Stanton, afterward Secretary of War, failed to discover the least maladministration or misappropriation of funds by the rulers; and proved the integrity of all who had managed their extensive and complicated business from the beginning.

As Father Rapp grew older, his influence over his people became absolute. His long life among them bore fruit in an unwavering confidence in his sound judgment and unselfish devotion. He appears to have led them in right paths; for, though probably few will be found to subscribe to their peculiar religious tenets, all their neighbors hold them in the highest esteem, as just, honest, kindly, charitable, patriotic; good citizens, though they do not vote; careful of their servants and laborers; fair and liberal in their dealings with the world.

Of Economy as it now is, what I have written gives a sufficiently precise view. The great factories are closed, and the people live quietly in their pretty and simple homes. The energies put in motion by their large capital are to be found at a distance from their village. Their means give employment to many hundreds of people in different parts of Western Pennsylvania; and wherever I have come upon their traces, I have found the "Economites," as they are commonly called, highly spoken of. They have not sought to accumulate wealth; but their reluctance to enter into new enterprises has probably made them in the long run only more successful, for it has made them prudent; and they have not been tempted to work on credit; while their command of ready money has opened to them the best opportunities.

The present managers or trustees ("*verwalter*") are Jacob Henrici and Jonathan Lenz. The first, who is also the religious head, being in this respect the successor of R. L. Bäker, who was the successor of Father Rapp, is a German by birth, and a man of culture and of deep piety. He was educated to be a teacher; and entered the Harmony Society in 1826, a year after its removal to Economy. Rapp appears to have appreciated from the first his gentle spirit, piety, and sincere devotion to the community, as well as the importance of his culture and talents. He lived long in the house with Father Rapp, and was his intimate and confidant. Upon Frederick Rapp's death, Father Rapp appointed Bäker and Henrici to attend to the temporal concerns with which he was then charged; and upon the Elder Rapp's death, these two were chosen to take his place. When Mr. Bäker died, Mr. Henrici was chosen to fill his place, and he selected Mr. Lenz to be his coadjutor.

Mr. Lenz was born in the society in 1807, and has lived in it all his life. He also is a man of some culture, of gentle and pleasant manners, and an excellent business man.

Both are aged, Henrici being seventy, and Lenz sixty·

seven. Both are tall, firmly built, and fine-looking men, with a peculiarly gentle and lovable expression of face. They live together in the house built for Father Rapp, where also live several of the older members, among them Miss Gertrude Rapp, a granddaughter of the founder, a charming old lady, with a very bright, intelligent face. All these old people are so well preserved, and have so free and wholesome an air, that intercourse with them is not a slight argument to the visitor in favor of their simple manner of life.

There is a council of seven persons, from among whom the trustees are chosen.

It is a curious fact that among the hired people of the society, living in Economy, are a number whom they adopted as children and brought up, and who conform their lives in all respects, even to the celibate condition, to the rules of the society, but prefer to labor for wages rather than become members.

The society does not seek new members, though I am told it would not refuse any who seemed to have a true vocation. As to its future, little is said. The people look for the coming of the Lord; they await the appearance of Christ in the heavens; and their chief aim is to be ready for this great event, when they expect to be summoned to Palestine, to be joined to the great crowd of the elect. Naturally there are not wanting, among their neighbors in Pittsburgh, people who are tormented with curiosity to know what is to become of the large property of the Harmonists when these old people finally, in the course of nature, pass away. "The Lord will show us a way," is the answer at Economy to such inquiries. "We have not trusted him in vain so far; we trust him still. He will give us a sign."

THE SOCIETY OF SEPARATISTS,

AT

ZOAR, OHIO.

THE SOCIETY OF SEPARATISTS AT ZOAR.

I.—HISTORY.

THE village of Zoar lies in Tuscarawas County, Ohio, about half-way between Cleveland and Pittsburgh, on a branch of the railroad which connects these two points. It is situated on the bank of the Tuscarawas Creek, which affords at this point valuable water-power. The place is irregularly built, and contains fewer houses than a village of the same number of inhabitants usually has; but the dwellings are mostly quite large, and each accommodates several families. There is a commodious brick church, a large and well-fitted brick school-house, an extensive country tavern or hotel, and a multitude of sheds and barns. There are, besides, several mills and factories; and in the middle of the village a somewhat elaborate, large, square house, which was the residence of the founder and head of the society until his death, and is now used in part as a storehouse.

Zoar is the home of a communistic society who call themselves "Separatists," and who founded the village in 1817, and have here become quite wealthy. They originated in Würtemberg, and, like the Harmony Society, the Inspirationists, and others, were dissenters from the Established Church. The Separatists of southern Germany were equivalent to what in New England are called "Come Outers"—protestants against the prevailing religious faith, or, as they would say, lack of faith.

These German "Come Outers" were for the most part mystics, who had read the writings of Jacob Boehm, Gerhard Terstegen, and Jung Stilling; they cherished different religious or doctrinal beliefs, were stigmatized as fanatics, but were usually, I judge, simple-hearted, pious people, desirous to lead a more spiritual life than they found in the churches.

Their refusal to send their children to the schools—which were controlled by the clergy—and to allow their young men to serve as soldiers, brought upon them persecution from both the secular and the ecclesiastical authorities, resulting in flogging, imprisonment, and fines. The people who finally emigrated to Zoar, after enduring these persecutions for ten or twelve years gathered together in an obscure part of Würtemberg, where, by the favor of a friend at court, they were permitted to settle. But even from this refuge they were hunted out after some years; and, finding no other resource left, they at last determined to remove in a body to America, those few among them who had property paying the passage of those who were without means.

Their persecutions had, it seems, attracted the attention of some English Quakers, who aided them to emigrate, and with kindly forethought sent in advance of them to certain Quakers in Philadelphia a sum of money, amounting, I have been told, to eighteen dollars for each person of the company, with which their Philadelphia friends provided for them on their landing. This kind care is still acknowledged at Zoar as an "inestimable blessing."

They arrived at Philadelphia in August, 1817, and almost immediately bargained with one Hagar for a tract of five thousand six hundred acres of land, which they were, with the help of their Quaker friends, enabled to buy on favorable terms. It was a military grant in the wilderness of Ohio, and they agreed to give for it three dollars per acre, with a credit of fifteen years, the first three years without interest.

Joseph Bäumeler, whom they had chosen to be their leader, went out to take possession with a few able-bodied men, and these built the first log-hut on the 1st of December, 1817. During the following spring the remainder of the society followed; but many were so poor that they had to take service with the neighboring farmers to earn a support for their families, and all lived in the poorest possible way.

At this time they had no intention of forming a communistic society. They held their interests separately; and it was expected that each member should pay for his own share of the land, which had been purchased in order to be thus subdivided. Their purpose was to worship God according to their faith, in freedom, and to live, for that end, in a neighborhood.

But, having among them a certain number of old and feeble people, and many poor who found it difficult to save money to pay for their land, the leading men presently saw that the enterprise would fail unless it was established upon a different foundation; and that necessity would compel the people to scatter. Early in 1819 the leaders after consultation determined that, to succeed, they must establish a community of goods and efforts, and draw in to themselves all whom poverty had compelled to take service at a distance. This resolution was laid before the whole society, and, after some weeks of discussion, was agreed to; and on the 15th of April articles of agreement for a community of goods were signed. There were then about two hundred and twenty-five persons—men, women, and children. The men were farm-laborers, weavers, carpenters, bakers, but at first they had not a blacksmith among them.

From this time they began to prosper. "We could never have paid for our land, if we had not formed a community," the older people told me; and, from all I could learn, I believe this to be true.

At first they prohibited marriage, and it was not until 1828 or 1830 that they broke down this rule.

On forming a community, Joseph Bäumeler, who had been a leading man among them, was chosen to be their spiritual as well as temporal head. His name probably proved a stumbling-block to his American neighbors, for he presently began to spell it Bimeler—a phonetic rendering. Thus it appears in deeds and other public documents; and the people came to be commonly spoken of as " Bimmelers." Bäumeler was originally a weaver, and later a teacher. He was doubtless a man of considerable ability, but not comparable, I imagine, with Rapp. He appears to have been a fluent speaker; and on Sundays he delivered to the society a long series of discourses, which were after his death gathered together and printed in German in three ponderous octavo volumes. They concern themselves not only with religious and communistic thoughts, but largely with the minor morals, manners, good order in housekeeping, cleanliness, health observances, and often with physiological details.

In March, 1824, an amended constitution was adopted. Between 1828 and 1830 they began to permit marriage, Bäumeler himself taking a wife. In 1832 the Legislature formally incorporated the " Separatist Society of Zoar," and a new constitution, still in force, was signed in the same year.

" As soon as we adopted community of goods we began to prosper," said one of the older members to me. Having abundance of hands, they set up shops; and, being poor and in debt, they determined to live rigidly within their means and from their own products. They crowded at first into a few small log-cabins; some of which are still standing, and are occupied to this day. They kept cattle; were careful and laborious farmers; and setting up blacksmith's, carpenter's, and joiner's shops, they began to earn a little money from work done for the neighboring farmers. Nevertheless their progress was slow, and they accounted it a great piece of good fortune when in 1827 a canal was built through their neighborhood. What with putting their own young men upon this work, and selling supplies to the contractors, they made enough money from this enterprise to pay for their land; and thenceforth, with free hands, they began to accumulate wealth.

They now own in one body over seven thousand acres of very fertile land, including extensive and valuable water-power, and have besides some land in Iowa. They have established a woolen factory, where they make cloth and yarn for their own use and for sale. Also two large flour-mills, a saw-mill, planing-mill, machine shop, tannery, and dye-house. They have also a country store for the accommodation of the neighborhood, a large hotel which receives summer visitors; and for their own use they maintain a wagon shop, blacksmith's and carpenter's shops, tailors, dressmakers, shoe-makers, a cider-mill, a small brewery, and a few looms for weaving linen. They employ constantly about fifty persons not members of the community, besides "renters," who manage some of their farms on shares.

They have now (in the spring of 1874) about three hundred members, and their property is worth more than a million dollars.

II.—Religious Faith and Practical Life.

The "Principles of the Separatists," which are printed in the first volume of Joseph Bäumeler's discourses, were evidently framed in Germany. They consist of twelve articles:

"I. We believe and confess the Trinity of God: Father, Son, and Holy Ghost.

"II. The fall of Adam, and of all mankind, with the loss thereby of the likeness of God in them.

"III. The return through Christ to God, our proper Father.

"IV. The Holy Scriptures as the measure and guide of our lives, and the touchstone of truth and falsehood.

"All our other principles arise out of these, and rule our conduct in the religious, spiritual, and natural life.

"V. All ceremonies are banished from among us, and we declare them useless and injurious; and this is the chief cause of our Separation.

"VI. We render to no mortal honors due only to God, as to uncover the head, or to bend the knee. Also we address every one as 'thou'—*du*.

"VII. We separate ourselves from all ecclesiastical connections and constitutions, because true Christian life requires no sectarianism, while set forms and ceremonies cause sectarian divisions.

"VIII. Our marriages are contracted by mutual consent, and before witnesses. They are then notified to the political authority; and we reject all intervention of priests or preachers.

"IX. All intercourse of the sexes, except what is necessary to the perpetuation of the species, we hold to be sinful and contrary to the order and command of God. Complete virginity or entire cessation of sexual commerce is more commendable than marriage.

"X. We can not send our children into the schools of Babylon [meaning the clerical schools of Germany], where other principles contrary to these are taught.

"XI. We can not serve the state as soldiers, because a Christian can not murder his enemy, much less his friend.

"XII. We regard the political government as absolutely necessary to maintain order, and to protect the good and honest and punish the wrong-doers; and no one can prove us to be untrue to the constituted authorities."

For adhering to these tolerably harmless articles of faith, they suffered bitter persecution in Germany in the beginning of this century.

Subject to the above declaration they have a formal constitution, which divides the members into two classes, the novitiates and the full associates. The former are required to serve at least one year before admission to the second class, and this is exacted even of their own children, if on attaining majority they wish to enter the society.

The members of the first or probationary class do not give up their property. They sign an agreement, " for the furtherance of their spiritual and temporal welfare and happiness," in which they " bind themselves to labor, obey, and execute all the orders of the trustees and their successors," and to " use all their industry and skill in behalf of the exclusive benefit of the said Separatist Society of Zoar;" and to put their minor children under the exclusive guardianship and care of the trustees.

The trustees on their part, and for the society, agree to secure to the signers of these articles " board and clothing free of cost, the clothing to consist of at any time no less than two suits, including the clothes brought by the said party of the first part to this society." Also medical attendance and nursing in case of sickness. " Good moral conduct, such as is enjoined by the strict observance of the principles of Holy Writ," is also promised by both parties; and it is stipulated that " no extra supplies shall be asked or allowed, neither in meat, drink, clothing, nor dwelling (cases of sickness excepted); but such, if any can be allowed to exist, may and shall be obtained [by the neophytes] through means of their own, and never out of the common fund."

All money in possession of the probationer must be deposited with the society when he signs the agreement; for it a receipt is given, making the deposit payable to him on his demand, without interest.

Finally, it is agreed that all disputes shall be settled by arbitration alone, and within the society.

When a member of the first or probationary class desires to

be received into full membership, he applies to the trustees, who formally hear his demand, inquire into the reasons he can give for it, and if they know no good cause why he should not be admitted, they thereupon give thirty days' notice to the society of the time and place at which he is to sign the covenant. If during that interval no member makes charges against him, and if he has no debts, and is ready to make over any property he may have, he is allowed to sign the following COVENANT:

" We, the subscribers, members of the Society of Separatists of the second class, declare hereby that we give all our property, of every kind, not only what we already possess, but what we may hereafter come into possession of by inheritance, gift, or otherwise, real and personal, and all rights, titles, and expectations whatever, both for ourselves and our heirs, to the said society forever, to be and remain, not only during our lives, but after our deaths, the exclusive property of the society. Also we promise and bind ourselves to obey all the commands and orders of the trustees and their subordinates, with the utmost zeal and diligence, without opposition or grumbling; and to devote all our strength, good-will, diligence, and skill, during our whole lives, to the common service of the society and for the satisfaction of its trustees. Also we consign in a similar manner our children, so long as they are minors, to the charge of the trustees, giving these the same rights and powers over them as though they had been formally indentured to them under the laws of the state."

Finally, there is a formal CONSTITUTION, which prescribes the order of administration; and which also is signed by all the members. According to this instrument, all officers are to be elected by the whole society, the women voting as well as the men. All elections are to be by ballot, and by the majority vote; and they are to be held on the second Tuesday in May. The society is to elect annually one trustee and one member of the standing committee or council, once in four years a cashier, and an agent whenever a vacancy occurs or is made. The time and place of the election are to be made public twenty days beforehand by the trustees, and four members are to be chosen at each election to be managers and judges at the next.

The trustees, three in number, are to serve three years, but may be indefinitely re-elected. They have unlimited power over all the temporalities of the society, but are bound to provide board, clothing, and dwelling for each member, " without respect of persons ;" and to use all confided to their charge for the best interests of the society. They are to manage all its industries and affairs, and to prescribe to each member his work ; " but in all they do they are to have the general consent of the society." They are to appoint subordinates and superintendents of the different industries ; are to consult in difficult cases with the Standing Committee of Five, and are with its help to keep the peace among the members.

The agent is the trader of the society, who is to be its intermediate with the outside world, to buy and sell. This office is now held by the leading trustee.

The standing committee is a high court of appeals in cases of disagreement, and a general council for the agent and trustees.

The cashier is to have the sole and exclusive control of all the moneys of the society, the trustees and agent being obliged to hand over to his custody all they receive. He is also the book-keeper, and is required to give an annual account to the trustees.

The constitution is to be read in a public and general meeting of the society at least once in every year.

The system of administration thus prescribed appears to have worked satisfactorily for more than forty years.

" Do you favor marriage ?" I asked some of the older members, trustees, and managers. They answered " No ;" but they exact no penalty nor inflict any disability upon those who choose to marry. "Marriage," I was told, "is on the whole unfavorable to community life. It is better to observe the celibate life. But it is not, in our experience, fatally adverse. It only makes more trouble; and in either case, whether a community permit or forbid marriage, it may lose members."

About half of their young people, who have grown up in the society, become permanent members, and as many young men as girls. They do not permit members to marry outside of the society; and require those who do to leave the place. "Men and women need to be trained to live peaceably and contentedly in a community. Those who have been brought up outside do not find matters to their taste here."

Bäumeler taught that God did not look with pleasure on marriage, but that he only tolerated it; that in the kingdom of heaven "husband, wife, and children will not know each other;" "there will be no distinction of sex there." Nevertheless he married, and had a family of children.

When a young couple wish to marry, they consult the trustees, whose consent is required in this as in the other emergencies of the community life; and the more so as they must provide lodgings or a dwelling for the newly married, and furniture for their housekeeping. Weddings, however, are economically managed, and the parents of the parties usually contribute of their superfluities for the young couple's accommodation.

When marriages began among them, a rule was adopted that the children should remain in the care of their parents until they were three years old; at which time they were placed in large houses, the girls in one, boys in another, where they were brought up under the care of persons especially appointed for that purpose; nor did they ever again come under the exclusive control of their parents. This singular custom, which is practiced also by the Oneida communists, lasted at Zoar until the year 1845, when it was found inconvenient.

CHURCH AT ZOAR.

SCHOOL-HOUSE AT ZOAR.

The sixty or seventy young persons under twenty-one now in the community live with their parents. Until the age of fifteen they are sent to school, and a school is maintained all the year round. Usually the instruction has been in German; but when I visited Zoar they had an American teacher.

On the blackboard, when I visited the school, a pupil had just completed an example in proportion, concerning the division of property among heirs; and I thought how remarkable it is that the community life ever lasts, in any experiment, beyond the first generation, when even the examples by which children of a community are taught arithmetic refer to division of property and individual ownership, and every piece of literature they read tends to inculcate the love of "me" and "mine." I do not wonder that general literary studies are not encouraged in many communities. As for the Zoar people, they are not great readers, except of the Bible and the few pious books which they brought over from Germany, or have imported since.

The Zoar communists belong to the peasant class of Southern Germany. They are therefore unintellectual; and they have not risen in culture beyond their original condition. Nor were their leaders men above the general level of the rank and file; for Bäumeler has left upon the society no marks to show that he strove for or desired a higher life here, or that he in the least valued beauty, or even what we Americans call comfort. The little town of Zoar, though founded fifty-six years ago, has yet no foot pavements; it remains without regularity of design; the houses are for the most part in need of paint; and there is about the place a general air of neglect and lack of order, a shabbiness, which I noticed also in the Aurora community in Oregon, and which shocks one who has but lately visited the Shakers and the Rappists.

The Zoarites have achieved comfort—according to the German peasant's notion — and wealth. They are relieved from severe toil, and have driven the wolf permanently from their doors. Much more they might have accomplished; but they have not been taught the need of more. They are sober, quiet, and orderly, very industrious, economical, and the amount of ingenuity and business skill which they have developed is quite remarkable.

Comparing Zoar and Aurora with Economy, I saw the extreme importance and value in such an experiment of leaders with ideas at least a step higher than those of their people. There is about Economy a tasteful finish which shows a desire for something higher than mere bread and butter, a neatness and striving for a higher kind of comfort, which makes Economy a model town, while the other two, though formed by people generally of the same social plane, are far below in the scale.

Yet, when I had left Zoar, and was compelled to wait for an hour at the railroad station, listening to men cursing in the presence of women and children; when I saw how much roughness there is in the life of the country people, I concluded that, rude and uninviting as the life in Zoar seemed to me, it was perhaps still a step higher, more decent, more free from disagreeables, and upon a higher moral scale, than the average life of the surrounding country. And if this is true, the community life has even here achieved moral results, as it certainly has material, worthy of the effort.

Moreover, considering the dull and lethargic appearance of the people, I was struck with surprise that they have been able to manage successfully complicated machinery, and to carry on several branches of manufacture profitably. Their machine shop makes and repairs all their own machinery; their grist-mills have to compete with those of the surrounding country; their cattle, horses, and sheep—of the latter they keep no less than 1400 head—are known as the best in the county; their hotel is a favorite summer resort; their store supplies the neighborhood; and they have found among themselves ability enough to conduct successfully all these and several other callings, all of which require both working skill and business acuteness.

They rise at six, or in summer at daylight, breakfast at seven, dine at twelve, and sup at six. During the long summer days they have two "bites" between meals. They do not eat pork, and a few refrain entirely from meat. They use both tea and coffee, and drink also cider and beer. Tobacco is forbidden, but it is used by some of the younger people. In the winter they labor in their shops after supper until eight o'clock.

Each family cooks for itself; but they have a general bakehouse, and make excellent bread. They have no general laundry. They have led water into the village from a reservoir on a hill beyond. Most of the houses accommodate several families, but each manages its own affairs. Tea, coffee, sugar, and other "groceries," are served out to all householders once a week. The young girls are taught to sew, knit, and spin, and to do the work of the household. The boys, when they leave school, are taught trades or put on the farm.

In their religious observances they studiously avoid forms. On Sunday they have three meetings. In the morning there is singing, after which the leading trustee reads one of Bäumeler's discourses, which they are careful not to call sermons. In the afternoon there is a children's meeting, where there is singing, and reading in the Bible. In the evening they meet to sing and hear reading from some work which interests them. They do not practice audible or public prayer. There are no religious meetings during the week; but the boys meet occasionally to practice music, as they have a band. The church has an organ, and several of the houses have pianos. They do not allow dancing. There is no "preacher," or clergyman. They have printed a hymn-book, which is used in their worship.

Bäumeler had some knowledge of homœopathy, and was during his life the physician of the community, and they still use the system of medicine which he introduced among them. Like all the communists I have known, they are long-lived. A number of members have lived to past eighty—the oldest now is ninety-one; and he, strangely enough, is an American, a native of New Hampshire, who, after a roving life in the West, at last, when past fifty, became a Shaker, and after eleven years among that people, came to Zoar twenty-eight years ago, and has lived here ever since.   The old fellow showed the shrewd intelligence of the Yankee, asking me whether we New-Yorkers were likely after all to beat the Tammany Ring; and declaring his belief that the Roman Catholics were the worst enemies of the United States.   He appeared to be, what a person of his age usually is if he retain his faculties, a sort of adviser-general; he sat in the common room of the hotel, and when any one came in he asked him about his business, and gave him advice what to do.

The oldest German member is now eighty-six; and there are still between thirty and forty people who came over from Germany with Bäumeler.   The latter died in 1853, at the age of seventy-five.

Most of the members now are middle-aged people, and the society is prosperous.   Thirty-five years ago, however, it had double the number it now counts.   Occasionally members leave; and in the society's early days it had much trouble and suffered some losses from suits for wages brought against it by dissatisfied persons.   Hence the stringent terms of the covenant.

They use neither Baptism nor the Lord's Supper.

In summer the women labor in the fields, to get in hay, potatoes, and in harvesting the grain.

They address each other only by the first name, use no title of any kind, and say thou (*du*) to all.   Also they keep their hats on in a public room. The church has two doors, one for the women, the other for the men, and the sexes sit on different sides of the house.

The hotel contains a queer, old-fashioned bar, at which the general public may drink beer, cider, or California wine. In the evening the sitting-room is filled with the hired laborers of the society, and with the smoke of their pipes.

Such is Zoar. Its people would not attract attention any where; they dress and look like common laborers; their leading trustee, Jacob Ackermann, who has carried on the affairs of the society for thirty years and more, might easily be taken for a German farm-hand. It is the more wonderful to compare the people with what they have achieved. Their leader and founder taught them self-sacrifice, a desire for heavenly things, temperance, or moderation in all things, preference of others to themselves, contentment—and these virtues, together with a prudence in the management of their affairs which has kept them out of debt since they paid for their land, and uprightness in their agents which has protected them against defalcations, have wrought, with very humble intelligence, and very narrow means at the beginning, the result one now sees at Zoar.

THE SHAKERS.

I

THE SHAKERS.

I.

THE Shakers have the oldest existing communistic societies on this continent. They are also the most thoroughly organized, and in some respects the most successful and flourishing.

Mount Lebanon, the parent society, and still the thriftiest, was established in 1792, eighty-two years ago.

The Shakers have eighteen societies, scattered over seven states; but each of these societies contains several families; and as each "family" is practically, and for all pecuniary and property ends, a distinct commune, there are in fact fifty-eight Shaker communities, which I have found to be in a more or less prosperous condition. These fifty-eight families contain an aggregate population of 2415 souls, and own real estate amounting to about one hundred thousand acres, of which nearly fifty thousand are in their own home farms.

Moreover, the Shakers have, as will be seen further on, a pretty thoroughly developed and elaborate system of theology; and a considerable literature of their own, to which they attach great importance.

The Shakers are a celibate order, composed of men and women living together in what they call "families," and having agriculture as the base of their industry, though most of them unite with this one or more other avocations. They have a uniform style of dress; call each other by their first names; say yea and nay, but not thee or thou; and their social habits have led them to a generally similar style of house architecture, whose peculiarity is that it seeks only the useful, and cares nothing for grace or beauty, and carefully avoids ornament.

They are pronounced Spiritualists, and hold that "there is the most intimate connection and the most constant communion between themselves and the inhabitants of the world of spirits."

They assert that the second appearance of Christ upon earth has been; and that they are the only true Church, "in which revelation, spiritualism, celibacy, oral confession, community, non-resistance, peace, the gift of healing, miracles, physical health, and separation from the world are the foundations of the new heavens." *

In practical life they are industrious, peaceful, honest, highly ingenious, patient of toil, and extraordinarily cleanly.

Finally, they are to a large extent of American birth, and English is, of course, their language.

II.—"MOTHER ANN."

The "Millennial Church, or United Society of Believers, commonly called Shakers," was formally organized at New Lebanon, a village in Columbia County, New York, in September, 1787, three years after the death of Ann Lee, whose followers they profess themselves, and whom they revere as the second appearance of Christ upon this earth, holding that Christ appeared first in the body of Jesus.

Ann Lee, according to the account of her accepted among and published by the Shakers, was an English woman, born of humble parents in Manchester, February 29th, 1736. Her father was a blacksmith; she was one of eight children; in her

---

* "Autobiography of a Shaker," etc., by Elder Frederick W. Evans.

A GROUP OF SHAKERS.

childhood she was employed in a cotton factory, and later as a cutter of hatters' fur. She was also at one time cook in a Manchester infirmary; and to the day of her death she could neither read nor write.

About the year 1747, some members of the Society of Quakers, under the influence of a religious revival, formed themselves into a society, at the head of which was a pious couple, Jane and James Wardley. To these people Ann Lee and her parents joined themselves in 1758, Ann being then twenty-three years of age and unmarried. These people suffered persecution from the ungodly, and some of them were even cast into prison, on account of certain unusual and violent manifestations of religious fervor, which caused them to receive the name of "Shaking Quakers;" and it was while Ann Lee thus lay in jail, in the summer of 1770, that "by a special manifestation of divine light the present testimony of salvation and eternal life was fully revealed to her," and by her to the society, "by whom she from that time was acknowledged as *mother* in Christ, and by them was called *Mother Ann.*"* She saw the Lord Jesus Christ in his glory, who revealed to her the great object of her prayers, and fully satisfied all the desires of her soul. The most astonishing visions and divine manifestations were presented to her view in so clear and striking a manner that the whole spiritual world seemed displayed before her. In these extraordinary manifestations she had a full and clear view of the mystery of iniquity, of the root and foundation of human depravity, and of the very act of transgression committed by the first man and woman in the garden of Eden. Here she saw whence and wherein all mankind were lost from God, and clearly realized the only possible way of recovery."† " By the immediate rev-

---

* " Shakers' Compendium of the Origin, History, etc., with Biographies of Ann Lee," etc. By F. W. Evans, 1859.

† " A Summary View of the Millennial Church," etc. Albany, 1848.

elation of Christ, she henceforth bore an open testimony against the lustful gratifications of the flesh as the source and foundation of human corruption; and testified, in the most plain and pointed manner, that no soul could follow Christ in the regeneration while living in the works of natural generation, or in any of the gratifications of lust."*

In a volume of " Hymns and Poems for the Use of Believers " (Watervhet, Ohio, 1833), Adam is made to confess the nature of his transgression and the cause of his fall, in a dialogue with his children:

" *First Adam being dead, yet speaketh, in a dialogue with his children.*

"*Children.* First Father Adam, where art thou ?
　　　　With all thy num'rous fallen race ;
　　　　We must demand an answer now,
　　　　　For. time hath stript our hiding-place.
　　　　Wast thou in nature made upright—
　　　　Fashion'd and plac'd in open light?

"*Adam.* Yea truly I was made upright :
　　　　This truth I never have deni'd,
　　　　And while I liv'd I lov'd the light,
　　　　　But I transgress'd and then I died.
　　　　Ye've heard that I transgress'd and fell—
　　　　This ye have heard your fathers tell.

"*Ch.* Pray tell us how this sin took place—
　　　　This myst'ry we could never scan,
　　　　That sin has sunk the human race,
　　　　　And all brought in by the first man.
　　　　'Tis said this is our heavy curse—
　　　　Thy sin imputed unto us.

"*Ad.* When I was plac'd on Eden's soil,
　　　　I liv'd by keeping God's commands—
　　　　To keep the garden all the while,
　　　　　And labor, working with my hands.
　　　　I need not toil beyond my pow'r,
　　　　Yet never waste one precious hour.

* " A Summary View of the Millennial Church," etc.

"But in a careless, idle frame,
  I gazed about on what was made:
And idle hands will gather shame,
  And wand'ring eyes confuse the head:
I dropp'd my hoe and pruning-knife,
To view the beauties of my wife.

"An idle beast of highest rank
  Came creeping up just at that time,
And show'd to Eve a curious prank,
  Affirming that it was no crime:—
'Ye shall not die as God hath said—
'Tis all a sham, be not afraid.'

"All this was pleasant to the eye,
  And Eve affirm'd the fruit was good;
So I gave up to gratify
  The meanest passion in my blood.
O horrid guilt! I was afraid:
I was condemn'd, yea I was dead.

"Here ends the life of the first man,
  Your father and his spotless bride;
God will be true, his word must stand—
  The day I sinn'd that day I died:
This was my sin, this was my fall!—
This your condition, one and all.

"*Ch.* How can these fearful things agree
  With what we read in sacred writ—
That sons and daughters sprung from thee,
  Endu'd with wisdom, power, and wit;
And all the nations fondly claim
Their first existence in thy name?

"*Ad.* Had you the wisdom of that beast
  That took my headship by deceit,
I could unfold enough at least
  To prove your lineage all a cheat.
Your pedigree you do not know,
The Second Adam told you so.

"When I with guile was overcome,
　　And fell a victim to the beast,
My station first he did assume,
　　Then on the spoil did richly feast.
Soon as the life had left my soul,
He took possession of the whole.

"He plunder'd all my mental pow'rs,
　　My visage, stature, speech, and gait;
And, in a word, in a few hours,
　　He was first Adam placed in state:
He took my wife, he took my name;
All but his nature was the same.

"Now see him hide, and skulk about,
　　Just like a beast, and even worse,
Till God in anger drove him out,
　　And doom'd him to an endless curse.
O hear the whole creation groan!
The Man of Sin has took the throne!

"Now in my name this beast can plead,
　　How God commanded him at first
To multiply his wretched seed,
　　Through the base medium of his lust.
O horrid cheat! O subtle plan!
A hellish beast assumes the man!

"This is your father in my name:
　　Your pedigree ye now may know:
He early from perdition came,
　　And to perdition he must go.
And all his race with him shall share
Eternal darkness and despair."

The same theory of the fall* is stated in another hymn:

---

* It is curious that the Jewish Talmud (according to Eisenmenger) has a somewhat similar theory—namely, that Eve cohabited with devils for a period of one hundred and thirty years; and that Cain was not the child of Adam, but of one of these devils.

"We read, when God created man,
He made him able then to stand
United to his Lord's command
    That he might be protected ;
But when, through Eve, he was deceiv'd,
And to his wife in lust had cleav'd,
And of forbidden fruit receiv'd,
    He found himself rejected.

"And thus, we see, death did begin,
When Adam first fell into sin,
And judgment on himself did bring,
    Which he could not dissemble :
Old Adam then began to plead,
And tell the cause as you may read ;
But from his sin he was not freed,
    Then he did fear and tremble.

"Compell'd from Eden now to go,
Bound in his sins, with shame and woe,
And there to feed on things below—
    His former situation :
For he was taken from the earth,
And blest with a superior birth,
But, dead in sin, he's driven forth
    From his blest habitation.

"Now his lost state continues still,
In all who do their fleshly will,
And of their lust do take their fill,
    And say they are commanded :
Thus they go forth and multiply,
And so they plead to justify
Their basest crimes, and so they try
    To ruin souls more candid."

The "way of regeneration" is opened in another hymn in the same collection :

"Victory over the Man of Sin.

" Souls that hunger for salvation,
    And have put their sins away,
Now may find a just relation,
    If they cheerfully obey;
They may find the new creation,
    And may boldly enter in
By the door of free salvation,
    And subdue the Man of Sin.

" Thus made free from that relation,
    Which the serpent did begin,
Trav'ling in regeneration,
    Having pow'r to cease from sin;
Dead unto a carnal nature,
    From that tyrant ever free,
Singing praise to our Creator,
    For this blessed jubilee.

" Sav'd from passions, too inferior
    To command the human soul;
Led by motives most superior,
    Faith assumes entire control:
Joined in the new creation,
    Living souls in union run,
Till they find a just relation
    To the First-born two in one.

" But this prize can not be gained,
    Neither is salvation found,
Till the Man of Sin is chained,
    And the old deceiver bound.
All mankind he has deceived,
    And still binds them one and all,
Save a few who have believed,
    And obey'd the Gospel call.

" By a life of self-denial,
    True obedience and the cross,
We may pass the fiery trial,
    Which does separate the dross.

If we bear our crosses boldly,
Watch and ev'ry evil shun,
We shall find a body holy,
And the tempter overcome.
    *   *   *   *   *   *

" By a pois'nous fleshly nature,
This dark world has long been led ;
There can be no passion greater—
This must be the serpent's head :
On our coast he would be cruising,
If by truth he were not bound :
But his head has had a bruising,
And he's got a deadly wound.

" And his wounds can not be healed,
Light and truth do now forbid,
Since the Gospel has revealed
Where his filthy head was hid :
With a fig-leaf it was cover'd,
Till we brought his deeds to light :
By his works he is discover'd,
And his head is plain in sight."

It should be said that Ann Lee had married previously to
these manifestations, her husband being Abraham Stanley, like
her father, a blacksmith. By him she had four children, all of
whom died in infancy. It is related that she showed from girl-
hood a decided repugnance to the married state, and married
only on the long-continued and urgent persuasion of her friends ;
and after 1770 she seems to have returned to her parents.

She and her followers were frequently abused and persecuted ; and in 1773 " she was by a direct revelation instructed
to repair to America ;" and it is quaintly added that " permission was given for all those of the society who were able,
and who felt any special impressions on their own minds so
to do, to accompany her."* She had announced, says the

---

* " Shakers' Compendium."

same authority, that " the second Christian Church would be
established in America; that the colonies would gain their independence; and that liberty of conscience would be secured
to all people, whereby they would be able to worship God
without hinderance or molestation." Accordingly Ann Lee
embarked at Liverpool in May, 1774, eight persons accompany-
ing her, six men and two women, among them her husband
and a brother and niece. They landed in New York in August; and, after some difficulties and hardships on account of
poverty, finally settled in what appears to have been then a
wilderness, " the woods of Watervliet, near Niskeyuna, about
seven miles northwest of Albany." In the mean time Ann
Lee had supported herself by washing and ironing in New
York, and her husband had misconducted himself so grossly
toward her that they finally separated, he going off with another woman.

At Niskeyuna, Ann Lee and her companions busied themselves in clearing land and providing for their subsistence.
They lived in the woods, and Ann was their leader and preacher.
She foretold to them that the time was near when they should
see a large accession to their numbers; but they had so long to
wait that their hearts sometimes failed them. They settled
at Watervliet in September, 1775, and it was not until 1780
that, by a curious chance, their doctrines were at last brought
to the knowledge of persons inclined to receive them.

In the spring of that year there occurred at New Lebanon
a religious revival, chiefly among the Baptists, who had a
church in that neighborhood. Some of the subjects of this
revival wandered off, seeking light and comfort from strangers,
and found the settlement of which Ann Lee was the chief. Her
doctrines, which inculcated rigid self-denial and repression of
the passions, were at once embraced by them; they brought
others to hear Ann Lee's statements, and thus a beginning
was at last made.

New Lebanon, where the new converts lived, lies upon the border of Massachusetts and Connecticut; and into these states, particularly the first, the new doctrine spread. Ann Lee, now called by her people Mother Ann, or more often Mother, traveled from place to place, preaching and advising; in Massachusetts she appears to have remained two years. It is asserted, too, that she performed miracles at various places, healing the sick by laying on of hands, and revealing to others their wickedness and concealed sins. For instance:

"Mary Southwick, of Hancock [in Massachusetts, where there was a colony of Ann Lee's followers], testifies: That about the beginning of August, 1783 (being then in the twenty-first year of her age), she was healed of a cancer in her mouth, which had been growing two years, and which for about three weeks had been eating, attended with great pain and a continual running, and which occasioned great weakness and loss of appetite.

"That she went one afternoon to see Calvin Harlowe, to get some assistance; that Mother being at the house, Calvin asked her to look at it. That she accordingly came to her, and put her finger into her mouth upon the cancer; at which instant the pain left her, and she was restored to health, and was never afflicted with it afterward.

"Taken from the mouth of the said Mary Southwick, the 23d day of April, 1808. In presence of Jennet Davis, Rebecca Clarke, Daniel Cogswell, Daniel Goodrich, and Seth Y. Wells.   (Signed)   MARY SOUTHWICK."

The volume from which this formal statement is extracted* contains a number of similar affidavits, which show that miraculous powers of healing diseases are claimed to have been

---

* "Testimony of Christ's Second Appearing," etc. Published by the United Society of Shakers. Albany, 1856. [The first edition was printed in 1808.]

exercised during Ann Lee's life, not only by her, but by her chief followers, Elder William Lee her brother, John Hocknell, Joseph Markham, and others.

It does not appear that Ann Lee made any attempts to settle her followers in colonies or communities, or that she interrupted the family life, except that she insisted on celibacy. But she seems to have gathered her followers in congregations, because she from the first required, as a sign of true repentance and a condition of admission, that "oral confession of all the sins of the past life, to God, in the presence of an elder brother," which is still one of the most rigorous rules of the order.

She is reported to have said: "When I confessed my sins, I labored to remember the time when and the place where I committed them. And when I had confessed them [to Jane and James Wardley, in Manchester], I cried to God to know if my confession was accepted; and by crying to God continually I traveled out of my loss."[*] Also she said: "The first step of obedience that any of you can take is to confess your sins to God before his witnesses." "To those who came to confess to her she said: 'If you confess your sins, you must confess them to God; we are but his witnesses.' To such as asked her forgiveness, she used to say: 'I can freely forgive you, and I pray God to forgive you. It is God that forgives you; I am but your fellow-servant.'"[†]

Ann Lee died at Watervliet, N. Y., on the 8th of September, 1784, in the forty-ninth year of her age.

In the "Summary View of the Millennial Church," as well as in some other works published by the Shakers, there are recorded details of her life and conversation, from which one gets the idea that she was a woman of practical sense, sincerely pious, and humble-minded. She was "rather below the common stature of woman, thickset but straight, and other-

---

[*] "Shakers' Compendium."   [†] "Summary View," etc.

wise well-proportioned and regular in form and feature. Her complexion was light and fair, and her eyes were blue, but keen and penetrating; her countenance mild and expressive, but grave and solemn. Her manners were plain, simple, and easy. She possessed a certain dignity of appearance that inspired confidence and commanded respect. By many of the world who saw her without prejudice she was called beautiful; and to her faithful children she appeared to possess a degree of dignified beauty and heavenly love which they had never before discovered among mortals."* She never learned to read or write. Aside from her strictly religious teachings, she appears to have inculcated upon her followers the practical virtues of honesty, industry, frugality, charity, and temperance. "Put your hands to work and give your hearts to God." "You ought never to speak to your children in a passion; for if you do, you will put devils into them." "Do all your work as though you had a thousand years to live; and as you would if you knew you must die to morrow." "You can never enter the kingdom of God with hardness against any one, for God is love, and if you love God you will love one another." "Be diligent with your hands, for godliness does not lead to idleness." "You ought not to cross your children unnecessarily, for it makes them ill-natured." To a woman: "You ought to dress yourself in modest apparel, such as becomes the people of God, and teach your family to do likewise. You ought to be industrious and prudent, and not live a sumptuous and gluttonous life, but labor for a meek and quiet spirit, and see that your family is kept decent and regular in all their goings forth, that others may see your example of faith and good works, and acknowledge the work of God in your family." To some farmers who had gathered at Ashfield, in Massachusetts, in the winter, to listen to her instructions: "It is now spring

---

* "Summary View."

of the year, and you have all had the privilege of being taught the way of God; and now you may all go home and be faithful with your hands. Every faithful man will go forth and put up his fences in season, and will plow his ground in season, and put his crops into the ground in season; and such a man may with confidence look for a blessing."

These are some of the sayings reported of her. They are not remarkable, except as showing that with her religious enthusiasm she united practical sense, which gave her doubtless a power over the people with whom she came in contact, mostly plain farmers and laborers.

Mother Ann was succeeded in her rule over the society, or "Church," as they preferred to call it, by Elder James Whittaker, one of those who had come over with her. He was called Father James; and under his ministry was built, in 1785, "the

THE FIRST SHAKER CHURCH, AT MOUNT LEBA- NON, NOW A SEED-HOUSE.

first house for public worship ever built by the society." He died at Enfield in July, 1787, less than three years after Mother Ann; and was succeeded by Joseph Meacham, an American, a native of Connecticut, in early life a Baptist preacher; and with him was associated Lucy Wright, as "the first leading character in the female line," as the "Summary" quaintly expresses it. She was a native of Pittsfield, in Massachusetts. Joseph Meacham died in 1796, at the age of fifty-four, and it seems that Lucy Wright then succeeded to the entire administration and "lead of the society." She died in 1821, at the age of sixty-one. " During her administration the several societies in the states of Ohio and Kentucky were established, and large accessions were made to the Eastern societies."*

While Joseph Meacham was elder, and in the period between 1787 and 1792, eleven societies were formed, of which two were in New York, four in Massachusetts, two in New Hampshire, two in Maine, and one in Connecticut.

Meantime, in the first year of this century broke out in Kentucky a remarkable religious excitement, lasting several years, and attended with extraordinary and in some cases horrible physical demonstrations. Camp-meetings were held in different counties, to which people flocked by thousands; and here men and women, and even small children, fell down in convulsions, foamed at the mouth and uttered loud cries. " At first they were taken with an inward throbbing of the heart; then with weeping and trembling; from that to crying out in apparent agony of soul; falling down and swooning away, until every appearance of animal life was suspended, and the person appeared to be in a trance." " They lie as though they were dead for some time, without pulse or breath, some longer, some shorter time. Some rise with joy and triumph, others crying for mercy." " To these encampments the people flocked by hundreds and thousands—on foot, on horseback, and in wagons and other carriages." At Cabin Creek, in May, 1801, a " great number fell on the third night; and to prevent their being trodden under foot by the multitude, they were collected together and laid out in order in two squares of the meeting-house; which, like so many dead corpses, covered a considerable part of the floor." At Concord, in Bourbon County, in June, 1801, " no sex or color, class or description, were exempted from the pervading influence of the Spirit; even from the age of eight months to sixty years." In August, at Cane Ridge,

---

* " Shakers' Compendium."

in Bourbon County, "about twenty thousand people" were gathered; and "about three thousand" suffered from what was called "the falling exercise." These brief extracts are from the account of an eye-witness, and one who believed these manifestations to be of divine origin.* The accuracy of McNemar's descriptions is beyond question. His account is confirmed by other writers of the time.

Hearing of these extraordinary events, the Shakers at New Lebanon sent out three of their number—John Meacham, Benjamin S. Youngs, and Issachar Bates—to "open the testimony of salvation to the people, provided they were in a situation to receive it." They set out on New-Year's day, 1805, and traveled on foot about a thousand miles, through what was then a sparsely settled country, much of it a wilderness. They made some converts in Ohio and Kentucky, and were, fortunately for themselves, violently opposed and in some cases attacked by bigoted or knavish persons; and with this impetus they were able to found at first five societies, two in Ohio, two in Kentucky, and one in Indiana. The Indiana society later removed to Ohio; and two more societies were afterward formed in Ohio, and one more in New York.

All these societies were founded before the year 1830; and no new ones have come into existence since then.

Following the doctrines put forth by Ann Lee, and elaborated by her successors, they hold:

I. That God is a dual person, male and female; that Adam was a dual person, being created in God's image; and that "the distinction of sex is eternal, inheres in the soul itself; and that no angels or spirits exist who are not male and female."

II. That Christ is a Spirit, and one of the highest, who ap-

---

* "The Kentucky Revival, or a Short History of the late extraordinary Outpouring of the Spirit of God in the Western States of America," etc. By Richard McNemar. Turtle Hill, Ohio, 1807.

peared first in the person of Jesus, representing the male, and later in the person of Ann Lee, representing the female element in God.

III. That the religious history of mankind is divided into four cycles, which are represented also in the spirit world, each having its appropriate heaven and hell. The first cycle included the antediluvians—Noah and the faithful going to the first heaven, and the wicked of that age to the first hell. The second cycle included the Jews up to the appearance of Jesus; and the second heaven is called Paradise. The third cycle included all who lived until the appearance of Ann Lee; Paul being "caught up into the third heaven." The heaven of the fourth and last dispensation " is now in process of formation," and is to supersede in time all previous heavens. Jesus, they say, after his death, descended into the first hell to preach to the souls there confined; and on his way passed through the second heaven, or Paradise, where he met the thief crucified with him.

IV. They hold themselves to be the "Church of the Last Dispensation," the true Church of this age; and they believe that the day of judgment, or "beginning of Christ's kingdom on earth," dates from the establishment of their Church, and will be completed by its development.

V. They hold that the Pentecostal Church was established on right principles; that the Christian churches rapidly and fatally fell away from it; and that the Shakers have returned to this original and perfect doctrine and practice. They say: "The five most prominent practical principles of the Pentecost Church were, first, common property; second, a life of celibacy; third, non-resistance; fourth, a separate and distinct government; and, fifth, power over physical disease." To all these but the last they have attained; and the last they confidently look for, and even now urge that disease is an offense to God, and that it is in the power of men to be healthful, if they will.

VI. They reject the doctrine of the Trinity, of the bodily resurrection, and of an atonement for sins. They do not worship either Jesus or Ann Lee, holding both to be simply elders in the Church, to be respected and loved.

VII. They are Spiritualists. "We are thoroughly convinced of spirit communication and interpositions, spirit guidance and obsession. Our spiritualism has permitted us to converse, face to face, with individuals once mortals, some of whom we well knew, and with others born before the flood.* They assert that the spirits at first labored among them; but that in later times they have labored among the spirits; and that in the lower heavens there have been formed numerous Shaker churches. Moreover, "it should be distinctly understood that special inspired gifts have not ceased, but still continue among this people." It follows from what is stated above, that they believe in a "probationary state in the world of spirits."

VIII. They hold that he only is a true servant of God who lives a perfectly stainless and sinless life; and they add that to this perfection of life all their members ought to attain.

IX. Finally, they hold that their Church, the Inner or Gospel Order, as they call it, is supported by and has for its complement the world, or, as they say, the Outer Order. They do not regard marriage and property as crimes or disorders, but as the emblems of a lower order of society. And they hold that the world in general, or the Outer Order, will have the opportunity of purification in the next world as well as here.

In the practical application of this system of religious faith, they inculcate a celibate life; "honesty and integrity in all

---

* "Plain Talks upon Practical Religion; being Candid Answers," etc. By Geo. Albert Lomas (Novitiate Elder at Watervliet). 1873.

SHAKER DWELLING—MOUNT LEBANON.

GRANITE DWELLING, OF THE ENFIELD SHAKERS.

words and dealings;" "humanity and kindness to friend and foe;" diligence in business; prudence, temperance, economy, frugality, "but not parsimony;" "to keep clear of debt;" suitable education of children; a "united interest in all things," which means community of goods; suitable employment for all; and a provision for all in sickness, infirmity, and old age.

III.—THE ORDER OF LIFE AMONG THE SHAKERS.

A Shaker Society consists of two classes or orders: the Novitiate and the Church Order. There is a general similarity in the life of these two; but to the Novitiate families are sent all applicants for admission to the community or Church, and here they are trained; and the elders of these families also receive inquiring strangers, and stand in somewhat nearer relations with the outer world than the Church families.

To the Church family or commune belong those who have determined to seclude themselves more entirely from contact with the outer world; and who aspire to live the highest spiritual life. Except so far as necessary business obliges deacons and care-takers to deal with the world, the members of the Church Order aim to live apart; and they do not receive or entertain strangers or applicants for membership, but confine their intercourse to members of other societies.

Formerly there was a considerable membership living in the world, maintaining the family relation so far as to educate children and transact business, but conforming to the Shaker rule of celibacy. This was allowed because of the difficulty of disposing of property, closing up business affairs, and perhaps on account of the unwillingness of husband or wife to follow the other partner into the Shaker family. There are still such members, but they are fewer in number than formerly. The Novitiate elders and elderesses keep some oversight, by correspondence and by personal visits, over such outside members.

The Shaker family, or commune, usually consists of from thirty to eighty or ninety persons, men and women, with such children as may have been apprenticed to the society. These live together in one large house, divided as regards its upper stories into rooms capable of accommodating from four to eight persons. Each room contains as many simple cot-beds as it has occupants, the necessary washing utensils, a small looking-glass, a stove for the winter, a table for writing, and a considerable number of chairs, which, when not in use, are suspended from pegs along the wall. A wide hall separates the dormitories of the men from those of the women. Strips of home-made carpet, usually of very quiet colors, are laid upon the floors, but never tacked down.

On the first floor are the kitchen, pantry, store-rooms, and the common dining-hall; and in a Novitiate family there is also a small separate room, where strangers — visitors — eat, apart from the family.

Ranged around the family house or dwelling are buildings for the various pursuits of the society: the sisters' shop, where tailoring, basket-making, and other female industries are carried on; the brothers' shop, where broom-making, carpentry, and other men's pursuits are followed; the laundry, the stables, the fruit-house, wood-house, and often machine shops, saw-mills, etc.

If you are permitted to examine these shops and the dwelling of the family, you will notice that the most scrupulous cleanliness is every where practiced; if there is a stove in the room, a small broom and dust-pan hang near it, and a wood-box stands by it; scrapers and mats at the door invite you to make clean your shoes; and if the roads are muddy or snowy, a broom hung up outside the outer door mutely requests you to brush off all the mud or snow. The strips of carpet are easily lifted, and the floor beneath is as clean as though it were a

SHAKER WOMEN AT WORK.

table to be eaten from. The walls are bare of pictures; not only because all ornament is wrong, but because frames are places where dust will lodge. The bedstead is a cot, covered with the bedclothing, and easily moved away to allow of dusting and sweeping. Mats meet you at the outer door and at every inner door. The floors of the halls and dining-room are polished until they shine.

Moreover all the walls, in hall and rooms, are lined with rows of wooden pegs, on which spare chairs, hats, cloaks, bonnets, and shawls are hung; and you presently perceive that neatness, order, and absolute cleanliness rule every where.

The government or administration of the Shaker societies is partly spiritual and partly temporal. " The visible Head of the Church of Christ on earth is vested in a Ministry, consisting of male and female, not less than three, and generally four in number, two of each sex. The first in the Ministry stands as the leading elder of the society. Those who compose the Ministry are selected from the Church, and appointed by the last preceding head or leading character; and their authority is confirmed and established by the spontaneous union of the whole body. Those of the United Society who are selected and called to the important work of the Ministry, to lead and direct the Church of Christ, must be blameless characters, faithful, honest, and upright, clothed with the spirit of meekness and humility, gifted with wisdom and understanding, and of great experience in the things of God. As faithful embassadors of Christ, they are invested with wisdom and authority, by the revelation of God, to guide, teach, and direct his Church on earth in its spiritual travel, and to counsel and advise in other matters of importance, whether spiritual or temporal.

" To the Ministry appertains, therefore, the power to appoint ministers, elders, and deacons, and with the elders to assign offices of care and trust to such brethren and sisters as they shall judge to be best qualified for the several offices to which they may be assigned. Such appointments, being communicated to the members of the Church concerned, and having received the mutual approbation of the Church, or the family concerned, are thereby confirmed and established until altered or repealed by the same authority."*

" Although the society at New Lebanon is the centre of union to all the other societies, yet the more immediate duties of the Ministry in this place extend only to the two societies of New Lebanon and Watervliet. [Groveland has since been added to this circle.] Other societies are under the direction of a ministry appointed to preside over them; and in most instances two or more societies constitute a bishopric, being united under the superintendence of the same ministry."

---

* " Summary View," etc.

Each society has ministers, in the Novitiate family, to instruct and train neophytes, and to go out into the world to
preach when it may be desirable. Each family has two elders,
male and female, to teach, exhort, and lead the family in spiritual concerns. It has also deacons and deaconesses, who
provide for the support and convenience of the family, and
regulate the various branches of industry in which the members are employed, and transact business with those without.
Under the deacons are " care-takers," who are the foremen
and forewomen in the different pursuits.

It will be seen that this is a complete and judicious system
of administration. It has worked well for a long time. A
notable feature of the system is that the members do not appoint their rulers, nor are they consulted openly or directly
about such appointments. The Ministry are self-perpetuating;
and they select and appoint all subordinates, being morally,
but it seems not otherwise, responsible to the members.

Finally, " all the members are equally holden, according to
their several abilities, to maintain one united interest, and
therefore all labor *with their hands,* in some useful occupation, for the mutual comfort and benefit of themselves and
each other, and for the general good of the society or family
to which they belong. Ministers, elders, and deacons, all without exception, are industriously employed in some *manual* occupation, except in the time taken up in the necessary duties
of their respective callings." So carefully is this rule ob-
served that even the supreme heads of the Shaker Church—
the four who constitute the Ministry at Mount Lebanon, Daniel
Boler, Giles B. Avery, Ann Taylor, and Polly Reed—labor at
basket-making in the intervals of their travels and ministrations, and have a separate little "shop" for this purpose near the
church. They live in a house built against the church, and eat in
a separate room in the family of the first order; and, I believe,
generally keep themselves somewhat apart from the people.

The property of each society, no matter of how many families it is composed, is for convenience held in the name of the trustees, who are usually members of the Church family, or first order; but each family or commune keeps its own accounts and transacts its business separately.

The Shaker family rises at half-past four in the summer, and five o'clock in the winter; breakfasts at six or half-past six; dines at twelve; sups at six; and by nine or half-past all are in bed and the lights are out.

They eat in a general hall. The tables have no cloth, or rather are covered with oil-cloth; the men eat at one table, women at another, and children at a third; and the meal is eaten in silence, no conversation being held at table. When all are assembled for a meal they kneel in silence for a moment; and this is repeated on rising from the table, and on rising in the morning and before going to bed.

When they get up in the morning, each person takes two chairs, and, setting them back to back, takes off the bedclothing, piece by piece, and folding each neatly once, lays it across the backs of the chairs, the pillows being first laid on the seats of the chairs. In the men's rooms the slops are also carried out of the house by one of them; and the room is then left to the women, who sweep, make the beds, and put every thing to rights. All this is done before breakfast; and by breakfast time what New-Englanders call "chores" are all finished, and the day's work in the shops or in the fields may begin.

Each brother is assigned to a sister, who takes care of his clothing, mends when it is needed, looks after his washing, tells him when he requires a new garment, reproves him if he is not orderly, and keeps a general sisterly oversight over his habits and temporal needs.

In cooking, and the general labor of the dining-room and kitchen, the sisters take turns; a certain number, sufficient to

SHAKER COSTUMES.

make the work light, serving a month at a time. The younger sisters do the washing and ironing; and the clothes which are washed on Monday are not ironed till the following week.

Their diet is simple but sufficient. Pork is never eaten, and only a part of the Shaker people eat any meat at all. Many use no food produced by animals, denying themselves even milk, butter, and eggs. At Mount Lebanon, and in some of the other societies, two tables are set, one with, the other without meat. They consume much fruit, eating it at every meal; and the Shakers have always fine and extensive vegetable gardens and orchards.

After breakfast every body goes to work; and the "caretakers," who are subordinate to the deacons, and are foremen in fact, take their followers to their proper employments. When, as in harvest, an extra number of hands is needed at any labor, it is of course easy to divert at once a sufficient force to the place. The women do not labor in the fields, except in such light work as picking berries. Shakers do not toil severely.

They are not in haste to be rich; and they have found that for their support, economically as they live, it is not necessary to make labor painful.   Many hands make light work; and where all are interested alike, they hold that labor may be made and is made a pleasure.

Their evenings are well filled with such diversions as they regard wholesome.   Instrumental music they do not generally allow themselves, but they sing well; and much time is spent in learning new hymns and tunes, which they profess to receive constantly from the spirit world.   Some sort of meeting of the family is held every evening.   At Mount Lebanon, for instance, on Monday evening there is a general meeting in the dining-hall, where selected articles from the newspapers are read, crimes and accidents being omitted as unprofitable; and the selections consisting largely of scientific news, speeches on public affairs, and the general news of the world.   They prefer such matter as conveys information of the important political and social movements of the day; and the elder usually makes the extracts.   At this meeting, too, letters from other societies are read.   On Tuesday evening they meet in the assembly hall for singing, marching, etc.   Wednesday night is devoted to a union meeting for conversation.   Thursday night is a "laboring meeting," which means the regular religious service, where they "labor to get good."   Friday is devoted to new songs and hymns; and Saturday evening to worship.   On Sunday evening, finally, they visit at each other's rooms, three or four sisters visiting the brethren in each room, by appointment, and engaging in singing and in conversation upon general subjects.

In their religious services there is little or no audible prayer; they say that God does not need spoken words, and that the mental aspiration is sufficient.   Their aim too, as they say, is to "walk with God," as with a friend; and mental prayer may be a large part of their lives without interruption to usual avocations.   They do not regularly read the Bible.

The Sunday service is held either in the "meeting-house," when two or three families, all composing the society, join together; or in the large assembly hall which is found in every family house. In the meeting-house there are generally benches, on which the people sit until all are assembled. In the assembly hall there are only seats ranged along the walls; and the members of the family, as they enter, take their accustomed places, standing, in the ranks which are formed for worship. The men face the women, the older men and women in the front, the elders standing at the head of the first rank. A somewhat broad space or gangway is left between the two front ranks. After the singing of a hymn, the elder usually makes a brief address upon holiness of living and consecration to God; he is followed by the eldress; and thereupon the ranks are broken, and a dozen of the brethren and sisters, forming a separate square on the floor, begin a lively hymn tune, in which all the rest join, marching around the room to a quick step, the women following the men, and all often clapping their hands.

The exercises are varied by reforming the ranks; by speaking from men and women; by singing; and by dancing as they march, "as David danced before the Lord"—the dance being a kind of shuffle. Occasionally one of the members, more deeply moved than the rest, or perhaps in some tribulation of soul, asks the prayers of the others; or one comes to the front, and, bowing before the elder and eldress, begins to whirl, a singular exercise which is sometimes continued for a considerable time, and is a remarkable performance. Then some brother or sister is impressed to deliver a message of comfort or warning from the spirit-land; or some spirit asks the prayers of the assembly: on such occasions the elder asks all to kneel for a few moments in silent prayer.

In their marching and dancing they hold their hands before them, and make a motion as of gathering something to them-

SHAKER WORSHIP.—THE DANCE.

selves: this is called gathering a blessing. In like manner, when any brother or sister asks for their prayers and sympathy, they, reversing their hands, push toward him that which he asks.

All the movements are performed with much precision and in exact order; their tunes are usually in quick time, and the singers keep time admirably. The words of the elder guide the meeting; and at his bidding all disperse in a somewhat summary manner. It is, I believe, an object with them to vary the order of their meetings, and thus give life to them.

New members are admitted with great caution. Usually a person who is moved to become a Shaker has made a visit to the Novitiate family of some society, remaining long enough to satisfy himself that membership would be agreeable to him. During this preliminary visit he lives separately from the family, but is admitted to their religious meetings, and is fully informed of the doctrines, practices, and requirements of the Shaker people. If then he still desires admission, he is expected to set his affairs in order, so that he shall not leave any unfulfilled obligations behind him in the world. If he has debts, they must be paid; if he has a wife, she must freely give her consent to the husband leaving her; or if it is a woman, her husband must consent. If there are children, they must be provided for, and placed so as not to suffer neglect, either within the society, or with other and proper persons.

It is not necessary that applicants for admission shall possess property. The only question the society asks and seeks to be satisfied upon is, "Are you sick of sin, and do you want salvation from it?" A candidate for admission is usually taken on trial for a year at least, in order that the society may be satisfied of his fitness; of course he may leave at any time.

The first and chief requirement, on admission, is that the neophyte shall make a complete and open confession of the sins of his whole past life to two elders of his or her own sex; and the completeness of this confession is rigidly demanded. Mother Ann's practice on this point I have quoted elsewhere. As this is one of the most prominent peculiarities of the Shaker Society, it may be interesting to quote here some passages from their books describing the detail on which they insist. Elder George Albert Lomas writes:

"Any one seeking admission as a member is required, ere we can give any encouragement at all, to settle all debts and contracts to the satisfaction of creditors; and then our rule is: If candid seekers after salvation come to us, we neither accept nor reject them; we *admit* them, leaving the Spirit of Goodness to decide as to their sincerity; to bless their efforts, if such, or to make them very dissatisfied if hypocritical. After becoming thoroughly acquainted with our principles, we ask individuals to give evidence of their sincerity, if really sick of sin, by an honest confession of every improper transaction or sin that lies within the reach of their memory. This confession of sin to elders of their own sex, appointed for the purpose, *we* believe to be the door of hope to the soul, the Christian valley of Achor, and one which every sin-sick soul seizes with avidity, as being far more comforting than embarrassing. And this opportunity remains a permanent institution with us—to confess, retract our wrongs as memory may recall them; and aids individuals in so thoroughly repent-ing of past sins that they are enabled to leave them in the rear, while they pass on to greater salvations. It often takes years for individuals to complete this work of *thorough confession and repentance;* but upon this, more than upon aught else, depends their success as permanent and happy members. Those who choose to use deceit, often do so, but *never* make reliable members: always uncomfortable while they remain; and very few do or can remain, unless they fulfill this important demand of `opening the mind.' If *we* do not detect their insincerity, God does, and they are tempted of the devil beyond their wish to remain with the Shak-ers; while he that *confesseth* and *forsaketh* his sins shall find mercy. This is not a confession to mortality, but unto God, witnessed by those who have thoroughly experienced the practical results of the ordeal. 'My son, give glory to the God of heaven; *confess unto him,* and *tell* me what thou hast done.'"*

Another authority says on this subject:

"All such as receive the grace of God which bringeth salvation, first honestly bring their former deeds of darkness to the light, by confessing all their sins, with a full determination to forsake them forever. By so doing they find justification and acceptance with God, and receive that power by which they become dead indeed unto sin, and alive unto God, through Jesus Christ, and are enabled to follow his example, and walk even as he walked." †

A third writer reasons thus upon confession:

"As all the secret actions of men are open and known to God, therefore a confession made in secret, though professedly made to God, can bring nothing to light; and the sinner may perhaps have as little fear of God in confessing his sins in this manner as he had in committing them. And as nothing is brought to the light by confessing his sins in this manner, he feels no cross in it; nor does he thereby find any mortification to that carnal nature which first led him into sin; and is therefore liable to run again into the same acts of sin as he was before his confession. But let

---

* "Plain Talks on Practical Religion," etc.
† "Christ's First and Second Appearing. By Shakers."

the sinner appear in the presence of a faithful servant of Christ, and there confess honestly his every secret sin, one by one, of whatever nature or name, and faithfully lay open his whole life, without any covering or disguise, and he will then feel a humiliating sense of himself, in the presence of God, in a manner which he never experienced before. He will then, in very deed, find a mortifying cross to his carnal nature, and feel the crucifixion of his lust and pride where he never did before. He will then perceive the essential difference between confessing his sins in the dark, where no mortal ear can hear him, and actually bringing his evil deeds to the light of one individual child of God; and he will then be convinced that a confession made before the light of God in one of his true witnesses can bring upon him a more awful sense of his accountability both to God and man than all his confessions in darkness had ever done."*

Community of property is one of the leading principles of the Shakers. " It is an established principle of faith in the Church, that all who are received as members thereof do freely and voluntarily, of their own deliberate choice, dedicate, devote, and consecrate themselves, with all they possess, to the service of God forever." In accordance with this rule, the neophyte brings with him his property; but as he is still on trial, and may prove unfit, or find himself uncomfortable, he is not allowed to give up his property unreservedly to the society; but only its use, agreeing that so long as he remains he will require neither wages for his labor nor interest for that which he brought in. On these terms he may remain as long as he proves his fitness. But when at last he is moved to enter the higher or Church order, he formally makes over to the society, forever, and without power of taking it back, all that he owns. The articles of agreement by which he does this read as follows :

" We solemnly and conscientiously dedicate, devote, and give up ourselves and services, together with all our temporal interest, to God and his people; to be under the care and direction of such elders, deacons, or trustees as have been or may

---

* " Summary View," etc.

hereafter be established in the Church, according to the first article of this Covenant.

" We further covenant and agree that it is and shall be the special duty of the deacons and trustees, appointed as aforesaid, to have the immediate charge and oversight of all and singular the property, estate, and interest dedicated, devoted, and given up as aforesaid ; and it shall also be the duty of the said deacons and trustees to appropriate, use, and improve the said united interest for the benefit of the Church, for the relief of the poor, and for such other charitable and religious purposes as the Gospel may require and the said deacons or trustees in their wisdom shall see fit ; *Provided nevertheless,* that all the transactions of the said deacons or trustees, in their use, management, and disposal of the aforesaid united interest, shall be for the benefit and privilege, and in behalf of the Church (to which the said deacons or trustees are and shall be held responsible), and not for any personal or private interest, object, or purpose whatsoever.

" As the sole object, purpose, and design of our uniting in a covenant relation, as a Church or body of people, in Gospel union, was from the beginning, and still is, faithfully and honestly to receive, improve, and diffuse the manifold gifts of God, both of a spiritual and temporal nature, for the mutual protection, support, comfort, and happiness of each other, as brethren and sisters in the Gospel, and for such other pious and charitable purposes as the Gospel may require ; *Therefore* we do, by virtue of this Covenant, solemnly and conscientiously, jointly and individually, for ourselves, our heirs, and assigns, promise and declare, in the presence of God and each other, and to all men, that we will never hereafter, neither directly nor indirectly, make nor require any account of any interest, property, labor, or service which has been, or which may be devoted by us or any of us to the purposes aforesaid ; nor bring any charge of debt or damage, nor hold any demand whatever against the Church, nor against any member or members thereof, on account of any property or service given, rendered, devoted, or consecrated to the aforesaid sacred and charitable purpose."

As under this agreement or covenant no accounts can be demanded, so the societies and families have no annual or business meetings, nor is any business report ever made to the members.

Agriculture and horticulture are the foundations of all the communes or families; but with these they have united some small manufactures. For instance, some of the families make brooms, others dry sweet corn, raise and put up garden seeds, make medicinal extracts; make mops, baskets, chairs; one society makes large casks, and so on. A complete list of these industries in all the societies will be found further on. It will be seen that the range is not great.

Besides this, they aim, as far as possible, to supply their own needs. Thus they make all their own clothing, and formerly made also their own woolen cloths and flannels. They make shoes, do all their own carpentering, and, as far as is convenient, raise the food they consume. They have usually fine barns, and all the arrangements for working are of the best and most convenient. For instance, at Mount Lebanon the different families saw their firewood by a power-saw, and store it in huge wood-houses, that it may be seasoned before it is used. In their farming operations they spare no pains; but, working slowly year after year, redeem the soil, clear it of stones, and have clean tillage. They are fond of such minute and careful culture as is required in raising garden seeds. They keep fine stock, and their barns are usually admirably arranged to save labor.

Their buildings are always of the best, and kept in the best order and repair.

Their savings they invest chiefly in land; and many families own considerable estates outside of their own limits. In the cultivation of these outlying farms they employ hired laborers, and build for them comfortable houses. About Lebanon, I am told, a farmer who is in the employ of the Shakers is considered a fortunate man, as they are kind and liberal in their dealings. Every where they have the reputation of being strictly honest and fair in all their transactions with the world's people.

The dress of the men is remarkable for a very broad, stiff-brimmed, white or gray felt hat, and a long coat of light blue. The women wear gowns with many plaits in the skirt; and a singular head-dress or cap of light material, which so completely hides the hair, and so encroaches upon the face, that a stranger is at first unable to distinguish the old from the

SISTERS IN EVERY-DAY COSTUME.

young. Out of doors they wear the deep sun-bonnet known in this country commonly as a Shaker bonnet. They do not profess to adhere to a uniform ; but have adopted what they find to be a convenient style of dress, and will not change it until they find something better.

IV.—A VISIT TO MOUNT LEBANON.

It was on a bleak and sleety December day that I made my first visit to a Shaker family. As I came by appointment, a brother, whom I later found to be the second elder of the family, received me at the door, opening it silently at the precise moment when I had reached the vestibule, and, silently bowing, took my bag from my hand and motioned me to follow him. We passed through a hall in which I saw numerous bonnets, cloaks, and shawls hung up on pegs, and passed an empty dining-hall, and out of a door into the back yard, crossing which we entered another house, and, opening a door, my guide welcomed me to the " visitors' room." " This," said he, " is where you will stay. A brother will come in presently to speak with you." And with a bow my guide noiselessly slipped out, softly closed the door behind him, and I was alone.

I found myself in a comfortable low-ceiled room, warmed by an air-tight stove, and furnished with a cot-bed, half a dozen chairs, a large wooden spittoon filled with saw-dust, a looking-glass, and a table. The floor was covered with strips of rag carpet, very neat and of a pretty, quiet color, loosely laid down. Against the wall, near the stove, hung a dust-pan, shovel, dusting-brush, and small broom. A door opened into an inner room, which contained another bed and conveniences for washing. A closet in the wall held matches, soap, and other articles. Every thing was scrupulously neat and clean. On the table were laid a number of Shaker books and newspapers. In one corner of the room was a bell, used, as I after-ward discovered, to summon the visitor to his meals. As I looked out of a window, I perceived that the sash was fitted with screws, by means of which the windows could be so se-cured as not to rattle in stormy weather; while the lower sash of one window was raised three or four inches, and a strip of neatly fitting plank was inserted in the opening—this allowed ventilation between the upper and lower sashes, thus prevent-ing a direct draught, while securing fresh air.

I was still admiring these ingenious little contrivances, when, with a preliminary knock, entered to me a tall, slender young man, who, hanging his broad-brimmed hat on a peg, announced himself to me as the brother who was to care for me during my stay. He was a Swede, a student of the university in his own country, and a person of intelligence, some literary cult-ure, and I should think of good family. His attention had been attracted to the Shakers by Mr. Dixon's book, " The New America ;" he had come over to examine the organization, and had found it so much to his liking that, coming as a visitor, he had remained as a member. He had been here six or seven years. He had a fresh, fine complexion, as most of the Shaker men and women have—particularly the latter ; his hair was cut in the Shaker fashion, straight across the forehead, and suffered to grow long behind, and he wore the long, blue-gray coat, a collar without a neck-tie, and the broad-brimmed whitish-gray felt hat of the order. His voice was soft and low, his motions noiseless, his conversation in a subdued tone, his smile ready ; but his expression was that of one who guarded himself against the world, with which he was determined to have nothing to do. Frank and communicative he was, too, though I do not doubt that my tireless questioning sometimes bored him. Such as I have described him I have found all or nearly all the Shaker people—polite, patient, noiseless in their motions except during their " meetings" or worship, when they are

ELDER FREDERICK W. EVANS.

sometimes quite noisy; scrupulously neat, and much given to attend to their own business.

The Sabbath quiet and stillness which prevailed I attributed to the fact that there had been a death in the family, and the funeral was to be held that morning; but I discovered afterwards that an eternal Sabbath stillness reigns in a Shaker family—there being no noise or confusion, or hum of busy industry at any time, although they are a most industrious people.

While the Swedish brother was, in answer to my questions, giving me some account of himself, to us came Elder Frederick, the head of the North or Gathering Family at Mount Lebanon, and the most noted of all the Shakers, because he, oftener than any other, has been sent out into the world to make known the society's doctrines and practice.

Frederick W. Evans is an Englishman by birth, and was a "reformer" in the old times, when men in this country strove for "land reform," the rights of labor, and against the United States Bank and other monopolies of forty or fifty years ago. He is now sixty-six years of age, but looks not more than fifty; was brought to this country at the age of twelve; became a socialist in early life, and, after trying life in several communities which perished early, at last visited the Shakers at Mount Lebanon, and after some months of trial and examination, joined the community, and has remained in it ever since— about forty-five years.

He is both a writer and a speaker; and while not college bred, has studied and read a good deal, and has such natural abilities as make him a leader among his people, and a man of force any where. He is a person of enthusiastic and aggressive temperament, but with a practical and logical side to his mind, and with a hobby for science as applied to health, comfort, and the prolongation of life. In person he is tall, with a stoop as though he had overgrown his strength in early life;

with brown eyes, a long nose, a kindly, serious face, and an attractive manner. He was dressed rigidly in the Shaker costume.

VIEW OF A SHAKER VILLAGE.

Mount Lebanon lies beautifully among the hills of Berkshire, two and a half miles from Lebanon Springs, and seven miles from Pittsfield. The settlement is admirably placed on the hillside to which it clings, securing it good drainage, abundant water, sunshine, and the easy command of water-power. Whoever selected the spot had an excellent eye for beauty and utility in a country site. The views are lovely, broad, and varied; the air is pure and bracing; and, in short, a company of people desiring to seclude themselves from the world could hardly have chosen a more delightful spot.

As you drive up the road from Lebanon Springs, the first building belonging to the Shaker settlement which meets your eye is the enormous barn of the North Family, said to be the largest in the three or four states which near here come together, as in its interior arrangements it is one of the most complete. This huge structure lies on a hillside, and is two hundred and ninety-six feet long by fifty wide, and five stories high, the upper story being on a level with the main road, and the lower opening on the fields behind it. Next to this lies the sisters' shop, three stories high, used for the women's industries; and next, on the same level, the family house, one hundred feet by forty, and five stories high. Behind these buildings, which all lie directly on the main road, is another set—an additional dwelling-house, in which are the visitors' room and several rooms where applicants for admission remain while they are on trial; near this an enormous woodshed, three stories high; below a carriage-house, wagon sheds, the brothers' shop, where different industries are carried on, such as broom-making and putting up garden seeds; and farther on, the laundry, a saw-mill and grist-mill and other machinery, and a granary, with rooms for hired men over it. The whole establishment is built on a tolerably steep hillside.

THE HERB-HOUSE, MOUNT LEBANON.

A quarter of a mile farther on are the buildings of the Church Family, and also the great boiler-roofed church of the society; and other communes or families are scattered along, each having all its interests separate, and forming a distinct community, with industries of its own, and a complete organization for itself.

MEETING-HOUSE AT MOUNT LEBANON.

The illustrations show sufficiently the character of the different buildings and the style of architecture, and make more detailed description needless. It need only be said that whereas on Mount Lebanon they build altogether of wood, in other settlements they use also brick and stone. But the peculiar nature of their social arrangements leads them to build very large houses.

Elder Frederick came to give me notice that I was permitted to witness the funeral ceremonies of the departed sister, which were set for ten o'clock, in the assembly-room; and thither I was accordingly conducted at the proper time by one of the brethren. The members came into the room rapidly, and ranged themselves in ranks, the men and women on opposite sides of the room, and facing each other. All stood up, there being no seats. A brief address by Elder Frederick opened the serv-

INTERIOR OF MEETING-HOUSE AT MOUNT LEBANON.

ices, after which there was singing; different brethren and sisters spoke briefly; a call was made to the spirit of the departed to communicate, and in the course of the meeting a medium delivered some words supposed to be from this source; some memorial verses were read by one of the sisters; and then the congregation separated, after notice had been given that the body of the dead sister would be placed in the hall, where all could take a last look at her face. I, too, was asked to look; the good brother who conducted me to the plain, unpainted pine coffin remarking very sensibly that "the body is not of much importance after it is dead."

Afterwards, in conversation, Elder Frederick told me that the "spiritual" manifestations were known among the Shakers many years before Kate Fox was born; that they had had all manner of manifestations, but chiefly visions and communications through mediums; that they fell, in his mind, into three epochs: in the first the spirits laboring to convince unbelievers in the society; in the second proving the community, the spirits relating to each member his past history, and showing up, in certain cases, the insincerity of professions; in the third, he said, the Shakers reacted on the spirit world, and formed communities of Shakers there, under the instruction of living

Shakers. "There are at this time," said he, "many thousands of Shakers in the spirit world." He added that the mediums in the society had given much trouble because they imagined themselves reformers, whereas they were only the mouth-pieces of spirits, and oftenest themselves of a low order of mind. They had to teach the mediums much, after the spirits ceased to use them.

In what follows I give the substance, and often the words, of many conversations with Elder Frederick and with several of the brethren, relating to details of management and to doctrinal points and opinions, needed to fill up the sketch given in the two previous chapters.

As to new members, Elder Frederick said the societies had not in recent years increased—some had decreased in numbers. But they expected large accessions in the course of the next few years, having prophecies among themselves to that effect. Religious revivals he regarded as "the hot-beds of Shakerism:" they always gain members after a "revival" in any part of the country. "Our proper dependence for increase is on the spirit and gift of God working outside. Hence we are friendly to all religious people."

They had changed their policy in regard to taking children, for experience had proved that when these grew up they were oftenest discontented, anxious to gain property for themselves, curious to see the world, and therefore left the society. For these reasons they now almost always decline to take children, though there are some in every society; and for these they have schools—a boys' school in the winter and a girls' school in summer—teaching all a trade as they grow up. "When men or women come to us at the age of twenty-one or twenty-two, then they make the best Shakers. The society then gets the man's or woman's best energies, and experience shows us that they have then had enough of the world to satisfy their curiosity and make them restful. Of course we like to keep up our numbers; but of course we do not sacrifice our principles. You will be surprised to know that we lost most seriously during the war. A great many of our younger people went into the army; many who fought through the war have since applied to come back to us; and where they seem to have the proper spirit, we take them. We have some applications of this kind now."

A great many Revolutionary soldiers joined the societies in their early history; these did not draw their pensions; most of them lived to be old, and "I proved to Mr. Lincoln and Mr. Stanton once, when we were threatened with a draft," said Elder Frederick, "that our members had thus omitted to draw from the government over half a million of dollars due as pensions for army service."

With their management, he said, they had not much difficulty in sloughing off persons who come with bad or low motives; and in this I should say he was right; for the life is strictly ascetic, and has no charms for the idler or for merely sentimental or romantic people. "If one comes with low motives, he will not be comfortable with us, and will presently go away; if he is sincere, he may yet be here a year or two before he finds himself in his right place; but if he has the true vocation he will gradually work in with us."

He thought an order of celibates ought to exist in every Protestant community, and that its members should be self-supporting, and not beggars; that the necessities and conscience of many in every civilized community would be relieved if there were such an order open to them.

In admitting members, no property qualification is made; and in practice those who come in singly, from time to time, hardly ever possess any thing; but after a great revival of religion, when numbers come in, usually about half bring in more or less property, and often large amounts.

As to celibacy, he asserted in the most positive manner that it is healthful, and tends to prolong life; "as we are constantly proving." He afterward gave me a file of the *Shaker*, a monthly paper, in which the deaths in all the societies are recorded; and I judge from its reports that the death rate is low, and the people mostly long-lived.* "We look for a testimony against disease," he said; "and even now I hold that no man who lives as we do has a right to be ill before he is sixty; if he suffer from disease before that, he is in fault. My life has been devoted to introducing among our people a knowledge of true physiological laws; and this knowledge is spreading among all our societies. We are not all perfect yet in these respects; but we grow. Formerly fevers were prevalent in our houses, but now we scarcely ever have a case; and the cholera has never yet touched a Shaker village."

"The joys of the celibate life are far greater than I can make you know. They are indescribable."

The Church Family at Mount Lebanon, by the way, have built and fitted up a commodious hospital, for the permanently disabled of the society there. It is empty, but ready; and "better empty than full," said an aged member to me.

Among the members they have people who were formerly clergymen, lawyers, doctors, farmers, students, mechanics, sea-captains, soldiers, and merchants; preachers are in a much larger proportion than any of the other professions or callings. They get members from all the religious denominations except the Roman Catholic; they have even Jews. Baptists, Methodists, Presbyterians, and Adventists furnish them the greatest proportion. They have always received colored people, and have some in several of the societies.

"Every commune, to prosper, must be founded, so far as

---

* In nine numbers of the *Shaker* (year 1873), twenty-seven deaths are recorded. Of these, Abigail Munson died at Mount Lebanon, aged 101 years, 11 months, and 12 days. The ages of the remainder were 97, 93, 88, 87, 86, 82, six above 75, four above 70, 69, 65, 64, 55, 54, 49, 37, 31, and two whose ages were not given.

its industry goes, on agriculture. Only the simple labors and manners of a farming people can hold a community together. Wherever we have departed from this rule to go into manufacturing, we have blundered." For his part, he would like to make a law for the whole country, that every man should own a piece of land and work on it. Moreover, a community, he said, should, as far as possible, make or produce all it uses. "We used to have more looms than now, but cloth is sold so cheaply that we gradually began to buy. It is a mistake ; we buy more cheaply than we can make, but our home-made cloth is much better than that we can buy ; and we have now to make three pairs of trousers, for instance, where before we made one. Thus our little looms would even now be more profitable—to say nothing of the independence we secure in working them."

In the beginning, he said, the societies were desirous to own land ; and he thought immoderately so. They bought to the extent of their means ; being economical, industrious, and honest, they saved money rapidly, and always invested their surplus in more land. Then to cultivate these farms they adopted children and young people. Twenty years ago the Legislature of New York had before it a bill to limit

SHAKER TANNERY, MOUNT LEBANON.

the quantity of land the Shakers should be allowed to hold, and the number of apprentices they should take. It was introduced, he said, by their enemies, but they at once agreed to it, and thereupon it was dropped; but since then the society had come generally to favor a law limiting the quantity of land which any citizen should own to not more than one hundred acres.

SHAKER OFFICE AND STORE AT MOUNT LEBANON.

He thought it a mistake in his people to own farms outside of their family limits, as now they often do. This necessitates the employment of persons not members, and this he thought impolitic. " If every out-farm were sold, the society would be better off. They are of no real advantage to us, and I believe of no pecuniary advantage either. They give us a prosperous look, because we improve them well, and they do return usually a fair percentage upon the investment; but, on the other hand, this success depends upon the assiduous labor of some of our ablest men, whose services would have been worth more at home. We ought to get on without the use of outside labor. Then we should be confined to such enterprises as are best for us. Moreover we ought not to make money. We ought to make no more than a moderate surplus over our usual living, so as to lay by something for hard times. In fact, we do not do much more than this."

Nevertheless nearly all the Shaker societies have the reputation of being wealthy.

In their daily lives many profess to have attained perfection: these are the older people. I judge by the words I have heard in their meetings that the younger members have occasion to wish for improvement, and do discover faults in themselves. One of the older Shakers, a man of seventy-two years, and of more than the average intelligence, said to me, in answer to a direct question, that he had for years lived a sinless life. "I say to any who know me, as Jesus said to the Pharisees, 'which of you convicteth me of sin.'" Where faults are committed, it is held to be the duty of the offender to confess to the elder, or, if it is a woman, to the eldress; and it is for these, too, to administer reproof. "For instance, suppose one of the members to possess a hasty temper, not yet under proper curb; suppose he or she breaks out into violent words or impatience, in a shop or elsewhere; the rest ought to and do tell the elder, who will thereupon administer reproof. But also the offending member ought not to come to meeting before having made confession of his sin to the elder, and asked pardon of those who were the subjects and witnesses of the offense."

As to books and literature in general, they are not a reading people. "Though a man should gain all the natural knowledge in the universe, he could not thereby gain either the knowledge or power of salvation from sin, nor redemption from a sinful nature."* Elder Frederick's library is of extremely limited range, and contains but a few books, mostly concerning social problems and physiological laws. The Swedish brother, who had been a student, said in answer to my

---

* "Christ's First and Second Appearing."

question, that it did not take him long to wean himself from the habit of books; and that now, when he felt a temptation in that direction, he knew he must examine himself, because he felt there was something wrong about him, dragging him down from his higher spiritual estate. He did not regret his books at all. An intelligent, thoughtful old Scotchman said on the same subject that he, while still of the world, had had a hobby for chemical research, to which he would probably have devoted his life; that he still read much of the newest investigations, but that he had found it better to turn his attention to higher matters; and to bring the faculties which led him naturally toward chemical studies to the examination of social problems, and to use his knowledge for the benefit of the society.

The same old Scotchman, now seventy-three years old, and a cheery old fellow, who had known the elder Owen, and has lived as a Shaker forty years, I asked, "Well, on the whole, reviewing your life, do you think it a success?" He replied, clearly with the utmost sincerity: "Certainly; I have been living out the highest aspirations my mind was capable of. The best I knew has been realized for and around me here. With my ideas of society I should have been unfit for any thing in the world, and unhappy because every thing around me would have worked contrary to my belief in the right and the best. Here I found my place and my work, and have been happy and content, seeing the realization of the highest I had dreamed of."

Considering the homeliness of the buildings, which mostly have the appearance of mere factories or human hives, I asked Elder Frederick whether, if they were to build anew, they would not aim at some architectural effect, some beauty of design. He replied with great positiveness, "No, the beautiful, as you call it, is absurd and abnormal. It has no business with us. The divine man has no right to waste money upon what you would call beauty, in his house or his daily life, while there are people living in misery." In building anew, he would take

care to have more light, a more equal distribution of heat, and a more general care for protection and comfort, because these things tend to health and long life. But no beauty. He described to me amusingly the disgust he had experienced in a costly New York dwelling, where he saw carpets nailed down on the floor, " of course with piles of dust beneath, never swept away, and of which I had to breathe ;" and with

A SHAKER ELDER.

heavy picture-frames hung against the walls, also the receptacles of dust. "You people in the world are not clean according to our Shaker notions. And what is the use of pictures ?" he added scornfully.

They have paid much attention to the early Jewish policy in Palestine, and the laws concerning the distribution of land, the Sabbatical year, service, and the collection of debts, are praised by them as establishing a far better order of things for the world in general than that which obtains in the civilized world to-day.

They hold strongly to the equality of women with men, and look forward to the day when women shall, in the outer world

as in their own societies, hold office as well as men. " Here
we find the women just as able as men in all business affairs,
and far more spiritual." " Suppose a woman wanted, in your
family, to be a blacksmith, would you consent?" I asked; and
he replied, " No, because this would bring men and women
into relations which we do not think wise." In fact, while
they call men and women equally to the rulership, they very
sensibly hold that in general life the woman's work is in the
house, the man's out of doors; and there is no offer to confuse
the two.

Moreover, being celibates, they use proper precautions in the
intercourse of the sexes. Thus Shaker men and women do
not shake hands with each other; their lives have almost no
privacy, even to the elders, of whom two always room together;
the sexes even eat apart; they labor apart; they worship, standing and marching, apart; they visit each other only at stated
intervals and according to a prescribed order; and in all things
the sexes maintain a certain distance and reserve toward each
other. " We have no scandal, no tea-parties, no gossip."

Moreover, they mortify the body by early rising and by
very plain living. Few, as I said before, eat meat; and I was
assured that a complete and long-continued experience had
proved to them that young people maintain their health and
strength fully without meat. They wear a very plain and
simple dress, without ornament of any kind; and the costume
of the women does not increase their attractiveness, and makes
it difficult to distinguish between youth and age. They keep
no pet animals, except cats, which are maintained to destroy
rats and mice. They have, of course, none of the usual relations to children—and the boys and girls whom they take in
are in each family put under charge of a special " care-taker,"
and live in separate houses, each sex by itself.

Smoking tobacco is by general consent strictly prohibited.
A few chew tobacco, but this is thought a weakness, to be

A GROUP OF SHAKER CHILDREN.

SHAKER DINING-HALL.

left off as standing in the way of a perfect life. The following notice in the *Shaker* shows that even some very old sinners in this respect reform:

OBITUARY.

On Tuesday, Feb. 20th, 1873, *Died*, by the power of truth, and for the
cause of Human Redemption, at the Young Believers' Order, Mt. Lebanon,
in the following much-beloved Brethren, the

TOBACCO-CHEWING HABIT,
aged respectively,

In D. S. - - - - - - -	51 years' duration.
In C. M. - - - - - -	57 "
In A. G. - - - - - - -	15 "
In T. S. - - - - - -	36 "
In OLIVER PRENTISS - - - -	71 "
In L. S. - - - - - -	45 "
In H. C. - - - - - - -	53 "
In C. K. - - - - - -	12 "

No funeral ceremonies, no mourners, no grave-yard; but an honorable
RECORD thereof made in the Court above.   *Ed.*

Reviewing all these details, it did not surprise me when
Elder Frederick remarked, "Every body is not called to the
divine life." To a man or woman not thoroughly and earnestly in love with an ascetic life and deeply disgusted with
the world, Shakerism would be unendurable; and I believe insincerity to be rare among them. It is not a comfortable
place for hypocrites or pretenders.

The housekeeping of a Shaker family is very thoroughly
and effectively done. The North Family at Mount Lebanon
consists of sixty persons; six sisters suffice to do the cooking
and baking, and to manage the dining-hall; six other sisters in
half a day do the washing of the whole family. The deaconesses give out the supplies. The men milk in bad weather,
the women when it is warm. The Swedish brother told me
that he was this winter taking a turn at milking—to mortify
the flesh, I imagine, for he had never done this in his own
home; and he used neither milk nor butter. Many of the

brethren have not tasted meat in from twenty-five to thirty-five years. Tea and coffee are used, but very moderately.

There is no servant class.

" In a community, it is necessary that some one person shall always know where every body is," and it is the elder's office to have this knowledge; thus if one does not attend a meeting, he tells the elder the reason why.

Obedience to superiors is an important part of the life of the order.

Living as they do in large families compactly stowed, they have become very careful against fires, and " a real Shaker always, when he has gone out of a room, returns and takes a look around to see that all is right."

The floor of the assembly room was astonishingly bright and clean, so that I imagined it had been recently laid. It had, in fact, been used twenty-nine years; and in that time had been but twice scrubbed with water. But it was swept and polished daily; and the brethren wear to the meetings shoes made particularly for those occasions, which are without nails or pegs in the soles, and of soft leather. They have invented many such tricks of housekeeping, and I could see that they acted just as a parcel of old bachelors and old maids would, any where else, in these particulars—setting much store by personal comfort, neatness, and order; and no doubt thinking much of such minor morals. For instance, on the opposite page is a copy of verses which I found in the visitors' room in one of the Shaker families—a silent but sufficient hint to the careless and wasteful.

Like the old monasteries, they are the prey of beggars, who always receive a dole of food, and often money enough to pay for a night's lodging in the neighboring village; for they do not like to take in strangers.

The visiting which is done on Sunday evenings is perhaps as curious as any part of their ceremonial. Like all else in

TABLE MONITOR.

GATHER UP THE FRAGMENTS THAT REMAIN, THAT NOTHING BE LOST.—Christ.

Here then is the pattern
  Which Jesus has set;
And his good example
  We can not forget:
With thanks for his blessings
  His word we'll obey;
But on this occasion
  We've somewhat to say.

We wish to speak plainly
  And use no deceit;
We like to see fragments
  Left wholesome and neat:
To customs and fashions
  We make no pretense;
Yet think we can tell
  What belongs to good sense.

What we deem good order,
  We're willing to state—
Eat hearty and decent,
  And clear out our plate—
Be thankful to Heaven
  For what we receive,
And not make a mixture
  Or compound to leave.

We find of those bounties
  Which Heaven does give,
That some live to eat,
  And that some eat to live—
That some think of nothing
  But pleasing the taste,
And care very little
  How much they do waste.

Tho' Heaven has bless'd us
  With plenty of food:
Bread, butter, and honey,
  And all that is good;
We loathe to see mixtures
  Where gentle folks dine,
Which scarcely look fit
  For the poultry or swine.

We often find left,
  On the same china dish,
Meat, apple-sauce, pickle,
  Brown bread and minc'd fish;
Another's replenish'd
  With butter and cheese;
With pie, cake, and toast,
  Perhaps, added to these.

Now if any virtue
  In this can be shown,
By peasant, by lawyer,
  Or king on the throne,
We freely will forfeit
  Whatever we've said,
And call it a virtue
  To waste meat and bread.

Let none be offended
  At what we here say;
We candidly ask you,
  Is that the best way?
If not—lay such customs
  And fashions aside,
And take this Monitor
  Henceforth for your guide.

[Visitors' Eating-Room, Shaker Village.]

their lives, these visits are prearranged for them—a certain group of sisters visiting a certain group of brethren. The sisters, from four to eight in number, sit in a row on one side, in straight-backed chairs, each with her neat hood or cap, and each with a clean white handkerchief spread stiffly across her lap. The brethren, of equal number, sit opposite them, in another row, also in stiff-backed chairs, and also each with a white handkerchief smoothly laid over his knees. Thus arranged, they converse upon the news of the week, events in the outer world, the farm operations, and the weather; they sing, and in general have a pleasant reunion, not without gentle laughter and mild amusement. They meet at an appointed time, and at another set hour they part; and no doubt they find great satisfaction in this—the only meeting in which they fall into sets which do not include the whole family.

Since these chapters were written, Hervey Elkins's pamphlet, "Fifteen Years in the Senior Order of the Shakers," printed at Hanover, New Hampshire, in 1853, has come into my hands. Elkins gives some details out of his own experience of Shaker life which I believe to be generally correct, and which I quote here, as filling up some parts of the picture I have tried to give of the Shaker polity and life:

"The spiritual orders, laws, and statutes, never to be revoked, are in substance as follows: None are admitted within the walls of Zion, as they denominate their religious sphere, but by a confession to one or more incarnate witnesses of every debasing and immoral act perpetrated by the confessor within his remembrance; also every act which, though the laws of men may sanction, may be deemed sinful in the view of that new and sublimer divinity which he has adopted. The time, the place, the motive which produced and pervaded the act, the circumstances which aggravated the case, are all to be disclosed. No stone is to be left unturned—no filth is suffered to remain. The temple of God, or the soul, must be carefully swept and garnished, before the new man can enter it and there make his abode. (Christ, or the Divine Intelligence which emanated from God the Father, transforms the soul into the new man spoken of in the Scriptures.)

"Those who have committed deeds cognizable by the laws of the land, shall never be admitted, until those laws have dealt with their transgressions and acquitted them.

"Those who have in any way morally wronged a fellow-creature, shall make restitution to the satisfaction of the person injured.

"Wives who have unbelieving husbands must not be admitted without their husbands' consent, or until they are lawfully released from the marriage contract, and vice versa. They may confess their sins, but can not enter the sacred compact.

"All children admitted shall be bound by legal indentures, and shall, if refractory, be returned to their parents.

"There shall exist three Orders, or degrees of progression, viz.: The Novitiate, the Junior, and the Senior.

"All adults may enter the Novitiate Order, and then may progress to a higher, by faithfulness in supporting the Gospel requirements.

"When at the age of twenty-one, the Church Covenant is presented to all the young members to peruse, and to deliberate and decide whether or not they will maintain the conditions therein expressed. To older members it is presented after all legal embarrassments upon their estates are settled, and they desire to be admitted to full fellowship with those who have consecrated *all*. And whoever, after having escaped the servility of Egypt, shall again desire its taskmasters and flesh-pots, are unfit for the kingdom of God; and in case of secession or apostasy shall, by their own deliberate and matured act (that of placing their signatures and seals upon this instrument when in the full possession of all their mental powers), be debarred from legally demanding any compensation whatever for the property or services which they had dedicated to a holy purpose.

"This instrument is legally and skillfully formed, and none are permitted to sign it until they have counted well the cost; or, at least, pondered for a time upon its requirements.

"Members also stipulate themselves by this signature to yield implicit obedience to the ministry, elders, deacons, and trustees, each in their respective departments of authority and duty.

"The Shaker government, in many points, resembles that of the military. All shall look for counsel and guidance to those immediately before them, and shall receive nothing from, nor make application for any thing to those but their immediate advisers. For instance: No elder in either of the subordinate bishoprics can make application for any amendment, any innovation, any introduction of a new system, of however trivial a nature, to the ministry of the first bishopric; but he may desire and ask of his own ministry, and, if his proposal meet their concurrence, they will seek its sanction of those next higher. All are to regard their spiritual leaders as mediators between God and their own souls; and these links of divine communication, successively descending from Power and Wisdom, who constitute the dual God, to their Son and Daughter, Jesus and Ann, and from them to Ann's successors of the Zion of God on earth, down to the prattling infant who may have been gathered within this ark of safety—this concatenated system of spiritual delegation is the river of life, whose salutary waters flow through the celestial sphere for the cleansing and redemption of souls.

" Great humility and simplicity of life is practiced by the first ministry —two of each sex—upon whom devolves the charge of subordinate bishoprics, besides that of their own immediate care, the societies of Niskeyuna and Mount Lebanon. They will not even (and this is good policy) allow themselves those expensive conveniences of life which are so common among the laity of their sect. But extreme neatness is the most prominent characteristic of both them and their subordinates. They speak much of the model enjoined by Jesus, that whosoever would be the greatest should be the servant of all.

"A simple song, of a beautiful tune, inculcating this spirit, is often sung in their assemblies. The words are these :

> 'Whoever wants to be the highest
> Must first come down to be the lowest ;
> And then ascend to be the highest
> By keeping down to be the lowest.'

"It is common for the leaders to crowd down, by humiliation, and withdraw patronage and attention from those whom they intend to ultimately promote to an official station. That such may learn how it seems to be slighted and humiliated, and how to stand upon their own basis, work spiritually for their own food without being dandled upon the soft lap of affection, or fed with the milk designed for babes. That also they be not deceived by the phantoms of self-wisdom; and that they martyr not in themselves the meek spirit of the lowly Jesus. Thus, while holding one in contemplation for an office of care and trust, they first prove him—the cause unknown to himself—to see how much he can bear, without exploding by impatience or faltering under trial.

" Virtually for this purpose, but ostensibly for some other, have I known many promising young people moved to a back order, or lower grade of fellowship. By such trials the leaders think to try their souls in the furnace of affliction, withdraw them from earthly attachments, and imbue them with reliance upon God. In fact, to destroy terrestrial idols of every kind, to dispel the clouds of inordinate affection and concentrative love, which fascinatingly float around the mind and screen from its view the radiant brightness of heaven and heavenly things, is the great object of Shakerism.

" Whoever yields enough to the evil tempter to gratify in the least the sensual passions—either in deed, word, or thought—shall cónfess honestly the same to his elders ere the sun of another day shall set to announce a day of condemnation and wrath against the guilty soul. These vile passions are—fleshly lusts in every form, idolatry, selfishness, envy, wrath, malice, evil-speaking, and their kindred evils.

" The Sabbath shall be kept pure and holy to that degree that no books shall be read on that day which originated among the world's people, save those scientific books which treat of propriety of diction. No idle or vain stories shall be rehearsed, no unnecessary labor shall be performed—not even the cooking of food, the ablution of the body, the cutting of the hair, beard, or nails, the blacking and polishing of shoes or boots. All these things must be performed on Saturday, or postponed till the subsequent week. All fruit, eaten upon the Sabbath, must be carried to the dwelling-house on Saturday. But the dormitories may be arranged, the cows milked, all domestic animals fed, and food and drink warmed on Sunday. No one is allowed to go to his workshop, to walk in the gardens, the orchards, or on the farms, unless immediate duty requires; and those who of necessity go to their workshops, shall not tarry over fifteen minutes but by the direct liberty of the elders. The dwelling-house is the place for all to spend the Sabbath; and thither all concentrate—elders, deacons, brethren, and sisters. If any property is likely to incur loss—as hay and grain that is cut and remaining in the field, and is liable to be wet before Monday, it may be secured upon the Sabbath.

"All shall rise simultaneously every morning at the signal of the bell, and those of each room shall kneel together in silent prayer, strip from the beds the coverlets and blankets, lighten the feathers, open the windows to ventilate the rooms, and repair to their places of vocation. Fifteen minutes are allowed for all to leave their sleeping apartments. In the summer the signal for rising is heard at half-past four, in the winter

at half-past five.   Breakfast is invariably one and a half hours after rising
—in the summer at six, in the winter at seven ; dinner always at twelve ;
supper at six.   These rules are, however, slightly modified upon the Sabbath.   They rise and breakfast on this day half an hour later, dine light-
ly at twelve, and sup at four.   Every order maintains the same regularity
in regard to their meals.

"In the Senior Order, at the ringing of a large bell, ten minutes before
meal-time, all may gather into the saloons, and retire the ten minutes before the dining-hall alarm summons them to the table.   All enter four
doors and gently arrange themselves at their respective places at the
table, then all simultaneously kneel in silent thanks for nearly a minute,
then rise and seat themselves almost inaudibly at the table.   No talking,
laughing, whispering, or blinking are allowed while thus partaking of
God's blessings.   After eating, all rise together at the signal of the first
elder, kneel as before, and gently retire to their places of vocation, without stopping in the dining-hall, loitering in the corridors and vestibules,
or lounging upon the balustrades, doorways, and stairs.

"The tables are long, three feet in width, highly polished, without cloth,
and furnished with white ware and no tumblers.   The interdict which
excludes glass-ware from the table must be attributed to conservatism
rather than parsimony, for in *most* useful improvements the Shakers
strive to excel.   They tremble at adopting the *customs* of the world.   At
the tables, each four have all the varieties of food served for themselves,
which precludes the necessity of continual passing and reaching.

"At half-past seven P.M. in the summer, and at eight in the winter,
the large bell summons all of every order to their respective dwellings,
there to retire, each individual in his own room, half an hour before
evening worship.   To retire is for the inmates of every room—generally
from four to eight individuals—to dispose themselves in either one or
two ranks, and sit erect, with their hands folded upon their laps, without
leaning back or falling asleep ; and in that position labor for a true sense
of their privilege in the Zion of God—of the fact that God has prescribed
a law which humbles and keeps them within the hollow of his hand, and
has favored them with the blessing of worshiping him, with soul and
body, unmolested, and according to the dictation of an enlightened mind
and a tender and good conscience.   If any chance to fall asleep while
thus mentally employed, they may rise and bow four times, or gently
shake, and then resume their seats.

"The man who is now the archbishop of Shakerism was, when a youth, very apt to fall into a drowsy state in retiring time; but he broke up that habit by standing erect the half-hour before every meeting for six months. And there are many as zealous as he in supporting every order. No unnecessary walking in the corridors or passing in and out of doors are in this sacred time allowed. When the half-hour has expired, a small hand-bell summons all to the hall of worship. None are allowed to absent themselves without the elder's liberty. If any are unwell or tired, it is but a little matter to rap at the elder's door, or ask a companion to do it, where any one may receive liberty to retire to rest if it is expedient. All pass the stairs and corridors, and enter the hall, two abreast, upon tiptoe, bowing once as they enter, and pass directly to their place in the forming ranks.

"The house, of course, is vacated through the day, except by sisters, who take turns in cooking, making beds, and sweeping. When brethren and sisters enter, they must uncover their heads, and hang their hats and bonnets in the lower corridors, and walk softly, and open and shut doors gently, and in the fear of God. None are allowed to carry money into sacred worship. In a word, the sanctuary and the whole house shall be kept sacred and holy unto the Lord; and all shall spend the time allotted to be in the house mostly in their own rooms. Three evenings in the week are set apart for worship, and three for 'union meetings.' Monday evenings all may retire to rest at the usual meeting time, an hour earlier than usual. For the union meetings the brethren remain in their rooms, and the sisters, six, eight, or ten in number, enter and sit in a rank opposite to that of the brethren's, and converse simply, often facetiously, but rarely profoundly. In fact, to say 'agreeable things about nothing,' when conversant with the other sex, is as common there as elsewhere. And what of dignity or meaning could be said? where talking of sacred subjects is not allowed, under the pretext that it scatters those blessings which should be carefully treasured up; and bestowing much information concerning the secular plans of economy practiced by your own to the other sex is not approved; and where to talk of literary matters would be termed bombastic pedantry and small display, and would serve to exhibit accomplishments which might be enticingly dangerous. Nevertheless, an hour passes away very agreeably and even rapturously with those who there chance to meet with an especial favorite; succeeded soon, however, when soft words, and kind, concentrated looks become obvious to the jealous eye of a female espionage, by the agonies of a separation. For the tidings of such reciprocity, whether true or surmised, is sure before the lapse of many hours to reach the ears of the elders; in which case, the one or the other party would be subsequently summoned to another circle of colloquy and union.

"No one is permitted to make mention of any thing said or done in any of these sittings to those who attend another, for party spirit and mischief might be the result. Twenty minutes of the union hour may be devoted to the singing of sacred songs, if desired.

"All are positively forbidden ever to say aught against their brother or their sister, whatever may be their defects; but such defects shall be made known to the elders, and to none else. 'If nothing good can be said of one, say nothing,' is a Shaker maxim. If one member is known by another to violate an ordinance of the Gospel, the witness thereto shall gently remind the transgressor, and request him to confess the deed to the elder. If he refuses, the witness shall divulge it; if he consents, then is the witness free, as having performed his duty.

"Brethren and sisters shall not visit each other's rooms unless for errands; and in such cases shall tarry no more than fifteen minutes. A sister shall not go to the brethren's work places unless accompanied by another. Brethren's and sister's workshops shall not be under one or the same roof; they shall not pass each other upon the stairs; nor one of each converse together unless a third person be present of more than ten years of age. They shall in no case give presents to each other, nor lend with the intention of never again receiving. If a sister desires any assistance, or desires any article made by the brethren, she must make application to the female deaconesses or stewards, and they will convey her wishes to the male stewards, who will provide the article or assistance requested. The converse is required of a brother; although it is more common for the brother to express his requests direct to the female steward, thus excluding one link of the concatenation. In each order a brother is generally appointed to aid the sisters in doing the heavy work of the laundry, dairy, kitchen, and similar places. All are required to spend their mornings and evenings, and their leisure time, in the performance of some good act.

"No one shall leave the premises of the family in which he lives without the consent of the elders; and he shall obtain the consent by stating the purpose or business which calls him away. This interdiction includes the act of going from one family to another. But on their own grounds *brethren* may range at pleasure; and the families are so large that the territory included in the domain of each extends in some directions for miles around.

" No conversation is allowed between members of different families, unless it be necessary, succinct, and discreet.

" Before a brother enters a sister's apartment, or a sister enters a brother's, they shall rap and enter by permission. When they enter the apartment of their own sex, they may open the door and ask, ' May I come in ?'

" The name of a person shall never be used to designate a dumb beast. No one is allowed to play with or handle unnecessarily any beast whatever. Brethren and sisters may not unnecessarily touch each other. If a brother shakes hands with an unbelieving woman, or a sister with an unbelieving man, they shall make known the same to the elders before they attend worship. Such salutes are admissible, for the sake of civility or custom, if the world party first present the hand—never without. All visiting of the world's people, even their own relations, is forbidden, unless there exist a prospect of making converts, or of gathering some one into the fold. All visiting of other societies of their own sect is under the immediate superintendence of the ministry, who prescribe the number, select the persons, appoint the time, define the length of their stay, and the routes by which they may go and come.

" The deacons are empowered to change the employment of an individual for an hour, a day, or a week, to perform a necessary piece of labor. But a permanent removal to another vocation can be required only by the elders.

" No trading is to be done by any save the trustees, and those whom the trustees may license. No new literary work or new-fangled article can be admitted, unless it be first sanctioned by the ministry and elders. Trustees may purchase any thing they believe may be admissible, and present the same for the inspection of the leaders. If they disapprove it, it must be sold. The property is all legally held by trustees, who may at any time be removed by the ministry. The trustees are to supervise all financial transactions with the world and other families and societies of their own denomination, and do all by knowledge and union of the ministry and elders. There must be two trustees in every order, and they shall make their financial returns known to each other every journey they perform. An exact book account of every cent of disbursement and income shall be presented to the ministry at the close of every year. The deacons are also to keep an exact account of every thing manufactured or produced for sale in the family, and these two registers are compared by the ministry.

" Not a single action of life, whether spiritual or temporal, from the initiative of confession, or cleansing the habitation of Christ, to that of dressing the right side first, stepping first with the right foot as you ascend a flight of stairs, folding the hands with the right-hand thumb and fingers above those of the left, kneeling and rising again with the right leg first, and harnessing first the right-hand beast, but that has a rule for its perfect and strict performance.

"The children, or all under the age of sixteen, unless very precocious, live, eat, work, play, sleep, and worship, accompanied only by their care-takers. Once upon the Sabbath do they worship with the adults. Their meetings are not so long, neither do they retire but fifteen minutes before them. They never attend union meetings until they emerge into the adult's degree. Stubborn children are sometimes corrected with a rod; but any child or beast that requires an extreme severity of coercion to induce them to conform, the society are not allowed to keep. The contumacious child must be returned to his parents or guardian, and the perverse beast must be sold.

"Prayer, supplication, persuasion, and keen admonition constitute the only means used to incline the disposition and bend the will of those arrived to years of understanding and reason.

* * * * * * * * *

"The boys' shop, so called, is a building two stories in height. In the upper loft is a large room where the care-takers reside, and where the boys who wish to read, write, or reflect may retire from the jabbering and confusion below. Whenever they leave their house or shop, they are required to go two abreast and keep step with each other. No loud talking was allowable in the court-yards at any time. No talking or whispering when passing through the tasteful courts to their work, their school, their meetings, or their meals; a still, soft walk on tiptoe, and an indistinct closing of doors in the house; a gentle, yet a more brisk movement in the shops; a free and jovial conversation when by themselves in the fields; but not a word, unless when spoken to, when other brethren than their care-takers were present—such were the orders we saw rigorously enforced, and the lenities we freely granted. We allowed them to indulge in the *innocent* sports practiced elsewhere. But wrestling and scuffling were rarely permitted. No sports were allowed in the court-yards, unless all loud talk was suppressed. We a few times permitted them to roll trucks there, but allowed no verbal communication only by whispering.

"All were taught to confess all violations of their instructions, and a portion of every Saturday was set apart for that purpose. They enter one at a time, and kneel before the care-taker; and, after confessing their faults, the care-taker makes some necessary inquiries in relation to other boys, gives them generally some good advice, and they depart. After eighteen years of age they are not required to kneel during the act of confession. To watch over a company of boys like these is, with a little tact, an easy task. The vigils must be incessant; but there are in so large a number those upon whom the care-taker may rely; and if ill conduct or bad habits are creeping in, it may soon be detected by a shrewd observer."

The contracting of a special liking between individuals of opposite sexes is in some of the societies called "sparking."

Details of the Shaker Societies.

To describe particularly each of the eighteen Shaker societies would involve a great deal of unnecessary repetition. In their buildings, their customs, their worship, their religious faith, their extreme cleanliness, their costume, and in many other particulars, they are all nearly alike; and the Shaker of Kentucky does not to the cursory view differ from his brother of Maine. But I have thought it necessary, to a complete view of the order, to present some particulars of each society, as to its location, numbers, the quantity of land it owns, its industries, and present and past prosperity, as also peculiarities of thought or custom; and these details will be found below.

There are two Shaker societies in Maine—one at Alfred, the other at New Gloucester.

Alfred.

The society is near Alfred, in York County, about thirty miles southwesterly from Portland. Its estate of eleven hundred acres lies in a pretty situation, between hills, and includes a large pond and an important water-power. The land is not very fertile or easily cultivated. They sold off last year an outlying tract of timber-land for $28,000, and were glad to be rid of it.

The society consists now of two families, having between sixty-five and seventy members, of whom two fifths are men and the remainder women. They are all Americans but two, of whom one is Irish and one Welsh.

The society was "gathered" in 1794; there were then three families; and in 1823 it had two hundred members. Twelve years ago one of the families, being small, was drawn in to the others, and the buildings it occupied have since been let out. The decrease began to be rapid about thirty years ago, when the founders, who had become very aged, died off, and new members did not come in in sufficient numbers to take their places. Two thirds of the present members were brought into the society as children, many being brought by their parents; others, orphans, adopted. Twenty per cent of the present membership are over fifty years of age.

The two families now raise a few garden seeds, make brooms, hair sieves, dry measures, keep a tan-yard, and make besides most of their home supplies. They also farm their own land. They have leased to outside people a saw-mill and grist-mill which they own. The young women make small baskets, fans, and other fancy articles, which are sold during the summer at neighboring sea-side watering-places. They hire a few outside laborers.

About a quarter of the people eat no meat. They have improved their sanitary regulations in the last twenty years, and have almost extirpated fevers. Formerly cancer was a frequent disease among them, but since they ceased to eat pork this has disappeared.

They take nine or ten newspapers, and encourage reading; have a small library, and a good school, in which thirteen children are taught. The people have been long-lived; only a few weeks before I visited Alfred, died at the Church Family Lucy Langdon Nowell, aged ninety-eight. She was born on the 4th of July, 1776, and had lived almost all her life in the society, her father having been one of its founders, and the owner of some of the land on which the society now live. Had she lived long enough, she was to have been taken to the proposed Centennial Exhibition at Philadelphia.

In the last ten years this society has maintained its numbers, but has not gained. They do not receive many applications for membership; and of those who apply, not more than one in ten " makes a good Shaker."

The Alfred Society desired a year or two ago to remove to a milder climate; they offered their entire property for $100,-000, but found no purchaser at the price, and determined to remain. Their buildings are in excellent order; and they are prosperous, having, besides the income from their different industries, a fund at interest. They have never had any defalcation or loss from unfaithful agents or trustees, and they have no debt.

I was told that the first circular saw ever made in the United States was invented by a Shaker at Alfred.

New Gloucester.

The New Gloucester Society lies in Cumberland County, about twenty-five miles northwest of Portland. It consists of two families, having together about seventy members, of whom one third are men. In 1823 it had three families, the third being gathered in 1820, and broken up in 1831. The society had in 1823 one hundred and fifty members.

It was " gathered " in 1794; its members are now all Americans except two, who are Scotch. Among them are persons who were farmers, merchants, printers, wool-weavers, and some mechanics.

The Church Family lives in a valley, the Gathering Family on a high ridge, about a mile off, and overlooking an extensive tract of country. The society has two thousand acres of land, and owns a saw-mill, grist-mill, and a very complete machine shop. The people raise garden seeds, make brooms, dry measures, wire sieves, and the old-fashioned spinning-wheel, which, it seems, is still used in Maine and New Hampshire by country-women to make stocking yarn. But its most profitable industry is the manufacture of oak staves for molasses hogsheads, which are exported to the West Indies. One of the elders of this society, Hewitt Chandler, a man of uncommon mechanical ingenuity, and the inventor of a mowing-machine which was made here for some years, has contrived a way of bending staves without setting them up in the cask, which saves much time and labor, and makes this part of their business additionally profitable. They made last year also a thousand dollars' worth of pickles; and the women make fancy articles in their spare time.

They employ from fifteen to twenty laborers in their mills and other works, most of whom are boarded and lodged on the place.

The meeting-house at this place was built in 1794, and the dwelling of the Church Family in the following year. Both are of wood, are still in good order, and have never been re-shingled.

The second family at this place was "gathered" in 1808, at Gorham, in Maine, and removed to its present location in 1819. It had then twenty brethren and thirty-two sisters; and has now only twenty members in all.

Very few of the people here eat meat. Some drink tea, but coffee is not used. They have flower gardens, and would have an organ or melodeon if they could afford it. The young people promise well; and they have lately received several young men as members, sons of neighboring farmers, who had worked for them as hired people for a number of years.

This society is less prosperous than most of the others. It has met with several severe losses by unfaithful and imprudent agents and trustees, who in one case ran up large debts for several years, contrary to the wise rule of the Shakers to "owe no man any thing," and in another case brought loss by defalcation. The hill family have built a large stone house, but owing to losses have not been able to complete it. The buildings at New Gloucester show signs of neglect; but the people are very industrious, and have in the last three years paid off a large sum which they owed through the default of their agents; and they will work their way out in the next two years. To prevent their being entirely crippled, the other societies helped them with a subscription.

At New Gloucester, also, the people are long-lived, some having died at the age of eighty-six; and very many living beyond seventy.

The societies at Alfred and New Gloucester were founded after a "revival" among the Free-will Baptists; and of the present members who came in later, there were Universalists, Baptists, Methodists, and Adventists or Millerites.

There are two societies in New Hampshire, both prosperous: one at Canterbury, the other at Enfield.

Canterbury.

The society at Canterbury lies on high ground, about twelve miles north by east from Concord. It consists of three families, of which, however, two only are independent; the third, which has but fifteen members, receiving its supplies from the Church Family, which contains one hundred members. The three families have in all one hundred and forty-five members. In 1823 they had over two hundred, and forty years ago they had about three hundred.

Forty of the whole number are under twenty-one; and one

third are males, two thirds females. The majority are young and middle-aged people; the oldest member is now eighty-three, and half a dozen are near seventy. The people have been generally long-lived, and one member lived to over one hundred years of age.

The greater part grew up in the society; but they have five young Scotch people, brought over by their parents. Of those who have joined in later years, the most were Adventists; others Free-will Baptists and Methodists. They have not gained in numbers in ten years, and few applicants nowadays remain with them.

This society is prosperous. It owns three thousand acres of rather poor farming land, some of which is in wood and timber. It has also a farm in Western New York, where it maintains eight hundred sheep. Its industries are varied: they make large washing-machines and mangles for hotels and public institutions, weave woolen cloths and flannels, make sarsaparilla sirup, checkerberry oil, and knit woolen socks. They also make brooms, and sell hay; have a saw-mill; make much of what they use; and they keep excellent stock, having one enormous and admirably arranged barn. The sisters also make fancy articles, for which they have a good market from the summer visitors to the mountains, with whom the Canterbury Shakers are justly favorites.

Their buildings are very complete and in excellent order. They have a steam laundry, with mangle, and an admirably arranged ironing-room; a fine and thoroughly fitted school-house, with a melodeon, and a special music-room; an infirmary for the feeble and sick, in which there is a fearful quantity of drugs; and they take twelve or fifteen newspapers, and have a library of four hundred volumes, including history, voyages, travels, scientific works, and stories for children, but no novels.

The Canterbury Society was "gathered" in 1792; the leading men owned the farm on which the buildings now stand, and gave the land to the community. The old gambrel-roofed meeting-house was built in 1792, and still stands in good order. The founders and early members were Free-will Baptists, who became Shakers after a great " revival." They had some property originally; and soon began to manufacture spinning-wheels, whips, sieves, mortars, brooms, scythe-snaths, and dry measures; they established also a tannery. As times changed, they dropped some of these industries and took up others. One of their members invented the washing-machine which they now make, and they hold the patent-right for it.

They employ six mechanics, non-members, and occasionally others. The members mostly eat meat, drink tea but not coffee, and a few of the aged members are indulged in the use of chewing-tobacco. They take fewer children than formerly, and prefer to take young men and women from eighteen to twenty-four. They take great pains to amuse as well as instruct the children; for the girls, gymnastic exercises are provided as well as a flower garden; the boys play at ball and marbles, go fishing, and have a small farm of their own, where each has his own garden plot. Once a week there is a general " exercise " meeting of the children, and they are, of course, included in the usual meetings for worship, reading, and conversation.

The " shops " or work-rooms are all excellently fitted; in the girls' sewing-room I found a piano, and a young sister taking her music-lesson.

The children are trained to confess their sins to the elders, in the Shaker fashion, and this is thought to be a most important part of their discipline.

In the dwelling-house and near the kitchen I noticed a great number of buckets, hung up to the beams, one for each member, and these are used to carry hot water to the rooms for bathing. The dwellings are not heated with steam. The dining-room was ornamented with evergreens and flowers in pots.

They have no physician, but in the infirmary the sisters in charge have sufficient skill for ordinary cases of disease.

The people are not great readers. The Bible, however, is much read. They are fond of music.

In summer they entertain visitors at a set price, and have rooms fitted for this purpose. In the visitors' dining-room I saw this printed notice:

"At the table we wish all to be as free as at home, but we dislike the wasteful habit of leaving food on the plate. No vice is with us the less ridiculous for being fashionable.

"Married persons tarrying with us overnight are respectfully notified that each sex occupy separate sleeping apartments while they remain."

They had at Canterbury formerly a printing-press, and printed a now scarce edition of hymns, and several books. This press has been sold.

The trustees here give once a year an inventory and statement of accounts to the elders of the Church Family. In the years 1848–9 they suffered severe losses from the defalcation of an agent or trustee, but they have long ago recovered this loss, and now owe no debts.

Agriculture they believe to be the true base of community life, and if their land were fertile they would be glad to leave off manufacturing entirely. But on such land as they have they can not make a living.

The leading elder of the society remarked to me that, though in numbers they were less than formerly, the influence of the Canterbury Society upon the outside world was never so great as now: their Sunday meetings in summer are crowded by visitors, and they believe that often their doctrines sink deep into the hearts of these chance hearers.

Enfield, N. H.

The Society at Enfield lies in Grafton County, about twelve miles southeast from Dartmouth College, and two miles from Enfield Station, on the Northern New Hampshire Railroad. It is composed of three families, having altogether at this time one hundred and forty members, of whom thirty-seven are males and one hundred and three females. This preponderance arises chiefly, I was told, from the large number of young sisters. There are thirty-five youth under twenty-one years of age, of whom eight are boys and twenty-seven girls. In 1823 the Enfield Society had over two hundred members; thirty years ago it had three hundred and thirty members. They do not now receive many applications for membership, and of those who apply but few remain.

This society was "gathered" in 1793, and consisted then of but one family or community. It arose out of a general revival of religion in this region. A second family was formed in 1800, and the third, the "North Family," in 1812. They lost some members during the war of the Rebellion, young men who became soldiers, and some others who were drawn away by the general feeling of unrest which pervaded the country. They like to take children, but are more careful than formerly to ascertain the characters of their parents. "We want a good kind; but we can't do without some children around us," I was told.

The society has about three thousand acres of land, part of it being an outlying farm, ten or a dozen miles away. The buildings are remarkably substantial. The dwelling of the Church Family is of a beautiful granite, one hundred feet by sixty, and of four full and two attic stories; some of the shops are also of granite, others of brick, and in the other families stone and brick have also been used. There is an excellently arranged infirmary, a roomy and well-furnished school-room, a large music-room in a separate building; and at the Church Family they have a laundry worked by water-power, and use a centrifugal dryer, instead of the common wringer.

Nearly the whole of their present real estate was brought into the society as a free gift by the founders, who were farmers living there; and many of the early members brought in considerable means, for those days. When they gathered into a community they began to add manufacturing to their farming work, and the Enfield Shakers were among the first to put up garden seeds. Besides this, they made spinning-wheels, rakes, pitchforks, scythe-snaths, and had many looms. Until within thirty years they wove linen and cotton as well as woolen goods, and in considerable quantities.

At present they put up garden seeds, make buckets and tubs, butter-tubs, brooms, dry measures, gather and dry roots and herbs for medicinal use, make maple-sugar in the spring and apple-sauce in the winter; sew shirts for Boston, and keep several knitting-machines busy, making flannel shirts and drawers and socks. They also make several patent medicines, among which the " Shaker anodyne " is especially prized by them; and extracts, such as fluid valerian; and in one of the families the women prepare bread, pies, and other provisions, which they sell in a neighboring manufacturing village. Finally, they own a woolen-mill and a grist-mill; but these they have leased. One of their members has invented and patented for the society a folding pocket-stereoscope.

Besides all these industries, uncommonly varied and numerous even for the Shakers, they have carpenter, blacksmith, tailor, and shoemaker shops, and produce or make up a great part of what they consume. Moreover, as in most of the Shaker societies, the women make up fancy articles for sale.

The members of the society are almost all Americans, and the greater part of them came in as little children. Of foreigners, there are one Englishman, two of Irish birth, one of Welsh, and two French Canadians. As elsewhere, Baptists, Methodists, and Millerites or Second Adventists contributed the larger part of the membership.

They hire from twenty to thirty-five laborers, according to the season of the year.

Most of the members are under forty, and almost all are farmers. I heard of one lawyer; and one when he entered had been a law student. Almost all are meat eaters, and they use both tea and coffee. A few of the older men are allowed to chew tobacco. There are no fevers in the society, and their health is excellent, which arises partly I suppose from the fact that the ground upon which the buildings stand has thorough natural drainage. Some of their members have lived to the age of ninety—which is not an uncommon age, by the way, for Shakers—and on the register of deaths I found these ages: 89, 86, 86, 80, 80, 79, 76, 75, and so on.

They have a library of about two hundred volumes in each family, exclusive of strictly religious books; and almost all the younger people can read music, one of the members being a thorough teacher and good musical drill-master. They read the Bible a good deal, and sometimes pray aloud in their meetings. Once or twice a week they hold reading meetings, at which some one reads either from a book of history or biography, or extracts from newspapers.

There was some years ago a defalcation in one of the societies, which "came largely if not entirely through neglect of the rule not to owe money." The family which suffered in this case has not entirely recovered from the blow; it still owes a small debt.

An annual business report is now made by the trustees to the ministry who are set over this society and that at Canterbury.

There is but one Shaker Society in Connecticut, at

Enfield, Conn.

The Society is in Hartford County, about twelve miles from Springfield, Massachusetts. It was founded in 1792; and the meeting-house then built, of brick, is still standing, but is now used for other purposes. There were formerly five families, and in 1823 this society had two hundred members. At present there are but four families, one of which is small, and contains only a few aged people, too much attached to their old home to be removed. There are in the four families one hundred and fifteen persons, of whom the Church Family has sixty, and the Gathering Family twenty-five. One third are males and two thirds females; and there are forty-three children and youth under twenty-one, of whom eighteen are boys and twenty-four girls. So late as 1848 this society numbered two hundred persons.

They own about three thousand three hundred acres of land, and make their living almost entirely by farming. Before the rebellion they had built up a large trade in the Southern States in garden seeds; but the outbreak of the war not only lost them this trade, but in bad debts they lost nearly all they had saved in thirty years. They now breed fine stock, which they sell; and they sell some hay, but only to buy Indian corn in its stead. They are careful and excellent farmers. The women make some articles of fancy work. They employ fifteen hired men constantly.

This society is prosperous. One of the families has just erected a large and, for Shakers, uncommonly stylish dwelling; and all the buildings are in good repair and well painted. Nevertheless they have not had an easy task to make a living. "If we have got any thing here," said an elder to me, "it is because we saved it." They have, however, the advantage of an excellent farm. In the beginning they raised garden seeds, and were among the first in this country to establish this business, and at one time they made lead pipe—but the invention of machinery drove them out of that business.

They eat meat, and use tea and coffee moderately ; and a few of the old members take snuff. They are mostly Americans, with a few Scotch and English, and more than half of the adult members came in when they were full-grown. About forty years ago there was in Rhode Island a religious revival among a sect of Baptists who call themselves " Christians," and many of these entered the Enfield Society. They now adopt a good many children, and do not seem displeased at the result. They have a school, and are fond of music, having a cabinet-organ in their music-room, and holding a weekly singing-school for the young people. They take " a great many " newspapers and magazines, and have a variety of books, but no regular library. The elders have the selection of reading-matter, and, as in all the societies, exclude what they think injurious.

They have been, they told me, somewhat careless of sanitary regulations, and have had typhus fever in their houses ; but they are now generally healthy.

They make very few articles for themselves, but buy a good deal.

They make no regular business statement, and owe no debts. They once had a defalcation, but only of a trifling amount.

There are four Shaker societies in Massachusetts : at Harvard, Shirley, Tyringham, and Hancock.

Harvard.

The Harvard Society lies in Worcester County, about thirty miles northwest from Boston. It was founded in 1793; and had in 1823 two hundred members. It has now four families, containing in all ninety persons, of whom sixteen are children and youth under twenty-one—four boys and twelve girls. Of the seventy-four adult members, seventeen are men and fifty-seven women. The Church Family has fifty members, of whom forty-one are women and girls, and nine men and boys. It is usual among the Shakers to find more women than men in a society or family, but at Harvard the disproportion of the sexes is uncommonly great.

The members are mainly Americans, but they have some Scotch, Germans, and Welsh. A considerable proportion of the present membership came in as adults, and these were, before becoming Shakers, for the most part Adventists, some however coming from the Baptist and Methodist denominations. The elder of the Gathering Family was a Baptist, and the leading minister was an English Wesleyan. The people are mostly in middle life. The health of this society has always been good; the *average* age at death, I was assured, ranged for a great number of years between sixty to sixty-eight. One sister died at ninety-three, and other members died at from eighty to eighty-six.

Their home farm consists of about eighteen hundred acres; and they have besides a farm in Michigan, and another in Massachusetts. Their living is made almost entirely by farming; and they have drained very thoroughly a considerable piece of swamp, which yields them large crops of hay. They make brooms, have a nursery, and press and put up herbs; and employ sixteen or seventeen hired laborers.

They have a small library, but " do not let books interfere with work;" there is a school, but no musical instrument; most of the people eat meat, and drink tea and coffee; and a few are indulged in the practice of chewing tobacco. They are not very musical, but they take a great many newspapers.

" Do you like to take children?" I asked; and an eldress replied, " Yes, we like to take children—but we don't like to take monkeys;" and, in general, the Shakers have discovered that "blood will tell," and that they can do much better with the children of religious parents than with those whose fathers or mothers were dissolute or irreligious.

This society has no debt, and is prosperous, though its buildings are not all in first-rate order according to the Shaker standard, which is very high. It has suffered from one defalcation.

The ministry among the Shakers usually occupy their spare time in some manual labor, as I have explained in a previous chapter. The leading minister over Harvard and Shirley makes brooms; his predecessor made shoes. The leading female minister is a dress-maker.

Shirley.

The Society of Shirley lies about two miles from Shirley Station, on the Fitchburg Railroad. It was gathered in 1793, the meeting-house having been built the year before. Mother Ann Lee passed nearly two years among the people in this vicinity, preaching to them; and this accounts for the early building of the meeting-house. In 1823 the Shirley Society had one hundred and fifty members. At present it has two families, numbering altogether forty-eight persons; of these twelve are children and youth under twenty-one—eight girls and four boys. Of the adults, six are men and thirty women. Until a year ago there were three families, but decreasing numbers led them to call in one; and they now let the buildings formerly used by that one. Thirty-five years ago this society numbered one hundred and fifty persons; twenty-four years ago, seventy-five; twenty years ago it had sixty. As the old people, the founders, died off, new members did not come in. They have not now many applications for membership; and of the children they adopt and bring up, not one in ten becomes a Shaker.

The society owns two thousand acres of land, which includes several outlying farms. They employ nine or ten hired laborers; and their main business is to make apple-sauce, of which they sell from five to six tons every year. One family makes brooms; and they all preserve fruit, make jellies and pickles, dry sweet corn, and in the spring make maple-sugar. The women make fancy articles for sale. Farming is also a considerable business with them, and they have good orchards.

Most of the members grew up in the society, and the greater number of them are, I believe, past middle age. Like all the Shakers, they are long-lived—one sister, a colored woman, is eighty, and another eighty-eight—and their mortality rate is low. Most of the members are Americans, but they have a few Nova-Scotians. Most of them eat meat, and drink tea, but no coffee; and they are especially fond of oatmeal. One old member both smokes and snuffs, but none others use to-bacco in any shape. They are fond of flowers, but do not cultivate any; have "plenty" of books and newspapers, but no regular library; like music, but have no musical instrument; and they are fond of the Bible. Among their meetings is one for singing.

Their buildings are not so large as those of a Shaker settlement usually are, but they are in excellent order, and include an infirmary, a house for aged and feeble members, a nice school-room, and a laundry. They have the reputation in the neighborhood of being wealthy; and had the enterprise once to build a large cotton factory, on the shore of a pond which they then owned. This building they have sold. It ran them into debt; and this they did not like. They were poor at first; have never had any defalcation; have no debt now; and make no regular business statement, trusting to the ministry to keep a proper oversight of their accounts.

In the school at Shirley physiology was taught, and with remarkable success as it seemed to me, with the help of charts; the children seemed uncommonly intelligent and bright. The school is open three months in the summer and three in the winter—two hours in the forenoon and two in the afternoon; and the teacher, a young girl, was also the care-taker of the girls. Singing-school is held, for the children, in the evening.

The societies at Hancock and Tyringham lie near the New York State line, among the Berkshire hills. They are small, and have no noticeable features.

There are three Shaker societies in New York: at Mount Lebanon, Watervliet, and Groveland.

Mount Lebanon.

The Mount Lebanon Society lies in Columbia County, two miles from New Lebanon. It is the parent society among the Shakers, and its ministry has a general oversight over all the societies. It is also the most numerous.

The Mount Lebanon Society was founded in 1787. In 1823 it numbered between five hundred and six hundred persons; at this time it has three hundred and eighty-three, including forty-seven children and youth under fifteen. This society is divided into seven families; and its membership has one hundred and thirty-six males and two hundred and forty-seven females, including children and youth.

It owns about three thousand acres of land within the State of New York, besides some farms in other states; and several of its farms in its own neighborhood are in charge of tenants. The different families employ a considerable number of hired laborers. They raise and put up garden seeds, make brooms, dry medicinal herbs and make extracts, dry sweet corn, and make chairs and mops. The women in all the families also make mats, fans, dusters, and other fancy articles for sale; and one of the families keep some sheep.

In a previous chapter I have given so many details concerning the Mount Lebanon Society that I need here say nothing further about it, except that it is in a highly prosperous condition.

Watervliet.

The society at Watervliet lies seven miles northwest from Albany, and upon the ground where Ann Lee and her followers first settled when they came to America. Her body lies in the grave-yard at Watervliet. No monument is built over it.

The society there has now four families, containing two hundred and thirty-five persons, of whom sixty are children and youth under twenty-one. Of the adult members, seventy-five are men and one hundred women. In 1823 it had over two hundred members; between 1837 and 1850 it had three hundred and fifty.

It has in its home estate twenty-five hundred acres of land, and owns besides about two thousand acres in the same state, and thirty thousand acres in Kentucky. Its chief industry is farming, and the families keep a large number of sheep and cattle. They shear wool enough to supply all their own needs in cloth and flannel, but have these woven by an outside mill; they raise large crops of broom-corn and sweet corn: the first they make into brooms, and the other they put up dry in barrels for sale; they put up fruits and vegetables in tin cans, and also sell garden seeds. They have given up their tan-yard, which was once a source of income. Finally, they make in their own shops, for the use of the society, shoes, carpets, clothing, furniture, and almost all the articles of household use they require.

They hire about seventy-five laborers.

Most of the members are Americans, and three quarters of them grew up from childhood in the society. Among the membership are some Germans, English, Irish, Swedes, Scotch, and two or three French people. Some among them were originally clergymen, others lawyers, mechanics, and gardeners; but the greater number are farmers by occupation. Some of those who came in as adults had been " Infidels," some Adventists, others Methodists. The society at this time contains more young than old people.

Most of the people eat meat, and drink tea and coffee. Some use tobacco, but this is discouraged.

They had formerly a good many colored members; and have still some, as well as several mulattoes and quadroons.

One colored sister is ninety years of age.

The members here have been long-lived; the register proves this: it shows deaths at ninety-seven, ninety-four, ninety-three, ninety, and so on. They are careful to have thorough drainage and ventilation, and pay attention to sanitary questions. They were formerly subject to bilious fevers; but since rejecting the use of pork, these fevers have disappeared.

They take a number of newspapers, and have a library of four hundred volumes, but the people are not great readers, and are fonder of religious books and works of popular science than of any other literature. There is a school; and the children are now to have instruction in music, as one of the families has bought an organ, and asked a musical brother from New Hampshire to come down and give lessons. Instrumental music, however, has been opposed by the older members, and here as in some of the other societies it has been introduced only after prolonged discussion.

This society has no debts, and has never suffered from the unfaithfulness of agents or trustees. It is in a very prosperous condition. Each family makes a detailed annual report to the presiding ministry, and a *daily* diary of events is kept.

They have baths in the dwellings, and well-arranged laundries.

The Watervliet and Mount Lebanon Societies have a number of members living in the outer world, but holding to Shaker principles, and maintaining by correspondence a connection with them. Some of these are inhabitants of cities, and " above the average in wealth and culture," I was told. The Watervliet Society has also a branch at Philadelphia, consisting of twelve colored women, who live together in one house under the leadership of an old woman, who was moved about twenty years ago to leave this society and go to Philadelphia to preach among her people. The members find employment as day servants in different families, going home every night. They mainly support themselves, and have never asked for help from the society; but this occasionally makes them presents, and keeps a general oversight over them.

Groveland.

The Groveland Society lies near Sonyea, in Livingston County, thirty-seven miles from Rochester on the Dansville and Mount Morris branch of the Erie Railway. This society was founded at Sodus Point in 1826, and removed from there to its present location in 1836. They had at that time one hundred and fifty members; and were most numerous about twenty-five years ago, when they had two hundred members. At present they have two families, with fifty-seven members in all, of whom nine are children under twenty-one; of these last, six are girls and three boys. Of the adults, thirty are females and eighteen males.

They own a home farm of two thousand acres, and an outlying farm of two hundred and eighty acres, mostly good land, and very well placed, a canal and two railroads running through their home farm. They have a saw-mill and grist-mill, which are sources of income to them; and they raise broom-corn, make brooms, and dry apples and sweet corn. The women make fancy articles for sale. They also keep fine cattle, and sell a good deal of high-priced stock. Farming and gardening are their chief employments, as they have a ready sale for all they produce. They employ eight hired laborers.

The members are mostly Americans, raised in the society;

but they have French Canadians, Dutch, German, Irish, and English among them. The French Canadians were Catholics, and some of their other members were Episcopalians, Presbyterians, and Methodists. Most of those who came in as adults were farmers. They are long-lived—living to beyond seventy in a considerable number of cases.

They eat meat, drink tea and coffee, and some aged members who came in late in life, with confirmed habits, are allowed to use tobacco. One sister smokes.

They have a school, and a good miscellaneous library of about four hundred volumes, in a case in the dwelling-house of the Church Family. They sing finely, but are opposed to the introduction of musical instruments. In some of their evening meetings they read aloud, and the last book thus read was Mr. Seward's "Journey around the World."

They do not adopt as many children as formerly, and experience has taught them the necessity of knowing something of the parentage of children, in order to make judicious selections.

"Formerly we had one or two physicians among our members, and then there was much sickness; now that we have no doctor there is but little illness, and the health of the society is good."

One of the families is in debt, through an imprudent purchase of land made by a trustee, without the general knowledge of the society. Moreover they have suffered severely from fires and by a flood. Once seven of their buildings were burned down in a night. In this way a fund they had at interest was expended in repairs. But the society seems now to be prosperous; its buildings are in excellent order, and the brick dwelling of the Church Family, built in 1857, is well arranged and a fine structure. They have a steam laundry and a fine dairy. In their shops they carry on blacksmithing, carpentry, tailoring, and dress-making.

They make a regular annual business statement to the presiding ministry.

At intervals they send out one or two brethren to preach to the outer world upon Shakerism.

There are four Shaker societies in Ohio: Union Village, near Lebanon; North Union, near Cleveland; Watervliet, near Dayton; and Whitewater, near Harrison.

Union Village.

The society at Union Village lies four miles from Lebanon, in Warren County, Ohio. It is the oldest Shaker settlement in the West; the three " witnesses " sent out from Mount Lebanon in 1805 were here received by a prosperous farmer named Malchas Worley, who became a " Believer," and whose influence greatly helped to spread the Shaker doctrines among his neighbors. His small dwelling still stands near the large house of one of the families, and is kept in neat repair; it lies in the heart of the society's present estate.

The ministry of Union Village, while subordinate to that at Mount Lebanon, rules or has a general oversight of the western societies in Ohio and Kentucky; and in former times there has been a good deal of printing done there, a number of Shaker publications having been written and published at Union Village.

The society at Union Village consists of four families, containing at this time two hundred and fifteen persons, of whom ninety-five are males and one hundred and twenty females. Of the whole number, forty-eight are children and youth under twenty-one, and of these twenty are boys and twenty-eight girls. Between 1827 and 1830 it had six hundred members, and at that time there were six families. It had, however, about that time received sudden and considerable accessions from the dissolution of the Shaker Society in Indiana, which left that state on account of the unhealthfulness of the country, and whose members were divided among the Ohio societies. In the last ten years I was told there had been neither gain nor loss of numbers, taking the average of the year; for here, as elsewhere, there is usually a swelling of the ranks in the fall, from what are called " winter Shakers."

The society at Union Village was " gathered " between 1805 and 1810. The oldest building dates from 1807, and others, of brick and still in excellent preservation, bear the dates of 1810 and 1811. All the buildings are in good order; and this society is among the most prosperous in the order. Its families own a magnificent estate of four thousand five hundred acres lying in the famous Miami bottom, a soil much of which is so fertile that after sixty years of cropping it will still yield from sixty to seventy bushels of corn to the acre, and without manuring. They have also some outlying farms. They have no debt, and one of the families has a fund at interest.

They let much of their land to tenants, having not less than forty thus settled and working the soil on shares. Besides this, the different families employ about thirty hired laborers. Their industries are broom-making, raising garden seeds and medicinal herbs, and preparing medicinal extracts. They also make a sirup of sarsaparilla, and one or two other patent medicines; they have a saw and a grist mill; the women make small fancy articles and baskets. But their most profitable business is the growth of fine stock—thoroughbred Durham cattle chiefly. They have, of course, shops in which they make and mend what they need for themselves—tailor's, shoemaker's, blacksmith's, wagon-maker's, etc. Formerly they manufactured more than at present—having made at one time, for the general market, steel, leather, hollow-ware, pipes, and woolen yarn. Prosperity has lessened their enterprise. Three of the families have very complete laundries.

They eat meat, but no pork; and only a very few of the aged members use tobacco. They have an excellent school, of which one of the ministry, an intelligent and kindly man, is the teacher. They have a small library—"not so many books as we would like;" and one of the sisters told me that she got books from a circulating library at Lebanon, and as a special indulgence was allowed to read novels sometimes, which, she remarked, she found useful to set her to sleep. They have two cabinet-organs, and believe in cultivating music.

The founders of this society were mostly Presbyterians. Their successors have been Methodists, Baptists, Quakers, and I found, to my surprise, several Catholics, one of whom was originally a Spanish priest. Almost all are Americans, but there are a few Germans and English.

They do not care to take children unless they are accompanied by their parents; and refuse to take any under nine years, unless they come as part of a family. Not more than ten per cent. of the children they train up remain with them; but they said it was not uncommon to see them return after spending some years in the world, and in such cases they often made good Shakers. During the war a number of their young men went off to become soldiers. Several of those who survived returned, and are now among them.

They have no provision for baths.

In 1835 they suffered from the defalcation of a trustee, to the amount of between forty and fifty thousand dollars.

I looked over a list of deaths during the last thirty years, and was surprised to find how many members had lived to ninety and past, and how large a proportion died at over seventy.

"Are you all Spiritualists," I asked, and was answered, "Of course;" but presently one added, "We are all Spiritualists, in a general sense; but there are some *real* Spiritualists here;" and I judge that here as in some of the other societies Spiritualism is not much thought of. I saw the "Sacred Roll and Book" on a table, but was told it was not much read nowadays, but that they read the Bible a good deal.

I found that for the last three years they have had here what they call a Lyceum: a kind of debating club which meets once a week, for the discussion of set questions, reading, and the criticism of essays written by the members. The last question discussed was, "Whether it is best for the Shaker societies to work on cash or credit."

This Lyceum has produced another meeting in the Church Family, in which, once a week, all the members—male and female, young and old—are gathered to overhaul the accounts of the week, and to discuss all the industrial occupations of the family, agricultural and mechanical, as well as housekeeping and every thing relating to their practical life. These weekly meetings are found to give the younger members a greater interest in the society, and they were established because it was thought necessary to make efforts to keep the youth whom they bring up. "We will never change the fundamental principles and practices of Shakerism," said one of the older and official members, an uncommonly intelligent Shaker, to me. "Celibacy and the confession of sins are vital; but in all else we ought to be changeable, and may modify our practices; and we feel that we must do something to make home more pleasant for our young people—they want more music and more books, and shall have them; they are greatly interested in these weekly business meetings; and I am in favor of giving them just as much and as broad an education as they desire."

The business meeting lasts an hour, and the "Elder Brother in the Ministry" presides. I saw some evidences that this meeting aroused thought. Any member may bring up a subject for discussion; and I heard some of the sisters say that one matter which had occupied their thoughts was the too great monotony of their own lives—they desired greater variety, and thought women might do some other things besides cooking. One thought it would be an improvement to abolish the caps, and let the hair have its natural growth and appearance—but I am afraid she might be called a radical.

The founders of Union Village were evidently men who did their work thoroughly; the dwellings and houses they built early in the century, all of brick, have a satisfactory solidity, and are not without the homely charm which good work and plain outlines give to any building. Two of these old houses in the Church Family are now used as the boys' and the girls' houses, and are uncommonly good specimens of early Western architecture. The whole village is a pattern of neatness, with flagged walks and pleasant grassy court-yards and shade-trees; but I noticed here and there a slackness in repairs which seemed to show the want of a deacon's sharp eyes.

North Union.

The North Union Shaker Society lies eight miles northeast from Cleveland. It was founded in 1822, in what was then a thickly timbered wilderness, and the people lived for some years in log cabins. The society was most numerous about 1840, when it contained two hundred members. It is now divided into three families, having one hundred and two persons, of whom seventeen are children and youth under twenty-one. Of these last, six are boys and eleven girls. Of the adult members, forty-four are women and forty-one men. Their numbers have of late increased, but there was a gradual diminution for fifteen years before that.

About a third of the present members were brought up in the society; of the remainder, the most were by religious connection Adventists, Methodists, and Baptists. They have among them persons who were weavers, whalemen, and sailors, but most of them were farmers. The greater number are Americans, but they have some Swiss, Germans, and English. They do not like to take in children unless their parents come

with them. The health of the society has been very good.
Many of their people have lived to past eighty; one sister died
at ninety-eight. In the last fifty years they have buried just
one hundred persons.

They eat but little meat; use tea and coffee, but moderately, and "bear against tobacco," but permit its use in certain
cases. But they allow no one to both smoke and chew the
weed. They have a school, and like to sing, but do not allow
musical instruments.

Less than a quarter of the young people whom they bring
up remain with them.

They own 1355 acres of land in one body, and have no outlying farms. They have a saw-mill, and make brooms, broom-
handles, and stocking yarn. But their chief sources of income
arise from supplying milk and vegetables to Cleveland, as well
as fire-wood, and some lumber, and they keep fine stock. They
used to make wooden ware. Their dairy brought them in
$2300 last year. They employ nine hired men.

The buildings of this society are not in as neat order as those
of Groveland or others eastward. I missed the thorough covering of paint, and the neatness of shops. They have no steam
laundry, and make no provision for baths. But they have the
usual number of "shops," among them an infirmary, or in
Shaker language a "nurse-shop." They have a small library,
and take two daily newspapers, the New York *World* and *Sun.*
They read the Bible "when they have a gift for it," but depend much upon their own revelations from the spirit-land.

They owe no debts, and have a fund at interest. They
make a detailed annual report to the presiding ministry. They
have never suffered serious loss from mismanagement and defaulting agents or trustees.

Watervliet and Whitewater.

The two societies of Watervliet and Whitewater, in Ohio, I

did not visit. They are small, and subordinate to that of Union Village.

The society at Watervliet has two families, containing fifty-five members, of whom nineteen are males and thirty-six females; and seven are under twenty-one. They own thirteen hundred acres of land, much of which they let to tenants. They have a wool-factory, which is their only manufactory.

This society was founded a year after that at Union Village; it had in 1825 one hundred members; and is now prosperous, pecuniarily, having no debt, and money at interest. One of its families once suffered a slight loss from a defalcation.

The society at Whitewater has three families, and one hundred members, of whom fifteen are under twenty-one. There are forty males and sixty females. It was founded in 1827, and many among its members came from the society which broke up in Indiana. It had at one time one hundred and fifty members.

It owns fifteen hundred acres of land, and has no debt, but a fund at interest in each family. The families put up garden seeds, make brooms, raise stock, and farm.

There are two societies in Kentucky, one at South Union, in Logan County, on the line of the Nashville Railroad, and one at Pleasant Hill, in Mercer County, seven miles from Harrodsburg. They are both prosperous.

South Union.

The society at South Union was founded nearly on the scene of the wild "Kentucky revival" in the year 1807, the gathering taking place in 1809. Some of the log cabins then built by the early members are still standing, and the first meeting-house, built in 1810, bears that date on its front. I judge that the early members were poor, from the fact that they lived for some time in cabins. Some who came into the society at an early date were slaveholders; and as the Shakers have always consistently opposed slavery, these set their slaves free, but induced them to the number of forty to join them. For many years there was a colored family, with a colored elder, living upon the same terms as the whites. From time to time some of these fell away and left the society; but I was told that a number became and remained "good Shakers," and died in the faith; and when the colored family became too small, the remnant of members was taken in among the whites. There are at present several colored members.

There were originally three families, but now four, one of which, however, is small. The society numbers two hundred and thirty persons, of whom one hundred are males and one hundred and thirty females, and forty of these are under twenty-one—twenty-five girls and fifteen boys. In 1827 they were most numerous, having three hundred and forty-nine persons* in all the families; they had at one time but one hundred and seventy-five, and have risen from that in the last twenty years to their present number. For some years they have neither increased nor diminished, except by the coming and going of "winter Shakers," and "we sift pretty carefully," they told me. Most of the members are Americans, but they have some Germans and a few English, and they had at one time several French Catholics.

They own nearly six thousand acres of land, of which three thousand five hundred acres are in the home farm, the remainder about four miles off. The South Union Shakers were early famous for fine stock, which they sold in Missouri and in the Northwestern states and territories. They still raise fine breeds of cattle, hogs, sheep, and chickens, and this is a considerable source of income to them. Some of their land they let

---

* The "Millennial Church" gives their number at four hundred about 1825, but I follow the account given me at South Union.

to tenants, among whom I found several colored families; they have also extensive orchards; the remainder they cultivate, raising—besides the pasturage of their stock—corn, wheat, rye, and oats. They have also a good grist-mill, from which they ship flour; they own a large brick hotel at the railroad station, which, I was told, is a summer resort, there being a sulphur spring near it, also a store, both of which they rent to "world's people;" and they make brooms, put up garden seeds—which was formerly an important business with them—and prepare canned and preserved fruits, which they sell largely in the Southern States. I saw here on the table those very sweet " preserves " which a quarter of a century ago were to be found on every farmer's table in New England, if he had a thrifty wife, and which, after breeding a kind of epidemic of dyspepsia, have now, I think, entirely disappeared from our Northern tables. It seems they are still served on "company occasions" in the South.

They have for their home use a tannery, and shops for tailoring, shoemaking, carpentering, and blacksmithing; and they employ fifteen hired people, all negroes.

Their buildings, which are both brick and frame, are all in excellent condition; and the large pines and Norway spruces growing near the dwellings (and "trimmed up "—or robbed of their lower branches, as the abominable fashion has too long been in this country), show that the founders provided for their descendants some grateful shade. Near the Church Family they showed me two fine old oaks, under which Henry Clay once partook of a public dinner, while at another time James Monroe and Andrew Jackson stopped for a day at the country tavern which once stood near by, when the stage road ran near here. " Monroe," said one of the older members to me, " was a stout, thickset man, plain, and with but little to say; Jackson, tall and thin, with a hickory visage." Naturally, this being Kentucky, Clay was held to be the greatest character of the three.

Here, too, as I am upon antiquities, I saw old men who in

their youth had taken part in the great "revival," and had
seen the "jerks," which were so horrible a feature of that religious excitement, and of which I have previously quoted some
descriptions from McNemar's " Kentucky Revival." To dance,
I was here told, was the cure for the "jerks;" and men often
danced until they dropped to the ground. "It was of no use
to try to resist the jerks," the old men assured me. "Young
men sometimes came determined to make fun of the proceedings, and were seized before they knew of it." Men were "flung
from their horses;" "a young fellow, famous for drinking,
cursing, and violence, was leaning against a tree looking on,
when he was jerked to the ground, slam bang. He swore he
would not dance, and he was jerked about until it was a wonder he was not killed. At last he had to dance." "Sometimes
they would be jerked about like a cock with his head off, all
about the ground." The dancing I judge to have been an in-
voluntary convulsive movement, which was the close of the
general spasm. Of course, the people believed the whole was
a "manifestation of the power of God." There is no reason
to doubt that McNemar's descriptions are accurate; from what
I have heard at South Union, I imagine that his account is not
complete.

The South Union Shakers have no debt, and mean to obey
the rule in this regard; they have a very considerable fund
at interest. They eat meat, but no pork; drink tea and coffee,
and some of them use tobacco—even the younger members.
They have as their minister here a somewhat remarkable man,
who studied Latin while driving an ox team as a youngster,
and later in life acquired some knowledge of German, French,
and Swedish while laboring successively as seed-gardener,
tailor, and shoemaker. His mild face and gentle manners
pleased me very much; and I was not surprised to find him a
man greatly beloved in other societies as well as at South
Union. Nevertheless his example does not appear to have

been catching, for I was told that they have no library. They read a number of newspapers, but the average of culture is low.

They have no baths; have lately bought a piano, and had a brother from Canterbury to instruct some of the sisters in music. The singing was not so good as I have heard elsewhere among the Shakers. They have a school during five months of the year; and they like to take children—"would rather have bad ones than none." They have brought children from New Orleans and from Memphis after an epidemic which had left many orphans. The young people "do tolerably well."

The founders of this society were "New-Light Presbyterians;" since then they have been reinforced by "Infidels," Spiritualists, Methodists, and others.

It is certainly to their credit that, living in a slave state, and having up to the outbreak of the war a great part of their business with the states farther south, these Shakers were always anti-slavery and Union people. Formerly they hired negro laborers from their masters, which, I suppose, kept the masters quiet; it did not surprise me to hear that they always had their choice of the slave population near them. A negro knew that he would nowhere be treated so kindly as among the Shakers. During the war they suffered considerable losses. A saw-mill and grist-mill, with all their contents, were burned, causing a loss of seventy-five thousand dollars. They fed the troops of both sides, and told me that they served at least fifty thousand meals to Union and Confederate soldiers alike. There was guerrilla fighting on their own grounds, and a soldier was shot near the Church dwelling. "The war cost us over one hundred thousand dollars," said one of the elders; and besides this they lost money by bad debts in the Southern States. Since the war they lost seventy-five thousand dollars in bonds, which, deposited in a bank, were stolen by one of its officers; but the greater part of this they hope to recover.

Like all the Shakers, they are long-lived. A man was pointed out to me, now eighty-seven years of age, who plowed and mowed last summer; two revolutionary soldiers died in the society aged ninety-three and ninety-four; one member died at ninety-seven; and they have now people aged eighty-seven, eighty-five, eighty-two, eighty, and so on.

During "meeting" on Sunday I saw the children, many of them small, and all clean and neat, and looking happy in their prim way. They came in, as usual, the boys by one door, the girls by another, each side with its care-taker; and took part in the marching, kneeling, and other forms of the Shaker worship. After the war, the South Union elders sought out twenty orphans in Tennessee, whom they adopted. Last fall, when Memphis suffered so terribly from yellow fever, they tried to get fifty children from there, but were unsuccessful. Considering the small number who stay with them after they are grown up, this charity is surely admirable. And though the education which children receive among the Shaker people is limited, the training they get in cleanliness, orderly habits, and morals is undoubtedly valuable, and better than such orphans would receive in the majority of cases among the world's people. Nor must it be forgotten that the Shakers still, with great good sense, teach each boy and girl a trade, so as to fit them for earning a living.

Pleasant Hill.

The Pleasant Hill Society lies in Mercer County, seven miles from Harrodsburg, on the stage road to Nicholasville, and near the Kentucky River, which here presents some grand and magnificent scenery, deserving to be better known.

They have a fine estate of rich land, lying in the midst of the famous blue-grass region of Kentucky. It consists of four thousand two hundred acres, all in one body. They have five families; but the three Church families have their property in common.   In 1820 they had eight families, and between 1820 and 1825 they had about four hundred and ninety members. At present the society numbers two hundred and forty-five persons, of whom seventy-five are children or youth under twenty-one.   About one third are males and two thirds females.

Pleasant Hill was founded in 1805, and "gathered into society order" in 1809; at which time community of goods was established.

The members are mostly Americans, but they have in one family a good many Swedes.   These are the remnant of a large number whom the society brought out a number of years ago at its own expense, in the hope that they would become good Shakers.   The experiment was not successful.   They have also two colored members, and some English.   They have among them people who were Baptists, Methodists, Adventists, and Presbyterians.   A considerable number of the people, however, have grown up in the society, having come in as children of the founders; and one old lady told me she was born in the society, her parents having entered three months before she came into the world.

They eat meat, but no pork; use tea and coffee, and tobacco, but "not much;" have baths in all the families; have no library, except of their own publications, of which copies are put into every room, and a good supply is on hand, especially of the "Sacred Roll and Book," and the "Divine Book of Holy Wisdom," which appear to be more read here than elsewhere. They have no musical instruments, but mean to get an organ "to help the singing."   They receive twenty newspapers of different kinds; and they are Spiritualists.

The buildings at Pleasant Hill are remarkably good.   The dwellings have high ceilings, and large, airy rooms, well fitted and very comfortably furnished, as are most of the Shaker houses.   Most of the buildings are of stone or brick, and the stone houses in particular are well built.   In most of the dwellings I found two doorways, for the different sexes, as well as two staircases within. The walks connecting the buildings are here, as at South Union, Union Village, and elsewhere, laid with flagging-stones—but so narrow that two persons can not walk abreast.

Agriculture, the raising of fine stock, and preserving fruit in summer are the principal industries pursued at Pleasant Hill for income. They make some brooms also, and in one of the families they put up garden seeds. They have, however, very complete shops of all kinds for their own use, as well as a saw and grist mill, and even a woolen-mill where they make their own cloth. Formerly they had also a hatter's shop; and in the early days they labored in all their shops for the public, and kept besides a carding and fulling mill, a linseed-oil mill, as well as factories of coopers' ware, brooms, shoes, dry measures, etc. At present their numbers are inadequate to carry on manufactures, and their wealth makes it unnecessary. They let a good deal of their land, the renters paying half the crop; and they employ besides fifteen or twenty hired hands, who are mostly negroes.

Hired laborers among the Shakers are usually, or always so far as I know, boarded at the "office," the house of the trustees; and this often makes a good deal of hard work for the sisters who do the cooking there. At Pleasant Hill they had two colored women and a little boy in the "office" kitchen, hired to help the sisters; and this is the only place where I saw this done.

They have a school for the children, which is kept during five months of the year. They do not like to take children without their parents; and very few of those they take remain in the society after they are grown up. They are troubled also with "winter Shakers," whom they take "for conscience' sake," if they show even very little of the Shaker spirit, hoping to do them good. They were Union people during the war, and a few of their young men entered the army, and some of these returned after the war ended, and were reinstated in the society after examination and confession of their sins. During the war both armies foraged upon them, taking their horses and wagons; and they served thousands of meals to hungry soldiers of both sides. Their estate lies but a few miles from the field of the great battle of Perryville, and this region was for a while the scene of military operations, though not to so great an extent as the country about South Union. The Confederate general John Morgan, who was born near here, always protected them against his own troops, and they spoke feelingly of his care for them.

This society has no debt, and has never suffered from a defalcation or breach of trust. Some years ago they lost nearly ten thousand dollars from the carelessness of an aged trustee.

They are long-lived, many of their members having lived to past ninety. They have one now aged ninety-eight years.

SHAKER LITERATURE, SPIRITUALISM, ETC.

" It should be distinctly understood that special inspired gifts have not ceased, but still continue among this people:" so reads a brief note to the Preface of " Christ's First and Second Appearing," the edition of 1854.

In the " Testimonies concerning the Character and Ministry of Mother Ann Lee," a considerable number of her followers who had known her personally, being her contemporaries, relate particulars of her teaching and conduct, and not a few give instances of so-called miraculous cures of diseases or injuries, performed by her upon themselves or others.

The hymns or " spiritual songs " they sing are said by the Shakers to be brought to them, almost without exception, from the " spirit-land;" and the airs to which these songs are sung are believed to come from the same source. There are, how-

A SHAKER SCHOOL.

SHAKER MUSIC-HALL.

ever, two collections of Hymns, to most of whose contents this
origin is not attributed, though even in these some of the
hymns purport to have been "given by inspiration." In the
older of these collections, "A Selection of Hymns and Poems
for the Use of Believers," printed at Watervliet, in Ohio, 1833,
one can trace some of the earlier trials of the societies, and
the evils they had to contend with within themselves. The
Western societies, for instance, appear to have early opposed
the drinking of intoxicating beverages. Here is a rhyme,
dated 1817, which appeals to the members in the cause of
total abstinence:

"From all intoxicating drink
  Ancient Believers did abstain;
Then say, good brethren, do you think
  That such a cross was all in vain?

"Inebriation, we allow,
  First paved the way for am'rous deeds;
Then why should poisonous spirits now
  Be ranked among our common needs?

"As an apothecary drug,
  Its wondrous virtues some will plead;
And hence we find the stupid *Slug*
  A morning dram does often need.

"Fatigue or want of appetite
  At noon will crave a little more,
And so the same complaints at night
  Are just as urgent as before.

"By want of sleep, and this and that,
  His thirst for liquor is increased;
Till he becomes a bloated sot—
  The very scarlet-colored beast.

"Why, then, should any soul insist
  On such pernicious, pois'nous stuff?
Malignant *spirits*, you're dismissed!
  You have possessed us long enough."

As a note to this temperance rhyme, stands the following:

"Ch. Rule.—All spirituous liquors should be kept under care of the nurses, that no drams in any case whatever should be dispensed to persons in common health, and that frivolous excuses of being unwell should not be admitted. Union Village, 1826."

"Slug," in the third of the preceding verses, seems to have been a cant term among the early Shakers for a sluggard and selfish fellow, a kind of creature they have pretty thoroughly extirpated; and presumably by such free speech as is used in the following amusing rhymes:

> "The depth of language I have dug
> To show the meaning of a Slug;
> And must conclude, upon the whole,
> It means a stupid, lifeless soul,
> Whose object is to live at ease,
> And his own carnal nature please;
> Who always has some selfish quirk,
> In sleeping, eating, and at work.

> "A lazy fellow it implies,
> Who in the morning hates to rise;
> When all the rest are up at four,
> He wants to sleep a little more.
> When others into meeting swarm,
> He keeps his nest so good and warm,
> That sometimes when the sisters come
> To make the beds and sweep the room,
> Who do they find wrap'd up so snug?
> Ah! who is it but Mr. Slug.

> "A little cold or aching head
> Will send him grunting to his bed,
> And he'll pretend he's sick or sore,
> Just that he may indulge the more.
> Nor would it feel much like a crime
> If he should sleep one half his time.

"When he gets up, before he's dress'd
He's so fatigued he has to rest;
And half an hour he'll keep his chair
Before he takes the morning air.
He'll sit and smoke in calm repose
Until the trump for breakfast blows—
His breakfast-time at length is past,
And he must wait another blast;
So at the sound of the last shell,
He takes his seat and all is well."

"Slug" at the table is thus satirized:

"To save his credit, you must know
That poor old Slug eats very slow;
And as in justice he does hate
That all the rest on him should wait,
Sometimes he has to rise and kneel
Before he has made out his meal.
Then to make up what he has miss'd,
He takes a luncheon in his fist,
Or turns again unto the dish,
And fully satisfies his wish;
Or, if it will not answer then,
He'll make it up at half-past ten.

"Again he thinks it quite too soon
To eat his dinner all at noon,
But as the feast is always free,
He takes a snack at half-past three.
He goes to supper with the rest,
But, lest his stomach be oppress'd,
He saves at least a piece of bread
Till just before he goes to bed;
So last of all the wretched Slug
Has room to drive another plug.

"To fam'ly order he's not bound,
But has his springs of union round;
And kitchen sisters ev'ry where
Know how to please him to a hair:

Sometimes his errand they can guess,
If not, he can his wants express;
Nor from old Slug can they get free
Without a cake or dish of tea."

"Slug" at work, or pretending to work, gets a fling also:

"When call'd to work you'll always find
The lazy fellow lags behind—
He has to smoke or end his chat,
Or tie his shoes, or hunt his hat:
So all the rest are busy found
Before old Slug gets on the ground;
Then he must stand and take his wind
Before he's ready to begin,
And ev'ry time he straights his back
He's sure to have some useless clack;
And tho' all others hate the Slug,
With folded arms himself he'll hug.

"When he conceits meal-time is near,
He listens oft the trump to hear;
And when it sounds, it is his rule
The first of all to drop his tool;
And if he's brisk in any case,
It will be in his homeward pace."

Here, too, is a picture of "Slug" shirking his religious duties:

"In his devotions he is known
To be the same poor lazy drone:
The sweetest songs Believers find
Make no impression on his mind;
And round the fire he'd rather nod
Than labor in the works of God.

"Some vain excuse he'll often plead
That he from worship may be freed—
He's bruis'd his heel or stump'd his toe,
And can not into meeting go;
And if he comes he's half asleep,
That no good fruit from him we reap:

He'll labor out a song or two,
And so conclude that that will do;
[And, lest through weariness he fall,
He'll brace himself against the wall],
And well the faithful may give thanks
That poor old Slug has quit the ranks.

"When the spectators are address'd,
Then is the time for Slug to rest—
From his high lot he can't be hurl'd,
To feel toward the wicked world;
So he will sit with closed eyes
Until the congregation rise;
And when the labor we commence,
He moves with such a stupid sense—
It often makes spectators stare
To see so dead a creature there."

The satire closes with a hit at "Slug's" devotion to tobacco:

"Men of sound reason use their pipes
For colics, pains, and windy gripes;
And smoking's useful, we will own,
To give the nerves and fluids tone;
But poor old Slug has to confess
He uses it to great excess,
And will indulge his appetite
Beyond his reason and his light.
If others round him do abstain,
It keeps him all the time in pain;
And if a sentence should be spoke
Against his much-beloved smoke,
Tho' it be in the way of joke,
He thinks his union's almost broke.
In all such things he's at a loss,
Because he thinks not of the cross,
But yields himself a willing slave
To what his meaner passions crave.

"This stupid soul in all his drift
Is still behind the proper gift—

With other souls he don't unite,
Nor is he zealous to do right.
Among Believers he's a drug,
And ev'ry elder hates a Slug.

"When long forbearance is the theme,
A warm believer he would seem—
For diff'rent tastes give gen'rous scope,
And he is full of faith and hope;
But talk about some good church rule,
And his high zeal you'll quickly cool.
Indulge him, then, in what is wrong,
And Slug will try to move along;
Nor will he his own state mistrust,
Until he gets so full of lust
His cross he will no longer tug,
Then to the world goes poor old Slug."

"Hoggish nature" comes in for a share of denunciation next in these lines:

"In the increasing work of the gospel we find,
The old hoggish nature we will have to bind—
To starve the old glutton, and leave him to shift.
Till in union with heaven we eat in a gift.

"What Father will teach me, I'll truly obey;
I'll keep Mother's counsel, and not go astray;
Then plagues and distempers they will have to cease,
In all that live up to the gospel's increase.

"The glutton's a seat in which evil can work,
And in hoggish nature diseases will lurk:
By faith and good works we can all overcome,
And starve the old glutton until he is done.

"But while he continues to guzzle and eat,
All kinds of distempers will still find a seat—
The plagues of old Egypt—the scab and the bile,
At which wicked spirits and devils will smile.

"Now some can despise the good porridge and soup,
And by the old glutton they surely are dup'd—
☞ To eat seven times in a day! what a mess!
I hate the old glutton for his hoggishness.

" No wonder that plagues and distempers abound,
  While there is a glutton in camp to be found,
  To spurn at the counsel kind Heaven did give—
  And guzzle up all, and have nothing to save.

" When glutton goes in and sits down with the rest,
  His hoggish old nature it grabs for the best—
  The cake and the custard, the crull and the pie—
  He cares not for others, but takes care of I.

" His stomach is weak, being gorg'd on the best,
  He has had sev'ral pieces secret from the rest;
  He'll fold up his arms, at the rest he will look,
  Because they do eat the good porridge and soup.

" Now all that are wise they will never be dup'd;
  They'll feed the old glutton on porridge and soup,
  Until he is willing to eat like the rest,
  And not hunt the kitchen to find out the best.

" We'll strictly observe what our good parents teach:
  Not pull the green apple, nor hog* in the peach;
  We'll starve the old glutton, and send him adrift;
  Then like good Believers we'll eat in a gift."

Following these verses are some reflections, concluding:

> " Away with the sluggard, the glutton, and beast,
>   For none but the bee and the dove
> Can truly partake of this heavenly feast,
>   Which springs from the fountains of love."

Obedience to the elders and ministry also appears to have
been difficult to bring about, for several verses in this collection
inculcate this duty. In one, called " Gospel-virtues illustrated," an old man is made the speaker, in these words:

> " Now eighteen hundred seventeen—
>   Where am I now? where have I been?
>   My age about threescore and three,
>   Then surely thankful I will be.

---

* To eat like a hog.

" I thank my parents for my home,
I thank good Elder Solomon,
I thank kind Eldress Hortency,
And Eldress Rachel kind and free.

" Good Elder Peter with the rest—
By his good works we all are blest;
His righteous works are plainly shown—
I thank him kindly for my home.

" From the beginning of this year,
A faithful cross I mean to bear,
To ev'ry order I'll subject,
And all my teachers I'll respect.

" With ev'ry gift I will unite—
They are all good and just and right;
If mortifying they do come,
I'll still be thankful for my home.

" When I'm chastis'd I'll not complain,
Tho' my old nature suffer pain;
Tho' it should come so sharp and hot,
Even to slay me on the spot.

" I will no longer use deceit,
I will abhor the hypocrite;
His forged lies I now will hate—
His portion is the burning lake.

" My vile affections they shall die,
And ev'ry lust I'll crucify;
I'll labor to be clean and pure,
And to the end I will endure.

" Th' adulterous eye shall now be blind—
It shall not feed the carnal mind;
My looks and conduct shall express
That holy faith that I possess.

" I will not murmur, 'tis not right,
About my clothing or my diet,
For surely those who have the care,
Will give to each their equal share.

" I will take care and not dictate
　　The fashion of my coat or hat;
But meet the gift as it may come,
　　And still be thankful for my home.

" I will be careful and not waste
　　That which is good for man or beast;
Or any thing that we do use—
　　No horse or ox will I abuse.

" I will be simple as a child;
　　I'll labor to be meek and mild;
In this good work my time I'll spend,
　　And with my tongue I'll not offend."

Again, in " Repentance and Confession," a sinner confesses
his misdeeds in such words as these:

" But still there's more crowds on my mind
　　And blacker than the rest—
They look more dark and greater crimes
　　Than all that I've confess'd
With tattling tongues and lying lips
　　I've often bore a part:
I frankly own I've made some slips
　　To give a lie a start.

" But worse than that I've tri'd to do,
　　When darken'd in my mind;
I've tri'd to be a Deist too—
　　That nothing was divine.
But O, good elders, pray for me!
　　The worst is yet behind—
I've talk'd against the ministry,
　　With malice in my mind.

" O Lord forgive! for mercy's sake,
　　And leave me not behind;
For surely I was not awake,
　　Else I had been consign'd.
Good ministry, can you forgive,
　　And elders one and all?
And, brethren, may I with you live,
　　And be the least of all?"

In "A Solemn Warning" there is a caution against the wiles of Satan, who tries Believers with a spirit of discontent:

"This cunning deceiver can't touch a Believer,
    Unless he can get them first tempted to taste
Some carnal affection, or fleshly connection,
    And little by little their power to waste.
The first thing is blinding, before undermining,
    Or else the discerning would shun the vile snare;—
Thus Satan hath frosted and artfully blasted
    Some beautiful blossoms that promis'd most fair.

"This wily soul-taker and final peace-breaker
    May take the unwary before they suspect,
And get them to hearken to that which will darken,
    And next will induce them their faith to reject;
He'll tell you subjection affords no protection—
    These things you've been tau't are but notions at best;
Reject your protection, and break your connection,
    And all you call'd faith you may scorn and detest."

"The Last Woe" denounces various sins of the congrega-tion:

"In your actions unclean, you are openly seen,
    And this truth you may ever remark,
That in anguish and woe, to the saints you must go,
    And confess what you've done in the dark.

"From restraint you are free, and no danger you see,
    Till the sound of the trumpet comes in,
Crying 'Woe to your lust—it must go to the dust,
    With the unfruitful pleasures of sin.'

"And a woe to the liar—he is doom'd to the fire,
    Until all his dark lies are confess'd—
Till he honestly tell, what a spirit from hell
    Had its impious seat in his breast.

"And a woe to the thief, without any relief—
    He is sentenc'd in body and soul,
To confess with his tongue, and restore ev'ry wrong,
    What he ever has robbed or stole.

"Tho' the sinner may plead, that it was not decreed
  For a man to take up a full cross,
Yet in hell he must burn, or repent and return,
  And be sav'd from the nature of loss."

In the following "Dialogue" "confession of sins" is urged
and enforced:

"Q. Why did you choose this way you're in, which all mankind
    despise?
A. It was to save my soul from sin, and gain a heav'nly prize.

Q. But could you find no other way, that would have done as well?
A. Nay, any other way but this would lead me down to hell.

Q. Well, tell me how did you begin to purge away your dross?
A. By honestly confessing sin, and taking up my cross.

Q. Was it before the Son of man you brought your deeds to light?
A. That was the mortifying plan, and surely it was right.

Q. But did you not keep something back, or did you tell the whole?
A. I told it all, however black—I fully freed my soul.

Q. Do you expect to persevere, and ev'ry evil shun?
A. My daily cross I mean to bear, until the work is done.

Q. Well, is it now your full intent all damage to restore?
A. If any man I've wrong'd a cent, I'll freely give him four.

Q. And what is now the greatest foe with which you mean to war?
A. The cursed flesh—'tis that, you know, all faithful souls abhor.

Q. Have you none of its sly deceit now lurking in your breast?
A. I say there's nothing on my mind but what I have confess'd.

Q. Well, what you have proclaim'd abroad, if by your works you show,
    You are prepar'd to worship God, so, at, it, you, may, go."

"The Steamboat" seems to me a characteristic rhyme, which
no doubt came home to Believers on the western rivers, when
they were plagued with doubters and cold-hearted adherents:

"While our steamboat, Self-denial,
  Rushes up against the stream,
Is it not a serious trial
  Of the pow'r of gospel steam?

When Self-will, and Carnal Pleasure,
  And Freethinker, all afloat,
Come down snorting with such pressure,
  Right against our little boat.

" Were there not some carnal creatures
  Mixed with the pure and clean,
When we meet those gospel-haters,
  We might pass and not be seen;
But the smell of kindred senses
  Brings them on us fair broadside,
Then the grappling work commences—
  They must have a fair divide.

" All who choose the tide of nature,
  Freely take the downward way;
But the doubtful hesitater
  Dare not go, yet hates to stay.
To the flesh still claiming kindred,
  And their faith still hanging to—
Thus we're held and basely hinder'd,
  By a double-minded few.

" Wretched souls, while hesitating
  Where to fix your final claim,
Don't you see our boiler heating,
  With a more effectual flame !—
When the steam comes on like thunder,
  And the wheels begin to play,
Must you not be torn asunder,
  And swept off the downward way?

" Tho' Self-will and Carnal Reason,
  Independence, Lust, and Pride,
May retard us for a season,
  Saint and sinner must divide;
When releas'd from useless lumber—
  When the fleshly crew is gone—
With our little faithful number,
  O how swiftly we'll move on !"

The " Covenant Hymn" was publicly sung in some of the
Western societies, "so that no room was left for any to say

that the Covenant [by which they agree to give up all property and labor for the general use] was not well understood." I quote here several verses:

" You have parents in the Lord, you honor and esteem,
But your equals to regard a greater cross may seem.
Where the gift of God you see,
Can you consent that it should reign?
Yea I can, and all that's free may jointly say—Amen.

" Can you part with all you've got, and give up all concern,
And be faithful in your lot, the way of God to learn?
Can you sacrifice your ease,
And take your share of toil and pain?
Yea I can, and all that please may freely say—Amen.

"Can you into union flow, and have your will subdu'd?
Let your time and talents go, to serve the gen'ral good?
Can you swallow such a pill—
To count old Adam's loss your gain?
Yea I can, and yea I will, and all may say—Amen.

"I set out to bear my cross, and this I mean to do:
Let old Adam kick and toss, his days will be but few.
We're devoted to the Lord,
And from the flesh we will be free;
Then we'll say with one accord—Amen, so let it be."

It is evident from these verses that the early Shakers had among them men who at least could make the rhymes run glibly, and who besides had a gift of plain speech. Here, for instance, is a denunciation of a scandal-monger:

"In the Church of Christ and Mother,
Carnal feelings have no place;
Here the simple love each other,
Free from ev'ry thing that's base.
Therefore when the flesh is named,
When impeachments fly around,
Honest souls do feel ashamed—
Shudder at the very sound.

"Ah! thou foul and filthy stranger!
　　What canst thou be after here?
Thou wilt find thyself in danger,
　　If thou dost not disappear.
Vanish quick, I do advise you!
　　For we mean to let you know
Good Believers do despise you,
　　As a dang'rous, deadly foe.

"Dare you, in the sight of heaven,
　　Show your foul and filthy pranks?
Can a place to you be given
　　In the bright angelic ranks?
Go! I say, thou unclean devil!
　　Go from this redeemed soil,
If you think you can not travel
　　Through a lake of boiling oil."

In those earlier days, as in these, idle persons seem to have troubled the Shakers with the question "What would become of the world if all turned Shakers," to which here is a sharp reply:

"The multiplication of the old creation
　　They're sure to hold forth as a weighty command;
And what law can hinder old Adam to gender,
　　And propagate men to replenish the land?
But truly he never obey'd the lawgiver,
　　For when the old serpent had open'd his eyes,
He sought nothing greater than just to please nature,
　　And work like a serpent in human disguise."

"Steeple houses" are as hateful to the Shakers as to the Quakers and the Inspirationists of Amana, and they are excluded in an especial manner from the Shakers' Paradise:

"No sin can ever enter here—
　　Nor sinners rear a steeple;
'Tis kept by God's peculiar care,
　　For his peculiar people.

One faith, one union, and one Lord,
   One int'rest all combining,
Believers all, with one accord,
   In heav'nly concert joining.

"Far as the gospel spirit reigns,
   Our souls are in communion;
From Alfred to South Union's plains,
   We feel our love and union.
Here we may walk in peace and love,
   With God and saints uniting;
While angels, smiling from above,
   To glory are inviting."

Occasionally the book from which I am quoting gives one of those lively brief verses to which the Shaker congregation marches, with clapping hands and skipping feet; as these, for instance:

"I mean to be obedient,
   And cross my ugly nature,
And share the blessings that are sent
   To ev'ry honest creature;
With ev'ry gift I will unite,
   And join in sweet devotion—
To worship God is my delight,
   With hands and feet in motion."

"Come, let us all be marching on,
   Into the New Jerusalem;
The call is now to ev'ry one
   To be alive and moving.
This precious call we will obey—
We love to march the heav'nly way,
And in it we can dance and play,
   And feel our spirits living."

In the newer collection, entitled "Millennial Hymns, adapted to the present Order of the Church," and printed at Canterbury, New Hampshire, in 1847, a change is noticeable. The hymns are more devotional and less energetic. There are many praises of Mother Ann—such lines as these:

"O Mother, blest Mother! to thee I will bow;
Thou art a kind Mother, thou dost teach us how
Salvation is gained, and how to increase
In purity, union, in order and peace.

"I love thee, O Mother; thy praise I will sound—
I'll bless thee forever for what I have found;
I'll praise and adore thee, to thee bow and bend,
For Mother, dear Mother, thou art my known friend."

Or these:

"I will walk in true obedience, I will be a child of love;
And in low humiliation I will praise my God above.
I will love my blessed Mother, and obey her holy word,
In submission to my elders, this will join me to the Lord.

"I will stand when persecution doth around like billows roll;
I will bow in true subjection, and my carnal will control.
I will stand a firm believer in the way and work of God,
Doubts and fears shall never, never in me find a safe abode.

"When temptations do surround me, floods of evil ebb and flow,
Then in true humiliation I will bow exceeding low.
I will fear the God of heaven, I will keep his holy laws,
Treasure up his blessings given in this pure and holy cause.

"Tho' beset by wicked spirits, men and devils all combin'd,
Yet my Mother's love will save me if in faithfulness I stand:
No infernal crooked creature can destroy or harm my soul,
If I keep the love of Mother and obey her holy call."

Or this hymn, which is called " Parents' Blessing :"

"My Father does love me, my Mother also
Does send me her love, and I now feel it flow;
These heavenly Parents are kind unto me,
And by their directions my soul is set free.

"They fill up my vessel with power and strength—
Yea, make my cross easy, my peace of great length;
My joy full and perfect, my trouble but light,
My gifts very many in which I delight.

"I truly feel thankful for what I receive,
 In each holy promise I surely believe;
 They're able and willing to do all they've said,
 And by my kind Parents I choose to be led.

"I love to feel simple, I love to feel low,
 I love to be kept in the path I should go;
 I love to be taught by my heavenly lead,
 That I may be holy and perfect indeed."

I add another, which has the lively, quick rhythm in which the Shakers delight. It is called "Wisdom's Path:"

"I'll learn to walk in wisdom's ways,
 And in her path I'll spend my days;
 I'll learn to do what Mother says
  And follow her example.
 All pride and lust this will subdue,
 And every hateful passion too;
 This will destroy old Satan's crew
  That's seated in the temple.

"Come, honest souls, let us unite
 And keep our conscience clear and white,
 For surely Mother does delight
  To own and bless her children.
 In Father's word let us go on,
 And bear our cross and do no wrong,
 In faith and love then we'll be strong
  To conquer every evil.

"For love and union is our stay,
 We'll be strong and keep it day by day;
 Then we shall never go astray,
  We'll gain more love and union.
 Obedience will still increase,
 And every evil work will cease,
 We'll gain a true and solid peace,
  We'll live in Mother's union."

I make no excuse for these quotations of Shaker hymns, for the books from which they are taken have been seen by very few outside of the order, and not even by all its members, as they are not now in common use.

The Shakers have always professed to have intimate intercourse with the "spirit world." Elder Frederick Evans says in his autobiography that from the beginning the exercises in Shaker meetings were "singing and dancing, shaking, turning, and shouting, *speaking with new tongues and prophesying.*" Elder Frederick himself, as he remarks, "was converted to Shakerism in 1830 by spiritual manifestations," having "visions" for three weeks, which converted him, as he relates, from materialism. He adds:

"In 1837 to 1844 there was an influx from the 'spirit world,' 'confirming the faith of many disciples' who had lived among Believers for years, and extending throughout all the eighteen societies, making media by the dozen, whose various exercises, not to be suppressed even in their public meetings, rendered it imperatively necessary to close them all to the world during a period of seven years, in consequence of the then unprepared state of the people, to which the whole of the manifestations, and the meetings too, would have been as unadulterated 'foolishness,' or as inexplicable mysteries."

In a recent number of the *Shaker and Shakeress* (1874), Elder James S. Prescott, of the North Union Society, gave a curious account of the first appearance of this phenomenon at that place, from which I quote what follows:

"It was in the year 1838, in the latter part of summer, some young sisters were walking together on the bank of the creek, not far from the hemlock grove, west of what is called the Mill Family, where they heard some beautiful singing, which seemed to be in the air just above their heads.

"They were taken by surprise, listened with admiration, and then hastened home to report the phenomenon. Some of them afterwards were chosen mediums for the 'spirits.' We had been informed, by letter, that there was a marvelous work going on in some of the Eastern societies, particularly at Mt. Lebanon, New York, and Watervliet, near Albany. And when it reached us in the West we should all know it, and we did know it;

in the progress of the work, every individual, from the least to the greatest, did know that there was a heart-searching God in Israel, who ruled in the armies of heaven, and will yet rule among the inhabitants of earth.

"It commenced among the little girls in the children's order, who were assembled in an upper room, the doors being shut, holding a meeting by themselves, when the invisibles began to make themselves known. It was on the Sabbath-day, while engaged in our usual exercises, that a messenger came in and informed the elders in great haste that there was something uncommon going on in the girls' department. The elders brought our meeting to a close as soon as circumstances would admit, and went over to witness the singular and strange phenomena.

"When we entered the apartment, we saw that the girls were under the influence of a power not their own—they were hurried round the room, back and forth as swiftly as if driven by the wind—and no one could stop them. If any attempts were made in that direction, it was found impossible, showing conclusively that they were under a controlling influence that was irresistible. Suddenly they were prostrated upon the floor, apparently unconscious of what was going on around them. With their eyes closed, muscles strained, joints stiff, they were taken up and laid upon beds, mattresses, etc.

"They then began holding converse with their guardian spirits and others, some of whom they once knew in the form, making graceful motions with their hands—talking audibly, so that all in the room could hear and understand, and form some idea of their whereabouts in the spiritual realms they were exploring in the land of souls. This was only the beginning of a series of 'spirit manifestations,' the most remarkable we ever expected to witness on the earth. One prominent feature of these manifestations was the gift of songs, hymns, and anthems—new, heavenly, and melodious. The first inspired song we ever heard from the 'spirit world,' with words attached, was the following, sung by one of the young sisters, while in vision, with great power and demonstration of the spirit, called by the invisible

'THE SONG OF A HERALD.

'Prepare, O ye faithful,
  To fight the good fight;
Sing, O ye redeemed,
  Who walk in the light.
Come low, O ye haughty,
  Come down, and repent.
Disperse, O ye naughty,
  Who will not relent.

> ' For Mother is coming—
> Oh, hear the glad sound—
> To comfort her children
> Wherever they're found ;
> With jewels and robes of fine linen
> To clothe the afflicted withal.'

" Given by inspiration, at North Union, August, 1838, ten years prior to the ' Rochester Rappings.'

" The gifts continued increasing among the children. Among these were the gift of tongues, visiting the different cities in the ' spirit world,' holding converse with the indwellers thereof, some of whom they once knew in the body. And in going to these cities they were accompanied by their guardian angels, and appeared to be flying, using their hands and arms for wings, moving with as much velocity as the wings of a bird.

" All of a sudden they stopped, and the following questions and answers were uttered through their vocal organism : *Question*—What city is this ? *Answer*—' The City of Delight.' *Question*—Who live here ? *Answer*—The colored population. *Question*—Can we go in and see them ? *Answer*—Certainly. For this purpose you were conducted here. They were admitted, their countenances changed. *Question*—Who are all these ? *Answer*—They are those who were once slaves in the United States. *Question*—Who are those behind them ? *Answer*—They are those who were once slaveholders. *Question*—What are they doing here ? *Answer* —Serving the slaves, as the slaves served them while in the earth life. God is just ; all wrongs have to be righted. *Question*—Who are those in the corner ? *Answer*—They are those slaveholders who were unmerciful, and abused their slaves in the world, and are too proud to comply with the conditions. *Question*—What were the conditions ? *Answer*— To make confession and ask forgiveness of the slaves, and right their wrongs ; and this they are too proud to do. *Question*—What will be done with them ? *Answer*—When their time expires they will be taken away and cast out, and will have to suffer until they repent ; for all wrongs must be righted, either in the form or among the disembodied spirits, before souls can be happy. And when the girls came out of vision, they would relate the same things, which corresponded with what they had previously talked out.

" Now, we will leave the girls for the present and go into the boys' department. Here we find them holding meetings by themselves, under

the safe guidance of their care-takers, going in vision, some boys and
some girls, for the work had progressed so as to reach adults, and all
were called immediately into the work whose physical organizations
would possibly admit of mediumship. The peculiar gift at this time was
in visiting the different cities in the 'spirit world,' and in renewing acquaintances with many of their departed friends and relatives, who were
the blissful and happy residents therein.

"But before we go any further we will let our mediums describe the
first city they came to after crossing the river. *Question*—What city is
this? *Answer*—The Blue City. *Question*—Who lives here? *Answer*—
The Indians. *Question*—What Indians? *Answer*—The American Indians.
Question—Why are they the first city we come to in the spirit-land, on
the plane, and most accessible? *Answer*—Because the Indians lived
more in accordance with the law of nature in their earth life, according
to their knowledge, and were the most abused class by the whites except
the slaves, and many of them now are in advance of the whites in ' spirituality,' and are the most powerful ministering spirits sent forth to minister
to those who shall be heirs of salvation.

"At another time these same mediums, fifteen in number, of both sexes,
sitting on benches in the meeting-house, saw a band of Indian spirits
coming from the 'Blue City' in the spirit world to unite with them
in their worship, and said, ' They are coming;' and as soon as the spirits
entered the door they entered the mediums, which moved them from
their seats as quick as lightning. Then followed the Indian songs and
dances, and speaking in the Indian tongue, which was wholly unintelligi-
ble to us except by spiritual interpreters."

Some of the most curious literature of the Shakers dates
from this period; and it is freely admitted by their leading
men that they were in some cases misled into acts and publications which they have since seen reason to regret. Their
belief is that they were deceived by false spirits, and were unable, in many cases, to distinguish the true from the false.
That is to say, they hold to their faith in "spiritual communications," so called; but repudiate much in which they formerly had faith, believing this which they now reject to have
come from the Evil One.

Little has ever become authentically known of the so-called

"spiritual" phenomena, which so profoundly excited the Shaker societies during seven years that, as Elder Frederick relates, they closed their doors against the world. Hervey Elkins, a person brought up in the society at Enfield, New Hampshire, in his pamphlet entitled "Fifteen Years in the Senior Order of Shakers," from which I have already quoted, gives some curious details of this period. It will be seen, from the passages I extract from Elkins, that he came under what he supposed to be "spiritual" influences himself:

"In the spring succeeding the winter of which I have treated, a remarkable religious revival began among all the Shakers of the land, east and west. It was announced several months prior to its commencement that the holy prophet Elisha was deputized to visit the Zion of God on earth, and to bestow upon each individual those graces which each needed, and to baptize with the Holy Ghost all the young who would prepare their souls for such a baptism.

"The time at length arrived. No one knew the manner in which the prophet would make himself known. The people were grave and concerned about their spiritual standing. Two female instruments from Canterbury, N. H., were at length ushered into the sanctuary. Their eyes were closed, and their faces moved in semigyrations. Their countenances were pallid, as though worn by unceasing vigils. They looked as though laden with a momentous and impending revelation. Throughout the assembly, pallid faces, tears, and trembling limbs were visible. Anxiety and excitement were felt in every mind, as all believed the instruments sacredly and superhumanly inspired. The alternate redness and pallor of every countenance revealed this anxiety. For the space of five minutes the spacious hall was as silent as the tomb. One of the mediums then advanced in the space between the ranks of brethren and sisters, and announced with a clear, deep, and sonorous voice, and in sublime and authoritative language, the mission of the holy prophet. The ministry then bade the instruments to be free and proceed as they could answer to God; and conferred on them plenary power to conduct the meetings as the prophet should direct.

"After marching a few songs, the prophet requested the formation of two circles, one containing all the brethren, the other the sisters. The two mediums were first inclosed by the circle of brethren. They both were young women between twenty and twenty-five years of age, and had never before been at Enfield. They had probably never heard the names of two thirds of the younger members. They moved around in these circles, stopping before each one as though reading the condition of every heart. As they passed some, they evinced pleasure; as they passed others, they bespoke grief; others, yet, an obvious contempt; by which it seemed they looked within, and saw with delight or horror the state of all. From our knowledge of the members, we knew they passed and noticed them as their works merited. Little was said to separate individuals in the first meeting. In the second, we were requested to form six circles, three of each sex, and those of a circle to be connected together by the taking hold of hands; and in this manner to bow, bend, and dance. In this condition an influence was felt, upon which psychologists and biologists would differ. It would be needless to enumerate the many gifts, the prophecies, the extempore songs, the revelations, the sins exposed, and the hypocrites ejected from the society during this period of two months. But, as near as we could estimate, four hundred new songs were sung in that time, either by improvisation or inspiration, of which I have my opinion. I doubt not but that many were inspired by spirits congenial with themselves, and consequently some of the songs evinced a fatuity and simplicity peculiar to the instrument. On the other hand, many songs were given from spheres above, higher in melody, sentiment, and pathos than any originating with earth's inhabitants.

"I recollect that the first spiritual gift presented to me was a 'Cup of Solemnity.' I drank the contents, and felt for a season the salutary effects. During the revival I became sincerely converted. I for a time, by reason of prejudice and distrust, resisted the effect of the impressions, which at length overwhelmed me in a flood of tears, shed for joy and gladness, as I more and more turned my thoughts to the Infinite. At last a halo of heavenly glory seemed to surround me. I drank deep of the cup of the waters of life, and was lifted in mind and purpose from this world of sorrow and sin. I soared in thought to God, and enjoyed him in his attributes of purity and love. I was wafted by angels safely above the ocean of sensual enjoyment which buries so many millions, but into which I had never fallen. I explored the beauties of ineffable bliss, and caught a glimpse of that divinity which is the culmination of science and the end of the world. The adoration and solemnity of the sanctuary enveloped me as with a mantle, even when employed in manual labor and in the company of my companions. The frivolity of some of my companions disgusted me. The extreme and favorable change wrought within me in so short a time was often remarked by the elders and members of the society; but the praise or the censure of mortals were to me like alternate winds, and of little avail.

"Two years thus passed, in which my highest enjoyments and pleasures were an inward contemplation of the beauty, love, and holiness of God, and in the ecstatic impressions that I was in the hollow of his hand, and owned and blessed of him.   Still later in life I retained and could evoke at times the same profoundly religious impressions, contaminated, however, by other favorite objects of study and attachment. Even the expression of my countenance wore an aspect of deep, tender, and benignant gravity, which the reflection of less holy subjects could not produce.   It was my delight to pray fervently and *tacitly*, and this I often did besides the usual time allotted for such devotion. (Vocal prayer is not admissible among the Shakers.)   I loved to unite in the dance, and give myself up to the operations of spirits even, if it would not thwart my meditative communion with God and with God alone.   Though instruments or mediums were multiplied around me, dancing in imitation of the spirits of all nations, singing and conversing in unknown tongues, some evincing a truly barbarian attitude and manners, I stood in mute thanksgiving and prayer.   At times I was asked by the elders if I could not unite and take upon me an Indian, a Norwegian, or an Arabian spirit? I would then strive to be impressed with their feelings, and act in conformity thereto.   But such inspiration, I found, was not the revelation of the Holy Ghost.   It was not that which elevated and kept me from all trials and temptations.   But my inward spontaneous devotion was the kind I needed.   I informed the elders of my opinion, and they concurred in it, only they regarded the inspiration of simple and unsophisticated spirits as a stepping-stone to a higher revelation, by virtue of removing pride, vanity, and self-will, those great barriers against the accession of holy infusions.

*   *   *   *   *   *   *   *   *

"In the fall of that season this revival redoubled its energy.   The gifts were similar to those of the spring previous, but less charity was shown to the hypocrite and vile pretender.   It was announced that Jehovah— Power and Wisdom—the dual God, would visit the inhabitants of Zion, and bestow a blessing upon each individual as their works should merit. A time was given for us to prepare for his coming.   Every building, every apartment, every lane, field, orchard, and pasture, must be cleansed of all rubbish and needless encumbrance; so that even a Shaker village, so notorious for neatness, wore an aspect fifty per cent. more tidy than usual. To sweep our buildings, regulate our stores, pick up and draw to a circular wood-saw old bits of boards, stakes, and poles that were fit for naught but fuel, and collect into piles to be burned upon the spot all such as were unfit for that, was the order of the day. Even the sisters debouched by scores to help improve the appearance of the farm and lake shores, on which were quantities of drift-wood. Thus was passed a fortnight of pleasant autumnal weather. As the evenings approached, we set fire to the piles of old wood, which burned, the flames shooting upward, in a serene evening, like the innumerable bonfires which announce the ingress of a regal visitant to monarchical countries. Viewed from the plain below, in the gray, dim twilight of a soft and serene atmosphere, when all nature was wrapped in the unique and beautiful solemnity of an unusually prorogued autumn, these fires, emerging in the blue distance from the vast amphitheatre of hills, were picturesque in the highest degree. How neat! how fascinating! and how much like our conceptions of heaven the whole vale appeared! And then to regard this work of cleansing and beautifying the domains of Mount Zion as that preparatory to the visitation of the Most High, is something which speaks to the heart and says: 'Dost thou appear as beautiful, as clean, and as comely in the sight of God as do these elements of an unthinking world? Is thine heart also prepared to be searched with the candles of him from whom no unclean thing is hidden?'

"The following words were said to have been brought by an angel from Jehovah, and accompanied by a most beautiful tune of two airs:

> 'I shall march through Mount Zion,
> With my angelic band;
> I shall pass through the city
> With my fan in my hand;
> And around thee, O Jerusalem,
> My armies will encamp,
> While I search my Holy Temple
> With my bright burning lamp.'

"It was during this revival that Henry, of whom I have spoken, was ejected from the society. During this, as also during the previous excitement, he had exhibited an aversion which often found vent in bitter taunts and jeers. Sometimes, however, a simulated unity of feeling had prevented his publicly incurring the imputation of open rebellion. He had learned some scraps of the Latin language, and on the occasion of the evening worship in which he was expelled, he afterward informed us that, at the time he was arraigned for expulsion, he was pretendedly uniting with those who were speaking in unknown languages by employing awful oaths and profanity in the Latin tongue. A female instrument, said to be employed by the spirit of Ann Lee, approached him while thus engaged, and uttered in a low, distinct, and funereal accent a denunciation which severed him as a withered branch from the tree of life. He suddenly bowed as if beneath the weight of a terrible destiny, smiting his breast and ejaculating, 'Pardon! pardon! Oh, forgive—forgive me my transgressions!' The elders strove to hush his cries, and replied that 'all forbearance is at an end.' His ardent vociferations now degenerated into inarticulate yells of horror and demoniacal despair. He rushed from the group which surrounded him, he glided like one unconscious of the presence of others from one extremity of the hall to another, he smote with clenched fists the walls of the apartment, and reeled at last in convulsive agony, uttering the deep, hollow groan of inexorable expiation. In this situation he was hurried for the last time from the sanctuary which he had so often profaned, and from the presence of those moistened eyes and commiserative looks which he never would again behold. The confession of his blasphemous profanity he made at the trustees' office prior to his leaving the society, which occurred the subsequent morning."

At another time such scenes as the following are described:

"Shrieks of some one, apparently in great distress, first announced a phenomenon, which caused the excitement. The screeching proceeded from a girl of but thirteen years of age, who had previously among the Shakers been a clairvoyant, and who has since been a powerful medium for spiritual manifestation elsewhere. She soon fell upon the floor, uttering awful cries, similar to those we had often heard emanating from instruments groaning under the pressure of some hidden abomination in the assembly. She plucked out entire handfuls of her hair, and wailed and shrieked like one subjected to all the conceived agonies of hell. The ministry and elders remarked that they believed that something was wrong; something extremely heinous was covered from God's witnesses somewhere in the assembly. All were exhorted to search themselves, and see if they had nothing about them that God disowns. The meeting was soon dismissed, but the medium continued in her abnormal and deplorable condition. Near the middle of the succeeding night we were all

awakened by the ringing of the alarm, and summoned quickly to repair to the girls' apartments. We obeyed. The same medium lay upon
a bed, uttering in the name of an apostate from the Shaker faith, and
who was still living in New England, tremendous imprecations against
himself, warning all to beware of what use they make of their privilege
in Zion, telling us of his awful torments in hell, how his flesh (or the substance of his spiritual body) was all to strings and ringlets torn, how he
was roasted in flames of brimstone and tar, and, finally, that all these calamities were caused by his doleful corruptions and pollutions while a
member, and professedly a brother to us. This, it was supposed by many,
was by true revelation the anticipation of the future state of this victim
of apostasy and sin. Two or three more girls were soon taken in the
same manner, and became uncontrollable. They were all instruments for
reprobated spirits, and breathed nothing but hatred and blasphemy to
God. They railed, they cursed, they swore, they heaped the vilest epithets
upon the heads of the leaders and most faithful of the members, they pulled
each other's and their own hair, threw knives, forks, and the most dangerous of missiles. When the instruments were rational, the elders entreated
them to keep off such vile spirits. They would weep in anguish, and
reply that, unless they spoke and acted for the spirits, they would choke
them to death. They would then suddenly swoon away, and in strug-
gling to resist them would choke and gasp, until they had the appearance of a victim strangled by a rope tightly drawn around her neck. If
they would then speak, the strangulation would cease. In the mean time
two females of adult age, and two male youths, were seized in the same
manner. Unless confined, they would elope, and appear to all intents the
victims of insanity. One of the young women eloped, fled to a lake
which was covered with ice, was pursued by some of the ox teamsters,
and carried back to the infirmary. Two men could with difficulty hold
a woman or a child when thus influenced. To prevent mischief and
elopement, we were obliged to envelop their bodies and their arms
tightly in sheets, and thus sew them up and confine them until the spell
was over. Such delirium generally lasted but a few hours. It would
seize them at any time and at any place.

"The phenomena to which we allude was the source of much facetious
pleasantry with the young brethren. One of the infernal spirits had one
evening declared that 'before morning they would have the deacon and
Lupier.' 'Deacon' was an epithet applied to myself, as a token of fa-
miliarity. The tidings of the declaration of this infernal agent were soon

conveyed to me. It happened that my companion of the dormitory, a middle-aged man, had that evening gone to watch with the mediums, and I was left alone. I replied to my companions, who interrogated and sarcastically congratulated me on my prospects for the night, that 'if the corporeal influence of incarnate devils could be kept from the room, I would combat without aid all other influences and answer for my own safety.' I accordingly locked myself into my room, and enjoyed, unmolested for the night, except by occasional raps upon the door by my passing comrades, some of whom were up all night by reason of the excitement, a sound and pleasant sleep. One or two instances occurred in which a superhuman agency was indubitably obvious. One of the abnormal males lay in a building at some distance from the infirmary where the female instruments were confined. Suddenly one of the last, who had been for some time in a quiescent state and rational, was seized by one of these paroxysms, which were always accompanied by dreadful contortions and sudden twitchings of the body, and, speaking for the spirit, said that ' Old S—— had bound him with a surcingle, and he had left E——,' one of the male instruments. The physician instantly repaired to the building where E—— lay, and he was perfectly rational. S——, the watch, informed the physician that E—— raved so violently a moment before that he bound his arms to his body by passing a surcingle around both, and he quickly became himself. At another time one of the females took a handful of living coals in her bare hands, and thus carried them about the room without even injuring the cuticle of the skin.

"The phenomena and excitement soon dwindled away by the tremendous opposition directed against them ; and when afterward spoken about, were designated by the sinister phrase—'The Devil's Visitation.'

"Other ministrations and gifts, original and perfectly illustrative of the inspirations of crude and uncivilized spirits, continued as usual to exist. They were truly ludicrous. I have seen female instruments in uncouth habits, and in imitation of squaws, and a few males acting as suneps, glide in groups on a stiffly frozen snow, shouting, dancing, yelling, and whooping, and others acting precisely the peculiar traits of a Negro, an Arab, a Chinese, an Italian, or even the polite gayety of a Frenchman. And, what is still more astounding, speaking the vernacular dialects of each race. Their confabulation, aided by inspired interpreters, was truly amusing and interesting. On one occasion I saw a sister, inspired by a squaw, her head mounted with an old hat of felt, cocked, jammed, and indented in no geometrical form, rush to a pan containing a collection of the amputated legs of hens, seize a handful of the raw delicacy, and devour them with as much alacrity as a Yankee woman would an omelet or a doughnut."

In general, Elkins relates:

"I have myself seen males, but more frequently females, in a superinduced condition, apparently unconscious of earthly things, and declaring in the name of departed spirits important and convincing revelations. Speaking in foreign tongues and prophesying were the most common gifts. In February, 1848, a medium became abstracted from earthly scenes, and announced the presence of an angel of God. The angel declared, through her, that he was sent on a mission to France, and that before many days we should hear of his doings in that nation. This announcement was in presence of the whole family, and it was then and there noted down. France at that time was, for aught we knew, resting upon a permanent political basis; or as nearly in that condition as she ever was. In a few days the revolution of the 24th of February precipitated the monarchy into an interregnum, which philanthropists hoped was bottomless.

"Turning rapidly upon the toes, bowing, bending, twisting, and reeling like one a victim to the fumes of intoxication; swooning and lying prostrate with limbs stiff and unyielding, like a corpse, and to all outward appearance the vital spark extinct; then suddenly resuscitating— the mind still abstracted from scenes below—and rising to join in the jubilancy of the dance, in company with and in imitation of the angels around the throne of God, singing extemporaneous anthems and songs, or those learned direct of seraphs in the regions of bliss—such are the many exercises, effusions of devotion, and supernatural illapses of which I was for fifteen years at intervals an eye and ear witness. Also the exposure of sin, designating in some cases the transgressor, the act, and the place of perpetration, of which the accused was most generally found culpable.

"More than a score of new dances were performed, with an attitude of grace and with the precision of a machine, by about twenty female clairvoyants. They *said* they learned them of seraphs before the throne of God.

"I was doubtful of their assertions, for such things were to me novel. I however determined not to overstep the bounds of prudence, and declare the work an illusion, for fear that I might blaspheme a higher power. I communicated my doubts to a few of my companions, and one, less cautious than myself, immediately broke forth in imprecations against it. I never was secretly opposed, but a turbulent disposition or a love for dramatic scenes, prompted by the hope of detecting either the validity or deception of such phenomena, impelled me to wink opposition to my reckless companion. In the devotional exercises, which served as a preliminary to the entrance of the mind into a superior condition, such as whirling, twisting, and reeling, we all took a part. Henry, for that was the name of the youth who was so zealous in his aspersions, united awkwardly and derisively in these exercises. Amid so many arms, legs, and bodies, revolving, oscillating, staggering, and tripping, it is not remarkable that a few should be thrown prostrate (not violently, however) upon the floor. One evening, in a boy's meeting at a time of great excitement, when the spirits of some of our companions were reported to be in spiritual spheres, and other departed spirits were careering their mortal ladies in the graceful undulations of a celestial dance, Henry and many others, among whom I was seen, were whirling, staggering, and rolling, striving in vain, by all the humility we could assume, to be also admitted into the regions of spiritual recognition, Henry suddenly tripped and fell. One of his visionary companions instantly sprang, passed his hands with great rapidity over him, as though binding him with invisible cords, and then returned to his graceful employment. The clairvoyant's eyes were closed, as indeed were the eyes of all while in that condition. In vain Henry struggled to rise, to turn, or hardly to move. He was fettered, bound fast by invisible manacles. The brethren were summoned to witness the sight. In the space of perhaps half an hour the clairvoyant returned, loosened his fetters, and he arose mortified and confounded. Singularly disposed, he ever after treated these gifts with virulent ridicule, and never was heard to utter any serious remarks concerning this transaction. The clairvoyant after this event was the butt of his satire and jests, and received them without revenge so long as Henry remained, which was about five years—a reckless, abandoned, evil-minded person, eventually severed by that same power which he strove incessantly to ridicule. All these strange operations and gifts are attributed by the Shakers to the influence of superhuman power like that manifested in the Primitive Church."

Some of the hymns which date from this period have fragments of the "strange tongues" in which the "mediums" spoke. Here is one, dated at New Lebanon, and printed in the collection called " Millennial Hymns :"

"HEAVENLY GUIDE.

" Lo all vo, hark ye, dear children, and listen to me,
  For I am that holy Se lone′ se ka′ ra an ve′;
  My work upon earth is holy, holy and pure,
  That work which will ever, forever endure.

" Yea, my heavenly Father hath se-ve′-ned to you
  That power which is holy and that faith which is true;
  O then, my beloved, why will ye delay?
  O la ho′ le en se′ ren, now while it is day.

" The holy angels in heaven their trumpets do raise,
  And with saints upon earth sound endless praise.
  Blessed, most blessed, your day, and holy your call,
  O ven se′ ne ven se′ ne, yea every soul.

" All holy se ka′ ren are the free blessings given
  And bestowed on you from the fountain of heaven;
  Yea, guardian spirits from the holy Selan′,
  Bring you heavenly love, vi′ ne see′, Lin′ se van′.

" Press ye on, my dear children, the holy Van′ la hoo′
  Is your heavenly guide, and will safely bear you through
  All vo′len tribulation you meet here below;
  Then be humble, dear children, be faithful and true.

" For God, your holy, holy HEAVENLY FATHER, will never,
  Never forsake his holy house of Israel on e.a.r.t.h.,
  But the blessings of heaven will continue to flow
  On you, my beloved Ar′ se le be low. (*n-o-t-e-s.*)"

The most curious relics of those days are two considerable volumes, which have since fallen into discredit among the Shakers themselves, but were at the time of their issue regarded as highly important. One of these is entitled " *A Holy, Sacred, and Divine Roll and Book, from the Lord God of Heaven to the Inhabitants of Earth :* Revealed in the United Society at New Lebanon, County of Columbia, State of

New York, United States of America. Received by the
Church of this Communion, and published in union with the
same." It is dated Canterbury, N. H., 1843 ; contains 405
pages ; and is in two parts. The first part contains the revelation proper ; the second, various " testimonies " to its accuracy
and divine origin. Of these evidences, some purport to be by
the prophets Elisha, Ezekiel, Malachi, Isaiah, and others ; from
Noah, St. Peter, St. John ; by " Holy and Eternal Mother Wisdom," and a " holy and mighty angel of God," whose name
was *Ma'ne Me'rah Vak'na Si'na Jah ;* but the greater number are by living Shakers. As a part of the revelation, the
Shakers were commanded to print, " in their own society, five
hundred copies " of this book, to be " given to the children of
men," and " it is my requirement that they be printed before
the 22d of next September. To be bound in yellow paper,
with red backs ; edges yellow also." Moreover, missionary societies were commanded to translate the book into foreign
tongues, and I have heard that a copy was sent to every ruler
or government which could be reached by mail.

The body of the book is a mixture of Scripture texts and
" revelations of spirits ;" and the absurdity of it appears to
have struck even the so-called " holy angel " who was supposed to have superintended the writing, as appears from the
following passage :

" We are four of the holy and mighty angels of God, sent from before
his throne, to pass and repass through the four quarters of the earth ;
and many are the holy angels that bear us company. And thus we shall
visit the earth in partial silence, as this Roll goes forth, until we have
marked the door-posts of all, as our God hath commanded, who shall
humble themselves and repent at his word, by proclaiming a solemn fast,
and cease from their awful crimes of wickedness, and turn to him in
righteousness.

" My name, says the angel whose quarter is eastward, and stands as
first, is HOLY ASSAN' DE LA JAH. The second, whose part is second, and quarter westward, is MI'CHAEL VAN' CE VA' NE. The

third, whose part is third, and quarter northward, is GA′ BRY VEN′ DO VAS′ TER REEN′. The fourth, whose part is fourth, and quarter southward, is VEN DEN′ DE PA′ ROL JEW′ LE JAH′.

" These are our names in our own tongues, and we are sent on earth to prepare the way for the Most High; and the whole human family will be convinced of this before the final event of our mission shall arrive.

" And although we know that the words of this book will be considered by many as being produced in the wildest of enthusiasm, madness, blasphemy, and fanaticism, and by others as solemn, sacred, and awful truths; yet do we declare unto all flesh that this Roll and Book contains the word of the God of heaven, your Almighty Creator, sent forth direct from his eternal throne now in this your day.

" And by this word shall every soul on earth be judged, in mercy or in judgment, whether they believe or disbelieve. We are not sent forth by our God to argue with mortals, but to declare his word and his work. And we furthermore declare unto all the inhabitants of earth that they have no time to lose in preparing for their God.

" If there be any who can not understand to their souls' satisfaction (though the requirements are plain), yet they may apply wheresoever they believe they can be correctly informed."

As a sample of the book, here is an account by one of the mediums of her " interview with a holy angel :"

" It was in the evening of the twenty-second of January, eighteen hundred and forty-two, while I was busily employed putting all things in readiness for the close of the week, that I distinctly heard my name called very loudly, and with much earnestness. I could not go so well at that moment, and I answered, ' I will come soon,' for I supposed it to be some one in the adjoining room that wished to see me; but the word was repeated three times, and I hastened to the place from whence the sound seemed to come, but there was no one present.

" I soon saw in the middle of the room four very large and bright lights, or balls of fire, as they appeared to be; they moved slowly each way, and after a little time joined together in one exceedingly large light, or pillar of fire. At this moment I heard a loud voice, which uttered many words with such mighty force that I feared to stay in the room, and attempted to go out; but found that I had not power to move my feet.

" For some time I could not understand one word that was sounded forth; but the first that I did understand were as follows: 'Hark! hark! hearken, O thou child of mortality, unto the word that is and shall be sounded aloud in thine ears, again and again, even until it is obeyed.

"'And lo, I say a time, and a time, and a half-time shall not pass by before my voice shall be heard, and my word sounded forth to the nations abroad. But in the Zion of my likeness and true righteousness shall it be received first, and from thence shall it go forth; for thus and thus hath the God of heaven and earth declared and purposed that it should be.

"'Then why will you, O why will you, yet fear to obey? What would you that your God would do in your presence, that you might fear his power rather than that of mortal man?'

"From this moment I was not sensible where I was; and after a little time of silence the body of light, or pillar of fire, dispersed, and I saw a mighty angel coming from the east, and I heard these words:

"'Woe, woe, and many woes shall be upon the mortal that shall see and will not stop to behold.'"

And so on, for a good many pages.

The second work is called "*The Divine Book of Holy and Eternal Wisdom, revealing the Word of God, out of whose mouth goeth a sharp Sword.* Written by Paulina Bates, at Watervliet, N. Y., United States of America; arranged and prepared for the Press at New Lebanon, N. Y. Published by the United Society called Shakers. Printed at Canterbury, N. H., 1849." This book contains 718 pages; and pretends also to be a series of revelations by angels and deceased persons of note. In the Preface by the editors its origin is thus described:

"During a number of years past many remarkable displays of divine power and heavenly gifts have been manifested among the children of Zion in all the branches of the United Society of Believers in the second appearing of Christ. Much increasing light has been revealed on many subjects which have heretofore remained as mysteries; and many prophetic revelations have been brought forth, from time to time, through messengers chosen and inspired by heavenly power and wisdom.

"Among these it has pleased God to select a female of the United Society at Wisdom's Valley (Watervliet), and indue her with the heavenly light of revelation as an instrument of divine Wisdom, to write by divine inspiration those solemn warnings, prophetic revelations, and heavenly instructions which will be found extensively diffused through the sacred pages of this book.

"These were written in a series of communications at various times during the year 1841, '42, '43, and '44, with few exceptions, which will be seen by their several dates. But the inspired writer had no knowledge that they were designed by the Divine Spirit to be published to the world until a large portion of the work was written; therefore, whenever she was called upon by the angel of God, she wrote whatever the angel dictated at the time, without any reference to the connective order and regular arrangement of a book; for she was not directed so to do, for reasons which were afterwards revealed to her and other witnesses then unknown to her.

"Hence it was made known to be the design of the Divine Spirit that these communications should be transmitted to the Holy Mount (New Lebanon), there to be prepared for publication by agents appointed for that purpose, in union with the leading authority of the Church. Accordingly they were conveyed to New Lebanon, and the subscribers were appointed as editors, to examine and arrange them in regular and convenient order for the press, and divine instructions were given for that purpose.

"Having therefore faithfully examined the manuscripts containing these communications, we have compiled them into one book, in two general divisions or volumes, agreeably to the instructions given. We have also, for convenient arrangement, divided the whole into seven parts, according to the relative connection which appeared in the different subjects. And for the convenience of the reader we have divided each part into chapters, prefixing an appropriate title to each.

"Some passages and annotations have been added by *The Angel of Prophetic Light*, who by inspiration has frequently assisted in the preparation and arrangement of the work, for the purpose of illustrating and confirming some of the original subjects by further explanations. A few notes have also been added by the editors for the information of the reader. These are all distinguished in their proper places from the original matter.

"But although it was found necessary to transcribe the whole, in order to prepare it properly and intelligibly for the press, yet we have used great care to preserve the sense of the original in its purity; and we can testify that the substance and spirit of the work have been conscientiously preserved in full throughout the whole.

"This work is called 'Holy Wisdom's Book,' because Holy and Eternal Wisdom is the Mother, or Bearing Spirit, of all the works of God; and because it was especially revealed through the line of the female, being WISDOM's *Likeness; and she lays special claim to this work*, and places her seal upon it.

"An *Appendix* is added, containing the testimonies of various divine and heavenly witnesses to the sacred truth and reality of the declarations and revelations contained in the work. The most of these were given before the inspired writers who received them had any earthly knowledge concerning the book or its contents. A *testimony* is also affixed to the work by the elders of the family in which the inspired writer resides, bearing witness to the honesty and uprightness of her character, and her faithfulness in the work of God."

The main object of the book is to warn sinners of all kinds from the "wrath to come." Especial woes, by the way, are denounced against slaveholders and slavetraders: "Whether they be clothed in tenements of clay, or whether they be stripped of their earthly tabernacles, the same hand of Justice shall meet them whithersoever they flee." It must be remembered to the honor of the Shakers that they have always and every where consistently opposed human slavery.

The "Divine Book of Holy Wisdom" contains the "testimonies" of the "first man, Adam," of the "first woman, Eve," of Noah and all the patriarchs, and of a great many other ancient worthies; but, alas! what they have to say is not new, and of no interest to the unregenerate reader.

These two volumes are not now, as formerly, held in honor by the Shakers. One of their elders declared to me that I ought never to have seen them, and that their best use was to burn them. But I found them on the table of the visitors' room in one or two of the Western societies, and I suppose they are still believed in by some of the people.

At this day most (but not all) of the Shaker people are sincere believers in what is commonly called Spiritualism. At a Shaker funeral I have heard what purported to be a message from the spirit whose body was lying in the coffin in the adjoining hall. In one of the societies it is believed that a magnificent spiritual city, densely inhabited, and filled with palaces and fine residences, lies upon their domain, and at but a little distance from the terrestrial buildings of the Church family; and frequent communications come from this spirit city to their neighbors. "When I was a little girl, I desired very much to have a hymn sent through me to the family from the spirit-land; and after waiting and wishing for a long time, one day when I was little expecting it, as I was walking about, a hymn came to me thus, to my inexpressible delight"—so said a Shaker eldress to me in all seriousness. "We have frequently been visited by a tribe of Indians (spirits of Indians), who used to live in this country, and whose spirits still come back here occasionally," said another Shaker sister to me.

On the other hand, when I asked one of the elders how far he believed that their hymns are inspired, he asked me whether it did not happen that I wrote with greater facility at one time than at another; and when I replied in the affirmative, he said, "In that case I should say you were inspired when your words come readily, and to that degree I suppose our hymn-writers are inspired. They have thought about the subject, and the words at last come to them."

I think I have before said that the Shakers do not attempt to suppress discussion of the relations of the sexes; they do not pretend that their celibate life is without hardships or difficulties; but they boldly assert that they have chosen the better life, and defend their position with not a little skill against all attacks. A good many years ago Miss Charlotte Cushman, after a visit to Watervliet, wrote the following lines, which were published in the *Knickerbocker Magazine:*

"Mysterious worshipers!
Are you indeed the things you seem to be,
Of earth—yet of its iron influence free—

From all that stirs
Our being's pulse, and gives to fleeting life
What well the Hun has termed "the rapture of the strife?"

"Are the gay visions gone,
Those day-dreams of the mind, by fate there flung,
And the fair hopes to which the soul once clung,
     And battled on;
Have ye outlived them? All that must have sprung,
And quicken'd into life, when ye were young?

"Does memory never roam
To ties that, grown with years, ye idly sever,
To the old haunts that ye have left forever—
     Your early homes?
Your ancient creed, once faith's sustaining lever,
The loved who erst prayed with you—now may never?

"Has not ambition's pæan
Some power within your hearts to wake anew
To deeds of higher emprise—worthier you,
     Ye monkish men,
Than may be reaped from fields? Do ye not rue
The drone-like course of life ye now pursue?

"The camp—the council—all
That woos the soldier to the field of fame—
That gives the sage his meed—the bard his name
     And coronal—
Bidding a people's voice their praise proclaim;
Can ye forego the strife, nor own your shame?

"Have ye forgot your youth,
When expectation soared on pinions high,
And hope shone out on boyhood's cloudless sky,
     Seeming all truth—
When all looked fair to fancy's ardent eye,
And pleasure wore an air of sorcery?

"You, too! What early blight
Has withered your fond hopes, that ye thus stand,
A group of sisters, 'mong this monkish band?

Ye creatures bright!
Has sorrow scored your brows with demon hand,
Or o'er your hopes passed treachery's burning brand?

"Ye would have graced right well
The bridal scene, the banquet, or the bowers
Where mirth and revelry usurp the hours—
Where, like a spell,
Beauty is sovereign—where man owns its powers,
And woman's tread is o'er a path of flowers.

"Yet seem ye not as those
Within whose bosoms memories vigils keep:
Beneath your drooping lids no passions sleep;
And your pale brows
Bear not the tracery of emotion deep—
Ye seem too cold and passionless to weep!"

A "Shaker Girl," in one of the Kentucky societies, published soon afterward the following "Answer to Charlotte Cushman," which is certainly not without spirit:

"We are, indeed, the things we seem to be,
Of earth, and from its iron influence free:
For we are they, or halt, or lame, or dumb,
'On whom the ends of this vain world are come.'
We have outlived those day-dreams of the mind—
Those flattering phantoms which so many bind;
All man-made creeds (your 'faith's sustaining lever')
We have forsaken, and have left forever!
To plainly tell the truth, we do not rue
The sober, godly course that we pursue;
But 'tis not we who live the dronish lives,
But those who have their husbands or their wives!
But if by drones you mean they're lazy men,
Then, Charlotte Cushman, take it back again;
For one, with half an eye, or half a mind,
Can there see industry and wealth combined.
If camps and councils—soldiers' 'fields of fame'—
Or yet a people's praise or people's blame,

Is all that gives the sage or bard his name,
We can 'forego the strife, nor own our shame.'
  What great temptations you hold up to view
For men of sense or reason to pursue!
The praise of mortals!—what can it avail,
When all their boasted language has to fail?
  And 'sorrow hath not scored with demon hand,'
Nor 'o'er our hopes pass'd treachery's burning brand;'
But where the sorrows and the treachery are,
I think may easily be made appear.
In 'bridal scenes,' in 'banquets and in bowers!' ⎫
'Mid revelry and variegated flowers, ⎬
Is where your mother Eve first felt their powers. ⎭
The 'bridal scenes,' you say, 'we'd grace right well!'
'Lang syne' there our first parents blindly fell!—
The bridal scene! Is this your end and aim?
And can you this pursue, 'nor own your shame?'
If so—weak, pithy, superficial thing—
Drink, silent drink the sick hymeneal spring.
  'The bridal scene! the banquet or the bowers,
Or woman's [bed of thorns, or] path of flowers,'
Can't all persuade our souls to turn aside
To live in filthy lust or cruel pride.
  Alas! your path of flowers will disappear;
E'en now a thousand thorns are pointed near;
Ah! here you find 'base treachery's burning brand,'
And sorrows score the heart, nor spare the hand;
But here 'Beauty's sovereign'—so say you—
A thing that in one hour may lose its hue—
It lies upon the surface of the skin—
Aye, Beauty's self was never worth a pin;
But still it suits the superficial mind—
The slight observer of the human kind;
The airy, fleety, vain, and hollow thing,
That only feeds on wily flattering.
'Man owns its powers?' And what will not man own
To gain his end—to captivate—dethrone?
The truth is this, whatever he may feign,
You'll find your greatest loss his greatest gain;

For like the bee, he will improve the hour,
And all day long he'll hunt from flower to flower,
And when he sips the sweetness all away,
For aught he cares, the flowers may all decay.
But here, each other's virtues we partake,
Where men and women all their ills forsake:
True virtue spreads her bright angelic wing,
While saints and seraphs praise the Almighty King.
And when the matter's rightly understood,
You'll find we labor for each other's good;
This, Charlotte Cushman, truly is our aim—
Can you forego this strife, 'nor own your shame?'
   Now if you would receive a modest hint,
You'd surely keep your name at least from print;
Nor have it hoisted, handled round and round,
And echoed o'er the earth from mound to mound,
As the great advocate of ———— (Oh, the name!).
Now can you think of this, 'nor own your shame?'
   But, Charlotte, learn to take a deeper view
Of what your neighbors say or neighbors do;
And when some flattering knaves around you tread,
Just think of what a SHAKER GIRL has said."

The *Shaker and Shakeress*, a monthly journal, edited by Elder Frederick Evans and Eldress Antoinette Doolittle, is the organ of the society; and in its pages their views are set forth with much shrewdness and ability. It is not so generally interesting a journal as the *Oneida Circular*, the organ of the Perfectionists, because the Shakers concern themselves almost exclusively with religious matters, and give in their paper but few details of their daily and practical life.

POPULATION RETURNS OF THE SHAKER SOCIETIES.

I give here, in a convenient tabular form, figures showing the present and past numbers of the different Shaker Societies—males, females, and children—the amount of land each society owns, and the number of laborers, not members, it employs:

Society.	No. of Families or Separate Communities.	Adults.		Youth under 21.		Total, 1874.	Population, 1823.	Greatest Population.	Acres of Land.	Hired Laborers.
		Male.	Female.	Male.	Female.					
Alfred, Me.	2	20	30	8	12	70	200	200	1100	15–20
New Gloucester, Me.	2	20	36	4	10	70	150	150	2000	15–20
Canterbury, N. H.	3	35	70	14	26	145	200	300	3000	6
Enfield, N. H.	3	29	76	8	27	140	200	330	3000	20–35
Enfield, Conn.	4	24	48	18	25	115	200	200	3300	15
Harvard, Mass.	4	17	57	4	12	90	200	200	1800	16
Shirley, Mass.	2	6	30	4	8	48	150	150	2000	10
Hancock, Mass.	3	23	42	13	20	98	—	300	3500	25
Tyringham, Mass.	1	6	11	0	0	17	—	—	1000	6
Mount Lebanon, N. Y.	7	115	221	21	26	383	500–600	600	3000	—
Watervliet, N. Y.	4	75	100	20	40	235	200	350	4500	75
Groveland, N. Y.	2	18	30	3	6	57	150 in 1836.	200	2280	8
North Union, O.	3	41	44	6	11	102	—	200	1355	9
Union Village, O.	4	75	92	20	28	215	600	600	4500	70
Watervliet, O.	2	16	32	3	4	55	100	100	1300	10
White Water, O.	3	34	51	6	9	100	150	150	1500	10
Pleasant Hill, Ky.	5	56	114	25	50	245	450	490	4200	20
South Union, Ky.	4	85	105	15	25	230	349	349	6000	15
Eighteen Societies.	58	695	1189	192	339	2415	—	—	49,335	—

The returns of land include, for the most part, only the home farms; and several of the societies own considerable quantities of real estate in distant states, of which I could get no precise returns.

THE PERFECTIONISTS

OF

ONEIDA AND WALLINGFORD.

THE PERFECTIONISTS OF ONEIDA AND WALLINGFORD.

I.—Historical.

The Oneida and Wallingford Communists are of American origin, and their membership is almost entirely American.

Their founder, who is still their head, John Humphrey Noyes, was born in Brattleboro, Vermont, in 1811, of respectable parentage. He graduated from Dartmouth College, began the study of the law, but turned shortly to theology; and studied first at Andover, with the intention of fitting himself to become a foreign missionary, and later in the Yale theological school. At New Haven he came under the influence of a zealous revival preacher, and during his residence there he "landed in a new experience and new views of the way of salvation, which took the name of Perfectionism."

This was in 1834. He soon returned to Putney, in Vermont, where his father's family then lived, and where his father was a banker. There he preached and printed; and in 1838 married Harriet A. Holton, the granddaughter of a member of Congress, and a convert to his doctrines.

He slowly gathered about him a small company of believers, drawn from different parts of the country, and with their help made known his new faith in various publications, with such effect that though in 1847 he had only about forty persons in his own congregation, there appear to have been small gatherings of "Perfectionists" in other states, in correspondence with Noyes, and inclined to take him as their leader.

Originally Noyes was not a Communist, but when his thoughts turned in that direction he began to prepare his followers for communal life; in 1845 he made known to them his peculiar views of the relations of the sexes, and in 1846 the society at Putney began cautiously an experiment in communal living.

Their views, which they never concealed, excited the hostility of the people to such a degree that they were mobbed and driven out of the place; and in the spring of 1848 they joined some persons of like faith and practice at Oneida, in Madison County, New York. Here they began community life anew, on forty acres of land, on which stood an unpainted frame dwelling-house, an abandoned Indian hut, and an old Indian saw-mill. They owed for this property two thousand dollars. The place was neglected, without cultivation, and the people were so poor that for some time they had to sleep on the floor in the garret which was their principal sleeping-chamber.

The gathering at Oneida appears to have been the signal for several attempts by followers of Noyes to establish themselves in communes. In 1849 a small society was formed in Brooklyn, N. Y., to which later the printing for all the societies was intrusted. In 1850 another community was begun at Wallingford, in Connecticut. There were others, of which I find no account; but all regarded Oneida as their centre and leader; and in the course of time, and after various struggles, all were drawn into the common centre, except that at Wallingford, which still exists in a flourishing condition, having its property and other interests in common with Oneida.

The early followers of Noyes were chiefly New England farmers, the greater part of whom brought with them some means, though not in any single case a large amount. Noyes himself and several other members contributed several thousand dollars each, and a "Property Register" kept from the beginning of the community experiment showed that up to the first of January, 1857, the members of all the associated

J. H. NOYES, FOUNDER OF THE PERFECTIONISTS.

communes had brought in the considerable amount of one hundred and seven thousand seven hundred and six dollars. I understand, however, that this sum was not at any one time in hand, and that much of it came in several years after the settlement at Oneida in 1848; and it is certain that in the early days, while they were still seeking for some business which should be at the same time agreeable to them and profitable, they had sometimes short commons. They showed great courage and perseverance, for through all their early difficulties they maintained a printing-office and circulated a free paper.

At first they looked toward agriculture and horticulture as their main-stays for income; but they began soon to unite other trades with these. Their saw-mill sawed lumber for the neighboring farmers; they set up a blacksmith shop, and here, besides other work, they began to make traps by hand, having at first no means to buy machinery, and indeed having to invent most of that which they now use in their extensive trap shop.

Like the Shakers with their garden seeds, and all other successful communities with their products, the Perfectionists got their start by the excellence of their workmanship. Their traps attracted attention because they were more uniformly well made than others; and thus they built up a trade which has become very large. They raised small fruits, made rustic furniture, raised farm crops, sold cattle, had at one time a sloop on the Hudson; and Noyes himself labored as a blacksmith, farmer, and in many other employments.

Working thus under difficulties, they had sunk, by January, 1857, over forty thousand dollars of their capital, but had gained valuable experience in the mean time. They had concentrated all their people at Oneida and Wallingford; and had set up some machinery at the former place. In January, 1857, they took their first annual inventory, and found themselves worth a little over sixty-seven thousand dollars. Their perseverance had conquered fortune, for in the next ten years the net profit of the two societies amounted to one hundred and eighty thousand five hundred and eighty dollars, according to this statement:

Net earnings in 1857.....$5,470 11	Net earnings in 1862....$9,859 78
" " 1858..... 1,763 60	" " 1863....44,755 30
" " 1859.....10,278 38	" " 1864....61,382 62
" " 1860.....15,611 03	" " 1865....12,382 81
" " 1861..... 5,877 89	" " 1866....13,198 74

During this time they made traps, traveling-bags and satchels, mop-holders, and various other small articles, and put up preserved fruits in glass and tin. They began at Wallingford, in 1851, making match-boxes, and the manufacture of traveling-bags was begun in Brooklyn, and later transferred to Oneida. Trap-making was begun at Oneida in 1855; fruit-preserving in 1858, and in 1866 the silk manufacture was established.

Meantime they bought land, until they have in 1874, near Oneida, six hundred and fifty-four acres, laid out in orchards, vineyards, meadows, pasture and wood land, and including several valuable water-powers; and at Wallingford two hundred and forty acres, mainly devoted to grazing and the production of small fruits. They have erected in both places commodious and substantial dwellings and shops, and carry on at this time a number of industries, of which some account will be found further on.

The two communities, whose members are interchangeable at will and whenever necessity arises, must be counted as one. At Oneida they have founded a third, on a part of their land, called Willow Place, but this too is but an offshoot of the central family. In February, 1874, they numbered two hundred and eighty-three persons, of whom two hundred and thirty-eight were at Oneida and Willow Place, and forty-five at Wallingford. Of these one hundred and thirty-one were males,

and one hundred and fifty-two females. Of the whole number, sixty-four were children and youth under twenty-one—
thirty-three males and thirty-one females. Of the two hundred and nineteen adults, one hundred and five were over forty-
five years of age—forty-four men and sixty-one women.

They employ in both places from twenty to thirty-five farm
laborers, according to the season, and a number of fruit-pickers
in the time of small fruits. Besides, at Oneida they employ
constantly two hundred and one hired laborers, of whom one
hundred and three are women, seventy-five of whom work in
the silk factory; sixty-seven of the men being engaged in the
trap works, foundry, and machine shops. At Wallingford the
silk works give employment to thirty-five hired women and girls.

Originally, and for many years, these Communists employed
no outside labor in their houses; but with increasing prosperity they have begun to hire servants and helpers in many
branches. Thus at Oneida there are in the laundry two men
and five women; in the kitchen three men and seven women;
in the heating or furnace room two men; in the shoemaker's
shop two; and in the tailor's shop two—all hired people. At
Wallingford they hire three women and one man for their
laundry.

These hired people are the country neighbors of the commune; and, as with the Shakers and the Harmonists, they
like their employers. These pay good wages, and treat their
servants kindly; looking after their physical and intellectual
well-being, building houses for such of them as have families
and need to be near at hand, and in many ways showing interest in their welfare.

The members of the two societies are for the most part
Americans, though there are a few English and Canadians.
There are among them lawyers, clergymen, merchants, physicians, teachers; but the greater part were New England farmers and mechanics. Former Congregationalists and Presbyte-

rians, Episcopalians, Methodists, and Baptists are among them —but no Catholics.

They have a great number of applications from persons desirous to become members. During 1873 they received over one hundred such by letter, besides a nearly equal number made in person. They are not willing now to accept new members; but I believe they are looking about for a place suitable for a new settlement, and would not be unwilling, if a number of persons with sufficient means for another colony should present themselves, to help them with teachers and guides.

In the year 1873 the Oneida Community produced and sold preserved fruits to the value of $27,417; machine and sewing silk and woven goods worth $203,784; hardware, including traps, chucks, silk-measuring machines and silk-strength testers (the last two of their own invention), gate-hinges and foundry castings, $90,447. They raised twenty-five acres of sweet corn, six acres of tomatoes, two acres of strawberries, two of raspberries; half an acre of currants, half an acre of grapes, twenty-two acres of apples, and three and a half acres of pears.

Silk-weaving has been abandoned, as not suitable to them.

At the beginning of 1874 they were worth over half a million of dollars.

From the beginning, Noyes and his followers have made great use of the press. Up to the time of their settlement at Oneida they had published " Paul not Carnal;" two series of *The Perfectionist; The Way of Holiness*, the *Berean*, and *The Witness*. From Oneida they began at once to issue the *Spiritual Magazine*, and, later, the *Free Church Circular*, which was the beginning of their present journal, the *Oneida Circular*. " Bible Communism" also was published at Oneida during the first year of their settlement there. They did not aim to make money by their publications, and the *Circular* was from the first published on terms probably unlike those of any other newspaper in the world. I take from an old number, of the year 1853, the following announcement, standing at the head of the first column:

"The *Circular* is published by Communists, and for Communists. Its main object is to help the education of several confederated associations, who are practically devoted to the Pentecost principle of community of property. Nearly all of its readers outside of those associations are Communists in principle. It is supported almost entirely by the free contributions of this Communist constituency. A paper with such objects and such resources can not properly be offered for sale. Freely we receive, and we freely give. Whoever wishes to read the *Circular* can have it WITHOUT PAYING, OR PROMISING TO PAY, by applying through the mail, or at 43 Willow Place, Brooklyn. If any one chooses to pay, he may send TWO DOLLARS for the yearly volume; but he must not require us to keep his accounts. We rely on the free gifts of the family circle for which we labor."

This paper was published on these terms, at one time semi-weekly, and at another three times a week. For some years past it has appeared weekly, printed on extremely good paper, and an admirable specimen of typography; and it has now at the head of its columns the following notice:

"The *Circular* is sent to all applicants, whether they pay or not. It costs and is worth at least two dollars per volume. Those who want it and ought to have it are divisible into three classes, viz.: 1, those who can not afford to pay two dollars; 2, those who can afford to pay *only* two dollars; and, 3, those who can afford to pay *more* than two dollars. The first ought to have it free; the second ought to pay the cost of it; and the third ought to pay enough more than the cost to make up the deficiencies of the first. This is the law of Communism. We have no means of enforcing it, and no wish to do so, except by stating it and leaving it to the good sense of those concerned. We take the risk of offering the *Circular* to all without price; but free subscriptions will be received only from persons making application for themselves, either directly or by giving express authority to those who apply for them.

"Foreign subscribers, except those residing in Canada, must remit with their subscriptions money to prepay the postage."

They print now about two thousand copies per week, and lost last year six hundred dollars in the enterprise, without reckoning what would have had to be paid in any other work of the kind for literary labor.

A list of the works they have issued will be found, with the titles of works issued by other communistic societies, at the end of the volume.

Aside from its religious and communistic teachings, the *Circular* has a general interest, by reason of articles it often contains relating to natural history and natural scenery, which, from different pens, show that there are in the society some close observers of nature, who have also the ability to relate their observations and experiences in excellent English.   In general, the style of the paper is uncommonly good, and shows that there is a degree of culture among the Oneida people which preserves them from the too common newspaper vice of fine English.

Their publications deal with the utmost frankness with their own religious and social theories and practices, and I suppose it may be said that they aim to keep themselves and their doctrines before the public.   In this respect they differ from all the other Communistic societies now existing in this country. That they are not without a sense of humor in these efforts, the following, printed as advertisements in the *Circular*, will show:

G RAND FIRE ANNIHILATOR!—AN INVENTION for overcoming Evil with Good.

MEEK & LOWLY.

T O JEWELERS.—A SINGLE PEARL OF GREAT PRICE!   This inestimable Jewel may be obtained by application to Jesus Christ, at the extremely low price of " all that a man hath !"

TO BROKERS.

W ANTED.—Any amount of SHARES OF SECOND-COMING STOCK, bearing date A.D. 70, or thereabouts, will find a ready market and command a high premium at this office.

ATTENTION!

SOLDIERS who claim to have "fought the fight of faith" will find it for their advantage to have their claims investigated. All who can establish said claim are entitled to a bounty land-warrant in the kingdom of Heaven, and a pension for eternity.

ROOMS TO LET in the "Many Mansions" that Christ has prepared for those that love him.

DIRECTIONS for cultivating the fruits of the Spirit may be obtained *gratis*, at   MEEK & LOWLY'S,
                    No. 1 Grace Court.

Practical Reflections on CHRIST'S SERMON ON THE MOUNT may be had also as above.

LEGAL NOTICE. — Notice is hereby given that all claims issued by the old firm of Moses and Law were canceled 1800 years ago. Any requirement, therefore, to observe as a means of righteousness legal enactments bearing date prior to A.D. 70, is pronounced by us, on the authority of the New Testament, a fraud and imposition.

THE EYES! THE EYES!!—It is known that many persons with two eyes habitually "see double." To prevent stumbling and worse liabilities in such circumstances, an ingenious contrivance has been invented by which the WHOLE BODY is filled with light. It is called the "SINGLE EYE," and may be obtained by applying to Jesus Christ.

WATER-CURE ESTABLISHMENT. — I will sprinkle clean water upon you, and ye shall be clean: from all your filthiness, and from all your idols, will I cleanse you. A new heart also will I give you, and a new spirit will I put within you: and I will take away the stony heart out of your flesh, and I will give you a heart of flesh.—Ezekiel xxxvi., 25, 26.

PATENT SIEVES.—The series of sieves for CRITICISM having been thoroughly tested, are now offered to the public for general use. They are warranted to sift the tares from the wheat, and in all cases to discriminate between good and evil. A person, after having passed through this series, comes out free from the incumbrances of egotism, pride, etc., etc. All persons are invited to test them gratuitously.

MAGNIFICENT RESTAURANT!—In Mount Zion will the Lord of hosts make unto all people a feast of fat things, a feast of wines on the lees; of fat things full of marrow, of wines on the lees well refined. And he will destroy in this mountain the face of the covering cast over all people, and the veil that is spread over all nations. He will swallow up death in victory; and the Lord God will wipe away tears from off all faces; and the rebuke of his people shall be taken away from off all the earth: for the Lord hath spoken it.—Isaiah xxv., 6–8.

PATENT SALAMANDER SAFES. — Lay not up for yourselves treasures upon earth, where moth and rust doth corrupt, and where thieves break through and steal: but lay up for yourselves treasures in heaven, where neither moth nor rust doth corrupt, and where thieves do not break through nor steal.—Matt. vi., 19, 20. This safe, having been submitted for 1800 years to the hottest fire of judgment, and having been through that time subject to constant attacks from the fiery shafts of the devil, is now offered to the public, with full confidence that it will meet with general approbation. Articles inclosed in this safe are warranted free from danger under any circumstances.

TO THE AFFLICTED!—WINE and MILK for the hungry, REST for the weary and heavy-laden, CONSOLATION and BALM for the wounded and invalids of every description—may be had *gratis*, on application to the storehouse of the Son of God.

The *Circular* contains each week extracts from journals kept in the two communities, and "Talks" by Noyes and others, with a variety of other matter relating to their belief and daily lives.

II.—RELIGIOUS BELIEF AND FAITH - CURES.

They call themselves "Perfectionists."

They hold to the Bible as the "text-book of the Spirit of truth;" to "Jesus Christ as the eternal Son of God;" to "the apostles and Primitive Church as the exponents of the everlasting Gospel." They believe that "the second advent of Christ took place at the period of the destruction of Jerusalem;" that "at that time there was a primary resurrection and judgment in the spirit world;" and "that the final kingdom of God then began in the heavens; that the manifestation of that kingdom in the visible world is now approaching; that its approach is ushering in the second and final resurrection and judgment; that a Church on earth is now rising to meet the approaching kingdom in the heavens, and to become its duplicate and representative; that inspiration, or open communication with God and the heavens, involving perfect holiness, is the element of connection between the Church on earth and the Church in the heavens, and the power by which the kingdom of God is to be established and reign in the world."*

They assert, further, that "the Gospel provides for complete salvation from sin"—hence the name they assume of "Perfectionists." "Salvation from sin," they say, "is the foundation needed by all other reforms."

"Do you, then, claim to live sinless lives?" I asked ; and received this answer :

"We consider the community to be a Church, and our theory of a Christian Church, as constituted in the apostolic age, is that it is a school, consisting of many classes, from those who are in the lowest degree of faith to those who have attained the condition of certain and eternal salvation from sin. The only direct answer, therefore, that we can give to your question is that some of us claim to live sinless lives, and some do not. A sinless life is the *standard* of the community, which all believe to be practicable, and to which all are taught to aspire. Yet we recognize the two general classes, which were characterized by Paul as the "nepiou" and the "teleioi." Our belief is that a Christian Church can exist only when the "teleioi" are in the ascendant and have control."

In compliance with my request, the following definition of "Perfectionism" was written out for me as authoritative :

"The bare doctrine of Perfectionism might be presented in a single sentence thus :

"As the doctrine of temperance is total abstinence from alcoholic drinks, and the doctrine of anti-slavery is immediate abolition of human bondage, so the doctrine of Perfectionism is immediate and total cessation from sin.

"But the analogy thus suggested between Perfectionism and two popular reforms is by no means to be regarded as defining the character and methods of Perfectionism. Salvation from

---

* Statement in the *Circular.*

sin, as we understand it, is not a system of duty-doing under a code of dry laws, Scriptural or natural; but is a special phase of *religious experience*, having for its basis spiritual intercourse with God. All religionists of the positive sort believe in a personal God, and assume that he is a sociable being. This faith leads them to seek intercourse with him, to approach him by prayer, to give him their hearts, to live in communion with him. These exercises and the various states and changes of the inner life connected with them constitute the staple of what is commonly called *religious experience.* Such experience, of course, has more or less effect on the character and external conduct. We can not live in familiar intercourse with human beings without becoming better or worse under their influence; and certainly fellowship with God must affect still more powerfully all the springs of action. Perfectionists hold that intercourse with God may proceed so far as to destroy selfishness in the heart, and so make an end of sin. This is the special phase of religious experience which we profess, and for which we are called Perfectionists."

Among other matters, they hold that " the Jews are, by God's perpetual covenant, the royal nation ;" that the obligation to observe the Sabbath passed away with the Jewish dispensation, and is " adverse to the advance of man into new and true arrangements ;" that " the original organization instituted by Christ [the Primitive Church] is accessible to us, and that our main business as reformers is to open communication with that heavenly body ;" and they " refer all their experience to the invisible hosts who are contending over them."

I must add, to explain the last sentence, that they are not Spiritualists in the sense in which that word is nowadays usually employed, and in which the Shakers are Spiritualists; but they hold that they are in a peculiar and direct manner under the guidance of God and good spirits. " Saving faith, according to the Bible, places man in such a relation to God that he is authorized to ask favors of him as a child asks favors of his father. Prayer without expectation of an answer is a performance not sanctioned by Scripture nor by common-sense. But prayer with expectation of an answer (that is, the prayer of faith) is impossible, on the supposition that 'the age of miracles is past,' and that God no longer interferes with the regular routine of nature." Hence their belief in what they call " Faith-cures," of which I shall speak further on.

Community of goods and of persons they hold to have been taught and commanded by Jesus : " Jesus Christ offers to save men from all evil—from sin and death itself ; but he always states it as a necessary condition of their accepting his help that they shall forsake all other ; and particularly that they shall get rid of their private property." Communism they hold therefore to be " the social state of the resurrection." " The account on the sides of life and death arranges itself thus :

APOSTASY,	RESTORATION,
UNBELIEF,	FAITH,
Obedience to	Obedience to
Mammon,	*Christ*,
PRIVATE PROPERTY,	COMMUNISM,
DEATH.	IMMORTALITY."

The community system, which they thus hold to have been divinely commanded, they extend beyond property—to persons ; and thus they justify their extraordinary social system, in which there is no marriage ; or, as they put it, " complex marriage takes the place of simple." They surround this singular and, so far as I know, unprecedented combination of polygamy and polyandry with certain religious and social restraints ; but affirm that there is " no intrinsic difference between property in persons and property in things ; and that the same spirit which abolished exclusiveness in regard to money would abolish, if circumstances allowed full scope to it, exclusiveness in regard to women and children."*

It is an extraordinary evidence of the capacity of mankind for various and extreme religious beliefs, that many men have brought their wives and young daughters into the Oneida Community.

They have no preaching; do not use Baptism nor the Lord's Supper; do not observe Sunday, because they hold that with them every day is a Sabbath; do not pray aloud; and avoid with considerable care all set forms. They read the Bible and quote it much.

They believe that the exercise of sufficient faith in prayer to God is capable of restoring the sick to health; and assert that there have been in their experience and among their membership a number of such cures. In a " Free-Church Tract," dated " Oneida Reserve, 1850," there is an account of such a cure of Mrs. M. A. Hall, ill of consumption, and given up by her physicians. In this case J. H. Noyes and Mrs. Cragin were those whose " power of faith " was supposed to have acted; and Mrs. Hall herself wrote, two years later: " From a helpless, bed-ridden state, in which I was unable to move, or even to be moved without excruciating pain, I was *instantly* raised to a consciousness of perfect health. I was constrained to declare again and again that I was perfectly well. My eyes, which before could not bear the light, were opened to the blaze of day and became strong. My appetite was restored, and all pain removed." This is said to have taken place in June, 1847. The following case is reported in the *Circular* for February 9th of the present year (1874), and the description of the injury, which immediately follows, is given by Dr. Cragin—a member of the Oneida Community—whom I understand to be a regularly educated physician. The sufferer was a woman, Mrs. M.

---

* " History of American Socialisms," by J. H. Noyes, p. 625.

"Her hand was passed between the rubber rollers of a wringing-machine. The machine was new, and the rollers were screwed down so that it brought a very heavy pressure on her hand, evidently crowding the bones all out of place and stretching the ligaments, besides seriously injuring the nerves of her hand and arm. When she came here from Wallingford Community, several weeks after the accident, not only the nerves of her hand were essentially paralyzed, but the trunk nerve of her arm was paralyzed and caused her a great deal of suffering. It was as helpless as though completely paralyzed: she had not sufficient control over her hand to bend her fingers.

"That was her condition up to the time of the cure. I could not see from the time she came here to the time of the cure that there was any change for the better. I told her the first time I examined her hand that, according to the ordinary course of such things, she must not expect to get the use of it under twelve months, if she did then. At the same time I told her I would not limit the power of God.

"Her general health improved, but her hand caused her the acutest suffering. It would awaken her in the night, and oblige her to get up and spend hours in rubbing it and trying to allay the pain. If any one has had a jumping toothache, he can imagine something what her suffering was, only the pain extended over the whole hand and arm, instead of being confined to one small place like a tooth. I have known of strong men who had the nervous system of an arm similarly affected, who begged that their arms might be taken off, and have indeed suffered amputation rather than endure the pain.

"For some time before her cure there had been considerable talk in the family about faith-cures, and persons had talked with her on the subject, and encouraged her to expect to have such a cure as Harriet Hall did. Finally Mr. Noyes's interest was aroused, and he invoked a committee for her—not so much to criticise as to comfort her, and bring to bear on her the concentrated attention and faith of the family. She was stimulated by this criticism to cheerfulness and hope, and to put herself into the social current, keeping around as much as she could where there was the most life and faith. A private criticism soon after penetrated her spirit, and separated her from a brooding influence of evil that she had come under in a heart affair.

"Still she suffered with her hand as much as ever, up to the time of her sudden cure. A few evenings after this private criticism we had a very interesting meeting, and she was present in the gallery. The subject was the power of prayer, and there was a good deal of faith experience related, and she appeared the next morning shaking hands with every body she met. Now you see her washing dishes and making beds.

"*Mrs. A.*—The morning she was cured I was at work in the hall, when she came running toward me, saying, 'I'm cured! I'm cured!' Then she shook hands with me, using the hand that had been so bad, and giving a hearty pressure with it.

"*Dr. C.*—To show that the case is not one of imagination, I will say that the day before the cure she could not have it *touched* without suffering pain. She had not been dressed for a week, but that morning she bathed and dressed herself and made her bed, and then went to Joppa.

"*Mr. N.*—She came down to Joppa with her hands all free, and went out on the ice; I don't know that she caught any fish, but she attended the 'tip-ups.'

"*Mrs. C.*—She said to me that she had attended to dieting and all the prescriptions that were given her, and got no help from them; and she had made up her mind that if there was any thing done for her, the community must take hold and do it.

"*W. A. H.*—Let us be united about this case; and if it be imagination, let us have more of it; and if it be the power of faith, let us have more faith.

"*C. W. U.*—Was Mrs. M. conscious of any precise moment when the pain left her in the night?

"*Mrs. M.* [the person who was cured].—After the meeting in which we talked about faith-cures, I went to my room and prayed to God to take the pain out of my hand, and told him if he did I would glorify him with it. The pain left me, and I could stretch out my arm farther than I had been able to since it was hurt. I went to bed, and slept until four o'clock without waking; then I awoke and found I was not in pain, and that I could stretch out my arm and move my fingers. Then I thought— 'I am well.' I got up, took a bath, and dressed myself. After this my arm ached some, but I said, 'I am well; I am made every whit whole.' I kept saying that to myself, and the pain left me entirely. My arm has begun to ache nearly every day since then, but I insist that I am well, and the pain ceases. That arm is not yet as strong as the other, but is improving daily.

"*Mrs. C.*—I have had considerable of that kind of experience during the last few years. For two years I raised blood a good deal, and thought a great many times that I was going to die—could not get that idea out of my mind. Mrs. M. talked with me about it, and told me I must not give up to my imaginations. I was put into business two years ago, and some days my head swam so that I could hardly go about, but I did what was given me to do ; and finally I came to a point in my experience where I said, 'I don't care if I do raise blood; I am not going to be frightened by it; I had as soon raise blood as do any thing else.' When I got there my trouble left me."

I have copied this account at some length, because it speaks in detail of a quite recent occurrence, and shows, in a characteristic way, their manner of dealing with disease.

They profess also to have wrought cures by what they call " Criticism," of which I shall speak further on.

Concerning their management of the intercourse of the sexes, so much has been written, by themselves and by others, that I think I need here say only that—

1st. They regard their system as part of their religion. Noyes said, in a " Home Talk," reported in the *Circular*, February 2, 1874: "Woe to him who abolishes the law of the apostasy before he stands in the holiness of the resurrection. The law of the apostasy is the law of marriage ; and it is true that whoever undertakes to enter into the liberty of the resurrection without the holiness of the resurrection, will get woe and not happiness. It is as important for the young now as it was for their fathers then, that they should know that holiness of heart is what they must have before they get liberty in love. They must put the first thing first, as I did and as their parents did ; they must be *Perfectionists* before they are *Communists*." He seems to see, too, that " complex marriage," as he calls it, is not without grave dangers to the community, for he added, in the same " Home Talk :" "We have got into the position of Communism, where without genuine salvation from sin our passions will overwhelm us, and nothing but confu sion and misery can be expected. On the other hand, we have got into a position where, if we do have the grace of God triumphant in our hearts and flowing through all our nature, there is an opportunity for harmony and happiness beyond all that imagination has conceived. So it is hell behind us, and heaven before us, and a necessity that we should *march !*"

2d. "Complex marriage" means, in their practice: that, within the limits of the community membership, any man and woman may and do freely cohabit, having first gained each other's consent, not by private conversation or courtship, but through the intervention of some third person or persons; that they strongly discourage, as an evidence of sinful selfishness, what they call "exclusive and idolatrous attachment" of two persons for each other, and aim to break up by "criticism" and other means every thing of this kind in the community; that they teach the advisability of pairing persons of different ages, the young of one sex with the aged of the other, and as the matter is under the control and management of the more aged members it is thus arranged; that "persons are not obliged, under any circumstances, to receive the attentions of those whom they do not like;" and that the propagation of children is controlled by the society, which pretends to conduct this matter on scientific principles: "Previous to about two and a half years ago we refrained from the usual rate of childbearing, for several reasons, financial and otherwise. Since that time we have made an attempt to produce the usual number of offspring to which people in the middle classes are able to afford judicious moral and spiritual care, with the advantage of a liberal education. In this attempt twenty-four men and twenty women have been engaged, selected from among those who have most thoroughly practiced our social theory."*

Finally, they find in practice a strong tendency toward what they call "selfish love"—that is to say, the attachment

---

* "Essay on Scientific Propagation," by John Humphrey Noyes.

of two persons to each other, and their desire to be true to each other; and there are here and there in their publications signs that there has been suffering among their young people on this account. They rebuke this propensity, however, as selfish and sinful, and break it down rigorously

III.—DAILY LIFE AND BUSINESS ADMINISTRATION.

The farm, or domain, as they prefer to call it, of the Oneida Community forms a part of the old Reservation of the Oneida Indians. It is a plain, the land naturally good and well watered; and it has been industriously improved by the communists. It lies four miles from Oneida on the New York Central Railroad, and the Midland Railroad passes through it.

The dwelling-house, a large brick building with some architectural pretensions, but no artistic merit, stands on the middle of a pleasant lawn, near the main road. It has some extensions in the rear, the chief of which is a large wing containing the kitchen and dining-room. The interior of the house is well arranged; the whole is warmed by steam; and there are baths and other conveniences. There is on the second floor a large hall, used for the evening gatherings of the community, and furnished with a stage for musical and dramatic performances, and with a number of round tables, about which they gather in their meetings. On the ground floor is a parlor for visitors; and a library-room, containing files of newspapers, and a miscellaneous library of about four thousand volumes.

There are two large family rooms, one on each story, around which a considerable number of sleeping-chambers are built; and the upper of these large rooms has two ranges of such dormitories, one above the other, the upper range being reached by a gallery.

All the rooms are plainly furnished, there being neither any attempt at costly or elegant furnishing, nor a striving for Shaker plainness.

Above the dining-room is the printing-office, where the *Circular* is printed, and some job printing is done.

Opposite the dwelling, and across the road, are offices, a school-building, a lecture-room with a chemical laboratory, and a room for the use of the daguerreotypist of the community; farther on to the right is a large carpenter's shop, and to the left are barns, stables, the silk-dye house, and a small factory where the children of the community at odd hours make boxes for the spool silk produced here. There is also a large and conveniently arranged laundry.

Somewhat over a mile from the home place are the factories of the community—consisting of trap works, silk works, a forge, and machine shops. These are thoroughly fitted with labor-saving machinery, and are extensive enough to produce three hundred thousand traps, and the value of over two hundred thousand dollars' worth of silk-twist in a year. Near these workshops is a dwelling inhabited by thirty or forty of the communists, who are particularly employed in the shops.

The farm has been put in excellent order: there are extensive orchards of large and small fruits; and plantations of ornamental trees shelter the lawn about the dwelling. This lawn is in summer a favorite resort for picnic parties from a distance. As Sunday-school picnics are also brought hither, I judge that the hostility which once existed in the neighborhood to the Oneida Communists has disappeared. Indeed, at Oneida all with whom I had occasion to speak concerning the communists praised them for honesty, fair dealing, a peaceable disposition, and great business capacity.

Their system of administration is perfect and thorough. Their book-keeping—in which women are engaged as well as men, a young woman being the chief—is so systematized that they are able to know the profit or loss upon every branch of industry they pursue, as well as the cost of each part of their living.

They have twenty-one standing committees: on finance; amusements; patent-rights; location of tenant houses; arbitration; rents; baths, walks, roads, and lawns; fire; heating; sanitary; education; clothing; real estate and tenant houses; water-works and their supplies; painting; forest; water and steam power; photographs; hair-cutting; arcade; and Joppa— the last being an isolated spot on Oneida Lake, to which they go to bathe, fish, shoot, and otherwise ruralize.

Besides these, they divide the duties of administration among forty-eight departments: *Circular;* publication; silk manufacture; hardware; fruit-preserving; paper-box; printing; dyeing; carpentry; business office; shoe shop; library; photographs; educational; science and art; laundry; furniture; legal; subsistence; Wallingford printing; agriculture; horticulture; medical; incidentals; dentistry; real estate; musical; amusements; quarry; housekeeping; repairs; traveling; watches; clocks; tin shop; porterage; lights; livery; clothing; stationery; floral; water-works; children's; landscape; forests; heating; bedding; coal.

At first view these many committees and departments may appear cumbrous; but in practice they work well.

Every Sunday morning a meeting is held of what is called a "Business Board." This consists of the heads of all the departments, and of whoever, of the whole community, chooses to attend. At this meeting the business of the past week is discussed; and a secretary notes down briefly any action deemed advisable. At the Sunday-evening meeting the secretary's report is read to all, and thereupon discussed; and whatever receives general or unanimous approval is carried out.

Once a year, in the spring, there is a special meeting of the Business Board, at which the work of the year is laid out in some detail.

At the beginning of the year an inventory is taken of all the possessions of the community.

Once a month the heads of the departments send in their accounts to the book-keepers, and these are then posted in the ledgers.

It is a principle with them to attempt nothing without the general consent of all the people; and if there is objection made, the matter proposed is put off for further discussion.

Shortly after New-Year, the Finance Committee sits and receives estimates. This means that each department sends in an estimate of the money it will require for the coming year. At the same time any one who has a project in his head may propose it, with an estimate of its cost. Thereupon the Finance Committee makes the necessary appropriations, revising the estimates in accordance with the general total which the society can afford to spend for the year. At or before this meeting the returns for the past year have been scrutinized.

All appointments on committees are made for a year; but there is a committee composed of men and women whose duty it is to appoint different persons to their work; and these may change the employments at any time. In practice, the foremen of the manufacturing establishments are not frequently changed. In appointing the labor of the members, their tastes as well as abilities are consulted, and the aim is to make each one contented.

The appointment of so many committees makes some one responsible for each department, and when any thing is needed, or any fault is to be found, the requisition can be directed to a particular person. Women, equally with men, serve on the committees.

They rise in the morning between five and half-past seven; this depending somewhat upon the business each is engaged in. The children sleep as long as they like. Breakfast is from eight to nine, and dinner from three to four; and they retire from half-past eight to half-past ten. The members do not now work very hard, as will appear from these hours; but they are steadily industrious; and as most of them superintend some department, and all of them work cheerfully, the necessary amount of labor is accomplished. Mere drudgery they nowadays put upon their hired people.

A square board, placed in a gallery near the library, tells at a glance where every body is. It contains the names of the men and women at the side, and the places where they can be found at the head; and a peg, which each one sticks in opposite his name, tells his whereabouts for the day.

There is no bell or other signal for proceeding to work; but each one is expected to attend faithfully to that which is given him or her to do; and here, as in other communities, no difficulty is found about idlers. Those who have disagreeable tasks are more frequently changed than others. Thus the women who superintend in the kitchen usually serve but a month, but sometimes two months at a time.

Children are left to the care of their mothers until they are weaned; then they are put into a general nursery, under the care of special nurses or care-takers, who are both men and women. There are two of these nurseries, one for the smaller children, the other for those above three or four years of age, and able somewhat to help themselves. These eat at the same time with the older people, and are seated at tables by themselves in the general dining-room. The children I saw were plump, and looked sound; but they seemed to me a little subdued and desolate, as though they missed the exclusive love and care of a father and mother. This, however, may have been only fancy; though I should grieve to see in the eyes of my own little ones an expression which I thought I saw in the Oneida children, difficult to describe—perhaps I might say a lack of buoyancy, or confidence and gladness. A man or woman may not find it disagreeable to be part of a great machine, but I suspect it is harder for a little child. However, I will not insist on this, for I may have been mistaken. I have seen, with similar misgivings, a lot of little chickens raised in an egg-hatching machine, and having a blanket for shelter instead of the wing of a mother: I thought they missed the cluck and the vigilant if sometimes severe care of the old hen. But after all they grew up to be hearty chickens, as zealous and greedy, and in the end as useful as their more particularly nurtured fellows.

In the dining-hall I noticed an ingenious contrivance to save trouble to those who wait on the table. The tables are round, and accommodate ten or twelve people each. There is a stationary rim, having space for the plates, cups, and saucers; and within this is a revolving disk, on which the food is placed, and by turning this about each can help himself.

They do not eat much meat, having it served not more than twice a week. Fruits and vegetables make up the greater part of their diet. They use tea, and coffee mixed with malt, which makes an excellent beverage. They use no tobacco, nor spirituous liquors.

The older people have separate sleeping-chambers; the younger usually room two together.

The men dress as people in the world do, but plainly, each one following his own fancy. The women wear a dress consisting of a bodice, loose trousers, and a short skirt falling to just above the knee. Their hair is cut just below the ears, and I noticed that the younger women usually gave it a curl. The dress is no doubt extremely convenient: it admits of walking in mud or snow, and allows freedom of exercise; and it is entirely modest. But it was to my unaccustomed eyes totally and fatally lacking in grace and beauty. The present dress of women, prescribed by fashion, and particularly the abominable false hair and the preposterously

COSTUMES AT ONEIDA.

ugly hats, are sufficiently barbarous; but the Oneida dress, which is so scant that it forbids any graceful arrangement of drapery, seemed to me no improvement.

As they have no sermons nor public prayers, so they have no peculiar mode of addressing each other. The men are called Mr., and the women Miss, except when they were married before they entered the society. It was somewhat startling to me to hear Miss ———— speak about her baby. Even the founder is addressed or spoken of simply as Mr. Noyes.

At the end of every year each person gives into the Finance Board a detailed statement of what clothing he or she requires for the coming year, and upon the aggregate sum is based the estimate. for the next year for clothing. At the beginning of 1874, the women proposed a different plan, which was thus described in the *Circular :*

"In our last woman's meeting, Mrs. C—— had a report to present for discussion and acceptance. A change of system was proposed. The plan that had been pursued for several years was to have a certain sum appropriated for clothing in the beginning of the year—so much for men, so much for women, and so much for children. Another sum was set apart for 'incidentals,' a word of very comprehensive scope. A woman of good judgment and great patience was appointed to the office of keeper and distributer of goods, and another of like qualifications was associated with a man of experience in doing the greater part of the buying. Each woman made out a list of the articles she needed, and selected them from the goods we had on hand, or sent or went for them to our neighboring merchants. This plan worked well in many respects, but it had some disadvantages. The women in charge had to be constantly adjusting and deciding little matters in order to make the wants coincide with the appropriated sum. Many unforeseen demands came in, and at the end of the year they inevitably exceeded their bounds. This year the Clothing Committee, in consultation with the financiers, proposed to adopt another plan. It was this: To appropriate a sum in the beginning of the year large enough to cover all reasonable demands, and then, after setting aside special funds for children's clothing, traveling wardrobes, infants' wardrobes and incidentals, to divide the remainder into as many equal portions as there were women in the family. Each woman then assumes for herself the responsibility of making the two ends meet at the close of the year. It was thought it would be a great advantage to each woman, and particularly to every young girl, to know what her clothing, from her hat to her shoes, costs. She would learn economy and foresight, and feel a new interest in the question of cost and payment. The plan, too, allows of great variations in the way of making presents and helping one another when there is a surplus, or, when there is no need, leaving it untouched in the treasury. After due explanations and discussions, the women voted unanimously to try the new plan."

It may interest some readers to know that the sum thus set aside for each woman's dress during the year, including shoes and hats, was thirty-three dollars. A member writes in explanation:

"Minus the superfluities and waste of fashion, we find thirty-three dollars a year plenty enough to keep us in good dresses, two or three for each season, summer, winter, fall, and spring (the fabrics are not velvets and satins, of course—they are flannels and merinos, the lighter kinds of worsted, various kinds of prints, and Japanese silk); to fill our drawers with the best of under-linen, to furnish us with hoods and sun-bonnets, beaver and broadcloth sacks, and a variety of shawls and shoulder-gear, lighter and pleasanter to wear, if not so ingrained with the degradation of toil as the costly Cashmere."

When a man needs a suit of clothes, he goes to the tailor and is measured, choosing at the same time the stuff and the style or cut.

There is a person called familiarly "Incidentals." To him is intrusted a fund for incidental and unforeseen expenses; and when a young woman wants a breast-pin—the only ornament worn—she applies to "Incidentals." When any one needs a watch, he makes his need known to the committee on watches.

For the children they have a sufficiently good school, in which the Bible takes a prominent part as a text-book. The young people are encouraged to continue their studies, and they have two or three classes in history, one in grammar, and several in French, Latin, geology, etc. These study and recite at odd times; and it is their policy not to permit the young men and women to labor too constantly. The Educational Committee superintends the evening classes.

They also cultivate vocal and instrumental music; and have several times sent one or two of their young women to New York to receive special musical instruction. Also for some years they have kept several of their young men in the Yale scientific school, and in other departments of that university. Thus they have educated two of their members to be physicians; two in the law; one in mechanical engineering; one in architecture; and others in other pursuits. Usually these have been young men from twenty-two to twenty-five years of age, who had prepared themselves practically beforehand.

It is their habit to change their young people from one employment to another, and thus make each master of several trades. The young women are not excluded from this variety; and they have now several girls learning the machinists' trade, in a building appropriated to this purpose; and their instructor told me they were especially valuable for the finer and more delicate kinds of lathe-work. A young man whom they sent to the Sheffield scientific school to study mechanical engineering had been for a year or two in the machine shop before he went to Yale; he is now at the head of the silk works. Their student in architecture had in the same way prepared himself in their carpenter's shop.

No one who visits a communistic society which has been for some time in existence can fail to be struck with the amount of ingenuity, inventive skill, and business talent developed among men from whom, in the outer world, one would not expect such qualities. This is true, too, of the Oneida

Communists. They contrived all the machinery they use for making traps—one very ingenious piece making the links for the chains. They had no sooner begun to work in silk than they invented a little toy which measures the silk thread as it is wound on spools, and accurately gauges the number of yards; and another which tests the strength of silk; and these have come into such general use that they already make them for sale.

So, too, when they determined to begin the silk manufacture, they sent one of their young men and two women to work as hands in a well-managed factory. In six months these returned, having sufficiently mastered the business to undertake the employment and instruction of hired operatives. Of the machinery they use, they bought one set and made all the remainder upon its pattern, in their own foundry and shops. A young man who had studied chemistry was sent out to a dye-house, and in a few months made himself a competent dyer. In all this complicated enterprise they made so few mistakes that in six months after they began to produce silk-twist their factory had a secure reputation in the market.

It is their custom to employ their people, where they have responsible places, in couples. Thus there are two house stewards, two foremen in a factory, etc.; both having equal knowledge, and one always ready to take the other's place if he finds the work wearing upon him.

They seemed to me to have an almost fanatical horror of forms. Thus they change their avocations frequently; they remove from Oneida to Willow Place, or to Wallingford, on slight excuses; they change the order of their evening meetings and amusements with much care; and have changed even their meal hours. One said to me, "We used to eat three meals a day—now we eat but two; but we may be eating five six months from now."

Very few of their young people have left them; and some

who have gone out have sought to return. They have expelled but one person since the community was organized. While they received members, they exacted no probationary period, but used great care before admission. Mr. Noyes said on this subject:

"There has been a very great amount of discrimination and vigilance exercised by the Oneida Community from first to last in regard to our fellowships, and yet it seems to me it is one of the greatest miracles that this community has succeeded as it has. Notwithstanding our discrimination and determination to wait on God in regard to those we receive, we scarcely have been saved."

New members sign a paper containing the creed, and also an agreement to claim no wages or other reward for their labor while in the community.

III.—SUNDAY AT THE ONEIDA COMMUNITY, WITH SOME ACCOUNT OF "CRITICISM."

I was permitted to spend several days at the Oneida Community, among which was a Sunday.

The people are kind, polite to each other and to strangers, cheerful, and industrious. There is no confusion, and for so large a number very little noise. Where two hundred people live together in one house, order, system, and punctuality are necessary; and loud voices would soon become a nuisance.

I was shown the house, the kitchen and heating arrangements, the barns with their fine stock, the various manufacturing operations; and in the evening was taken to their daily gathering, at which instrumental music, singing, and conversation engage them for an hour, after which they disperse to the private parlors to amuse themselves with dominoes or dancing, or to the library to read or write letters.   Cards are prohibited. The questions I asked were freely answered; and all the people in one way or another came under my eye.

Some of them have the hard features of toil-worn New England farmers; others look like the average business-men of our country towns or inland cities; others are students, and there are a number of college-bred men in the community. A fine collection of birds in a cabinet, skillfully stuffed and mounted, showed me that there is in the society a lively love of natural history.   The collection is, I should think, almost complete for the birds of the region about Oneida.

The people seem contented, and pleased with their success, as well they may be, for it is remarkable.   They use good language, and the standard of education among them is considerably above the average.   No doubt the training they get in their evening discussions, and in the habit of writing for a paper whose English is pretty carefully watched, has benefited them.   They struck me as matter-of-fact, with no nonsense or romance about them, by no means overworked, and with a certain, perhaps for their place in life high average of culture. I should say that the women are inferior to the men: examining the faces at an evening meeting, this was the impression I carried away.

If I should add that the predominant impression made upon me was that it was a common-place company, I might give offense; but, after all, what else but this could be the expression of people whose lives are removed from need, and narrowly bounded by their community; whose religious theory calls for no internal struggles, and, once within the community, very little self-denial; who are well-fed and sufficiently amused, and not overworked, and have no future to fear?   The greater passions are not stirred in such a life.   If these are once thoroughly awakened, the individual leaves the community.

On Sunday the first work is to sort and send away to the

laundry the soiled clothing of the week. After this comes the regular weekly meeting of the Business Board; and thereafter meetings for criticism, conducted in rooms apart.

The institution of Criticism, a description of which I have reserved for this place, is a most important and ingenious device, which Noyes and his followers rightly regard as the corner-stone of their practical community life. It is in fact their main instrument of government; and it is useful as a means of eliminating uncongenial elements, and also to train those who remain into harmony with the general system and order.

I am told that it was first used by Mr. Noyes while he was a divinity student at Andover, where certain members of his class were accustomed to meet together to criticise each other. The person to suffer criticism sits in silence, while the rest of the company, each in turn, tell him his faults, with, I judge, an astonishing and often exasperating plainness of speech. Here is the account given by Mr. Noyes himself:

"The measures relied upon for good government in these community families are, first, *daily evening meetings,* which all are expected to attend. In these meetings, religious, social, and business matters are freely discussed, and opportunity given for exhortation and reproof. Secondly, *the system of mutual criticism.* This system takes the place of backbiting in ordinary society, and is regarded as one of the greatest means of improvement and fellowship. All of the members are accustomed to voluntarily invite the benefit of this ordinance from time to time. Sometimes persons are criticised by the entire family; at other times by a committee of six, eight, twelve, or more, selected by themselves from among those best acquainted with them, and best able to do justice to their character. In these criticisms the most perfect sincerity is expected; and in practical experience it is found best for the subject to receive his criticism without replying. There is little danger that the general verdict in respect to his character will be unjust. This ordinance is far from agreeable to those whose egotism and vanity are stronger than their love of truth. It is an ordeal which reveals insincerity and selfishness; but it also often takes the form of commendation, and reveals hidden virtues as well as secret faults. It is always acceptable to those who wish to see themselves as others see them.

" These two agencies—daily evening meetings and criticism—are found quite adequate to the maintenance of good order and government in the communities. Those who join the communities understanding their principles, and afterward prove refractory and inharmonic, and also those who come into the communities in childhood, and afterward develop characters antagonistic to the general spirit, and refuse to yield to the governmental agencies mentioned, either voluntarily withdraw or are expelled. Only one case of expulsion is, however, recorded."

They depend upon criticism to cure whatever they regard as faults in the character of a member; for instance, idleness, disorderly habits, impoliteness, selfishness, a love of novel-reading, " selfish love," conceit, pride, stubbornness, a grumbling spirit—for every vice, petty or great, criticism is held to be a remedy. They have even a " criticism-cure," and hold that this is almost as effective as their " prayer-cure."

On Sunday afternoon, by the kindness of a young man who had offered himself for criticism, I was permitted to be present. Fifteen persons besides myself, about half women, and about half young people under thirty, were seated in a room, mostly on benches placed against the wall. Among them was Mr. Noyes himself, who sat in a large rocking-chair. The young man to be criticised, whom I will call Charles, sat inconspicuously in the midst of the company. When the doors were closed, he was asked by the leader (not Mr. Noyes) whether he desired to say any thing. Retaining his seat, he said that he had suffered for some time past from certain intellectual difficulties and doubts—a leaning especially toward positivism, and lack of faith; being drawn away from God; a tendency to think religion of small moment. But that he was combating the evil spirit within him, and hoped he had gained somewhat; and so on.

Hereupon a man being called on to speak, remarked that he thought Charles had been somewhat hardened by too great good-fortune; that his success in certain enterprises had somewhat spoiled him; if he had not succeeded so well, he would

have been a better man; that he was somewhat wise in his
own esteem; not given to consult with others, or to seek or
take advice. One or two other men agreed generally with the
previous remarks, had noticed these faults in Charles, and that
they made him disagreeable; and gave examples to show his
faults. Another concurred in the general testimony, but added that he thought Charles had lately made efforts to correct
some of his faults, though there was still much room for improvement.

A young woman next remarked that Charles was haughty
and supercilious, and thought himself better than others with
whom he was brought into contact; that he was needlessly
curt sometimes to those with whom he had to speak.

Another young woman added that Charles was a respecter
of persons; that he showed his liking for certain individuals
too plainly by calling them pet names before people; that he
seemed to forget that such things were disagreeable and wrong.

Another woman said that Charles was often careless in his
language; sometimes used slang words, and was apt to give a
bad impression to strangers. Also that he did not always conduct himself at table, especially before visitors, with careful
politeness and good manners.

A man concurred in this, and remarked that he had heard
Charles condemn the beefsteak on a certain occasion as tough;
and had made other unnecessary remarks about the food on
the table while he was eating.

A woman remarked that she had on several occasions found
Charles a respecter of persons.

Another said that Charles, though industrious and faithful
in all temporalities, and a very able man, was not religious at
all.

A man remarked that Charles was, as others had said, somewhat spoiled by his own success, but that it was a mistake for
him to be so, for he was certain that Charles's success came

mainly from the wisdom and care with which the society had surrounded him with good advisers, who had guided him; and that Charles ought therefore to be humble, instead of proud and haughty, as one who ought to look outside of himself for the real sources of his success.

Finally, two or three remarked that he had been in a certain transaction insincere toward another young man, saying one thing to his face and another to others; and in this one or two women concurred.

Amid all this very plain speaking, which I have considerably condensed, giving only the general charges, Charles sat speechless, looking before him; but as the accusations multiplied, his face grew paler, and drops of perspiration began to stand on his forehead. The remarks I have reported took up about half an hour; and now, each one in the circle having spoken, Mr. Noyes summed up.

He said that Charles had some serious faults; that he had watched him with some care; and that he thought the young man was earnestly trying to cure himself. He spoke in general praise of his ability, his good character, and of certain temptations he had resisted in the course of his life. He thought he saw signs that Charles was making a real and earnest attempt to conquer his faults; and as one evidence of this he remarked that Charles had lately come to him to consult him upon a difficult case in which he had had a severe struggle, but had in the end succeeded in doing right. " In the course of what we call stirpiculture," said Noyes, " Charles, as you know, is in the situation of one who is by and by to become a father. Under these circumstances, he has fallen under the too common temptation of selfish love, and a desire to wait upon and cultivate an exclusive intimacy with the woman who was to bear a child through him. This is an insidious temptation, very apt to attack people under such circumstances; but it must nevertheless be struggled against." Charles, he went on to say, had come to him for advice in this case, and he (Noyes) had at first refused to tell him any thing, but had asked him what he thought he ought to do; that after some conversation, Charles had determined, and he agreed with him, that he ought to isolate himself entirely from the woman, and let another man take his place at her side; and this Charles had accordingly done, with a most praiseworthy spirit of self-sacrifice. Charles had indeed still further taken up his cross, as he had noticed with pleasure, by going to sleep with the smaller children, to take charge of them during the night. Taking all this in view, he thought Charles was in a fair way to become a better man, and had manifested a sincere desire to improve, and to rid himself of all selfish faults.

Thereupon the meeting was dismissed.

All that I have recited was said by practiced tongues. The people knew very well how to express themselves. There was no vagueness, no uncertainty. Every point was made; every sentence was a hit—a stab I was going to say, but as the sufferer was a volunteer, I suppose this would be too strong a word. I could see, however, that while Charles might be benefited by the " criticism," those who spoke of him would perhaps also be the better for their speech; for if there had been bitterness in any of their hearts before, this was likely to be dissipated by the free utterance. Concerning the closing remarks of Noyes, which disclose so strange and horrible a view of morals and duty, I need say nothing.

Here are a few specimens of criticisms which have been printed in the *Circular*. The first concerns a young woman:

" What God has done for U. is wonderful; her natural gifts and attractions are uncommon; but she has added very little to them. She is spoiling them by indolence and vanity. The gifts we have by nature do not belong to us. We shall have to give account for them to God as his property. All that we can expect any reward for is what we add to that which he gives us."

The next seems to point at troubles of a kind to which the community is, I suppose, more or less subject:

"I wish I could entirely change public opinion among us in regard to the matter of keeping secrets. The fact that a person is of such a character that others associated with him are afraid that he will finally expose their wrong-doing is the highest credit to him. I would earnestly exhort all lovers of every degree, young and old, and especially the young, to consider the absolute impossibility of permanently keeping secrets. It is not for us to say whether we will keep other folks' secrets or not. It is for God to say. We are in his hands, and he will make us tell the truth even though we say we won't. He has certainly made it his programme and eternal purpose that every secret thing shall come to light. What is done in darkness shall be published on the house-top. This is sure to come, because it is God's policy, and it is vain for us to seek to evade and thwart it. Two persons get together with shameful secrets, and promise and protest and pledge themselves never to turn on each other. What is the use? It is not for them to say what they will do. They *will* finally turn on one another. It is a mercy to them that they must. The best thing to be said of them is that they are likely to turn on one another and betray their secrets. They will, if there is any honesty or true purpose in them. This keeping secrets that are dishonest, profane, and infernal, and regarding them as sacred, is all wrong. It is the rule of friendship and honor in the world, but to let the daylight in on every thing is the rule for those who want to please God."

What follows relates to a man who was cast down because of criticism, and whose fault Noyes says is excessive sensitiveness:

"Excessive sensitiveness is a great fault. Every one should strive to get where he can judge himself, look at himself truthfully by the grace of God, and cultivate what may be called the superior consciousness, looking at his own fault as he would at another person's, and feeling no more pain in dissecting his own character than he would that of any one else. This superior consciousness takes us into fellowship with God and his judgment; and in that condition it is possible to rejoice in pulling to pieces our own works. Paul says: 'Other foundation can no man lay than that is laid, which is Jesus Christ. Now if any man build upon this foundation gold, silver, precious stones, wood, hay, stubble, every man's work shall be made manifest—for the day shall declare it, because it shall be revealed by fire; and the fire shall try every man's work, of what sort it is. If any man's work abide which he hath built thereupon, he shall receive a reward. If any man's work shall be burned, he shall suffer loss; but he himself shall be saved, yet so as by fire.' There is a great amount of poor building upon that good foundation; a great number of structures that are wood, hay, and stubble, and which in the day of fire will be burned up. The main point to be gained by those who have thus built is to get into such sympathy with God that they can stand by when the day of fire comes, and help on the destruction—poke the wood, hay, and stubble into the flame, rejoicing that they have a good foundation, and are to be saved not only from the fire, but by the fire."

Finally, they use criticism as a remedy for diseases. I take this example from the *Circular* for June 4, 1853:

" S. P., having a bad cold and symptoms of a run of fever, tried the criticism-cure, and was immediately relieved. She was on the bed in a state of pain and restlessness, when a friend mentioned to her the above remedy as having been successfully applied in similar cases. Having some faith in it, she arose immediately and made her wishes known to the family physician, that is, to the *family*, who kindly administered the remedy without delay. The operation was not particularly agreeable—there is no method of cure that is; but it was short and speedily efficacious. One secret of its efficacy is, it stops the flow of thought toward the seat of difficulty, and so tends directly to reduce inflammation. At the same time it has a very bracing, invigorating effect. In the present case, it went right to the cause of the disease, which was discovered to be a spirit of *fear*, throwing open the pores and predisposing the subject to the attack. S. P. had been brought up in a bad habit in this respect, expecting with every exposure to take cold—and then expecting to have it go on to a serious cough, and so on—fear realizing itself. Criticism stopped this false action, and not only made her well in the first instance, but by breaking up this fear it has given her comparative security against future attacks. It requires some fortitude and self-denial in the patient, when he thinks he needs sympathy and nursing, to take criticism instead; but it is well known that to rouse the will to strong exertion is more than half a cure. The criticism remedy professes to be universal, and is recommended for trial to all the afflicted."

The *Circular* for December, 1863, reports:

" It is a common custom here for every one who may be attacked with any disorder to apply this remedy by sending for a committee of six or eight persons, in whose faith and spiritual judgment he has confidence, to come and criticise him. The result, when administered sincerely, is almost universally to throw the patient into a sweat, or to bring on a re-action of his life against disease, breaking it up, and restoring him soon to usual health. We have seen this result produced without any other agency except the use of ice, in perhaps twenty cases of sore throat within a few weeks. We have seen it take effect at an advanced stage of chronic disease, and raise a person up apparently from death's door. It seems a somewhat heroic method of treatment when a person is suffering in body to apply a castigation to the character through the spiritual or moral part; but this is precisely the thing needed to cleanse and purify the system from disease. We have tried it, and found it to be invaluable. To all who have faith in Christ as a physician we can commend this pre-scription as a medium for conveying his healing life. If you are sick, seek for some one to tell you your faults, to find out your weakest spot in character or conduct; let them put their finger on the very sore that you would best like to keep hid. Depend upon it, there is the avenue through which disease gets access to you. And if the sincerity which points this out and opens it to the light hurts, and is mortifying for the time being, it is only a sign that the remedy is applied at the right place and is taking effect."

In a recent number of the *Circular* (1874) a "criticism of a sick man " is reported in full. It is too long to give here; but I quote a few of the remarks, to show the style of attack in such cases. The report opens with this statement:

"[L. has been quite prostrate for months with some kind of spinal af-fection, complicated with chills and fever. In presenting himself for criticism, he was invited, as the subject generally is, to open his own case. He said he was under a spirit of depression and discouragement, particu-larly about his health. He thought he should be better off if he did not know so much about his disease. Dr. Pope had pronounced it incur-able.]"

W. said :

"I think that L. is troubled with false imaginations, and that he has inherited this tendency. His father was subject to the hypo—always a prey to imaginations. I question whether the root of L.'s whole difficulty does not lie in his imagination. I don't doubt but that he feels what he thinks he does, but imagination has terrible power to make us feel. Christ can cast down imaginations, and every high thing that exalteth itself against the knowledge of God."

J. said :

" He talks a great deal about his symptoms. If he would talk on the side of faith, I think he would be a well man right off. He is as well as any body when he *is* well, and there is no reason why he should not be well all the time. He is a very valuable member of the community, and I don't like to see him lie on his back so much.

" *M.*—I have thought that his knowledge of physiology, as he uses it, is really a hinderance to him : he knows too much about his case.

" *C.*—I thought I had the heart disease when I was about nineteen years of age. My heart would beat so when I went up stairs that I had to sit down at the top. I remember that I said to my aunt one day I was sure that I had got that disease, because my heart had such times of beating. ' O la !' she answered, 'I guess you would not live long if it did not beat.'

" *N.* [probably Mr. Noyes]—I have good reason to believe that a great many diseases which doctors pronounce incurable are so so far as their powers are concerned, and yet can be cured by exorcism. Doctors do not believe in possession by the devil, and of course have no means of curing diseases of that nature. They accordingly pronounce some diseases incurable. Yet these diseases are not incurable by persons who understand the nature of them, and that they are spiritual obsessions. I do not care what the doctors say about L.'s back. It is very likely incurable so far as they know, and yet it may be very easily curable to any body who knows about the doctrine of the possession of the devil. There is a range of science beyond the routine of the doctors which we must take into the account in all this dealing with disease. Just look at the case of Harriet Hall, and see what incurable diseases she had. Two doctors certified that she ought to be dead twenty years ago, and here she is alive and waiting on her father. Those doctors are dead, and she is trotting around.

" *E.*—I have been associated a good deal with L. in business and now in this sickness. I have studied his case some. His attitude toward disease is very much like his attitude in business. When he has been well and able to do his best, he has been in the past an autocrat in our businesses. If he said a thing would not go, or would go, his dictum was always accepted. He has a good deal of pride in having what he predicts turn out to be true. I have sometimes thought that he was willing to

have things break down in order to demonstrate his infallibility as an oracle. He shows the same trait in regard to disease. If he has a symp-
tom, and makes up his mind that he is going to have a certain disease,
he notifies his friends of it, and seems bound to have his prophecy come
true any way.

"*N.*—He would rather have a good chill, I suppose, than have his prediction prove false.

"*E.*—I think he really knows but very little about his case. He lost
his health, and took up the study of medicine to find out what ailed him.
It may seem paradoxical, but I think that he is suffering for want of
work; his brain is suffering for want of some healthy action. If he would
use his brain about something for only half an hour a day, he would find
himself improving right along.

"*A.*—I remember L. had the reputation of being an ingenious boy; but
he used to seem old even then—he had the rheumatism or some such
complaint. In thinking about him, it seems to me that the instinct of
his life is to find a soft place in the world: he is hunting up cushions and
soft things to surround himself with. His bent is rather scientific than
religious. A man that is an oracle surrounds himself with something soft
in having people defer to him. I must say I think he is too oracular
about disease, considering the amount of study he has given to the science
of medicine. He went into the study of medicine in a sort of self-cod-
dling way, to find out what the matter was with himself. I have realized
that it is not good for a man in this world to hunt for a soft spot."

And so on.   Mr. Noyes closed the session with this remark:

"*N.*—Christ's words, 'Because I live ye shall live also,' may be thrust
in the face of all incurable diseases. There is no answer to that. No incurable disease can stand against it."

I do not know whether L. recovered or not.

On Sunday evening, about half-past six o'clock, there was a
gathering in the large hall to hear some pieces of music from
the orchestra. After half an hour's intermission, the people
again assembled, this time for a longer session. A considerable number of round tables were scattered about the large hall;
on these were lamps; and around them sat most of the women,
old and young, with sewing or knitting, with which they busied

themselves during the meeting. Others sat on benches and chairs, irregularly ranged about.

After the singing of a hymn, a man rose and read the report of the business meeting held that morning, the appointment of some committees, and so on; and this was then put to vote and accepted, having elicited no discussion, and very little interest apparently. Next a man, who sat near Mr. Noyes in the middle of the room, read some extracts from newspapers, which had been marked and sent in to him by different members for that purpose. Some of these were mere drolleries, and raised laughter. Others concerned practical matters.

To this reading, which was brief, followed a discussion of the power of healing disease by prayer. It was asserted to be " necessary to regard Christ as powerful to-day over diseases of the body as well as of the spirit." When several had spoken very briefly upon this subject, and the conversation was evidently closed, a considerable number of the people concurred in what had been said by short ejaculations, as " I confess the power of Christ in my heart;" " I confess the power of healing;" " I confess to a tender conscience;" " I confess Christ;" " I confess a love for all good people," and so on.

Next a hymn was sung relating to community life, which I copy here as a curiosity:

> " Let us sing, brothers, sing,
>   In the Eden of heart-love—
> Where the fruits of life spring,
>   And no death e'er can part love;
> Where the pure currents flow
>   From all gushing hearts together,
> And the wedding of the Lamb
>   Is the feast of joy forever.
>   Let us sing, brothers, sing.

> " We have built us a dome
>   On our beautiful plantation,
> And we all have one home,
>   And one family relation;

> We have battled with the wiles
> Of the dark world of Mammon,
> And returned with its spoils
> To the home of our dear ones.
> Let us sing, brothers, sing.

> "When the rude winds of wrath
> Idly rave round our dwelling,
> And the slanderer's breath
> Like a simoon was swelling,
> Then so merrily we sung,
> As the storm blustered o'er us,
> Till the very heavens rung
> With our hearts' joyful chorus.
> Let us go, brothers, go.

> "So love's sunshine begun:
> Now the spirit-flowers are blooming,
> And the feeling that we're one
> All our hearts is perfuming;
> Toward one home we have all
> Set our faces together,
> Where true love doth dwell
> In peace and joy forever.
> Let us sing, brothers, sing."

This was presently followed by another song peculiar to the Oneida people. A man sang, looking at a woman near him:

> "I love you, O my sister,
> But the love of God is better;
> Yes, the love of God is better—
> O the love of God is best."

To this she replied:

> "I love you, O my brother,
> But the love of God is better;
> Yes, the love of God is better—
> O the love of God is best."

Then came the chorus, in which a number of voices joined:

"Yes, the love of God is better,
O the love of God is better;
Hallelujah, Hallelujah—
Yes, the love of God is best."

Soon after the meeting broke up; but there was more singing, later, in the private parlors, which I did not attend.
Thus ended Sunday at the Oneida Community; and with this
picture of their daily life I may conclude my account of these
people.

THE AURORA AND BETHEL

COMMUNES.

THE AURORA AND BETHEL COMMUNES.

Twenty-nine miles south of Portland, on the Oregon and California Railroad, lies the village of Aurora, more commonly known along the road as "Dutchtown." As you approach it on the train, you will notice on an eminence to the left a large wooden church; in the deep ravine which is spanned by a railroad-bridge, a saw-mill; and, scattered irregularly over the neighboring country, a number of houses, most of them differing from usual village dwellings in the United States, mainly because of their uncommon size, and the entire absence of ornament. They are three stories high, sometimes nearly a hundred feet deep, and look like factories.

Opposite the railroad station, upon elevated ground, stands one of these houses, which is called the hotel, and is an excellent, clean country inn, famous all over Oregon for good living. When I mentioned to an acquaintance in Portland my purpose to spend some days at Aurora, he replied, "Oh, yes—Dutchtown; you'll feed better there than any where else in the state;" and on further inquiry I found that I might expect to see there also the best orchards in Oregon, the most ingenious expedients for drying fruits, and an excellent system of agriculture. Beyond these practical points, and the further statement that "these Dutch are a queer people," information about them is not general among Oregonians. The inn, or "hotel," however, at Aurora, is used as a summer resort by residents of Portland; the Aurora band is employed at festivities in Portland; the pleasure-grounds of the community are opened to Sunday-school and other picnics from the city in summer and fall; and at the State Agricultural Fair, held at Salem, the Aurora Community controls and manages the restaurant, and owns the buildings in which food is prepared and sold. In these ways it comes into direct communication with the outside world.

I found the hotel a plainly furnished but scrupulously neat and clean house, at which I was received with very little ceremony. Nor did any one volunteer to guide me about or give me information concerning the society: curiosity does not seem to be a vice of the place. A note of introduction to that member of the society who acts as its purchasing agent, with which fortunately I was provided, secured me his attention after I had found him. He was just then at work as a carpenter, putting up a small house for a newly married couple.

The Aurora Commune is an offshoot of a society formed upon the same principles in Bethel, Shelby County, Missouri. Dr. Keil, the President of Aurora, was the founder of Bethel, and still rules both communities. He removed from Missouri to Oregon because he imagined that there would be a larger field for his efforts in a new state; and also, I imagine, because of an innate restlessness of disposition.

Dr. Keil is a Prussian, born in 1811; and was a man-milliner in Germany. He became a mystic, and he seems to have dealt also in magnetism, and used this as a curative agent for diseases. After living for some time in New York, he came to Pittsburgh, where he gave himself out as a physician, and showed, it is said, some knowledge of botany. He professed also to be the owner of a mysterious volume, written with human blood, and containing receipts for medicines which enabled him, as he professed, to cure various diseases. Presently he became a Methodist, and thereupon burned this book with certain awe-inspiring formalities. He seems to have been a fanatic in religious matters, for he soon left the Methodists to form a sect of his own; and it is related that he gathered a number of Germans about him, to whom he gave himself out as a being to be worshiped, and later as one of the two witnesses in the Book of Revelation; and in this capacity he gave public notice that on a certain day, after a fast of forty days, he would be slain in the presence of his followers.

While he was thus engaged in forming a following for himself among the ignorant and simple-minded Germans, the rogue who called himself Count Leon came over and joined Rapp's colony at Economy; and when Leon, after quarreling with Rapp and removing to Phillipsburg, ran away from there to Louisiana, Keil managed to secure some of Leon's people as his adherents, and thereupon began to plan a communistic settlement, somewhat upon the plan of Rapp's, but with the celibate principle left out. In the year 1844, his followers, among whom were by good luck some of the seceders from Economy, began a settlement in accordance with these plans in Missouri. They were all either Germans or "Pennsylvania Dutch," and people of limited means. It is probable that Keil had nothing, for he appears for some years previously to have followed no regular business or profession. They removed to Bethel, a point forty-eight miles from Hannibal, in Missouri, and thirty-six miles from Quincy; and began in very humble style. Not all the colonists came out at once. He took with him at first two families and a number of young people. These broke ground in the new settlement, and others followed as they sold their property at home.

Shelby County, Missouri, was then a new country. The colonists took up four sections, or two thousand five hundred and sixty acres of land, to which they added from time to time until they possessed four thousand acres. Upon a part of this estate they gradually established a distillery, grist-mill, saw-mill, carding machinery, a woolen-mill, and all the mechanical trades needed by the farmers in their neighborhood, and thus they made a town. As soon as they were able they set up a general store, and a post-office was of course established by the government. Among their first buildings was a church; for Dr. Keil was their spiritual as well as temporal head.

At Bethel they prospered; and there four hundred of these Communists still live. I shall give an account of them later.

Keil's ideas grew with the increasing wealth of the people; and his unrestful spirit longed for a new and broader field of labor. He imagined that on the Pacific coast he might found a larger communistic society upon a broader domain; and he did not find it difficult to persuade his people that the attempt ought to be made.

In 1855, accordingly, Dr. Keil set out with ten or twelve families, eighty persons in all, across the plains, carrying along household utensils and some cattle. A few families started later, and crossed the Isthmus; and all gathered at Shoalwater Bay, north of the mouth of the Columbia River, and in Washington Territory. There a few families belonging to Aurora still live, managing farms of the community; but in June, 1856, the main body of the society removed to Aurora, and began there, with tedious and severe labor, a clearing among the firs.

The upper part of the Willamette Valley is a broad, open plain, easy to till, and inviting to the farmer. Dr. Keil and his companions avoided this plain: they chose to settle in a region pretty densely grown over with timber. I asked him why he did so. He replied that, meaning to establish a saw-mill, they wished to use the trees cut down in clearing the land to make into lumber for houses and fences. There was at that time no railroad, and lumber in the open prairie was expensive. "The end proved that we were right," said he; "for, though we had hard work at first, and got ahead slowly, we were soon able to buy out the prairie farmers, who had got into debt and were shiftless, while we prudent Germans were building our place." He added a characteristic story of their early days—that when they first settled at Aurora, having no fruit of their own, he used to buy summer apples for his people from the nearest farmers for a dollar a bushel. These were eaten in the families; but he taught them to save the apple-parings, and make them into vinegar, which he then sold to the wives of his American farming neighbors at a dollar and a half per gallon.

In order to make intelligible the means as well as the ways of their success, I must here explain what are the social principles to which they agree, and in accordance with which they have worked since 1844. They are remarkable chiefly for their simplicity. Dr. Keil teaches, and they hold that—

1st. All government should be parental, to imitate, as they say, the parental government of God.

2d. That therefore societies should be formed upon the model of the family, having all interests and all property absolutely in common; all the members laboring faithfully for the general welfare and support, and drawing the means of living from the general treasury.

3d. That, however, neither religion nor the harmony of nature teaches community in any thing further than property and labor. Hence the family life is strictly maintained; and the Aurora Communists marry and are given in marriage, and raise and train children precisely as do their neighbors the Pike farmers. They reject absolutely all sexual irregularities, and inculcate marriage and support the family relation as religious duties, as the outside world does. Each family has its own house, or separate apartments in one of the large buildings.

4th. Dr. Keil, who is not only their president, but also their preacher, holds the fundamental truth of Christianity to be, " Love one another," and interprets this in so broad and literal a sense as requires a community of goods and effects. His sermons are exhortations and illustrations of this principle, and warnings against "selfishness" and praise of self-sacrifice. Service is held in a very commodious and well-built church twice a month, and after the Lutheran style: opening with singing, prayer, and reading of the Scriptures; after which the president preaches from a chosen text.

To me he spoke with some vehemence against sects and creeds as anti-Christian. Sunday is usually a day of recreation and quiet amusement, with music and visiting among the people.

5th. The children of the community are sent to school, there being at Aurora a common or free school, in which an old man, a member of the society, who bears a remarkable resemblance to the late Horace Greeley, is teacher. The school is supported as other free schools of the state are; but it is open all the year round, which is not the case generally with country schools. They aim to teach only the rudimentary studies —reading, writing, and arithmetic.

6th. The system of government is as simple as possible. Dr. Keil, the founder, is president of the community, and autocrat. He has for his advisers four of the older members, who are selected by himself. In the management of affairs he consults these, whose opinions, I imagine, usually agree with his. When any vitally important change or experiment is contemplated, the matter is discussed by the whole community, and nothing is done then without a general assent.

7th. Every man is expected to labor for the general good, but there are no established hours of work, nor is any one compelled to labor at any special pursuit.

8th. Plain living and rigid economy are inculcated as duties from each to the whole; and to labor regularly, and to waste nothing, are important parts of the "whole duty of man."

9th. Each workshop has its foreman, who comes, it would

seem, by natural selection. That is to say, here, as elsewhere, the fittest man comes to the front. But it is a principle of their polity that men shall not be confined to one kind of labor. If brickmakers are needed, and shoemakers are not busy, the shoe shop is closed, and the shoemakers go out and make brick. During the spring and summer months a large proportion of the people are engaged in the cultivation of crops. After harvest these are drawn into the town, and find winter employment in the saw-mill and the different shops. It is to accommodate these temporary sojourners that the large houses are built. Here they have apartments allotted to them, and the young people board with the different families, the young girls being employed chiefly in household duties.

These are the extremely simple principles and practical rules which guide the Aurora Community. Their further application I will show in detail hereafter. I wish first to show the dollar-and-cent results.

Coming to Aurora in 1856, they have held together, with some outside gains, and some additions from the Bethel Society, until there are now nearly four hundred people in the settlement, who own about eighteen thousand acres of land, scattered over several counties. They have established a saw-mill, a tan-yard, and cabinet-maker's, blacksmith's, wagon-maker's, tailor's, shoemaker's, carpenter's, and tin shops. Also a grist-mill, carding machinery, some looms for weaving wool; drying houses for fruit; and there is a supply store for the community, a drug store kept by the doctor of the society, and a general country store, at which the neighboring farmers, not Communists, deal for cash.

They have besides the most extensive orchards in the state, in which are apples, pears of all kinds, plums, prunes, which do admirably here, and all the commoner large and small fruits. There is also a large vegetable garden, for the use of those who have none at their houses. The orchards are in fine order, and were laden with fruit when I saw them in June, 1873. Near the orchard is a large, neatly kept house, in which the people gather during the fruit-harvest to prepare it for market, and to pare that which is to be dried. Beyond the orchard is a public ground of a dozen acres, for Sunday assemblies; and here, too, are houses for eating and dancing, with a kitchen and bake-ovens commodious enough to cook a meal for the whole settlement, or for a large picnic party.

Thus far they have brought their affairs in seventeen years, without any peculiar religious belief, any interference with the marriage or family relation, without a peculiar dress, or any other habit to mark them as Separatists, or " Come-outers," to use a New England phrase. It must be admitted also that they have achieved thus much without long or exhausting or enforced labor.

Their living is extremely plain. The houses and apartments are without carpets; the women wear calico on Sunday as well as during the week, and the sun-bonnet is their head-covering. The men wear ready-made clothing of no particular style. Cleanliness is, so far as I saw, a conspicuous virtue of the society. Dr. Keil, the president, was the only person with whom I came in contact who was not very neat. He is a snuff-taker; and he walked over the orchard with me in an untidy pair of carpet slippers.

They appear to be people of few ceremonies. On a Sunday I attended a wedding; the marriage took place in the school-house, and was witnessed by a small congregation of young people, friends of the bride and groom. The young girls came to the wedding in clean calico dresses and sun-bonnets; and I noticed that even the bride wore only a very plain woolen dress, with a bit of bright ribbon around her neck. The ceremony was performed by the schoolmaster, who is also a justice of the peace; when it was over, the company quietly and somewhat shyly walked up to congratulate the newly married, some of the young women kissing the bride. Then there was an immediate adjournment to the house of the bride's father, a mile off in the country. I was hospitably invited to go to the feast; and found a small log cabin, with kitchen and bedroom below, and a loft above, standing near a deep ravine, and with a neat garden and small orchard back of it.

In front a bower had been formed of the boughs of ever-greens, beneath which were two or three tables, which were presently spread with a plain but wholesome and bountiful feast, to which the strangers present and the older people were first invited to sit down, the younger ones waiting on the table, and with laughter and joking taking their places afterward. Meantime the village band played; after dinner we all walked into the garden, and in a pretty little summer-house discussed orchards, bees, and other country living, and by and by return-ed to the village. The young people were to have some danc-ing, and altogether it was a very pretty, rather quiet country wedding. It struck me that the young women were under-sized, and did not look robust or strong; there were no rosy cheeks, and there was a very subdued air upon all the congre-gation. The poor little bride looked pale and scared; but the bridegroom, a stout young fellow, looked proud and happy, as was proper. Dr. Keil was not present, but drove out in a very plain country wagon as the weddingers entered the school-room.

The community occasionally employs outside laborers; and when a man or woman applies to join the society, he or she is at first employed at wages, and at some trade. "We will em-ploy and pay you as long as we need your labor," the council says in such a case; "if after a while you are thoroughly sat-isfied that this is the best life, and if we approve of you, we will take you in." It is not necessary that the new-comer should bring money with him; but if he has means, he is required to put them into the common treasury, for he *must* believe that "all selfish accumulation is wrong, contrary to God's law and to natural laws."

Occasionally, I was told, they have had as members idle or drunken men. Such are admonished of their wrong courses; and if they are incorrigible, they always, I was assured, leave the place. "An idler or dissolute person has not the sympathies of our people; he has no connection with the industries of the society; as he does not work, he can hardly be so brazen as to ask for supplies. The practical result is that presently he disappears from among us."

"Do you have no disagreements from envy or jealousy among you," I asked Dr. Keil; who replied, "Very seldom now; the people have been too long and too thoroughly trained; they are too well satisfied of the wisdom of our plan of life; they are practiced in self-sacrifice, and know that selfishness is evil and the source of unhappiness. In the early days we used sometimes to have trouble. Thus a man would say, 'I brought money into the society, and this other man brought none; why should he have as much as I;' but my reply was, 'Here is your money—take it; it is not necessary; but while you remain, remember that you are no better than he.' Again, another might say, 'My labor brings one thousand dollars a year to the society, *his* only two hundred and fifty;' but my answer was, 'Thank God that he made you so much abler, stronger, to help your brother; but take care lest your poorer brother do not some day have to help you, when you are crippled, or ill, or disabled.'"

The children who have in these years, since 1844, grown up in the community generally remain. I spoke with a number of men who had thus passed all but their earliest years in the society, and who were content. Men sometimes return, repentant, after leaving the society. "The boys and girls know that they can leave at any time; there is no compulsion upon any one; hence no one cares to go. But they generally see that this is the best place. We are as prosperous and as happy as any one; we have here all we need."

As all work for the common good, so all are supplied from the common stores. I asked the purchasing agent about the book-keeping of the place; he replied, "As there is no trading, few accounts are needed. Much of what we raise is consumed on the place, and of what the people use no account is kept. Thus, if a family needs flour, it goes freely to the mill and gets what it requires. If butter, it goes to the store in the same way. We need only to keep account of what we sell of our own products, and of what we buy from abroad, and these accounts check each other. When we make money, we invest it in land." Further, I was told that tea, coffee, and sugar are roughly allowanced to each family.

Each family has either a house, or apartments in one of the large houses. Each has a garden patch, and keeps chickens; and every year a number of pigs are set apart for each household, according to its number. These are fed with the leavings of the table, and are fattened and killed in the winter, and salted down. Fresh beef is not commonly used. If any one needs vegetables, he can get them in the large garden. There seemed to be an abundance of good plain food every where.

Originally, and until 1872, all the property stood in Dr. Keil's name; but in that year he, finding himself growing old, and urged too, I imagine, by some of the leading men, made a division of the whole estate, and gave a title-deed to each head of a family of a suitable piece of property—to a farmer a farm, to a carpenter a house and shop, and so on. If there was any heart-burning over this division, I could not hear of it; and it appears to have made no difference in the conduct of the society, which labors on as before for the common welfare.

I asked, "What, then, if you have divided all the property, will you do for the young people as they grow up?"

Dr. Keil replied, "Dear me!—in the beginning we had nothing, now we have a good deal: where did it all come from? We earned and saved it. Very well; we are working just the same—we shall go on earning money and laying it by for those who are growing up; we shall have enough for all." I give below some further details, which I elicited from Dr. Keil, preferring to give them in the form of questions and answers:

Question. I have noticed that when young girls grow up they usually manifest a taste for ribbons and finery. How do you manage with such cases?

Answer. Well, they get what they want. They have only to ask at the supply store; only if they go too far—if it amounts to vanity—they are admonished that they are not acting according to the principles of love and temperance; they are putting undue expense on the society; they are making themselves different from their neighbors. It is not necessary to say this, however, for our people are now all trained in sound principles, and there is but little need for admonition.

Q. But suppose such a warning as you speak of were not taken?

A. Well, then they have leave to go into the world. If they want to be like the world, that is the place for them. And don't you see that if they are so headstrong and full of vanity they would not stay with us anyhow? They would not feel at home with us.

Q. Suppose one of your young men has the curiosity to see the world, as young men often have?

A. We give him money; he has only to ask the council. We say to him: "You want to live in the world; well, you must earn your own living there; here is money, however, for your journey." And we give him according to his character and worth in the society.

Q. Suppose a young man wanted to go to college?

A. If any one of our people wanted to train himself in some practical knowledge or skill for the service of the community, and if he were a proper person in stability of character and capacity, we would send him, and support him while he was learning. This we have repeatedly done. In such cases our experience is that when such young men return to us they bring back, not only all the money we have advanced for their support, but generally more besides. Suppose, for instance, one wanted to learn how to dye woolens; we would give him sufficient means to learn his calling thoroughly. But he would probably soon be receiving wages; and, as our people are economical, he would lay aside from his wages most likely more even than we had advanced him; and this he would be proud to bring into the common treasury on his return. [Dr. Keil gave me several instances of such conduct; and then proceeded, with a contemptuous air.] But if a young man wants to study languages, he may do so here, as much as he likes—no one will object; but if he wanted to go to college for that—well, we don't labor here to support persons in such undertakings, which have no bearing on the general welfare of the society.

In fact there is little room for poetry or for the imagination in the life of Aurora. What is not directly useful is sternly left out. There are no carpets, even in Dr. Keil's house; no sofas or easy chairs, but hard wooden settles; an immense kitchen, in which women were laboring, with short gowns tucked up; a big common room, where apparently the Doctor lives with the dozen unmarried old men who form part of his household; a wide hall full of provision safes, flour-bins, barrels, etc.; but no books, except a Bible and hymn-book, and a few medical works; no pictures—nothing to please the taste; no pretty outlook, for the house lies somewhat low down. Such was the house of the founder and president of the community; and the other houses were neither better nor much worse. There is evidently plenty of scrubbing in-doors, plenty of plain cooking, plenty of every thing that is absolutely necessary to support life—and nothing superfluous.

When I remarked upon this to some of the men, and urged them to lay out the village in a somewhat picturesque style, to which the ground would readily lend itself, and explained that a cottage might be plain and yet not ugly, the reply invariably came: "We have all that is necessary now; by and by, if we are able and want them, we may have luxuries." "For the present," said one, "we have duties to do: we must support our widows, our orphans, our old people who can no longer produce. No man is allowed to want here amongst us; we all work for the helpless." It was a droll illustration of their devotion to the useful, to find in the borders of the garden, where flowers had been planted, these flowers alternating with lettuce, radishes, and other small vegetables.

Dr. Keil is a short, burly man, with blue eyes, whitish hair, and white beard. I took him to be a Swiss from his appearance, but his language—he spoke German with me—showed him to be a Prussian. He seemed excitable and somewhat suspicious; gave no tokens whatever of having studied any book but the Bible, and that only as it helped him to enforce his own philosophy. He was very quick to turn every thought toward the one subject of community life; took his illustrations mostly from the New Testament; and evidently laid much stress on the parental character of God. As he discussed, his eyes lighted up with a somewhat fierce fire; and I thought I could perceive a fanatic, certainly a person of a very determined, imperious will, united to a narrow creed.

As to that creed: He said it was desirable and needful so to arrange our lives as to bring them into harmony with natural laws and with God's laws; that we must all trust in Him for strength and wisdom; that we all needed his protection—and as he thus spoke we turned suddenly into a little inclosure where I saw an uncommon sight, five graves close together, as sometimes children's are made; but these were evidently the graves of grown persons. " Here," he said, " lie my children—all I had, five; they all died after they were men and women, between the ages of eighteen and twenty-one. One after the other I laid them here. It was hard to bear; but now I can thank God for that too. He gave them, and I thanked him; he took them, and now I can thank him too." Then, after a minute's silence, he turned upon me with sombre eyes and said: " To bear all that comes upon us in silence, in quiet, without noise, or outcry, or excitement, or useless repining—that is to be a man, and that we can do only with God's help."

As we walked along through the vegetable garden and vineyard, I saw some elderly women hoeing the vines and clearing the ground of weeds. I must not forget to say that the culture of their orchards, vineyards, and gardens is thorough and admirable. Dr. Keil said, nodding to the women, " They like this work; it is their choice to spend the afternoon thus. If I should tell them to go and put on fine clothes and lounge around, they would be very much aggrieved."

The members are all Germans or Pennsylvanians. They are of several Protestant sects; and there is even one Jew, but no Roman Catholics.

The band played on Sunday evening for an hour or more, but did not attract many people. Boys were playing ball in the street at the same time. Some *bought* tobacco; which led me to ask again about the use of money. The question was not in any case satisfactorily answered; but I have reason to believe that a little selfish earning of private spending money is winked at. For instance, the man whose daughter's wedding I attended kept a few hives of bees; and in answer to a question I was told he did not turn their honey into the general treasury; what he did not consume he was allowed to sell.

"In such ways we get a little finery for our daughters," said one. Again, when apples are very abundant, and a sufficient supply has been dried for market, the remainder of the crop is divided among the householders, with the understanding that they may eat or sell them as they prefer.

There is an air of untidyness about the streets of the settlement which is unpleasing. There is a piece of water, which might easily be made very pretty, but it is allowed to turn into a quagmire. But few of the door-yards are neatly kept. The village seems to have been laid out at haphazard. Moreover, their stock is of poor breeds ; the pigs especially being wretched razor-backed creatures.

As to the people—there can be no doubt that they are happy and contented. In a country where labor is scarce and highly paid, and where the rewards of patient industry in any calling are sure and large, it is not to be supposed that such a society as Aurora would have held together nineteen years if its members were not in every way satisfied with their plan of life, and with the results they have attained under it.

What puzzled me was to find a considerable number of people in the United States satisfied with so little. What they have secured is neighbors, sufficient food probably of a better kind than is enjoyed by the ordinary Oregon farmer, and a distinct and certain provision for their old age, or for helplessness. The last seemed, in all their minds, a source of great comfort. Pecuniarily their success has not been brilliant, for if the property were sold out and the money divided, the eighty or ninety families would not receive more than three thousand or thirty-five hundred dollars each ; and a farmer in Oregon must have been a very unfortunate man, who, coming here nineteen years ago with nothing, should not be worth more than this sum now, if he had labored as steadily and industriously, and lived as economically as the Aurora people have.

It is probable, however, that in the minds of most of them, the value of united action, the value to each of the example of the others, and the security against absolute poverty and helplessness in the first years of hard struggle, as well as the comfort of social ties, has counted for a great deal.

Nor ought I to forget the moral advantages, which appear to me immense and not to be underrated. Since the foundation of the colony, it has not had a criminal among its numbers; it has sent no man to jail; it has not had a lawsuit, neither among the members nor with outside people; it has not an insane person, nor one blind or deaf and dumb; nor has there been any case of deformity. It has no poor; and the support of its own helpless persons is a part of its plan.

This means that the Aurora community has not once in nineteen years of its existence used the courts, the jails, or the asylums of the state; that it has contributed nothing to the criminal or the pauper parts of the population.

This result in a newly settled state, and among a rude society, will appear not less remarkable when I add that the community has no library; that its members, so far as I could see, lack even the most common and moderate literary culture, aspiring to nothing further than the ability to read, write, and cipher; that from the president down it is absolutely without intellectual life. Moreover, it has very few amusements. Dancing is very little practiced; there is so little social life that there is not even a hall for public meetings in the village; apple-parings and occasional picnics in the summer, the playing of a band, a sermon twice a month, and visiting among the families, are the chief, indeed the only excitements in their monotonous lives. With all this there is singularly little merely animal enjoyment among them: they do not drink liquor; the majority, I was told, do not even smoke tobacco; there is no gayety among the people. Doubtless the winter, which brings them all together in the village, leads to some amusements; but I could hear of nothing set, or looked forward to, or elaborately planned. "The women talk, more or less," said one man to me, when I asked if there were never disagreements and family jars; "but we have learned to bear that, and it makes no trouble."

It seemed to me that I saw in the faces and forms of the people the results of this too monotonous existence. The young women are mostly pale, flat-chested, and somewhat thin. The young men look good-natured, but aimless. The older women and men are slow in their movements, placid, very quiet, and apparently satisfied with their lives.

I suppose the lack of smart dress and finery among the young people on Sunday, and at the wedding, gave a somewhat monotonous and dreary impression of the assemblage. This was probably strengthened in my mind by the fact that the somewhat shabby appearance of the people was only of a piece with the shabby and neglected look of their village, so that the whole conveyed an impression of carelessness and decay. Nineteen years of steady labor ought to have brought them, I could not but think, a little further: ought to have given them tastefully ornamented grounds, pretty houses, a public bath, a library and assembly-room, and neat Sunday clothing. It appeared to me that the stern repression of the whole intellectual side of life by their leader had borne this evil fruit. But it may be that the people themselves were to blame: they are Germans of a low class, and "Pennsylvania Dutch"—people, too often, who do not aim high. Then, too, it must be admitted that farm-life in Oregon is not, in general, above the plane of Aurora. Dutchtown is an Oregonian paradise; and the Aurora people are commonly said to "have every thing very nice about them."

Moreover, I could see that such a community must, unless it has for its head a person of strong intellectual life, advance more slowly and with greater difficulty than its members might, if they were living in the great world and thrown upon their individual resources.

Economically, I think there is no doubt that in the clearing up of their land, and the establishment of orchards and other productive industries, these Communists had a decided and important advantage over farmers undertaking similar enterprises with the help of laborers to whom they must have paid wages. For, though the wages of a day-laborer nowhere yield much more than his support and that of his family, they yield this in an uneconomical manner, a part of the sum earned being dropped on the way to middlemen, and a part going for whisky, sprees, blue Mondays, and illness arising out of bad situation, improper food, etc. The Aurora colonists labored without money wages; they could economize to the last possible degree in order to tide over a difficult place; they at all times measured their outlay by their means on hand; and I do not doubt that they made Aurora, with its orchards and other valuable improvements, for half what it would have cost by individual effort.

Nor can it be safely asserted that there is no higher future for Aurora. Dr. Keil can not carry them further—but he is sixty-four years old; if, when he dies, the presidency should fall into the hands of a person who, with tact enough to keep the people together, should have also intellectual culture enough to desire to lift them up to a higher plane of living, I can see nothing to prevent his success. The difficulty is that Dr. Keil's system produces no such man. Moses was brought up at Pharaoh's court, and not among the Israelites whom he liberated, and who made his whole life miserable for him.

II.—BETHEL.

Bethel is, of course, the older community; I describe it here after Aurora, because my visit to it was made after I had seen the Oregon community, and also because here is shown to what Aurora tends. The two societies are still one, having their efforts in common; and I was told that if the people at Bethel could sell their property, they would all remove to Oregon.

The Bethel Community now owns about four thousand acres of good land, exclusive of a tract of thirteen hundred acres at Nineveh, in the neighboring county of Adair, where six families of the community live, who are engaged chiefly in farming, having, however, also an old saw-mill and a tannery, and a shoemaker's and a blacksmith's shop. These families were removed thither twenty-five years ago, because it was thought the land there had a valuable water-power.

Bethel has now above two hundred members, and about twenty-five families. There are fifty children in the school, I was told.

They have a saw-mill and grist-mill, a tannery, a few looms, a general store, and a drug-store, and shops for carpenters, blacksmiths, coopers, tinners, tailors, shoemakers, and hatters, all on a small scale, but sufficient to supply not only themselves but the neighboring farmers. They had formerly a distillery, but that and a woolen factory were burned down a few years ago. They mean to rebuild the last.

All the people are Germans, and I found here many relatives of persons I had met at Aurora.

The town has much the same characteristic features as Aurora, except that it has not the exceptionally large and factory-like dwellings. It has one main street, poorly kept, and in parts even without a sidewalk; cattle and pigs were straying

THE BETHEL COMMUNE, MISSOURI.

about it, too, and altogether it did not look very prosperous. But the brick dwellings which lined the street were substantially built, and the saw and grist mill which lies at the lower end is a well-constructed building of brick. Half-way up the main street was a drug-store, large enough I should have said to accommodate with purges and cathartics a town of twenty-five hundred inhabitants ; and on a cross-street was another. Besides the chief store, I was surprised to see two other smaller shops; and still more surprised to be told that they belonged to and were kept by persons who had left the community, but who remained here in its midst. Of these I shall have something to say by and by.

At the head of the street stands the tavern or hotel, kept in the German or Pennsylvania Dutch way—with a bed in the large common room, and meals served in the kitchen. The German cooking was substantial and good. To the right of the hotel, at some distance, stands the church, placed in the middle of a young grove of trees planted much too thickly ever to prosper. The church has a floor of large red tiles ; a narrow pulpit at one end ; a place railed off at the other end, where the band plays on high festivals, and two doors for the entrance of the sexes, who sit on separate sides of the house. From the tower I had a view of the greater part of the community's territory, which lies finely, and is evidently a well-selected and valuable tract of land.

As in Aurora, they have preaching here every other Sunday, and no week-day meetings or assemblages of any kind. They told me, however, that they have a Sunday-school for the children, where they are instructed in the Bible.

The preacher and head of this society is a Mr. Giese, appointed by Dr. Keil; he keeps also the drug-store, where I was sorry to see liquor sold to laboring men and others, but in a very quiet way.

The Bethel Society has six trustees, chosen by the members,

but holding office during good behavior. As in Aurora, no business report is made to the society. Giese is cashier and book-keeper, and the trustees examine his accounts once a year.

The real estate in Bethel is held upon a very extraordinary tenure. It appears that—the settlement having begun in 1844—by 1847 there were in the society some dissatisfied persons, who clamored for a partition of the property. Dr. Keil thereupon determined to divide it, and to each member or householder a certain part was made over as his own. Out of the gains of the community in the three years was reserved sufficient to support the aged and infirm, and I believe the mills were also kept as part of the common stock. Thereupon some dissatisfied persons sold their shares and went off. The remainder lived on in common, and without changing their relations. To each person a deed was given of his share; but those who remained in the society were told—so the matter was explained to me by two of the trustees — not to put their deeds on record; and later a deed of the whole property of the community, including the individual holdings, was made out in the name of the president, Mr. Giese. I did not see this document, but presume, of course, that it gave him a title only in trust for all.

"Why did you partition the property?" I asked, curiously; and was answered, "In order to let every one be absolutely free, and to see who were inclined to a selfish life, and who for the community or unselfish life." Moreover, I was assured that any one who wished might at any time put his deed on record, and its validity would be acknowledged.

Now among the persons who left the society, six families were allowed to retain their property, and of these several at this day live in the midst of the village. One is a mechanic, who pursues his trade for wages; and two others keep small shops. This appeared to me a really extraordinary instance of liberality or carelessness; but no one of the community seemed to think it strange. There are also one or two farmers, not members; with one of these, a young man, I rode into Shelbina. He told me that he had grown up in the society; that he had gone into the army, where he served during the war; and when he returned he had got tired of community life. He had also got some business notions into his head, and thought the community affairs were too loosely managed. The members, he thought, had not sufficient knowledge of business; in which I agreed with him. But his house stood at the end of the village, and the relations between him and his former associates were at least so far amicable that one of the trustees took me to him to engage my passage to the railroad station.

The society was strongest before Dr. Keil went to Oregon; he drew away, between 1854 and 1863, about four hundred of the six hundred and fifty persons who were gathered in Bethel in 1855; and among these were, it seems, a large number of young men who did not want to serve in the war, the society being non-resistants, and slipped off to Oregon to avoid the draft. There are no accessions from outside, or at any rate so few as to count for nothing. But, on the other hand, they assured me that they keep most of their young people.

When one of the younger generation—for whom no property has been set apart—wishes to leave, a sum of money is given. While I was there a young girl was about to sever her connection with the society, and she received, besides her clothing, twenty-five dollars in money. If she had been older she would have received more, on the ground that she would have earned more by her labor, beyond the cost to the society of her care from childhood.

Some years ago they were subjected to a troublesome lawsuit, brought by a seceding member to recover both wages and the property of his parents. Thereupon, for the first time, they drew up a Constitution, which all signed, and which binds them to claim no wages.

Clothing is served to all the members alike from a common store. As to food: as at Aurora, each family receives pigs enough for meat, and cows enough for milk and butter; and adjoining each house is a garden of from a quarter to half an acre, in which the women work to raise vegetables for the home supply—the men helping at odd hours. But it is plainly understood that each may, and indeed is expected to raise a surplus of chickens, eggs, vegetables, fruits, etc., which is sold at the store for such luxuries as coffee, sugar, and articles of food brought from a distance. The calves are raised for the community. I found that one member was a silversmith and photographer; and all that he sold to his fellow-members of course they paid for with the surplus products of their small holdings. Flour and meal they take from the mill as they please, and no account is kept of it.

The trustees are also foremen, and lay out the work. The people rise with the sun, and have three meals a day. Before every house, neatly piled up in the street, I noticed large supplies of fire-wood, sawed and split. They hire a few laborers to cut wood for them; it is then drawn into town and to each man's door by the community teams; and thereupon each family is expected to saw and split its own supplies. In fact, they make a general effort, and with singing and much merriment the wood-piles are properly prepared. This certainly is a convenience which the backwood's farmer's wife is often without; but the untidy look of a great wood-pile before each house vexed my eyes.

The older men complained to me that the emigration to Oregon of so many of their young people had crippled them; and, indeed, I saw many signs of neglect—buildings in want of repair, and a lack of tidiness. But still they appear to be making money; for they have recently rebuilt their grist-mill,

CHURCH AT BETHEL, MISSOURI.

and have also within a few years paid off a debt of between three and four thousand dollars.

The religious belief of the Bethel Communists is, of course, the same with their Aurora brethren. They venerate Dr. Keil as the wisest of mankind, and abhor all ceremonies and sects. I was told that they celebrate the Lord's Supper at irregular intervals, and then by a regular supper, held either in the church or in a private house.

The people, like those of Aurora, are simple Germans of the lower class, and they live comfortably after their fashion. They have no library, and read few books except the Bible. They have never printed any thing. In many of the houses I noticed two beds in one room, and that the principal sitting-room of the family. Dr. Giese, the president, has living with him most of the young men who are without family connections in the society. There are usually no carpets in the houses. But every thing is clean; the beds are neat; and it is only out of doors that litter is to be found.

The people have but little ingenuity; there is a lack of labor-saving devices; indeed, the only thing of the kind I saw was a wash-house, through which the hot water from the boiler of the mill is led; but the house itself was badly arranged and comfortless. The young people have a band of music, but no other amusement that I could hear of. Tobacco they use freely, and strong drink is allowed; but they have no drunkards.

As their future is secure, the people marry young, and this probably does much to bind them to the place. No restriction is placed upon marriage, except that if one marries out of the community, he must leave it.

The extraordinary feature of the Bethel and Aurora communities is the looseness of the bond which keeps the people together. They might break up at any time; but they have remained in community for thirty years. Their religious belief is extremely simple, and yet it seems to suffice to hold them. They have not had among them any good business-men, yet they have managed to make a reasonably fair busi-ness success; for though, as I remarked concerning Aurora, almost any farmer industrious and economical as they are would have been pecuniarily better off after so many years, still these people, but for their determination to have their goods in common, would for the most part to-day have been day-laborers.

In weighing results, one should not forget the character of those who have achieved them; and considering what these people are, it can not be denied that they have lived better in community than they would have lived by individual effort.

THE ICARIANS,

NEAR

CORNING, IOWA.

THE ICARIANS.

ETIENNE CABET had a pretty dream; this dream took hold of his mind, and he spent sixteen years of his life in trying to turn it into real life.

One can not help respecting the handful of men and women who, in the wilderness of Iowa, have for more than twenty years faithfully endeavored to work out the problem of Communism according to the system he left them; but Cabet's own writings persuade me that he was little more than a vain dreamer, without the grim patience and steadfast unselfishness which must rule the nature of one who wishes to found a successful communistic society.

Cabet was born at Dijon, in France, in 1788. He was educated for the bar, but became a politician and writer. He was a leader of the Carbonari; was a member of the French Legislature; wrote a history of the French Revolution of July; established a newspaper; was condemned to two years' imprisonment for an article in it, but evaded his sentence by flying to London; in 1839 returned to France, and published a history of the French Revolution in four volumes; and the next year issued a book somewhat famous in its day—the voyage to Icaria. In this romance he described a communistic Utopia, whose terms he had dreamed out; and he began at once to try to realize his dream. He framed a constitution for an actual Icaria; sought for means and members to establish it; selected Texas as its field of operations, and early in 1848 actually persuaded a number of persons to set sail for the Red River country.

Sixty-nine persons formed the advance guard of his Utopia. They were attacked by yellow fever, and suffered greatly; and by the time next year when Cabet arrived at New Orleans with a second band, the first was already disorganized. He heard, on his arrival, that the Mormons had been driven from Nauvoo, in Illinois, leaving their town deserted; and in May, 1850, he established his followers there.

They bought at Nauvoo houses sufficient to accommodate them, but very little land, renting such farms as they needed. They lived there on a communal system, and ate in a great dining-room. But Cabet, I have been told, did not intend to form his colony permanently there, but regarded Nauvoo only as a rendezvous for those who should join the community, intending to draft them thence to the real settlements, which he wished to found in Iowa.

If Cabet had been a leader of the right temper, he might, I believe, have succeeded; for he appears to have secured the only element indispensable to success—a large number of followers. He had at Nauvoo at one time not less than fifteen hundred people. With so many members, a wise leader with business skill ought to be able to accomplish very much in a single year; in ten years his commune, if he could keep it together, ought to be wealthy.

The Icarians labored and planted with success at Nauvoo; they established trades of different kinds, as well as manufactures; and Cabet set up a printing-office, and issued a number of books and pamphlets in French and German, intended to attract attention to the community. Among these, a pamphlet of twelve pages, entitled, "Wenn ich $500,000 hätte" ("If I had half a million dollars"), which bears date Nauvoo, 1854, gives in some detail his plans and desires. It is a statement of what he could and would achieve for a commune if some one would start him with a capital of half a million; and the fact that four years after he came to Nau-

voo he should still have spent his time in such an impractica-
ble dream, shows, I think, that he was not a fit leader for the
enterprise. For nothing appears to me more certain than that
a communistic society, to be successful, needs above all things
to have the training, mental and physical, which comes out of
a life of privation, spent in the patient accumulation of property by the labors of the members.

Moreover, in Cabet's first paragraph he shows contempt for
one of the vital principles of a communistic society. "If I
had five hundred thousand dollars," he writes, "this would
open to us an immense credit, and in this way vastly increase
our means." But it is absolutely certain that debt is the bane
of such societies; and the remnant of Icarians who have so
tenaciously and bravely held together in Iowa would be the
first to confess this, for they suffered hardships for years because of debt.

If he had half a million, Cabet goes on to say, he would be
able to establish his commune upon a broad and generous
scale; and he draws a pretty picture of dwellings supplied
with gas and hot and cold water; of factories fitted up on the
largest scale; of fertile farms under the best culture; of
schools, high and elementary; of theatres, and other places
of amusement; of elegantly kept pleasure-grounds, and so on.
Alas for the dreams of a dreamer! I turned over the leaves
of his pamphlet while wandering through the muddy lanes of
the present Icaria, on one chilly Sunday in March, with a keen
sense of pain at the contrast between the comfort and elegance
he so glowingly described and the dreary poverty of the life
which a few determined men and women have there chosen
to follow, for the sake of principles which they hold both true
and valuable.

I have heard that Cabet developed at Nauvoo a dictatorial
spirit, and that this produced in time a split in the society.
The leader and his adherents went off to St. Louis, where he

died in 1856. Meantime some of the members were already settled in Iowa, and those who remained at Nauvoo after Cabet's desertion or flight dispersed; the property was sold, and the Illinois colony came to an end. The greater part of the members went off, more or less disappointed. Between fifty and sixty settled upon the Iowa estate, and here began life, very poor and with a debt of twenty thousand dollars in some way fixed upon their land.

Their narrow means allowed them to build at first only the meanest mud hovels. They thought themselves prosperous when they were able to build log-cabins, though these were so wretched that comfort must have been unknown among them for years. They were obliged to raise all that they consumed; and they lived, and indeed still live, in the narrowest way.

The Icarian Commune lies about four miles from Corning, a station on the Burlington and Missouri River Railroad, in Iowa. They began here with four thousand acres of land, pretty well selected, and twenty thousand dollars of debt. After some years of struggle they gave up the land to their creditors, with the condition that they might redeem one half of it within a certain stipulated time. This they were able to do by hard work and pinching economy; and they own at present one thousand nine hundred and thirty-six acres, part of which is in timber, and valuable on that account.

There are in all sixty-five members, and eleven families. The families are not large, for there are twenty children and only twenty-three voters in the community.

They possess a saw-mill and grist-mill, built out of their savings within five years, and now a source of income. They cultivate three hundred and fifty acres of land, and have one hundred and twenty head of cattle, five hundred head of sheep, two hundred and fifty hogs, and thirty horses. Until within three years the settlement contained only log-cabins, and these very small, and not commodiously arranged. Since then they

have got entirely out of debt, and have begun to build frame
houses. The most conspicuous of these is a two-story building, sixty by twenty-four feet in dimensions, which contains
the common dining-room, kitchen, a provision cellar, and up
stairs a room for a library, and apartments for a family. In
the spring of 1874 they had nearly a dozen frame houses,
which included the dining-hall, a wash-house, dairy, and school-
house. All the dwellings are small and very cheaply built.
They have small shops for carpentry, blacksmithing, wagon-
making, and shoemaking; and they make, as far as possible,
all they use.

Most of the people are French, and this is the language
mainly spoken, though I found that German was also understood. Besides the French, there are among the members one
American, one Swiss, a Swede, and a Spaniard, and two Germans. The children look remarkably healthy, and on Sunday
were dressed with great taste. The living is still of the plainest. In the common dining-hall they assemble in groups at
the tables, which were without a cloth, and they drink out of
tin cups, and pour their water from tin cans. "It is very
plain," said one to me; "but we are independent—no man's
servants—and we are content."

They sell about two thousand five hundred pounds of wool
each year, and a certain number of cattle and hogs; and these,
with the earnings of their mills, are the sources of their income.

Their number does not increase, though four or five years
ago they were reduced to thirty members; but since then
seven who went off have returned. I should say that they had
passed over the hardest times, and that a moderate degree of
prosperity is possible to them now; but they have waited long
for it. I judge that they had but poor skill in management
and no business talent; but certainly they had abundant courage and determination.

They live under a somewhat elaborate constitution, made

for them by Cabet, which lays down with great care the equality and brotherhood of mankind, and the duty of holding all things in common; abolishes servitude and service (or servants); commands marriage, under penalties; provides for education; and requires that the majority shall rule. In practice they elect a president once a year, who is the executive officer, but whose powers are strictly limited to carrying out the commands of the society. " He could not even sell a bushel of corn without instructions," said one to me. Every Saturday evening they hold a meeting of all the adults, women as well as men, for the discussion of business and other affairs. Officers are chosen at every meeting to preside and keep the records ; the president may present subjects for discussion; and women may speak, but have no vote. The conclusions of the meeting are to rule the president during the next week. All accounts are made up monthly, and presented to the society for discussion and criticism. Besides the president, there are four directors—of agriculture, clothing, general industry, and building. These carry on the necessary work, and direct the other members. 'They buy at wholesale twice a year, and just before these purchases are made each member in public meeting makes his or her wants known. Luxury is prohibited in the constitution, but they have not been much tempted in that direction so far. They use tobacco, however.

They have no religious observances. Sunday is a day of rest from labor, when the young men go out with guns, and the society sometimes has theatrical representations, or music, or some kind of amusement. The principle is to let each one do as he pleases.

They employ two or three hired men to chop wood and labor on the farm.

They have a school for the children, the president being teacher.

The people are opposed to what is called a " unitary home," and prefer to have a separate dwelling for each family.

The children are kept in school until they are sixteen; and the people lamented their poverty, which prevented them from providing better education for them.

Members are received by a three-fourths' majority.

This is Icaria. It is the least prosperous of all the communities I have visited; and I could not help feeling pity, if not for the men, yet for the women and children of the settlement, who have lived through all the penury and hardship of these many years. A gentleman who knew of my visit there writes me: " Please deal gently and cautiously with Icaria. The man who sees only the chaotic village and the wooden shoes, and only chronicles those, will commit a serious error. In that village are buried fortunes, noble hopes, and the aspirations of good and great men like Cabet. Fertilized by these deaths, a great and beneficent growth yet awaits Icaria. It has an eventful and extremely interesting history, but its future is destined to be still more interesting. It, and it alone, represents in America a great idea—rational democratic communism."

I am far from belittling the effort of the men of Icaria. They have shown, as I have said, astonishing courage and perseverance. They have proved their faith in the communistic idea by labors and sufferings which seem to me pitiful. In fact, communism is their religion. But their long siege at fortune's door only shows how important, and indeed indispensable to the success of such an effort, it is to have an able leader, and to give to him almost unlimited power and absolute obedience.

THE BISHOP HILL COMMUNE.

THE BISHOP HILL COMMUNE.

I HAVE determined to give a brief account of the Swedish colony at Bishop Hill, in Henry County, Illinois, because, though it has now ceased to exist as a communistic society, its story yields some instructive lessons in the creation and maintenance of such associations. These Swedes began in abject poverty, and in the course of a few years built up a prosperous town and settlement. They rashly went into debt: debt brought lawsuits and disputes into the society, and all three broke it up.

The people of Bishop Hill came from the region of Helsingland, in Sweden. In their own country they were Pietists, and Separatists from the State Church, mostly farmers, scattered over a considerable district, but united by their peculiar doctrines, and by the efforts of their preachers. I am told that they came into existence as a sect about 1830; in 1843 their chief preacher was a man of some energy, Eric Janson by name; and he taught them the duty of living after the manner of the Primitive Christian Church, inculcating humble and prayerful lives, equality of conditions, and community of property.

Their refusal to attend church, and to submit themselves to its ordinances, excited the attention of the government, which, probably also alarmed at the phrase "community of goods," began to persecute them with fines and imprisonment. Police officers were sent to break up their congregations; they imagined themselves threatened with confiscation; and in 1845 they sent one of their number, Olaf Olson, to the United States, to see if they could not here find land on which to live in peace and freedom. Olson's inquiries led him to Illinois; he selected Henry County as a favorable situation; and in 1846, on his report, the people determined to emigrate in a body, the few wealthy agreeing to pay the expenses of the poor. They say that when they were ready to embark, they were refused permission to leave their country, and Jonas Olson, one of their leaders, had to go to the king, who, on his prayer, finally allowed them to depart.

The first ship-load left Galfa in the summer of 1846, and arrived at Bishop Hill in October of that year. Others followed, until by the summer of 1848 they had eight hundred people on this spot—which they named from an eminence in their own country.

They appear to have spent most of their means in the emigration, for they were able during the first year to buy only forty acres of land, and for eighteen months they lived in extreme poverty—in holes in the ground, and under sheds built against hillsides; and ground their corn for bread in hand-mills, often laboring at this task by turns all night, to provide meal for the next day. A tent made of linen cloth was their church during this time; and they worked the land of neighboring farmers on shares to gain a subsistence. Living on the prairie, fever and ague attacked them and added to their wretchedness.

By 1848 they had acquired two hundred acres of land, but were $1800 in debt, which they had borrowed to keep them from starving; but in this year they built a brick church, and they now worked a good deal of land on shares. In 1849 they began to build a very long brick house, still standing, which served them as kitchen and dining-hall. In the same year Jonas Olson, a preacher, took eight young men, and with the consent of the society went to California to dig gold for the common interest. He returned after a year, unsuccessful.

In 1850 Eric Janson, their leader, was shot in the Henry
County court-house, while attending a trial in which a young
man, not a member of the community, claimed his wife, a girl
who was a member, and whom he wished to take away. I do
not know the merits of the case, nor is it important here. During this year Olaf Janson returned from Sweden with several
thousand dollars which he had been sent to collect—being debts
due some of the members; and this money, which enabled them
to buy land, appears to have given them their first fair start.

At this time, though they were still poor, they had built a
number of brick dwellings, had set up shops for carpentry,
blacksmithing, wagon-making, etc.; were raising flax, selling
the seed, and making the fibre into linen, some of which they
sold; and they had a few cattle, and a worn-out saw-mill.
They had set up a school, even while they lived " in the caves,"
and now hired an American teacher.

In 1853 they got an act of incorporation from the Illinois
Legislature, which enabled them to hold land and transact business as an association, and in the name of trustees; until that
time all they owned was held in the name of individual members. In the same year they made a contract to raise, during
two years, seven hundred acres of broom-corn, for which they
received in cash on delivery fifty dollars a ton. As yet they
had no railroad, and had to haul their corn fifty miles. At
this time, too, they began to improve their breeds of cattle;
paid high prices for one or two short-horn bulls, and were soon
famous in their region for the excellence of their stock. They
also made wagons for the neighboring farmers, and established
a grist-mill.

In 1854–5 they took a contract to grade a part of the Chicago, Burlington, and Quincy Railroad line, and to build some
bridges; and as they were able to put a considerable body of
their young men upon this work, it brought them in a good
deal of money. They now began to erect brick dwellings, a

town-hall, and a large hotel, where they for a while did a good business. They made excellent brick, and all their houses are very solidly built, plain, but of pleasing exteriors. The most remarkable one is the long dining-hall and kitchen, with a bakery and brewery adjoining. In the upper story of this building a considerable number of families lived; in the lower story all the people—to the number of a thousand at one time—ate three times a day.

They were now prospering. In 1859 they owned ten thousand acres of land, and had it all neatly fenced and in excellent order. They had the finest cattle in the state; and their shops and mills earned money from the neighboring farmers.

The families lived separately, but all ate together. They received their clothing supplies at a common storehouse as they needed them, and labored under the direction of foremen. Their business organization was always loose. They had no president or single head. A body of trustees transacted business, and made reports to the society, not regularly, but at irregular intervals. There seems, too, to have been a speculative spirit among them, for while in 1859 they owned ten thousand acres of land and a town, which must have been worth at least three hundred thousand dollars, as the land was all fenced and improved, and the town was uncommonly well built,* they owed at that time, or in 1860, between eighty and one hundred thousand dollars.

Their religious life was very simple. They had no paid preacher, but expected their leaders to labor during the week with the rest. On Sunday they had two services in the church—at ten in the morning, and between six and seven in the evening. At these, after singing and prayer, the preacher read the Bible, and commented on what he read. On every week-day

---

* Between four and five hundred thousand dollars was their own valuation; and in 1860 a report given in one of the briefs of a lawsuit gives their assets at $864,000, and their debts at less than $100,000.

evening, unless the weather was bad, they held a similar meeting, which lasted an hour and a half. They had no library, and encouraged no reading except in the Bible, teaching that the most important matter for every man was to get a thorough understanding of the commandments of God. They had for a little while a newspaper, and they printed at the neighboring town of Galva, which was their business centre, an edition of their hymn-book.* They discouraged amusements, as tending to worldliness; and though they appear to have lived happily and without disputes, about 1859 they discovered that their young people, who had grown up in the society, were discontented, found the community life dull, did not care for the religious views of the society, and were ready to break up the organization.

When this discontent arose, the looseness of the organization was fatal. With a more compact and energetic administration, either the dissatisfied elements would have been eliminated quietly, or the causes of dissatisfaction, mainly, as far as I could understand, the dullness of the life and the lack of amusements, would have been removed. But with a loose organization there appears to have been, what is not unnatural, rigidity of discipline. There was no power any where to make changes. "The discontented ones wanted a change, but no change was possible: it was often discussed." The young people persuaded some of the older ones to be of their mind, and thus two parties were formed; and after many meetings, in which I imagine there were sometimes bitter words, it was determined in the spring of 1860 to divide the property, the Olson party, as it was called, including two thirds of the membership, determining with their share to continue the community, while the Janson party determined on individual effort.

Hereupon two thirds of the real and personal property was

---

* " Några Sånger, samt Böner. Författade af Erik Janson. Förenade Staterna, Galva, Ills. S. Cronsioe, 1857."

set apart for the Olson party, but for a whole year the two parties lived together at Bishop Hill. In 1861 the Janson party divided their share among the families composing it; and in the same year the disorganization proceeded another step. The Olson party fell into three divisions. In 1862, finally, all the property was divided, and the commune ceased to exist.

In 1860 a receiver had been appointed. In 1861 Olaf Janson was appointed attorney in fact. This became necessary, because, besides the property, there were debts; and when the trustees were removed and a receiver was appointed, the question necessarily came up how the debts should be met. The division of the property was made by a committee of the society, who took a complete inventory, including even the smallest household articles; and at the time there seems to have been no complaint of unfairness. The whole was divided into shares, of which each man received one, and women and children fractional shares. A part of the property was set off, sufficient, as it was then believed, to pay off the indebtedness; but it proved insufficient, and finally each farm given to a member in the partition was saddled with a share of indebtedness; and as there was poor management after the disorganization began, and as the debt constantly increased by the non-payment of interest, there are now, thirteen years after the final partition, heavy lawsuits still pending in the courts against the colony and its trustees.

In 1861 the community raised a company of soldiers for the Union army, furnishing both privates and officers. These fought through the war, and one of the younger members after the war was, for meritorious conduct and promising intellect, taken as a scholar at West Point, where he was graduated with honor.

At present Bishop Hill is slowly falling into decay. The houses are still mostly inhabited; there are several shops and stores; but the larger buildings are out of repair; and business has centred at Galva, five or six miles distant. Most of the former communists live happily on their small farms. A Methodist church has been built in the village, and has some attendants, but a good many of the older members have adopted the Adventist or Millerite faith, which appears to revive after every failure of prediction, especially in the West, where people seem to look forward with a quite singular pleasure to the fiery end of all things.

On the whole, it is a melancholy story. It shows both what can be achieved by combined industry, and what trifles can destroy such an organization as a communistic society. It shows the extreme importance of a central authority, wisely administered but also implicitly obeyed; able therefore to yield, as well as to act, promptly. The history of these Bishop Hill Communists also shows the necessity of great caution in all financial affairs in a commune, which ought to avoid debt like the plague, and to live financially as though it might break up at any moment.

Not only were debt and the speculative spirit out of which debt arose the causes of the colony's failure, but they have brought great trouble on the people since. Had there been no debt, the commune could have divided its property among the members at any time, without loss or trouble; and I suspect that the possibility of such an immediate division might have induced the people to keep together.

At any rate, the story of Bishop Hill shows how important it would be to a community agreeing to labor and produce in common for a limited time to keep free from debt.

THE CEDAR VALE COMMUNITY.

THE CEDAR VALE COMMUNITY.

At Cedar Vale, in Howard County, Kansas, a communistic society has been founded, which, though its small numbers might make it insignificant, is remarkable by reason of the nationality of some of its members.

It was begun three years ago, and the purpose of its projectors was " to achieve both communism and individual freedom, or to lead persons of all kinds of opinions to labor together for their common welfare. If there was to be any law, it should be only for the regulation of industry or hours of work." I quote this from the letter of a gentleman who is familiar with this society, and who has been kind enough to send me its constitution, and to give me the following particulars : " It is now three years since the founders of the society settled in this domain, coming here entirely destitute, and building first as a residence a covered burrow in a hillside. Two of them had left affluence and position in Russia, and subjected themselves to this poverty for the sake of their principles. Of course they suffered here from fever, from insufficient food, and cold, and were not able to make much improvement on the place. The practical condition now, though insignificant from the common point of view, compared with what has been, is very satisfactory. There are at least comfortable shelter and enough to eat, and this year sufficient land will be fenced and planted to leave a surplus.

" The propaganda has been made among two essentially dif- fering classes of socialists—the Russian Materialists and the

American Spiritualists. Both these classes are represented in the community, and thus far seem to live in harmony. There are here a ' hygienic doctor' and a ' reformed clergyman,' both Spiritualists, and a Russian sculptor of considerable fame, a Russian astronomer, and a very pretty and devoted and wonderfully industrious Russian woman."

The printed statement made by the community I copy here, as a sufficient account of its numbers and possessions in April, 1874 :

" The PROGRESSIVE COMMUNITY is located near Cedar Vale, Howard County, Kansas, has three hundred and twenty acres of choice prairie land, with abundance of stock, water, and with all advantages for successful farming, stock and fruit raising.

" The nearest railroad station is Independence, Montgomery County, Kansas, fifty miles east from the place.

" The community was established in January, 1871. It is out of debt now, and has a fair prospect for success in the future.

" The business of the community consists chiefly in farming.

" Number of members : four males ; three females ; one child. Persons on probation : two males ; one female ; one child.

" Improvements : frame house ; stable ; forty acres under fence ; four acres of orchard and vines.

" Live stock and implements : four horses ; four oxen ; three cows and calves.

" The co-operation of earnest communists is wanted for the better realization of a true home based on Liberty, Equality, and Fraternity.

" No fee is required from those who visit the community, but their work for the community is regarded as equivalent to their current expenses.

" The principles and organization of the community can be seen from the following constitution.

" PREAMBLE.

" *Whereas*, we believe that man is not only an individual having rights as such, but also owing social duties to others, and that strict justice requires us to help each other, and that our highest happiness and development can only be attained by a union and co-operation of interests and efforts ; *Therefore*, we pledge ourselves to live

'For the cause that lacks assistance,
For the wrong that needs resistance,
For the future in the distance,
And the good that we can do.'

" And we, whose names are annexed, hereby organize ourselves under the name of the PROGRESSIVE COMMUNITY, and agree to devote our labor and means, to the full extent of our ability, to carry out the following

"CONSTITUTION.

"ARTICLE I.

" SEC. 1.—The community shall be considered as a family. The members shall unite in their labor and business, hold their property in common for the use of all, and dwell together in a unitary home.

" SEC. 2.—Each member shall be free to hold whatever opinions his conscience may dictate; and the community shall make no restriction or regulation interfering with the freedom of any, except when his actions conflict with the rights of others.

" SEC. 3.—All shall be alike responsible for the strict observance of this constitution. Equal rights and privileges shall be accorded to all members; but the community may temporarily withhold from a member the right to vote by the unanimous consent of the rest.

"ARTICLE II.

" SEC. 1.—All matters concerning the welfare of the community shall be decided by the members at their meetings, which shall be of the following kinds: (1) Daily business meetings for the decision of daily work; (2) Weekly meetings for the discussion of business questions, and for remarks on the general interests and welfare of the community.

" SEC. 2.—All decisions, except as herein otherwise provided for, shall be by a majority of three fourths of all the members.

" SEC. 3.—Debts may be contracted, or credit given, only by the unanimous vote of the community.

" SEC. 4.—The officers of the community shall consist of a president, secretary, treasurer, and managers. They shall be elected at the end of each year, and enter on the duties of their offices on the first of January following, being subject to removal at any time.

" SEC. 5.—The president shall preside at all meetings, shall see that the decisions of the community are carried out, and make temporary arrangements for the business of the day when necessary.

" SEC. 6.—The secretary shall record the proceedings of all the meetings of the community, attend to all its correspondence, and preserve all the valuable documents thereof.

"Sec. 7.—The treasurer shall hold the fund of the community, and keep an accurate account of all money received or expended; but no money shall be paid out except as appropriated by the community. He shall make a report at each business meeting.

"Sec. 8.—The managers shall control the different departments to which they are elected, decide all details of business, if not previously acted upon by the community, and make reports at each business meeting.

"ARTICLE III.

"Sec. 1.—Any person, after having lived in the community, and having become thoroughly acquainted with its members and the community life, may become a member by subscribing to this constitution; provided he is accepted by the unanimous vote of the community.

"Sec. 2.—All property which members may have, or may receive from any source or at any time, shall be given to the community without reservation or return.

"Sec. 3.—The members shall be furnished with food, clothing, and lodging, care and attention in sickness, misfortune, infancy, or old age, and the means and opportunity for a complete integral education, and for such other necessary requirements as the community can afford; and these benefits shall be guaranteed by the whole resources of the community.

"Sec. 4.—A withdrawing member shall not bring any claim against the community on account of any labor, services, or property given thereto; but his current expenses and the advantages of the community life shall be considered as an equivalent therefor. He shall be allowed to take from the common property only what may be decided upon by the community at the time of withdrawal.

"Sec. 5.—Children of the members, or those which may be adopted by the community, shall be considered as members thereof; they shall have equal rights as herein specified, except voting, to which privilege they shall be admitted when the community by unanimous consent shall think best, and after signing their names to this constitution.

"ARTICLE IV.

"Any amendments, additions to, or interpretations of this constitution may be made at any time by unanimous vote of the community."

THE SOCIAL FREEDOM COMMUNITY.

THIS is a communistic society, established in the beginning of the year 1874 in Chesterfield County, Virginia. It has as "full members" two women, one man, and three boys, with four women and five men as "probationary members." They have a farm of three hundred and thirty-three acres, unencumbered with debt, and with a water-power on it; and are attempting general farming, the raising of medicinal herbs, sawing lumber and staves, coopering, and the grinding of grain. The members are all Americans.

They hold, the secretary writes me, to "unity of interests, and political, religious, and social freedom; and believe that every individual should have absolute control of herself or himself, and that, so long as they respect the same freedom in others, no one has a right to infringe on that individuality." The secretary further writes: "We have no constitution or by-laws; ignore the idea of man's total depravity; and believe that all who are actuated by a love of truth and a desire to progress (and we will knowingly accept no others), can be better governed by love and moral suasion than by any arbitrary laws. Our government consists in free criticism. We have a unitary home."

COLONIES WHICH ARE NOT

COMMUNISTIC.

COLONIES—NOT COMMUNISTIC.

I HAVE noticed that not unfrequently Vineland, in New Jersey, and Anaheim, in California, are classed with Communistic Societies. They are nothing of the kind; and only one of the two—Anaheim, namely—was in the beginning even co-operative.

As, however, both these settlements were founded under peculiar circumstances, and as both show what can be achieved in a short time by men of narrow means, acting more or less in concert for certain purposes, I have determined to give here a brief history of the two places.

Anaheim.

Anaheim, the oldest of these two " colonies," lies in Los Angeles County, in Southern California, about thirty miles from the town of Los Angeles, and ten or twelve miles from the ocean, upon a fertile and well-watered plain. In its settlement it was strictly a co-operative enterprise.

In 1857 several Germans in San Francisco proposed to certain of their countrymen to purchase by a united effort a tract of land in the southern part of the state, cause it to be subdivided into small farms, and procure these to be fenced, planted with grape-vines and trees, and otherwise prepared for the settlement of the owners. After some deliberation, fifty men set their names to an agreement to buy eleven hundred and sixty-five acres of land, at two dollars per acre; securing water-rights for irrigation with the purchase, because in that region the dry summers necessitate artificial watering.

The originator of the enterprise, Mr. Hansen, of Los Angeles, a German lawyer and civil engineer, a man of culture, was appointed by his associates to select and secure the land; and eventually he became the manager of the whole enterprise, up to the point where it lost its co-operative features and the members took possession of their farms.

The Anaheim associates consisted in the main of mechanics, and they had not a farmer among them. They were all Germans. There were several carpenters, a gunsmith, an engraver, three watch-makers, four blacksmiths, a brewer, a teacher, a shoemaker, a miller, a hatter, a hotel-keeper, a bookbinder, four or five musicians, a poet (of course), several merchants, and some teamsters. It was a very heterogeneous assembly; they had but one thing in common: they were all, with one or two exceptions, poor. Very few had more than a few dollars saved; most of them had neither cash nor credit enough to buy even a twenty-acre farm; and none of them were in circumstances which promised them more than a decent living.

The plan of the society was to buy the land, and thereupon to cause it to be subdivided and improved as I have said by monthly contributions from the members, who were meantime to go on with their usual employments in San Francisco. It was agreed to divide the eleven hundred and sixty-five acres into fifty twenty-acre tracts, and fifty village lots, the village to stand in the centre of the purchase. Fourteen lots were also set aside for school-houses and other public buildings.

With the first contribution the land was bought. The fifty associates had to pay about fifty dollars each for this purpose. This done, they appointed Mr. Hansen their agent to make the projected improvements; and they, it may be supposed, worked a little more steadily and lived a little more frugally in San Francisco. He employed Spaniards and Indians as laborers; and what he did was to dig a ditch seven miles long to lead water out of the Santa Anna River, with four hundred and fifty miles of subsidiary ditches and twenty-five miles of feeders to lead the water over every twenty-acre lot. This done, he planted on every farm eight acres of grapes and some fruit-trees; and on the whole place over five miles of outside willow fencing and thirty-five miles of inside fencing. Willows grow rapidly in that region, and make a very close fence, yielding also fire-wood sufficient for the farmer's use.

All this had to be done gradually, so that the payments for labor should not exceed the monthly contributions of the associates, for they had no credit to use in the beginning, and contracted no debts.

When the planting was done, the superintendent cultivated and pruned the grape-vines and trees, and took care of the place; and it was only when the vines were old enough to bear, and thus to yield an income at once, that the proprietors took possession.

At the end of three years the whole of this labor had been performed and paid for; the vines were ready to bear a crop, and the division of lots took place. Each shareholder had at this time paid in all twelve hundred dollars; a few, I have been told, fell behind somewhat, but were helped by some of their associates who were in better circumstances. If we suppose that most of the members had no money laid by at the beginning of the enterprise, it would appear that during three years they saved, over and above their living, somewhat less than eight dollars a week—a considerable sum, but easily possible at that time in California to a good and steady mechanic.

It was inevitable that some of the small farms should be more valuable than others; and there was naturally a difference, too, in the village lots. To make the division fairly, all the places were viewed, and a schedule was made of them, on which each was assessed at a certain price, varying from six hundred to fourteen hundred dollars, according to its situation, the excellence of its fruit, etc.   They were then distributed by a kind of lottery, with the condition that if the farm drawn was valued in the schedule over twelve hundred dollars, he who drew it should pay into the general treasury the surplus; if it was valued at less, he who drew it received from the common fund a sum which, added to the value of his farm, equaled twelve hundred dollars.   Thus A, who drew a fourteen-hundred-dollar lot, paid two hundred dollars; B, who drew a six-hundred-dollar lot, received six hundred dollars additional in cash.

The property was by this time in such a state of improvement that money could readily be borrowed on the security of these small farms.   Moreover, when the drawing was completed, there was a sale of the effects of the company—horses, tools, etc.; and on closing all the accounts and balancing the books, it was found that there remained a sum of money in the general treasury sufficient to give each of the fifty shareholders a hundred dollars in cash as a final dividend.

When this was done, the co-operative feature of the enterprise disappeared.   The members, each in his own good time, settled on their farms.   Lumber was bought at wholesale, and they began to build their houses.   Fifty families make a little town in any of our Western States, suffiicently important to attract traders.   The village lots at once acquired a value, and some were sold to shopkeepers.   A school was quickly established; mechanics of different kinds came down to Anaheim to work for wages; and the colonists in fact gathered about them at once many conveniences which, if they had settled singly, they could not have commanded for some years.

They were still poor, however.   But few of them were able even to build the slight house needed in that climate without running into debt.   For borrowed money they had to pay from two to three per cent. per month interest.   Moreover, none of them were farmers; and they had to learn to cultivate, prune, and take care of their vines, to make wine, and to make a vegetable garden. They had from the first to raise and sell enough for their own support, and to pay at least the heavy interest on their debts. It resulted that for some years longer they had a struggle with a burden of debt, and had to live with great economy. But the people told me that they had always enough to eat, a good school for their children, and the immense satisfaction of being their own employers. "We had music and dancing in those days; and, though we were very poor, I look back to those times as the happiest in all our lives," said one man to me.

And they gradually got out of debt. Not one failed. The sheriff has never sold out any one in Anaheim; and only one of the original settlers had left the place when I saw it in 1872. They have no destitute people. Their vineyards give them an annual *clear* income of from two hundred and fifty to one thousand dollars over and above their living expenses; their children have enjoyed the advantages of a social life and a fairly good school. And, finally, the property which originally cost them an average of one thousand and eighty dollars for each, is now worth from five to ten thousand dollars. They live well, and feel themselves as independent as though they were millionaires.

Now this was an enterprise which any company of prudent mechanics, with a steadfast purpose, might easily imitate. The founders of Anaheim were not picked men. I have been told that they were not without jealousies and suspicions of each other and of their manager, which made his life often uncomfortable, and threatened the life of the undertaking. They had grumblers, fault-finders, and wiseacres in their company, as probably there will be among any company of fifty men; and I have heard that Mr. Hansen, who was their able and honest manager, declared that he would rather starve than conduct another such enterprise.

They were extremely fortunate to have for their manager an honest, patient, and sufficiently able man ; and such a leader is indeed the corner-stone of an undertaking of this kind. Granted a man sufficiently wise and honest, in whom his associates can have confidence, and there needs only moderate patience, perseverance, and economy, in the body of the company, to achieve success. Nor could I help noticing, when I was at Anaheim, that the experience and training which men gain in carrying to success—no matter through what struggles of poverty, self-denial, and debt—such an enterprise, has an admirable effect on their characters. The men of Anaheim were originally a very common class of mechanics ; they have stepped up to a higher plane of life—they are masters of their own lives. This result—namely, the training of families in the hardier virtues, their elevation to a higher moral as well as physical standard—is certainly not to be overlooked by any thoughtful man.

Vineland.

Vineland was not a co-operative enterprise. It is the land-speculation of a long-headed, kind-hearted man, who believed that he could form a settlement profitable and advantageous to many people, and with pecuniary benefit to himself. Until the year 1861, the southern part of New Jersey contained a large region known as " the Barrens," and very sparsely settled with a rude and unthrifty population. The light soil was supposed to be unfit for profitable agriculture ; and the country for miles was covered with scrub pine and small oak timber, used chiefly for charcoal, and as fuel for some glass factories at Millville and Glassborough. Much of this land was owned in large tracts, and brought in but a small revenue. When the West Jersey Railroad, connecting Cape May with Philadelphia, was completed, it ran through many miles of these " Barrens," and some of the owners, tired of a property which in their hands had little value, were ready to sell out.

Charles K. Landis had conceived the idea of forming a colony, upon certain plans which he had matured in his own mind. His attention was attracted to this region, and after examining the soil and the general character of the region, he bought sixteen thousand acres in one parcel. To this he added, soon after, another purchase of fourteen thousand acres, making thirty thousand in all. He has bought lately (in 1874) twenty-three thousand acres more.

The country is a rolling plain, densely overgrown with small wood, with one or two streams running through it; with water obtainable at from fifteen to thirty feet every where, and perfectly healthy. Mr. Landis took possession in August, 1861, and at once began to develop the land according to his own ideas. He laid out, first, the town site of Vineland, in the centre of the tract; next had the adjacent plain surveyed, and laid out into tracts of ten, twenty, and fifty acres; laid out and opened roads, so as to make these small parcels accessible; and then he began to advertise for settlers.

His offer was to sell the land, lying within thirty-four miles of Philadelphia by railroad, in tracts of from ten to forty or sixty acres, at twenty-five dollars per acre, guaranteeing a clear title, and giving reasonable credit, but requiring the purchasers to make certain improvements within a year after buying. These consisted of a house—which need not be costly—the clearing of some acres of ground, and the planting of shade-trees along the road-side, and sowing a strip of this road-side with some kind of grass. It was also stipulated that if the owner, in after-years, neglected his road-side adornment, it should be kept in order by the town at his cost.

Mr. Landis had procured the passage of a law prohibiting the straying of cattle within the limits of the township in which his estate lay; and consequently the new settlers were not obliged to build fences. This was an immense saving to the people, who came in mostly with small means. Vineland has to-day between eleven thousand and twelve thousand people; it has about one hundred and eighty miles of roads; and it is probable that the " no fence" regulation, as it is called, has saved the inhabitants at least a million and a half of dollars.

He prevented in the beginning, with the most solicitous care, the establishment of bar-rooms or dram-shops on the tract; the Legislature gave permission to the people of the township, by an annual vote, to decide whether the sale of liquor at retail should be allowed or forbidden, and they have constantly forbidden it, to their immense advantage.

He endeavored as soon as possible to establish factories in the village, and succeeded so well in this that there has long been a local market for a part of the products of the place.

He founded and encouraged library, horticultural, and other societies, helped in the building of churches, and paid particular attention to obtaining for the people facilities for marketing their products advantageously.

In all these concerns he sought the advantage of the settlers on his lands, knowing that their prosperity would make him also prosperous.

But one other part of his plan appears to me to have been of extraordinary importance, though usually it is not mentioned in descriptions of Vineland. Mr. Landis established the price of his own uncultivated lands at twenty-five dollars per acre. At that price he sold to the first settler; and that price he did not increase for many years. Any one could, within two or three years, buy wild land on the Vineland tract at twenty-five dollars per acre. This means that he did not speculate upon the improvements of the settlers. He gave to them the advantage of their labors. It resulted that many poor men bought, cleared, and planted places in Vineland on purpose to sell them, certain that they could, if they wished, buy more land at the same price of twenty-five dollars per acre which they originally paid.

In my judgment, this feature of the Vineland enterprise, more than any other, changed it from a merely selfish speculation to one of a higher order, in which the settlers, to a large extent, have a common interest with the proprietor of the land. He might have done all the rest—might have laid out roads, proclaimed a "no fence" law, prevented the establishment of dram-shops, helped on educational and other enterprises—and still, had he raised the price of his wild lands as the settlers increased, he would have been a mere land speculator, and I doubt if his scheme would have obtained more than a very moderate and short-lived success. But the undertaking to sell his wild land always at the one fixed price, not only gave later comers an advantage which attracted them with a constantly increasing force, but it gave the poorer settlers an occupation from which many of them gained handsomely—the improvement of places to sell to new-comers with capital. The result showed Mr. Landis's wisdom. Improved property, cleared and planted in fruit, has always borne a high price in Vineland, and has almost always had a ready sale, but there has never been any feverish land speculation there.

In twelve years the founder of Vineland was able to collect upon his tract—which had not a single inhabitant in 1861—about eleven thousand people. Most of these have improved their condition in life materially by settling there. Many of them came without sufficient capital, and no doubt suffered from want in the early days of their Vineland life. But if they persevered, two or three years of effort made them comfortable. Meantime they had, what our American farmers have not in general, easy access to good schools for their children, to churches and an intelligent society, and the possibility of good laws regarding the sale of liquor.

Vineland was settled largely by New England people. They are more restless and changeable than the Germans of Anaheim: less easily contented with mere comfort. The New-

Englander seems to me to like change, often, for its own sake; the German too frequently goes to the other extreme, and so greatly abhors change that he does without conveniences which he might well afford. Anaheim and Vineland differ in these respects, as the character of their inhabitants differs. But in both, no one can doubt that the people have been greatly benefited by the colonizing experiment; that they not merely live better, but have a higher standard of thinking as well, and are thus better citizens than they would have been had they remained in their original employments and abodes.

Some of the striking practical and moral results of the Vineland plan of colonization were set forth by Mr. Landis in a speech before the Legislature of New Jersey last year; and the following extracts from this address are of interest in this place. He said:

"When I first projected the colony, in 1861, what is now Vineland lay before me an unbroken wilderness. Nothing was to be heard but the song of birds to break the silence, which at times was oppressive. It was necessary that the fifty square miles of territory should be suddenly, thoroughly, and permanently improved. The land was in good part to be paid for out of the proceeds of sale. One hundred and seventy miles of public roads and other improvements were to be made, and the improvements were to be such as to insure the prosperity of the colonist in future years, as my outlay was in the early start of the settlement, and my returns were not to be realized for years to come. If the settlement should not be prosperous in these years to come, I could never realize my reward, and besides, ruin, involving character and fortune, stared me in the face. It was by no temporary efforts or expedients that I could succeed, but by fixing upon certain principles, calculated to be creative, healthful, and permanent in their influences—principles which, while they benefited each colonist day by day, would have a growing influence in developing the prosperity of the colony. What were these principles?

"1. That no land should be sold to speculators who would not improve, but only to persons who would agree to improve in a specified time, and also to plant shade-trees in front of their places, and seed the road-sides to grass for purposes of public utility and ornamentation.

"2. That no man should be compelled to erect fences, that his neighbor's cattle might roam at large; but that the old and shiftless and wasteful system should be done away with.

" 3. That the public sale of intoxicating drinks should be prohibited, and that this prohibition should be obtained by leaving it to a vote of the people.

" By the first principle, the continual improvement of the land was secured. Employment was furnished to laborers at remunerative prices. The value of the land was increased by the mutual effort of the colonists. The value of my land was also enhanced, and it was made more and more marketable.

" By the second principle, a vast and constant expense was saved— greater than the cost and annual interest upon all the railroads of the United States. Stock was improved, the cultivation of root crops was encouraged, and the economizing of fertilizers.

" By the third principle, the money, the health, and the industry of the people were conserved, that they might all be devoted to the work before them.

" I am in candor compelled to say that I did not introduce the local-option principle into Vineland from any motives of philanthropy. I am not a temperance man in the total-abstinence sense. I introduced the principle because in cool, abstract thought I conceived it to be of vital importance to the success of my colony. If in this thought I had seen that liquor made men more industrious, more skillful, more economical, and more æsthetic in their tastes, I certainly should then have made liquor-selling one of the main principles of my project.

*   *   *   *   *   *   *   *   *

" The question then came up as to how I could give such direction to public opinion as would regulate this difficulty. Many persons had the idea that no place could prosper without taverns—that to attract business and strangers taverns were necessary. I could not accomplish my object by the influence of total-abstinence men, as they were too few in numbers in proportion to the whole community. I had long perceived that there was no such thing as reaching the result by the moral influence brought to bear on single individuals—that to benefit an entire community, the law or regulation would have to extend to the entire community. In examining the evil, I found also that the moderate use of liquor was not the difficulty to contend against, but it was the immoderate use of it.

" The question, then, was to bring the reform to bear upon what led to the immoderate use of it. I found that few or none ever became intoxicated in their own families, in the presence of their wives and children, but that the drunkards were made in the taverns and saloons. After this conclusion was reached, the way appeared clear. It was not necessary to make a temperance man of each individual—it was not necessary to abridge the right or privilege that people might desire to have of keeping liquor in their own houses, but to get their consent to prevent the public sale of it by the small—that people in bartering would not be subject to the custom of dri nking—that they would not have the opportunity of drinking in bar-rooms, away from all home restraint or influence; in short, I believed that if the public sale of liquor was stopped either in taverns or beer saloons, the knife would reach the root of the evil. The next thing to do was to deal with settlers personally as they bought land, and to counsel with them as to the best thing to be done. In conversation with them I never treated it as a moral question—I explained to them that I was not a total-abstinence man myself, but that on account of the liability of liquor to abuse when placed in seductive forms at every street corner, and as is the usual custom that followed our barbarous law that it incited to crime, and made men unfortunate who would otherwise succeed; that most of the settlers had little money to begin with, sums varying from two hundred to one thousand dollars, which, if added to a man's labor, would be enough in many cases to obtain him a home, but which taken to the tavern would melt away like snow before a spring sun; that new places were liable to have this abuse to a more terrible extent than old places, as men were removed from the restraints of old associations, and in the midst of the excitement of forming new acquaintances; and that it was a notorious fact that liquor-drinking did not add to the inclination for physical labor. I then asked them—for the sake of their sons, brothers, friends—to help establish the new system, as I believed it to be the foundation-stone of our future prosperity.

"To these self-evident facts they would almost all accede. Many of them had witnessed the result of liquor-selling in the new settlements of the Far West, and were anxious to escape from it. The Local-Option Law of Vineland was not established, therefore, by temperance men or total-abstinence men only, but by the citizens generally, upon broad social and public principles. It has since been maintained in the same way. Probably not one tenth of the number of voters in Vineland are what may be called total-abstinence men. I explain this point to show that this reform was not the result of mere fanaticism, but the sense of the people generally, and that the people who succeed under it are such people as almost all communities are composed of. This law has been practically in operation since the beginning of the settlement in the autumn of 1861, though the act of the Législature empowering the people of Landis Township to vote upon license or no license was not passed until 1863. The vote has always stood against license by overwhelming majorities, there being generally only from two to nine votes in favor of liquor-selling. The population of the Vineland tract is about ten thousand five hundred people, consisting of manufacturers and business people upon the town plot in the centre, and, around this centre, of farmers and fruit-growers. The most of the tract is in Landis Township. I will now give statistics of police and poor expenses of this township for the past six years:

POLICE EXPENSES.		POOR EXPENSES.	
1867	$50 00	1867	$400 00
1868	50 00	1868	425 00
1869	75 00	1869	425 00
1870	75 00	1870	350 00
1871	150 00	1871	400 00
1872	25 00	1872	350 00

" These figures speak for themselves, but they are not all. There is a material and industrial prosperity existing in Vineland which, though I say it myself, is unexampled in the history of colonization, and must be due to more than ordinary causes. The influence of temperance upon the health and industry of her people is no doubt the principal of these causes. Started when the country was plunged in civil war, its progress was continually onward. Young as the settlement was, it sent its quota of men to the field, and has paid over $60,000 of war debts. The settlement has built twenty fine school-houses, ten churches, and kept up one of the finest systems of road improvements, covering one hundred and seventy-eight miles, in this country. There are now some fifteen manufacturing establishments on the Vineland tract, and they are constantly increasing in number. Her stores in extent and building will rival any other place in South Jersey. There are four post-offices on the tract. The central one did a business last year of $4800 mail matter, and a money-order business of $78,922.

" Out of seventy-seven townships in the state, by the census of 1869 Landis Township ranked the fourth from the highest in the agricultural value of its productions. There are seventeen miles of railroad upon the tract, embracing six railway stations.

"The result of my project as a land enterprise has been to the interest of the colonists as well as my own. Town lots that I sold for $150 have been resold for from $500 to $1500, exclusive of improvements. Land that I sold for $25 per acre has much of it been resold at from $200 to $500 per acre. This rule will hold good for miles of the territory—all resulting from the great increase of population and the prosperity of the people.

"Were licenses for saloons and taverns obtainable with the same ease as in New York, Philadelphia, and many country districts, Vineland would probably have, according to its population, from one to two hundred such places. Counting them at one hundred, this would withdraw from the pursuits of productive industry about one hundred families, which would give a population of six hundred people. Each of these places would sell about $3000 worth of beer and liquor per annum, making $300,000 worth of stimulants a year. I include beer saloons, as liquor can be obtained in them all as a general thing, and in the electrical climate of America beer leads to similar results as spirits. Think of the effect of $300,000 worth of stimulants upon the health, the minds, and the industry of our people. Think of the increase of crime and pauperism—the average would be fully equal to other places in which liquor is sold. Instead of having a police expense of $50, and poor expenses of $400 per annum, the amount would be swollen to thousands. Homes that are now happy would be made desolate, and, instead of peace reigning in our midst, we should have war—the same war that is now carried on throughout the length and breadth of the land in the conflict that is waged with crime, where blood is daily shed, where houses are daily fired, where helpless people are daily robbed, and the darkest of crimes daily perpetrated. Concentrate the work of this war that is carried on throughout the land for one day, and you will have as many people killed and wounded, houses fired or plundered, as in the sack of a city.

"The results in Vineland have convinced me—

"1. That temperance does conserve the industry of the people.

"2. That temperance is conducive to a refined and æsthetical taste.

"3. That temperance can be sufficiently secured in a community by suppressing all the taverns and saloons, to protect it from the abuse of excessive liquor-drinking. Here is a community where crime and pauperism are almost unknown, where taxes are nominal, where night is not made hideous by the vilest of noises, where a man's children are not contaminated by the evil language and influence of drunkards."

The following letter from the deputy sheriff of Vineland gives the practical result of the Vineland system of moral co-operation, as it may be called:

"VINELAND, *December* 4, 1873.

"DEAR SIR,—*The poor tax in this township amounts to about five cents to each inhabitant per annum,* and our special expense for police matters, when any body happens to be engaged on an emergence, amounts to an average expense *of about one half cent each.* In fact, it may be said we have little or no crime or breach of the peace; and, though I am no total-abstinence man, I ascribe this state of things to the absence of liquor shops, and on this account have always voted against licensing. Before I came here I acted as constable in Massachusetts, and have been deputy sheriff and overseer of the poor for five years, and I know from actual ob-servation that more happiness is secured to men themselves, to their wives and children, and more peace to the home, than by any other cause in the world, not excepting all the churches—so help me God!

"Yours respectfully, T. T. CORTIS, Deputy Sheriff."

In the journal from which I take this letter it is stated that the poor and police expenses of Perth Amboy, also in New Jersey, amount in the same year to *two dollars* per head! The figures need no comment.

Prairie Home.

The Prairie Home Colony, in Franklin County, Kansas, was established by a French gentleman, E. V. Boissiere. He owns three thousand acres of land, and has been engaged during the last three years in putting it in order for settlement, upon a plan to which he gives the title, "Association and Co-opera-tion, based on Attractive Industry." So far as the details of his plan are developed, it appears that he wishes to secure to colonists constant employment at reasonable wages, and to en-able them to live in an economical manner. It is evident from what follows that he does not intend to establish a benevolent institution, and that at *Prairie Home* there will be no accom-modations for idlers. I reprint here a circular, which is issued by Mr. Boissiere, and parts of a private note from him, in which, in March, 1874, he gave me some particulars of the progress of his enterprise :

"A domain of more than three thousand acres, purchased about four years ago, and then called the ' Kansas Co-operative Farm,' but since named ' Silkville,' from the fact that the weaving of silk-velvet ribbons is one of its branches of industry, and silk-culture is contemplated, for which ten thousand mulberry-trees are now thriftily growing, having had two hundred and fifty acres subjected to cultivation, and several preliminary buildings erected upon it, it is now thought expedient to inform those who wish to take part in the associative enterprise for which the purchase was made, that the subscribers, as its projectors, will be prepared to receive persons the ensuing spring, with a view to their becoming associated for that purpose.

" A leading feature of the enterprise is to establish the ' Combined Household ' of Fourier—that is, a single large residence for all the associates. Its principal aim is to organize labor, the source of all wealth, first, on the basis of *remuneration proportioned to production*, and, second, in such manner as to make it both *efficient* and *attractive*. Guarantees of education and subsistence to all, and of help to those who need it, are indispensable conditions, to be provided as soon as the organization shall be sufficiently advanced to render them practicable.

" A spacious edifice, sufficient for the accommodation of eighty to one hundred persons, will be erected the ensuing season, its walls and principal partitions, which are to be of stone, being already contracted for, to be completed by the 1st of October. But the buildings already erected will furnish accommodations—less eligible, but perfectly comfortable except in severely cold weather—for at least an equal number.

" It is not, however, expected that the operations of the ensuing year will be any thing more than preparative ; they will be limited probably to collecting a few persons to form a nucleus of the institution to be gradually developed in the future. But, from the first, facilities will be furnished for industry on the principle of *remuneration proportioned to production*, by means of which, or otherwise, each candidate will be required to provide for his own support, and for that of such other persons as are admitted at his request as members of his family or other dependents.

" The means of support at present available for those who come to reside on the domain will be, as they may be stated in a general way, *op-*

portunities to engage, on liberal terms, in as many varieties as possible of productive industry; but, more particularly, first, an ample area of fertile land to cultivate; and, secondly, facilities for such mechanical work as can be executed with hand-tools, especially the making of clothes, boots and shoes, and other articles of universal consumption, not excluding, however, any article whatever for which a market, either internal or external, can be found. But, as far as income depends upon earnings, the most reliable resource will be agricultural and horticultural industry, as most of the mechanical work likely to be required for some time should perhaps be reserved for weather not suitable to out-door employments. Employment for wages at customary rates will be furnished to some extent to those who desire it for a part of their time, but can not be reliably promised. Steam-power will be provided as soon as warranted by a sufficient number of associates, and by the prospect of being applied to profitable production.

"Having provided the associates and candidates with these facilities for industry, and made them responsible each for his own support, and, at first, for that of his dependents, the projectors propose to have them distribute themselves into organizations for industrial operations, and select or invent their own kinds and mode of cultivation and other practical processes, under regulations prescribed by themselves. They will be indulged with the largest liberty, consistent with the protection of rights and the preservation of order, in choosing their own employments, and their own industrial and social companions; in appointing, concurrently with those with whom they are immediately associated, their own hours of labor, recreation, and repose; and, generally, in directing their activity in such manner and to such purposes as their taste or interest may induce them to prefer. We hope thus to demonstrate that interference with individual choice is necessary only to restrain people from transgressing their own proper sphere and encroaching upon that of others, and that restraints, even for that purpose, will seldom be required, and not at all except during the rudimentary stage of industrial organization.

" No efforts, therefore, will be made to select persons of similar views or beliefs, or to mould them afterward to any uniform pattern. That unanimity which is not expected in regard to practical operations, is much less expected in regard to those subjects transcending the sphere of human experience about which opinions are now so irreconcilably conflicting. All that will be required is that each shall accord to others as much freedom of thought and action as he enjoys himself, and shall respect the rights and interests of others as he desires his own to be respected by them.

"The apprehension that our experiment might be greatly embarrassed by admitting the totally destitute to participate in it, compels us to say that such can not at present be received. The means applicable to our purpose, considerable as they are, might become inadequate if subjected to the burden of maintaining objects of charity; while but few could be thus relieved, even if all the means at command were devoted to that single object. Our system, if we do not misapprehend it, will, in its maturity, provide abundantly for all.

"But though we insist that the first participators in our enterprise shall not be pecuniarily destitute, the amount insisted upon is not large. So much, however, as is required must be amply secured by the following cash advances:

"First: rent of rooms and board paid two months in advance for each person admitted to reside on the domain, including each member of the applicant's family; and at the end of the first month, payment of these items for another month, so that they shall again be paid two months in advance, and so from month to month indefinitely.

"Rent of rooms will be reasonable, and board will be finally settled for at its cost, as near as may be; but in computing it for advance payment, it will be rated rather above than below its expected cost, to provide against contingencies. If too much is advanced, the excess, when ascertained, will either be repaid or otherwise duly accounted for.

"Facilities for cheap boarding, and for tables graduated to suit different tastes and circumstances, will be limited at first, and until associates become numerous enough to form messes and board themselves.

"Second: each person so admitted will be required to deposit, as may be directed, the sum of one hundred dollars for himself, and an equal sum for every other person admitted with him at his request, on which interest will be allowed at the rate of six per cent. per annum. This deposit is expected to be kept unimpaired until the projectors think it may safely be dispensed with, but will be repaid, or so much thereof as is subject to no charges or offsets, whenever the person on whose account it was made withdraws from the enterprise and ceases to reside on the domain; as will also any unexpended residue of the amount advanced for rooms and board.

"This deposit, besides furnishing a guarantee against the destitution of the person making it, is recommended by another consideration not less important—it secures him, in case he wishes to retire from the enterprise, because he can find no satisfactory position in it, or for any other reason, against retiring empty-handed, or remaining longer than he wishes for want of means to go elsewhere.

" In addition to these cash advances, each person admitted as an associate or candidate will be required to provide furniture for his room, and all other articles needed for his personal use, including, generally, the hand-tools with which he works. But some of these articles may, in certain cases, be rented or sold on certain cases, be rented or sold on credit to persons of good industrial capacity who have complied with the other conditions.

" We should esteem, as especially useful, a class of residents who, having an income, independent of their earnings, adequate to their frugal support at least, can devote themselves as freely as they please to attractive occupations which are not remunerative, it being such occupations probably that will furnish the first good examples of a true industrial organization. Next to be preferred are those having an independent income which, though not adequate to their entire support, is sufficient to relieve them from any considerable anxiety concerning it; for they can, to a greater or less extent, yield to the impulses of attraction with comparative indifference to the pecuniary results of their industry.

" It is hoped and expected that the style of living, at least in the early stages of the experiment, will be frugal and inexpensive. Neatness and good taste, and even modest elegance, will be approved and encouraged; but the projectors disapprove of superfluous personal decorations, and of all expense incurred for mere show without utility, and in this sentiment they hope to be sustained by the associates.

" As a general rule, applicants who comply with the pecuniary conditions will be admitted on trial as candidates, to the extent of our accommodations, without formal inquisition of other particulars; but each applicant should state his age and occupation, and the ages and industrial capacities of others, if any, whom he desires to have admitted with him, and whether any of them are permanently infirm. References are also requested, and photographs if possible.

" The cardinal object of our enterprise being, as has been said, to organize labor on the basis of rewarding it according to the value of its product, and in such manner as to divest it of the repugnance inseparable from it as now prosecuted, the policy to which recourse will first be had to effect this object will be to throw upon the associates the chief responsibility of selecting functions and devising processes, as well as of marshaling themselves into efficient industrial organizations. Freedom to select their preferred occupations and modes of proceeding is proposed, with the expectation that a diversity of preferences will be developed in both, the respective partisans of which will vie with each other to demonstrate the superior excellence of their chosen specialties. Among the numerous merits which recommend this policy, not the least important is that it will, as is believed, give full play to all varieties of taste and capacity, and secure a more perfect correspondence of functions with aptitudes than exists in the present system of labor. But we are not so committed to any policy as to persist in it, if, after being fairly tested, it fails of its purpose. In that event new expedients will be resorted to, and others again, if necessary, for we should not abandon our enterprise, though our first efforts should prove unsuccessful. The failure of any particular policy, therefore, does not involve a final failure, of which indeed the danger, if any, is remote, inasmuch as care will be taken not to exhaust the means applicable to our main purpose in a first trial, or in a second, or even any number of trials. But we have great confidence that not many trials will be necessary to construct a system of industry and of social life far in advance of any form of either now prevailing in the world.

" The lowest degree of success—we will not say with which we shall be satisfied, but to which we can be reconciled—is that the experiment shall be SELF-SUSTAINING. By this we mean that the associates, aided by the facilities furnished them, shall produce enough not only to supply their own consumption, including education for children and subsistence for all, and to repair the waste, wear, and decay of tools, machines, and other property used, but enough also to reasonably compensate those who furnish the capital for the use of it. Less production than this implies a waning experiment, which must, sooner or later, terminate adversely. But even though this low degree of success should be delayed, the domain is indestructible, and being dedicated forever to associative purposes, must remain unimpaired for repeated trials.

" An ample sufficiency of land will be conveyed to trustees in such manner as to secure the perpetual use of it to the associates and their successors. The land to be thus appropriated has on it a large peach orchard now in full bearing, which yielded last season a large crop of excellent peaches ; 400 selected apple-trees, which have four years' thrifty growth from the nursery, and a considerable number of other fruit-trees ;

and a vineyard of about 1200 young grape-vines. A library of 1200 volumes in English, besides a large number in French and other languages, is now here, intended for the use of future associates and residents.

" No fund is set apart for the gratuitous entertainment of visitors. Those not guests of some one here who will be chargeable for them, will be expected to pay a reasonable price for such plain and cheap accommodations as can be afforded them.

" For a more extended explanation of the principles and aim of our enterprise, and of some of the details of the mode of proceeding, persons interested are referred to a treatise on ' Co-operation and Attractive Industry,' published under the auspices of the departed and lamented Horace Greeley, for which send fifty cents to the *Tribune*, New York, or to either of the subscribers.

" [*Note.* — It should be understood that the foregoing exposition of principles and policy, though the best that our present knowledge enables us to make, is provisional only, and liable to be modified from time to time as experience makes us wiser.]   E. V. BOISSIERE.

" Williamsburg P. O., Franklin Co., Kansas."

On the back of the circular is the following description of Silkville's position and other particulars :

" Silkville, at which ' The Prairie Home ' is located, is near the southwest corner of Franklin County, Kansas, three miles south of Williamsburg, at present the nearest post-office ; about twelve miles nearly west of Princeton, on the L. L. and G. Railroad, the nearest railroad station ; and about twenty miles southwest of Ottawa, the county seat. An open wagon, which carries passengers and the mail between Williamsburg and Princeton, connects with the cars at the latter place every Monday, Wednesday, and Friday, at about 2 o'clock P. M., which (by special arrangement) will carry passengers with ordinary baggage between Princeton and Silkville for sixty-five cents each. Fare from Ottawa to Princeton, nine miles, fifty cents. Persons coming here frequently hire a private conveyance from Ottawa.

" Through tickets to Kansas City and Lawrence (and perhaps to Ottawa) can be purchased at the principal railroad stations. Fare from Kansas City to Ottawa, fifty-three miles, $2 90 ; from Lawrence to Ottawa, twenty-seven miles, $1 60."

Under date of March 30, 1874, Mr. Boissiere writes me:

"The unitary building is complete so far as masonry and carpenter work goes, but the plastering and painting will require two months to complete. Our neighborhood has not settled as fast as I expected, and will not afford a market for small industries. I would not invite associates to come on until I establish more firmly the silk business and some other industries. The country has not yet learned what crops will pay best. Farmers are now trying the castor-bean and flax for seed, with some promise of success. I had information about an oil-mill, but find it gives occupation to only a very few operators. I think now of a factory for working the flax-tow into twine and rope, bagging, or mats.

"I have plenty of patience, having lived a farmer's life; and I like better to go surely than too fast. We have plenty of good coal around us, selling at fourteen cents per bushel of eighty pounds. We had the prospect of a railroad crossing our grounds from Ottawa to Burlington, but the hard times prevent it. Yours, E. V. BOISSIERE."

It is difficult to foretell what will be the outcome of Mr. Boissiere's effort. The offer he makes to "associates" is not very promising. Land and employment outside of the great cities are both so plentiful in this country that men who have capital enough to make the deposit required by Mr. Boissiere are more likely to settle upon public land under the homestead act, and carve out their own future.

A COMPARATIVE VIEW

OF THE

CUSTOMS AND PRACTICES

OF THE

AMERICAN COMMUNES.

COMPARATIVE VIEW.

I.—Statistical.

Though brief accounts are given in the preceding pages of several recently established communistic societies, it is evident that only those which have been in practical operation during a term of years are useful for purposes of comparison, and to show the actually accomplished results of communistic effort in the United States, as well as the means by which these results have been achieved.

The societies which may thus be properly used as illustrations of successful communism in this country are the Shakers, established in the Eastern States in 1794, and in the West about 1808; the Rappists, established in 1805; the Bäumelers, or Zoarites, established in 1817; the Eben-Ezers, or Amana Communists, established in 1844; the Bethel Commune, established in 1844; the Oneida Perfectionists, established in 1848; the Icarians, who date from 1849; and the Aurora Commune, from 1852.

Though in name there are thus but eight societies, these consist in fact of not less than seventy-two communes: the Shakers having fifty-eight of these; the Amana Society seven; and the Perfectionists two. The remaining societies consist of but a single commune for each.

It will be seen that the oldest of these communes have existed for eighty years; the youngest cited here for review has been founded twenty-two years. Of all, only two societies remain under the guidance of their founders; though it may be said that the Amana Communes have still the advantage of the presence among them of some of the original leading members. The common assertion that a commune must break up on the death of its founder would thus appear to be erroneous.

These seventy-two communes make but little noise in the world; they live quiet and peaceful lives, and do not like to admit strangers to their privacy. They numbered in 1874 about five thousand persons, including children, and were then scattered through thirteen states, in which they own over one hundred and fifty thousand acres of land—probably nearer one hundred and eighty thousand, for the more prosperous frequently own farms at a distance, and the exact amount of their holdings is not easily ascertained. As they have sometimes been accused of being land monopolists, it is curious to see that even at the highest amount I have given they would own only about thirty-six acres per head, which is, for this country, a comparatively small holding of land.

It is probably a low estimate of the wealth of the seventy-two communes to place it at twelve millions of dollars. This wealth is not equally divided, some of the older societies holding the larger share. But if it were, the members would be worth over two thousand dollars per head, counting men, women, and children. It is not an exaggeration to say that almost the whole of this wealth has been created by the patient industry and strict economy and honesty of its owners, without a positive or eager desire on their part to accumulate riches, and without painful toil.

Moreover—and this is another important consideration—I am satisfied that *during its accumulation* the Communists enjoyed a greater amount of comfort, and vastly greater security against want and demoralization, than were attained by their neighbors or the surrounding population, with better schools and opportunities of training for their children, and far less exposure for the women, and the aged and infirm.

In origin the Icarians are French; the Shakers and Perfectionists Americans; the others are Germans; and these outnumber all the American communists. In fact, the Germans make better communists than any other people — unless the Chinese should some day turn their attention to communistic attempts. What I have seen of these people in California and the Sandwich Islands leads me to believe that they are well calculated for communistic experiments.

All the communes under consideration have as their bond of union some form of religious belief. It is asserted by some writers who theorize about communism that a commune can not exist long without some fanatical religious thought as its cementing force; while others assert with equal positiveness that it is possible to maintain a commune in which the members shall have diverse and diverging beliefs in religious matters. It seems to me that both these theories are wrong; but that it is true that a commune to exist harmoniously, must be composed of persons who are of one mind upon some question which to them shall appear so important as to take the place of a religion, if it is not essentially religious; though it need not be fanatically held.

Thus the Icarians reject Christianity; but they have adopted the communistic idea as their religion. This any one will see who speaks with them. But devotion to this idea has supported them under the most deplorable poverty and long-continued hardships for twenty years.

Again, the Bethel and Aurora Communes, whose members make singularly little of outward religious observances, are held together by their belief that the essence of all religion, and of Christianity, is unselfishness, and that this requires community of goods.

I do not think that any of these people can be justly called fanatics.

On the other hand, the Shakers, Rappists, Bäumelers, Eben-

Ezers, and Perfectionists have each a very positive and deeply rooted religious faith; but none of them can properly be called fanatics, except by a person who holds every body to be a fanatic who believes differently from himself. For none of these people believe that they are alone good or alone right; all admit freely that there is room in the world for various and varying religious beliefs; and that neither wisdom nor righteousness ends with them.

It is also commonly said that all the communistic societies in this country oppose the family-life, and that in general they advocate some abnormal relation of the sexes, which they make a fundamental part of their communistic plan. This, too, is an error. Of all the communes I am now considering, only the Perfectionists of Oneida and Wallingford have established what can be fairly called unnatural sexual relations.

At Icaria, Amana, Aurora, Bethel, and Zoar the family relation is held in honor, and each family has its own separate household. The Icarians even forbid celibacy. None of these five societies maintain what is called a "unitary household;" and in only two, Icaria and Amana, do the people eat in common dining-halls.

The Shakers and Rappists are celibates; and it is often said by the Shakers that communism can not be successful except where celibacy is a part of the system. It is not unnatural that they should think so; but the success of those societies which maintain the family relation would seem to prove the Shakers mistaken. And it is useful to remember that even the Rappists were successful before they determined, under deep religious influences, to give up marriage, and adopt celibacy. Moreover, the Rappists have never used the "unitary home" or the common dining-hall; they have always lived in small "families," composed of men, women, and children.

It seems to me a fair deduction from the facts, that neither religious fanaticism nor an unnatural sexual relation (unless voluntary celibacy is so called) is necessary to the successful prosecution of a communistic experiment. What *is* required I shall try to set forth in another chapter.

The Eben-Ezers and the Perfectionists are the only communes which are at this time increasing in numbers. At Icaria, Bethel, Aurora, and Zoar, they hold their own; but they, too, have lost strength during the last twenty years. The Shakers and Rappists, the only celibate communists, are decreasing, and have lost during a number of years; and this in spite of their benevolent custom of adopting and training orphan children, to whom they devote money and care with surprising and creditable liberality. The Eben-Ezers get the greater part of their accessions from among the brethren of their faith in Germany; and they live in Iowa in such rigorous seclusion, and so entirely conceal themselves and their faith and plan from the general public, that it is evident they do not wish to recruit their membership from the surrounding population. The Perfectionists publish a weekly journal, send this and their pamphlets to all who wish them, and have always used the press freely. Their peculiar doctrines are widely known, and they receive constantly applications from persons desirous to join their communes. I believe the greater number of these applicants are men; and I do not doubt that the peculiar sexual relations existing at Oneida and Wallingford are an element of attraction to a considerable proportion of the persons who apply for membership, and who are almost without exception rejected; for it is right that I should here prevent a misconception by saying that the Perfectionists are sincerely and almost fanatically attached to their peculiar faith, and accept new members only with great care and many precautions.

The Perfectionists are essentially manufacturers, using agriculture only as a subsidiary branch of business. All the other societies have agriculture as their industrial base, and many of them manufacture but little, though all have some branch of manufacture. Also, it is the aim of all to produce and make, as far as possible, every thing they consume. To limit the expenditures and increase the income is the evident road to wealth, as they have all discovered.

Much ingenuity has been exercised by all these communists in establishing profitable branches of manufacture; and they have had the good sense and courage in whatever they undertook to make only a good article, and secure trade by rigid honesty. Thus the Shaker garden seeds have for nearly three quarters of a century been accepted as the best all over the United States; the Oneida Perfectionists established the reputation of their silk-twist in the market by giving accurate weight and sound material; the woolen stuffs of Amana command a constant market, because they are well and honestly made; and in general I have found that the communists have a reputation for honesty and fair dealing among their neighbors, and wherever their products are bought and sold, which must be very valuable to them.

Saw and grist mills, machine shops for the manufacture and repair of agricultural implements, and woolen factories, are the principal large manufacturing enterprises in which they are engaged; to these must be added the preserving of fruits, broom and basket making, the preparation of medicinal extracts, and the gathering and drying of herbs, garden seeds, and sweet corn, chair-making, and a few other small industries. One Shaker community manufactures washing-machines and mangles on a large scale, and another makes staves for molasses hogsheads. Indeed, the Shakers have shown more skill in contriving new trades than any of the other societies, and have among their members a good deal of mechanical ingenuity.

All the communes maintain shops for making their own clothing, shoes, and often hats; as well as for carpentry, blacksmithing, wagon-making, painting, coopering, etc., and have the reputation among their neighbors of keeping excellent breeds of cattle. The small shops and the improved cattle are important advantages to their country neighbors; and a farmer who lives within half a dozen miles of a commune is fortunate in many ways, for he gains a market for some of his produce, and he has the advantage of all their mechanical skill. I did not specially investigate the question, but I have reason to believe that land in the neighborhood of a communistic society is always more valuable for these reasons; and I know of some instances in which the existence of a commune has added very considerably to the price of real estate near its boundaries.

Almost without exception the communists are careful and thorough farmers. Their barns and other farm-buildings are usually models for convenience, labor-saving contrivances, and arrangements for the comfort of animals. Their tillage is clean and deep; and in their orchards one always finds the best varieties of fruits. In their houses they enjoy all the comforts to which they are accustomed or which they desire, and this to a greater degree than their neighbors on the same plane of life; and, especially, they are always clean. The women of a commune have, without exception, I think, far less burdensome lives than women of the same class elsewhere. This comes partly because the men are more regular in their hours and habits, and waste no time in dram-shops or other and less harmful places of dissipation; partly, too, because all the industries of a commune are systematized, and what Yankees call " chores," the small duties of the household, such as preparing and storing firewood, providing water, etc., which on our farms are often neglected by the men, and cause the women much unnecessary hardship and toil, are in a commune brought into the general plan of work, and thoroughly attended to

Of course, the permanence of a commune adds much to the comfort of the women, for it encourages the men in providing many small conveniences which the migratory farmer's wife sighs for in vain. A commune is a fixture; its people build and arrange for all time; and if they have an ideal of comfort they work up to it.

II.—Communal Politics and Political Economy.

Nothing surprised me more, in my investigations of the communistic societies, than to discover—

1st. The amount and variety of business and mechanical skill which is found in every commune, no matter what is the character or intelligence of its members; and,

2d. The ease and certainty with which the brains come to the top. Of course this last is a transcendent merit in any system of government.

The fundamental principle of communal life is the subordination of the individual's will to the general interest or the general will : practically, this takes the shape of unquestioning obedience by the members toward the leaders, elders, or chiefs of their society.

But as the leaders take no important step without the unanimous consent of the membership; and as it is a part of the communal policy to set each member to that work which he can do best, and so far as possible to please all; and as the communist takes life easily, and does not toil as severely as the individualist — so, given a general assent to the principle of obedience, and practically little hardship occurs.

The political system of the Icarians appears to me the worst, or most faulty, and that of the Shakers, Rappists, and Amana Communists the best and most successful, among all the societies.

The Icarian system is as nearly as possible a pure democracy. The president, elected for a year, is simply an executive officer to do the will of the majority, which is expressed or ascertained every Saturday night, and is his rule of conduct for the following week. "The president could not sell a bushel of corn without instructions from the meeting of the people," said an Icarian to me—and thereby seemed to me to condemn the system of which he was evidently proud.

At Amana, and among the Shaker communes, the "leading characters," as the Shakers quaintly call them, are selected by the highest spiritual authority, are seldom changed, and have almost, but not quite, unlimited power and authority. The limitations are that they shall so manage as to preserve harmony, and that they shall act within the general rules of the societies—shall not contract debts, for instance, or enter upon speculative or hazardous enterprises.

The democracy which exists at Oneida and Wallingford is held in check by the overshadowing conservative influence of their leader, Noyes; it remains to be seen how it will work after his death. But it differs from the Icarian system in this important respect, that it does give large powers to leaders and executive officers. Moreover, the members of these two Perfectionist communes are almost all overseers of hired laborers; and Oneida is in reality more a large and prosperous manufacturing corporation, with a great number of partners all actively engaged in the work, than a commune in the common sense of the word.

At Economy the chiefs have always been appointed by the spiritual head, and for life; and the people, as among the Shakers and Eben-Ezers, trouble themselves but little about the management. The same is true of Zoar and Bethel, practically, though the Bäumelers elect trustees. Aurora is still under the rule of its founder.

Aside from the religious bond, and I believe of equal strength with that in the minds of most communists, is the fact that in a commune there is absolute equality. The leader is only the chief servant; his food and lodgings are no better than those of the members. At Economy, the people, to be sure, built a larger house for Rapp, but this was when he had become old, and when he had to entertain strangers — visitors. But even there the garden which adjoins the house is frequented by the whole society—is, in fact, its pleasure-ground; and the present leaders live in the old house as simply and plainly as the humblest members in theirs. At Zoar, Bäumeler occupied a commodious dwelling, but it was used also as a storehouse. At Aurora, Dr. Keil's house accommodates a dozen or twenty of the older unmarried people, who live in common with him. At Amana, the houses of the leaders are so inconspicuous and plain that they are not distinguishable from the rest. A Shaker elder sits at the head of the table of his family or commune, and even the highest elder or bishop of the society has not a room to himself, and is expected to work at some manual occupation when not employed in spiritual duties.

In a commune no member is a servant; if any servants are kept, they are hired from among the world's people. When the Kentucky Shakers organized, they not only liberated their slaves, but such of them as became Shakers were established in an independent commune or family by their former masters. They "ceased to be servants, and became brethren in the Lord."

Any one who has felt the oppressive burden of even the highest and best-paid kinds of service will see that independence and equality are great boons, for which many a man willingly sacrifices much else.

Moreover, the security against want and misfortune, the sure provision for old age and inability, which the communal system offers—is no doubt an inducement with a great many to whom the struggle for existence appears difficult and beset by terrible chances.

I do not mean here to undervalue the higher motives which lead men and women into religious communities, and which control the leaders, and no doubt a considerable part of the membership in such communes; but not all. For even among the most spiritual societies there are, and must be, members controlled by lower motives, and looking mainly to sufficient bread and butter, a regular and healthful life, easy tasks, and equality of condition.

Finally, the communal life secures order and system—certainly at the expense of variety and amusement; but a man or woman born with what the Shakers would call a gift of order, finds, I imagine, a singular charm in the precision, method, regularity, and perfect system of a communal village. An eternal Sabbath seems to reign in a Shaker settlement, or at Economy, or Amana. There is no hurly-burly. This systematic arrangement of life, combined with the cleanliness which is a conspicuous feature in every commune which I have visited, gives a decency and dignity to humble life which in general society is too often without.

"How do you manage with the lazy people?" I asked in many places; but there are no idlers in a commune. I conclude that men are not naturally idle. Even the " winter Shakers"—the shiftless fellows who, as cold weather approaches, take refuge in Shaker and other communes, professing a desire to become members; who come at the beginning of winter, as a Shaker elder said to me, " with empty stomachs and empty trunks, and go off with both full as soon as the roses begin to bloom"—even these poor creatures succumb to the systematic and orderly rules of the place, and do their share of work without shirking, until the mild spring sun tempts them to a freer life.

The character of the leaders in a commune is of the greatest importance. It affects, in the most obvious manner, the development of the society over which they rule. The "leading character" is sure to be a man of force and ability, and he forms the habits, not only of daily life, but even of thought, of those whom he governs—just as the father forms the character of his children in a family, or would if he did not give his whole life to "business."

But origin, nationality, and previous social condition are, of course, still greater powers. Thus the German communists in the United States, who came for the most part from the peasant class in their country, retain their peculiar habits of life, which are often singular, and sometimes repulsive to an American. They enjoy doubtless more abundant food than in their old homes; but it is of the same kind, and served in the same homely style to which they were used. Their dwellings may be more substantial; but they see nothing disagreeable in two or three families occupying the same house. At Icaria I saw French sabots, or wooden shoes, standing at the doors of the houses; and at dinner the water was poured from a a vessel of tin—not, I imagine, because they were too poor to afford a pitcher, but because this was the custom at home.

So, too, among the American societies there are great differences. To the outer eye one Shaker is much like another; but the New Hampshire and Kentucky Shakers are as different from each other as the general population of one state is from that of the other, both in intellectual character and habits of life; and the New York Shaker differs again from both. Climate, by the habits it compels, makes trivial but still conspicuous differences; it is not possible that the Kentucky Shaker, who hears the mocking-bird sing in his pines on every sunny day the winter through, and in whose woods the blue-jay is a constant resident, should be the same being as his brother in Maine or New Hampshire, who sees the mercury fall to twenty degrees below zero, and stores his winter's firewood in a house as big as an ordinary factory or as his own meeting-house.

I was much struck with the simplicity of the book-keeping in most of the communities, which often made it difficult for me to procure such simple statistics as I have given in previous pages. Sometimes, as at Zoar, Aurora, and Bethel, it was with great trouble that I could get even approximate figures; and this not entirely because they were unwilling to give the information, but because it was nowhere accessible in a condensed and accurate shape. "If a man owes no money—if he pays and receives cash—he needs to keep but few accounts," said a leading man at Aurora to me.

In most of the communes there is no annual or other business statement made to the members; and this plan, which at first seems to be absurdly insecure and unbusiness-like, works well in practice. Among the Shakers, the ministry, whenever they wish to, and usually once a year, overhaul the accounts of the trustees. The extensive business affairs of the Rappists have always been carried on by two leading men, without supervision, and without loss or defalcation. At Amana it is the same, as well as at Zoar, Bethel, and Aurora. The fixed rule of the communes, not to run in debt, is a wholesome check on trustees; and though defalcations have occurred in several of the Shaker communes, they remain satisfied that their plan of account-keeping is the best.

At Oneida they have a very thorough system of book-keeping—more complete than would be found, I suspect, in most large manufacturing establishments; and there I received definite and accurate statistical information with but little delay. But the Perfectionists have a more keenly mercantile spirit than any of the other communal societies; they are, as I said before, essentially a manufacturing corporation.

It is an important part of the commune's economies in living that it buys its supplies at wholesale. Oddly enough, a person at Buffalo, with whom I spoke of the Eben-Ezer people, remarked that they were disliked in the city, because, while they sold their products there, they bought their supplies at wholesale in New York. The retailer and middle-man appear to have vested rights nowadays. People seem to have thought in Buffalo that they obliged the Eben-Ezer men by buying their vegetables. I have heard the same objection made in other states to the Shaker societies: "They are of no use to the country, for they buy every thing in the city at wholesale." As though they did not pay taxes, besides setting an excellent example of virtuous and moderate living to their neighbors.

The simplicity of dress usual among communists works also an economy not only in means, but what is of equal importance, and might be of greater, a saving of time and trouble and vexation of spirit to the women. I think it a pity that all the societies have not a uniform dress; the Shakers and Rappists have, and it is an advantage in point of neatness. The slop-made coats and trousers worn in many societies quickly turn shabby, and give a slouchy appearance to the men, which is disagreeable to the eye, and must be more or less demoralizing to the wearers. The blue jacket of the Rappist is a very suitable and comfortable working garment; and the long coat of the Shaker always looks decent and tidy.

As to the dress of the women—in Amana, and also among the Shakers, the intention seems to be to provide a style which shall conceal their beauty, and make them less attractive to male eyes; and this is successfully achieved. At Economy no such precautions are taken; the women wear the honest dress of German peasants, with a kind of Norman cap, and the dress is sensible, convenient, and by no means uncomely. At Oneida the short dress, with trousers, and the clipped locks, though convenient, are certainly ugly. Elsewhere dress is not

much thought of. But in all the societies stuffs of good quality are used; and none are the slaves of fashion. I need not
point out how much time and trouble are saved to women by
this alone.

The societies have generally as good schools as the average
of the common schools in their neighborhoods, and often better. None but the Oneida and Wallingford Communists favor
a "liberal" or extended education; these, however, have sent
a number of their young men to the Sheffield scientific school
at New Haven. The Shakers and Rappists teach musical notation to the children; and all the communes, except of course
Icaria, give pretty careful religious instruction to the young.

But, besides the "schooling," they have all preserved the
wholesome old custom of teaching the boys a trade, and the
girls to sew, cook, and wash. "Our boys learn as much, perhaps more than the farmer's or village boys, in our schools;
and we make them also good farmers, and give them thorough
knowledge of some useful trade:" this was often said to me—
and it seemed to me a good account to give of the training of
youth.

III. — Character of the People; Influences of Communistic Life.

I remark, in the first place, that all the successful communes are composed of what are customarily called "common
people."

You look in vain for highly educated, refined, cultivated, or
elegant men or women. They profess no exalted views of humanity or destiny; they are not enthusiasts; they do not speak
much of the Beautiful with a big B. They are utilitarians.
Some do not even like flowers; some reject instrumental music.
They build solidly, often of stone; but they care nothing for

architectural effects. Art is not known among them; mere beauty and grace are undervalued, even despised. Amusements, too, they do not value; only a few communes have general libraries, and even these are of very limited extent, except perhaps the library at Oneida, which is well supplied with new books and newspapers. The Perfectionists also encourage musical and theatrical entertainments, and make amusement so large a part of their lives that they have nearly half a dozen committees to devise and superintend them.

At Amana and Economy, as well as among the Shakers, religious meetings are the principal recreations; though the Shaker union meetings, where the members of a family visit each other in small groups, may be called a kind of diversion. At Economy, in the summer, the people enjoy themselves in flower-gardens, where they gather to be entertained by the music of a band.

2. The communists do not toil severely. Usually they rise early—among the Shakers at half-past four in the summer, and five in winter; and in most of the other communes before or about sunrise. They labor industriously, but not exhaustingly, all the day; and in such ways as to make their toil comfortable and pleasant. "Two hired workmen would do as much as three of our people," said a Shaker to me; and at Amana they told me that three hired men would do the work of five or even six of their members. " We aim to make work not a pain, but a pleasure," I was told; and I think they succeed. The workshops are usually very comfortably arranged, thoroughly warmed and ventilated, and in this they all display a nice care.

3. They are all very cleanly. Even in those communes, as at Aurora, where the German peasant appears to have changed but very little most of his habits, cleanliness is a conspicuous virtue. The Shaker neatness is proverbial; at Economy every thing looks as though it had been cleaned up for a Sunday ex-

amination. In the other German communes the neatness is as conspicuous within the houses, but it does not extend to the streets and spaces out of doors. The people do not appear to be offended at the sight of mud in winter, and, like most of our Western farmers, do not know what good roads are. The Perfectionists pay a little attention to landscape-gardening, and have laid out their grounds very tastefully.

4. The communists are honest. They like thorough and good work; and value their reputation for honesty and fair dealing. Their neighbors always speak highly of them in this respect.

5. They are humane and charitable. In Kentucky, during the slavery period, the Shakers always had their pick of negroes to be hired, because they were known to treat them well. At New Lebanon I was told that a farm-hand was thought fortunate who was engaged by the Mount Lebanon Shakers. At Amana and at Economy the hired people value their situations so highly that they willingly conform to the peculiarities of the commune, so far as it is demanded. At Oneida, where a large number of men and women are employed in the factories, they speak very highly of their employers, though these are the objects of prejudice on account of their social system. So, too, the animals of a commune are always better lodged and more carefully attended than is usual among its neighbors.

6. The communist's life is full of devices for personal ease and comfort. At Icaria, owing to their poverty, comfort was, until within a year or two, out of the question—but they did what they could. Among the other and more prosperous communes, a good deal of thought is given to the conveniences of life. One sees very perfectly fitted laundries; covered ways by which to pass from house to outhouses in stormy weather; ingenious contrivances for ventilation, and against drafts, etc.

7. They all live well, according to their different tastes.

Food is abundant, and well cooked. In some Shaker communes a part of the family eat no meat, and special provision is made for these. Fruit is every where very abundant, and forms a large part of their diet; and this no doubt helps to keep them healthy. They take a pride in their store-rooms and kitchens, universally eat good bread and butter, and live much more wholesomely than the average farmer among their neighbors.

8. They are usually healthy, though in some communes they have a habit of doctoring themselves for fancied diseases. In almost all the Shaker communes I found hospitals, or "nurse-shops," as they call them, but oftenest they were empty. In the other societies I saw no such special provision for serious or chronic diseases.

9. I have no doubt that the communists are the most long-lived of our population. This is natural; they eat regularly and well, rise and retire early, and do not use ardent spirits; they are entirely relieved of the care and worry which in individual life beset every one who must provide by the labor of hand or head for a family; they are tenderly cared for when ill; and in old age their lives are made very easy and pleasant. They live a great deal in the open air also. Moreover, among the American communists, health and longevity are made objects of special study; and the so-called health journals are read with great interest. It results that eighty is not an uncommon age for a communist; and in every society, except perhaps in Icaria, I saw or heard of people over ninety, and still hale and active.

10. They are temperate in the use of wine or spirits, and drunkenness is unknown in all the communes, although among the Germans the use of wine and beer is universal. The American communes do not use either at all. But at Economy or Amana or Zoar the people receive either beer or wine daily, and especially in harvest-time, when they think

these more wholesome than water. At Economy they have very large, substantially built wine-cellars, where some excellent wine is stored.

Is it not possible that the general moderation with which life is pursued in a commune, the quiet, absence of exciting or worrying cares, regularity of habit and easy work, by keeping their blood cool, decrease the tendency to misuse alcoholic beverages? There is no doubt that in the German communes wine and beer are used, and have been for many years, in a way which would be thought dangerous by our temperance people; but I have reason to believe without the occurrence of any case of habitual intemperance. Possibly scientific advocates of temperance may hereafter urge a more temperate and sensible pursuit of wealth and happiness, a less eager life and greater contentment, as more conducive to what we narrowly call "temperance" than all the total-abstinence pledges.

11. It is a fixed principle in all the communes to keep out of debt, and to avoid all speculative and hazardous enterprises. They are content with small gains, and in an old-fashioned way study rather to moderate their outlays than to increase their profits. Naturally—as they own in common—they are not in haste to be rich. Those of them who have suffered from debt feel it to be both a danger and a curse. None of the communes make the acquisition of wealth a leading object of life. They have greater regard to independence and comfort. Their surplus capital they invest in land or in the best securities, such as United States bonds.

12. In those communes where the family relation is upheld, as the people are prosperous, they marry young. At Amana they do not permit the young men to marry before they reach the age of twenty-four.

In the celibate societies a number of precautions are used to keep the sexes apart. Among the Shakers, especially, there are usually separate doors and stairways in the dwelling-houses;

the workshops of the sexes are in different buildings; they eat at separate tables; and in their meetings men and women are ranged on opposite sides of the hall. Moreover, no one is lodged alone, even the elders and ministry sharing the sleeping-room with some other brother. It is not even permitted that a man and woman shall stand and talk together on the public walk. In most of their schools the sexes are also separated. In some of their dwellings, where but a single staircase exists, there is a rule that two persons of opposite sexes shall not pass each other on the stairs. They are not allowed to keep pet animals; nor to enter the room of another sex without knocking and receiving permission; nor to visit, except by appointment of the elders or ministry; nor to make presents to each other; nor to visit the shops of the other sex alone. At Economy there are separate entrance-ways to the dwellings for the two sexes.

It is not pretended in the celibate communes that the celibate life is easy; they confess it to be a sacrifice; but as they are moved to it by their religious faith, they rigorously maintain their rule. I am satisfied that very few cases of sexual irregularity have occurred among them, and they rigorously expel all those who transgress their rules.

It is natural that they should assert that celibacy is healthful; and, indeed, they point to the long life and general good health of their members in proof; and the fresh and fair complexions of a great number of their middle-aged people might be cited as another proof. Yet I have been told that the women are apt to suffer in health, particularly at the critical period of life. I must add, however, that I could hear of no cases of insanity or idiocy traceable to the celibate condition. Of course there is no force used to keep members in a commune; and those who are uncomfortable leave and go out into the world. The celibate communes keep very few of the young people whom they train up.

13. The communal life appears to be, at first view, inexorably dull and dreary; and the surprise was the greater to a visitor like myself to find the people every where cheerful, merry in their quiet way, and with a sufficient number and variety of healthful interests in life. But, after all, the life of the communist has much more varied interests and excitements than that of the farmer or his family; for a commune is a village, and usually forms a tolerably densely crowded aggregation of people—more like a small section cut out of a city than like even a village. There is also a wholesome variety of occupations; and country life, to those who love it, presents an infinite fund of amusement and healthful work.

That this is a correct view is shown by the curious fact that at Amana, when the farmers of the surrounding country bring in their wool, which they sell to the society, they bring with them their wives and children, who find enjoyment in a stay at the little inn; at Zoar the commune's hotel is a favorite resort of the country people; the neighbors of the Icarians come from miles around to attend the school exhibitions and other diversions of these communists; and about Aurora, in Oregon, the farmers speak of the commune's life as admirably arranged for amusement and variety.

14. Several of the societies have contrived ingenious mechanical means for securing harmony and eliminating without violence improper or rather uncongenial members; and these appear to me to be of high importance. The Shakers use what they call "Confession of sins to the elders;" the Amana people have an annual "*untersuchung*," or inquiry into the sins and the spiritual condition of the members; the Perfectionists use what they rightly call "Criticism"—perhaps the most effective of all, as in it the subject is not left to tell his own tale, but sits at the *oyer* of his sins and disagreeable conduct, being judge rather than witness. But all these devices are meritorious, because by their means petty disputes

are quieted, grievances are aired and thus dispersed, and harmony is maintained; while to one not in general agreement with the commune either is unbearable, and will drive him off. As I have described these practices in detail, under their proper heads, I need not here do more than mention them.

In judging of the *quality* of the communal life, I have found myself constantly falling into the error of comparing it with my own, or with the life of men and women in pleasant circumstances in our great cities. Even when thus studied it has merits—for the commune gives its members serenity of spirit, and relieves them from many of the follies to which even the most sensible men and women nowadays are reluctantly compelled to submit; not to speak of the petty and lowering cares which these follies and the general spirit of society bring to almost every one. It is undoubtedly an advantage to live simply, not to be the slave of fashion or of the opinion of others, and to keep the body under control.

But to be fairly judged, the communal life, as I have seen and tried to report it, must be compared with that of the mechanic and laborer in our cities, and of the farmer in the country; and when thus put in judgment, I do not hesitate to say that it is in many ways—and in almost all ways—a higher and better, and also a pleasanter life.

It provides a greater variety of employment for each individual, and thus increases the dexterity and broadens the faculties of men. It offers a wider range of wholesome enjoyments, and also greater restraints against debasing pleasures. It gives independence, and inculcates prudence and frugality. It demands self-sacrifice, and restrains selfishness and greed; and thus increases the happiness which comes from the moral side of human nature. Finally, it relieves the individual's life from a great mass of carking cares, from the necessity of over-severe and exhausting toil, from the dread of misfortune or exposure in old age.

If the communal life did not offer such or equivalent rewards, no commune could exist. For though in almost all of those I have described a religious thought and theory enter in, it may nevertheless be justly said that all arose out of a deepseated dissatisfaction with society as it is constituted—a feeling which is well-nigh universal, and affects men and women more the more thoughtful they are; that they continue only because this want of something better is gratified; but that a commune could not long continue whose members had not, in the first place, by adverse circumstances, oppression, or wrong, been made to feel very keenly the need of something better. Hence it is that the German peasant or weaver makes so good a communist; and hence, too, the numerous failures of communistic experiments in this country, begun by people of culture and means, with a sincere desire to live the "better life." J. H. Noyes, the founder of the Perfectionist communes, gives, in his book on "American Socialisms," brief accounts of not less than forty-seven failures,* many of them experiments which promised well at first, and whose founders were high-minded, highly cultivated men and women, with sufficient means, one would think, to achieve success.

Now, why these successes in the face of so many failures? Certainly there was not among the Shakers, the Rappists, the Bäumelers, the Eben-Ezers, the Perfectionists, greater business

---

* Here is a list of titles, which I take from Noyes: The Alphadelphia Phalanx, Hopedale Community, Leroysville Phalanx, Bloomfield Association, Blue Springs Community, North American Phalanx, Ohio Phalanx, Brook Farm, Bureau County Phalanx, Raritan Bay Union, Wisconsin Phalanx; the Clarkson, Clermont, Columbian, Coxsackie, Skaneateles, Integral, Iowa Pioneer, Jefferson County, La Grange, Turnbull, Sodus Bay, and Washtenaw Phalanxes; the Forrestville, Franklin, Garden Grove, Goose Pond, Haverstraw, Kendall, One Mentian, and Yellow Springs Communities; the Marlborough, McKean County, Mixville, Northampton, Spring Farm, and Sylvania Associations; the Moorehouse and the Ontario Unions; the Prairie Home; New Harmony, Nashoba, New Lanark, the Social Reform Unity, and the Peace Union Settlement.

ability or more powerful leadership? Greater wealth there was not, for most of the successful societies began poor. If education or intellectual culture are important forces, the unsuccessful societies had these, the successful ones had them not.

Mr. Noyes believes that religion must be the base of a successful commune. Mr. Greeley agreed with him. I believe that religion must be the foundation of every human society which is to be orderly, virtuous, and therefore self-denying, and so far I do not doubt that they are right. But if it is meant, as I understand them, that in order to success there must be some peculiar religious faith, fanatically held, I do not believe it at all.

I believe that success depends—together with a general agreement in religious faith, and a real and spiritual religion leavening the mass—upon another sentiment—upon a feeling of the unbearableness of the circumstances in which they find themselves. The general feeling of modern society is blindly right at bottom: communism is a mutiny against society.

Only, whether the communist shall rebel with a bludgeon and a petroleum torch, or with a plow and a church, depends upon whether he has not or has faith in God—whether he is a religious being or not. If priestcraft and tyranny have sapped his faith and debauched his moral sense, then he will attack society as the French commune recently attacked Paris—animated by a furious envy of his more fortunate fellow-creatures, and an undiscriminating hatred toward every thing which reminds him of his oppressors, or of the social system from which he has or imagines he has suffered wrong. If, on the contrary, he believes in God, he finds hope and comfort in the social theory which Jesus propounded; and he will seek another way out, as did the Rappists, the Eben-Ezers, the Jansenists, the Zoarites, and not less the Shakers and the Perfectionists, each giving his own interpretation to that brief narrative of Luke in which he describes the primitive Christian Church:

" And all that believed were together, and had all things in common ; and sold their possessions and goods ; and parted them to all men as every man had need."

These words have had a singular power over men in all ages since they were written. They form the charter of every communistic society of which I have spoken—for even the Icarians recall them.

IV.—CONDITIONS AND POSSIBILITIES OF COMMUNISTIC LIVING.

Reviewing what I have seen and written, these questions occur:

I. On what terms, if at all, could a carefully selected and homogeneous company of men and women hope to establish themselves as a commune ?

II. Would they improve their lives and condition ?

III. Have the existing societies brought communal life to its highest point; or is a higher and more intellectual life compatible with that degree of pecuniary success and harmonious living which is absolutely indispensable ?

I. I doubt if men and women in good circumstances, or given to an intellectual life, can hope to succeed in such an experiment. In the beginning, the members of a commune must expect to work hard ; and, to be successful, they ought always to retain the frugal habits, the early hours, and the patient industry and contentment with manual labor which belong to what we call the working class. Men can not play at communism. It is not amateur work. It requires patience, submission ; self-sacrifice, often in little matters where self-sacrifice is peculiarly irksome; faith in a leader; pleasure in plain living and healthful hours and occupations.

"Do you have no grumblers?" I asked Elder Frederick Evans at Mount Lebanon; and he replied, "Yes, of course—and they grumble at the elder. That is what he is for. It is necessary to have some one man to grumble at, for that avoids confusion."

"Do you have no scandal?" I asked at Aurora, and they said, "Oh yes—women will talk; but we have learned not to mind it."

"Are you not troubled sometimes with disagreeable members?" I asked at Oneida; and they answered, "Yes; but what we can not criticise out of them we bear with. That is part of our life."

"*Bear ye one another's burdens*" might well be written over the gates of every commune.

Some things the communist must surrender; and the most precious of these is solitude.

The man to whom at intervals the faces and voices of his kind become hateful, whose bitterest need it is to be sometimes alone—this man need not try communism. For in a well-ordered commune there is hardly the possibility of privacy. You are part of a great family, all whose interests and all whose life must necessarily be in common. At Oneida, when a man leaves the house he sticks a peg in a board, to tell all his little world where he is to be found. In a Shaker family, the elder is expected to know where every man is at all hours of the day. Moses, wandering over the desert with his great commune, occasionally went up into a mountain; but he never returned to the dead level of his Israelites without finding his heart fill with rage and despair. Nor is this surprising; for in the commune there must be absolute equality; there can be no special privileges; and when the great Leader, resting his spirit on the mountain, and enjoying the luxury of solitude

and retirement from the hateful sight and sounds of human
kind, "delayed to come down," his fellow-communists began
at once to murmur, "As for this Moses, the man who brought
us up out of the land of Egypt, we wot not what is become of
him."

Fortunately — else there would be no communes — to the
greater part of mankind the faces and voices of their kind are
necessary.

A company of fifty, or even of twenty-five families, well
known to each other, belonging to the same Christian Church,
or at least united upon some one form of religious faith, composed of farmers or mechanics, or both, and strongly desirous
to better their circumstances, and to live a life of greater independence and of greater social advantages than is attainable
to the majority of farmers and mechanics, could, I believe, if
they were so fortunate as to possess a leader of sufficient wisdom and unselfishness, in whom all would implicitly trust,
make an attempt at communistic living with strong hopes of
success; and they would undoubtedly, if they maintained their
experiment only ten years, materially improve their condition;
and, what to me seems more important, the life would affect
their characters and those of their children in many ways
beneficially.

I think it would be a mistake in such a company of people
to live in a "unitary home." They should be numerous
enough to form a village; they should begin with means sufficient to own a considerable tract of land, sufficient to supply
themselves with food, and to keep as much stock as they required for their own use. They should so locate their village
as to make it central to their agricultural land. They should
determine, as the Rappists did, upon a uniform and simple
dress and house, and upon absolute equality of living. They
should place *all* the power in the hands of their leader, and
solemnly promise him unhesitating trust and obedience; spec-

ifying only that he should contract no debts, should attempt no new enterprise without unanimous consent, and should at all times open his purposes and his acts to the whole society. Finally, they should expect in the beginning to live economically—*very* economically, perhaps; and in every case within their income.

They would, of course, adopt rules as to hours of labor and of meals; but if they had the spirit which alone can give success, these matters would be easily settled—for in a community men are more apt to over-work than to be idle. The lazy men, who are the bugbears of speculative communists, are not, so far as I have heard, to be found in the existing communes, and I have often and in different places been told, especially of the early days: "We worked late and early, each trying how much he could accomplish, and singing at our work."

In a commune, which is only a large family, I think it a great point gained for success to give the women equal rights in every respect with the men. They should take part in the business discussions, and their consent should be as essential as that of the men in all the affairs of the society. This gives them, I have noticed, contentment of mind, as well as enlarged views and pleasure in self-denial. Moreover, women have a conservative spirit, which is of great value in a communistic society, as in a family; and their influence is always toward a higher life.

Servants are inadmissible in a commune; but it may and ought to possess conveniences which make servants, with plain living, needless. For instance, a common laundry, a common butcher's shop, a general barn and dairy, are contrivances which almost every commune possesses, but which hardly any village in the country has. A clean, hard road within the communal village limits, and dry side-walks, would be attainable with ease. A church and a school-house ought to be the first buildings erected; and both being centrally placed, either could be used for such evening meetings as are essential to happy and successful community living.

Finally, there should be some way to bring to the light the dissatisfaction which must exist where a number of people attempt to live together, either in a commune or in the usual life, but which in a commune needs to be wisely managed. For this purpose I know of no better means than that which the Perfectionists call "criticism"—telling a member to his face, in regular and formal meeting, what is the opinion of his fellows about him—which he or she, of course, ought to receive in silence. Those who can not bear this ordeal are unfit for community life, and ought not to attempt it. But, in fact, this "criticism," kindly and conscientiously used, would be an excellent means of discipline in most families, and would in almost all cases abolish scolding and grumbling.

A commune is but a larger family, and its members ought to meet each other as frequently as possible. The only advantage of a unitary home lies in this, that the members may easily assemble in a common room every evening for an hour, not with any set or foreordained purpose, but for that interchange of thought and experience which makes up, or should, a large and important part of family life. Hence every commune ought to have a pleasantly arranged and conveniently accessible meeting-room, to which books and newspapers, music, and cheap, harmless amusements should draw the people— women and children as well as men—two or three times a week. Nor is such meeting a hardship in a commune, where plain living, early hours, and good order and system make the work light, and leave both time and strength for amusement.

Tobacco, spirituous liquors, and cards ought to be prohibited in every commune, as wasteful of money, strength, and time.

The training of children in strict obedience and in good habits would be insisted on by a wise leader as absolutely necessary to concord in the society; and the school-teacher ought to have great authority. Moreover, the training of even little children, during some hours of every day, in some manual occupation, like knitting—as is done at Amana—is useful in several ways. Regular and patient industry, not exhausting toil, is the way to wealth in a commune; and children—who are indeed in general but too proud to be usefully employed, and to have the sense of accomplishing something—can not be brought into this habit of industry too early.

What now might the members of such a community expect to gain by their experiment? Would they, to answer the second question above, improve their lives and condition?

Pecuniarily, they would begin at once a vast economy and saving of waste, which could hardly help but make them prosperous, and in time wealthy. A commune pays no wages; its members "work for their board and clothes," as the phrase is; and these supplies are either cheaply produced or bought at wholesale. A commune has no blue Mondays, or idle periods whatever; every thing is systematized, and there is useful employment for all in all kinds of weather and at all seasons of the year. A commune wastes no time in "going to town," for it has its own shops of all kinds. It totally abolishes the middle-man of every kind, and saves all the large percentage of gain on which the "store-keepers" live and grow rich elsewhere. It spends neither time nor money in dram-shops or other places of common resort. It secures, by plain living and freedom from low cares, good health in all, and thus saves "doctors' bills." It does not heed the changes in fashion, and thus saves time and strength to its women. Finally, the communal life is so systematized that every thing is done well, at the right time, and thus comes another important saving of time and material. The communal wood-house is always full of well-seasoned firewood: here is a saving of time and temper which almost every Western farmer's wife will appreciate.

If you consider well these different economies, it will cease to be surprising that communistic societies become wealthy; and this without severe or exhausting toil. The Zoarites acknowledge that they could not have paid for their land had they not formed themselves into a commune; the Amana Inspirationists confess that they could not have maintained themselves near Buffalo had they not adopted the communal system.

I have said nothing about the gain of the commune by the thorough culture it is able and likely to give to land; its ability to command at any moment a large laboring force for an emergency, and its advantage in producing the best, and selling its surplus consequently at the highest market price. But these are not slight advantages. I should say that the reputation for honesty and for always selling a good article is worth to the Shakers, the Amana and other communes, at least ten per cent. over their competitors.

On the moral side the gain is evidently great. In a society so intimately bound together, if there are slight tendencies to evil in any member, they are checked and controlled by the prevailing public sentiment. The possibility of providing with ease and without the expenditure of money good training and education for children, is an immense advantage for the commune over the individualist who is a farmer or mechanic in a new country. The social advantages are very great and evident. Finally, the effect of the communal life upon the character of the individual is good. Diversity of employments, as I have noticed in another chapter, broadens the men's faculties. Ingenuity and mechanical dexterity are developed to a surprising degree in a commune, as well as business skill. The constant necessity of living in intimate association with others, and taking into consideration their prejudices and weaknesses, makes the communist somewhat a man of the world; teaches him self-restraint; gives him a liberal and tolerant spirit; makes him an amiable being. Why are *all* communists remarkably cleanly? I imagine largely because filth or carelessness would be unendurable in so large a family, and because system and method are absolutely necessary to existence.

But, to come to my third question, the communes I have visited do not appear to me to make nearly as much of their lives as they might. Most of them are ascetics, who avoid the beautiful as tending to sin; and most of them, moreover, out of the force of old habits, and a conservative spirit which dreads change, rigidly maintain the old ways.

In the beginning, a commune must live with great economy, and deny itself many things desirable and proper. It is an advantage that it should have to do this, just as it is undoubtedly an advantage to a young couple just starting out in life to be compelled by narrow circumstances to frugal living and self-denial. It gives unselfishness and a wholesome development of character. But I can not see why a prosperous commune should not own the best books; why it should not have music; why it should not hear the most eloquent lecturers; why it should not have pleasant pleasure-grounds, and devote some means to the highest form of material art—fine architecture. It seems to me that in these respects the communes I have visited have failed of their proper and just development; and I believe this inattention to the higher and intellectual wants of men to be the main reason of their generally failing numbers. They keep their lives on the plane of the common farmer's life out of which most of the older members were gathered — and their young people leave them, just as the farmers of our country complain that their boys run off to the cities. The individual farmer or country mechanic can not control this; he can not greatly beautify his life, or make it intellectually richer. But to the commune, once well established and prosperous, all needful things are possible, so far as money cost is concerned; and it is my belief that neither books nor music, nor eloquence nor flowers, nor finely kept pleasure-grounds nor good architecture would be dangerous to the success of a commune.

In another respect, the communistic societies fall short of what they ought to be and do. The permanence of their establishments gives them extraordinary advantages for observing the phenomena of climate and nature; and it would add greatly to the interest of their lives did they busy and interest themselves with observations of temperature, and of the various natural phenomena which depend upon or denote climate: the arrival and departure of birds; the first and last frosts; the blossoming of flowers and trees. A Shaker family ought to produce records of this kind of great value and interest; and I wonder that such a book as White's "Selborne" has not tempted some communist to such observations. But I nowhere, except at Oneida, found more than a very superficial interest in natural phenomena.

It is easy to see that here is a field of innocent and healthful amusement which, with the abundant leisure the members of a prosperous commune enjoy, could be worked so as to give a new and ever-fresh interest to the lives of young and old.

I find fault also with the isolation in which communal societies live. They would be the better if they communicated fully and frequently among each other, and interchanged thoughts and experiences. Not only do the different societies hold aloof from each other, but among the Shakers even families do not communicate or advise with others living at a distance. But I believe this is to be remedied.

Finally, I repeat that one can not play at communism. It is earnest work, and requires perseverance, patience, and all other manly qualities. But if I compare the life in a contented and prosperous, that is to say a successful commune, with the life of an ordinary farmer or mechanic even in **our** prosperous country, and more especially with the lives of the working-men and their families in our great cities, I must confess that the communist life is so much freer from care and risk, so much easier, so much better in many ways, and in all material aspects, that I sincerely wish it might have a farther development in the United States.

With this wish I conclude a work which has interested me extremely—the record of an investigation which was certainly the strangest and most remarkable I ever made, and which forced me to take some views of the nature and capacities of the average man which I had not before.

That communistic societies will rapidly increase in this or any other country, I do not believe. The chances are always great against the success of any newly formed society of this kind. But that men and women can, if they *will*, live pleasantly and prosperously in a communal society is, I think, proved beyond a doubt; and thus we have a right to count this another way by which the dissatisfied laborer may, if he chooses, better his condition. This seems to me a matter of some importance, and justifies, to myself at least, the trouble I have taken in this investigation.

BIBLIOGRAPHY.

BIBLIOGRAPHY.

THE following list does not pretend to be a complete bibliography of Socialism or Communism. It contains the titles of all the works which have fallen under my own observation relating to the Communistic Societies now existing in the United States, and referred to in this book. Most of these are in my own collection; a few I found in the Congressional Library or in the hands of friends. To a few of the titles I have appended remarks explanatory of their contents.

1. A Brief Account of a Religious Scheme taught and propagated by a number of Europeans who lately lived in a place called Nisqueunia, in the State of New York, but now residing in Harvard, Commonwealth of Massachusetts, commonly called Shaking Quakers. By Valentine Rathbone, Minister of the Gospel. To which is added a Dialogue between George the Third of Great Britain and his Minister, giving an account of the late London mob, and the original of the Sect called Shakers. The whole being a discovery of the wicked machinations of the principal enemies of America. Worcester, 1782.

[This is the earliest printed mention I have found of the Shakers. The pamphlet is in the Congressional Library, and came from the Force Collection. Its intention was to make the Shakers odious as British spies; and in the "Dialogue" between the king and his minister, "Lord Germain" is made to comfort the king with an account of "the persons who were sent to propagate a new religious scheme in America," whose accounts, he says, are "very flattering," and upon whom he depends to mislead the ignorant Americans into opposition to the "rebels." The "Dialogue" pretends to have been "printed London; reprinted Worcester, 1782."]

2. Testimony of Christ's Second Appearing, exemplified by the Principles and Practice of the Church of Christ. History of the Progressive Work of God, extending from the Creation of Man to the Harvest, comprising the Four Great Dispensations now consummating in the Millennial Church. Antichrist's Kingdom or Churches, contrasted with the Church

of Christ's First and Second Appearing, the Kingdom of the God of Heaven. Published by the United Society called Shakers. No date. (The Preface to the first edition is dated "Lebanon, O., 1808." Of the fourth, "Watervliet, N. Y., 1854;" pp. 632.)

3. Autobiography of a Shaker, and Revelation of the Apocalypse, with an Appendix. By Frederick W. Evans. New York, American News Company, 1869, pp. 162.

4. *The Same.* London, J. Burns, 1871, with a photographic portrait of the author.

5. Shaker's Compendium of the Origin, History, Principles, Rules and Regulations, Government and Doctrines of the United Society of Christ's Second Appearing, with Biographies of Ann Lee, William Lee, James Whittaker, J. Hocknell, J. Meacham, and Lucy Wright. By F. W. Evans. New York, D. Appleton & Co., 1859, pp. 189.

6. The Nature and Character of the True Church of Christ proved by Plain Evidences, and showing whereby it may be known and distinguished from all others. Being Extracts from the Writings of John Dunlavy. New York, printed by George W. Wood, 1850, pp. 93.

7. The Kentucky Revival; or a Short History of the late Extraordinary Outpouring of the Spirit of God in the Western States of America, agreeably to Scripture Promises and Prophecies concerning the Latter Day, with a Brief Account of the Entrance and Purposes of what the World call Shakerism, among the Subjects of the late Revival in Ohio and Kentucky. Presented to the *True Zion Traveler* as a Memorial of the Wilderness Journey. By Richard McNemar. New York. Reprinted by Edward O. Jenkins, 1846. pp. 156. (The Preface is dated "Turtle Creek, 1807.")

8. *The Same.* Press of John W. Brown, Liberty Hall, Cincinnati, 1807.

9. *The Same.* Albany, 1808.

10. A Short Treatise on the Second Appearing of Christ in and through the Order of the Female. By F. W. Evans, New Lebanon, N. Y. Boston, 1853, pp. 24.

11. A Brief Exposition of the Established Principles and Regulations of the United Society of Believers called Shakers. New York, 1851, pp. 30.

12. *The Same.* Watervliet, Ohio, 1832.

13. *The Same.* Canterbury, N. H., 1843.

14. Shaker Communism; or Tests of Divine Inspiration. The Second Christian or Gentile Pentecostal Church, as exemplified by Seventy Communities of Shakers in America. By F. W. Evans. London, James Burns, 1871, pp. 120.

15. Religious Communism. A Lecture by F. W. Evans (Shaker), of Mount Lebanon, Columbia Co., New York, U. S. A., delivered in St. George's Hall, London, Sunday evening, August 6th, 1871; with Introductory Remarks by the Chairman of the Meeting, Mr. Hepworth Dixon. Also some Account of the Extent of the Shaker Communities, and a Narrative of the Visit of Elder Evans to England. An abstract of a Lecture by Rev. J. M. Peebles, and his Testimony in regard to the Shakers.

16. Plain Talks upon Practical Religion. Being Candid Answers to Earnest Inquirers. By Geo. Albert Lomas, Shaker. (Watervliet), N. Y.. 1873, pp. 24.

17. Ann Lee, the Founder of the Shakers. A Biography, with Memoirs of her Companions. Also a Compendium of the Origin, History, Principles, Rules and Regulations, Government and Doctrines of the United Society of Believers in Christ's Second Appearing. By F. W. Evans. London, J. Burns. (The same as No. 5.)

18. The Shaker and Shakeress. A monthly paper. Published by the United Society, Mount Lebanon, N. Y. F. W. Evans, Editor.

19. Social Gathering Dialogue between Six Sisters of the North Family of Shakers, Mount Lebanon, N. Y. Albany, 1873, pp. 18.

20. Shakerism, the Possibility of the Race. Being Letters of A. B. B. and Elder F. W. Evans. Office of the *Shaker*, 1872, pp. 14.

21. The Universal Church. By F. W. Evans. Office of the *Shaker*, 1872, pp. 16.

22. Catalogue of Medicinal Plants, Barks, Roots, Seeds, Flowers, and Select Powders, with their Therapeutic Qualities and Botanical Names; also Pure Vegetable Extracts, prepared in vacuo; Ointments, Inspissated Juices, Essential Oils, Double-distilled and Fragrant Waters, etc., raised, prepared, and put up in the most careful manner by the United Society of Shakers at Mount Lebanon, N. Y. First established in 1800, being the oldest of the kind in the country. Albany, N. Y., 1873, pp. 58.

23. Plain Evidences by which the Nature and Character of the True Church of Christ may be known and distinguished from all others. Taken from a work entitled, " The Manifesto, or a Declaration of the Doctrines and Practice of the Church of Christ." Published at Pleasant Hill, Kentucky, 1818. By John Dunlavy. Printed by Hoffman & White, Albany, 1834, pp. 120.

24. A Collection of Millennial Hymns, adapted to the present Order of the Church. Printed in the United Society, Canterbury, N. H., 1847, pp. 200.

25. A Sacred Repository of Anthems and Hymns, for devotional Worship and Praise. Canterbury, N. H., 1852, pp. 222.

26. Testimonies concerning the Character and Ministry of Mother Ann Lee and the First Witnesses of the Gospel of Christ's Second Appearing, given by some of the aged Brethren and Sisters of the United Society; including a few Sketches of their own Religious Experiences. Approved by the Church. Albany, printed by Packard & Van Benthuysen, 1827, pp. 178.

27. Familiar Dialogues on Shakerism; in which the Principles of the United Society are illustrated and defended. By Fayette Mace. Portland, Charles Day & Co., Printers, 1838, pp. 120.

28. *The Same.* Concord, 1838.

29. A Discourse of the Order and Propriety of Divine Inspiration and Revelation, showing the Necessity thereof in all Ages to know the Will of God. Also, a Discourse on the Second Appearing of Christ in and through the Order of the Female. And a Discourse on the Propriety and Necessity of a United Inheritance in all Things in order to Support a true Christian Community. By William Leonard. Harvard (Mass.), published by the United Society, 1853, pp. 88.

30. A Brief Illustration of the Principles of War and Peace, showing the ruinous Policy of the former, and the superior Efficacy of the latter, for National Protection and Defense; clearly manifested by their practical Operations and opposite Effects upon Nations, Kingdoms, and People. By Philanthropos. Albany, printed by Packard & Van Benthuysen, 1831, pp. 112.

31. Some Lines in Verse about Shakers, not Published by Authority of the Society so called. New York, William Taylor & Co., No. 2 Astor House, 1846, pp. 56.

32. A Concise Answer to the General Inquiry who or what are the Shakers. First printed at Union Village, Ohio, 1823. Reprinted at Enfield, N. H., 1825. Albion Chase, Printer, pp. 14.

33. The Life of Christ is the End of the World. By George Albert Lomas. Watervliet, 1869, pp. 16.

34. The Higher Law of Spiritual Progression. Albany, 1868, pp. 32.

35. The Social Evil. By James J. Prescott. North Union (Ohio), 1870, pp. 14.

36. A Shaker's Answer to the oft-repeated Question " What would become of the World if all should become Shakers?" Orders supplied by John Whiteley, Shirley Village, Massachusetts. Boston, 1874, pp. 32.

37. *The Same.* By R. W. Pelham. Cincinnati, 1868, pp. 32.

38. Shakers : A Correspondence between Mary F. C., of Mount Holly City, and a Shaker Sister, Sarah L., of Union Village. Edited by R. W. Pelham. Union Village, Ohio, 1868, pp. 24.

39. Respect and Veneration due from Youth to Age. New Bedford, 1870, pp. 15.

40. The Universal Church. By F. W. Evans. Office of the *Shaker.* Shakers, N. Y., 1872, pp. 16.

41. Improved Shaker Washing-machine, etc. Manufactured and for sale by the United Society of Shakers, at Shaker Village, N. H., pp. 12.

42. The Divine Book of Holy and Eternal Wisdom, revealing the Word of God, out of whose Mouth goeth a sharp Sword. Written by Paulina Bates, at Watervliet, New York, United States of North America; including other Illustrations and Testimonies. Arranged and prepared for the Press at New Lebanon, N. Y. Published by the United Society called Shakers. Printed at Canterbury, N. H., 1849, pp. 718.

43. A Holy, Sacred, and Divine Roll and Book, from the Lord God of Heaven to the Inhabitants of Earth. Revealed in the United Society at New Lebanon, County of Columbia, State of New York, United States of America. Received by the Church of this Communion, and published in Union with the same. Printed in the United Society, Canterbury, N. H., 1843, pp. 412.

44. A Summary View of the Millennial Church, or United Society of Believers, comprising the Rise, Progress, and Practical Order of the Society, together with the general Principles of their Faith and Testimony, 1823. (2d edition, revised and improved) republished by the United Society with the approbation of the Ministry. Albany, printed by C. Van Benthuysen, 1848, pp. 384.

45. The Testimony of Christ's Second Appearing; containing a general Statement of all Things pertaining to the Faith and Practice of the Church of God in this Latter Day. Published in Union by Order of the Ministry. Lebanon, Ohio, from the Press of John M'Clean, office of the *Western Star*, 1808, pp. 618.

46. *The Same.* 2d edition, corrected and improved. Albany, 1810, pp. 660.

47. *The Same.* 3d edition, corrected and improved. Union Village, Ohio. B. Fisher & A. Burnett, Printers, 1823, pp. 621.

48. Account of some of the Proceedings of the Legislatures of the States of Kentucky and New Hampshire, 1828, etc., in Relation to the People called Shakers. Reprinted, New York, 1846, pp. 103.

49. A Selection of Hymns and Poems for the Use of Believers; collected from sundry Authors. By Philos - Harmoniæ. Watervliet, Ohio, 1833, pp. 186.

50. The Constitution of the United Society of Believers called Shakers; containing sundry Covenants and Articles of Agreement definitive of the Legal Grounds of the Institution. Watervliet, Ohio, 1833, pp. 16.

[Contains several forms of the Church Covenant, from 1810 down to 1833.]

51. Condition of Society and its only Hope in obeying the Everlasting Gospel, as now developing among Believers in Christ's Second Appearing. Printed and published at the *Day Star* Office, Union Village, Ohio, 1847, pp. 121.

52. A Juvenile Guide, or Manual of Good Manners, consisting of Counsels, Instructions, and Rules of Deportment for the Young, by Lovers of Youth. In Two Parts. Printed in the United Society, Canterbury, N. H., 1844, pp. 137.

53. Shakerism Detected, a Pamphlet published by Col. James Smith, of Kentucky, Examined and Confuted in Five Propositions. Published at Lebanon, Ohio, and Lexington, Kentucky, 1811, by Richard McNemar. Reprinted by Request. Watervliet, Ohio, May 2, 1833, pp. 12.

54. General Rules of the United Society, and Summary Articles of Mutual Agreement and Release, Ratified and Confirmed by the Society at Watervliet, Montgomery County, Ohio, January, 1833. Union Office, 1833, pp. 7.

[Contains the signatures of members.]

55. The Shakers: Speech of Robert Wickliffe in the Senate of Kentucky, January, 1831, on a Bill to Repeal an Act of the General Assembly of the State of Kentucky, entitled an Act to Regulate Civil Proceedings against certain Communities having Property in Common. Frankfort, Ky., 1832, pp. 32.

56. A Memorial Remonstrating against a certain Act of the Legislature of Kentucky entitled an Act to Regulate Civil Proceedings against certain Communities having Property in Common, and declaring that it shall and may be lawful to commence and prosecute suits, obtain decrees, and have execution against any of the Communities of People called Shakers, without naming or designating the individuals, or serving process on them otherwise than by fixing a Subpœna on the door of their Meeting-house, etc. Union Office, Harrodsburg, Ky., 1830, pp. 8.

57. An Address to the State of Ohio, Protesting against a certain Clause of the Militia Law enacted by the Legislature. Lebanon, Ohio, Office of the *Farmer*, 1818, pp. 24.

58. Investigator; or a Defense of the Order, Government, and Economy of the United Society called Shakers against sundry Charges and Legislative Proceedings. Addressed to the Political World by the Society of Believers at Pleasant Hill, Kentucky. Lexington, Ky., Smith & Palmer, 1828, pp. 57.

59. A Brief Statement of the Sufferings of Mary Dyer, occasioned by the Society called Shakers. Written by Herself. To which is added Affidavits and Certificates; also a Declaration from their own Publication. Concord, N. H., 1818, pp. 35.

60. A Compendious Narrative, Elucidating the Character, Disposition, and Conduct of Mary Dyer, from the Time of her Marriage, in 1799, till she left the Society called Shakers in 1815, etc. By her Husband, Joseph Dyer. To which is annexed a Remonstrance against the Testimony and Application of the said Mary for Legislative Interference. Concord, by Isaac Hill, for the Author, 1818, pp. 90.

61. The Memorial of the Society of People of Canterbury, in the County of Rockingham, and Enfield, in the County of Grafton, commonly called Shakers. (No date—but about 1818), pp. 13.

62. Tests of Divine Inspiration, or the Rudimental Principles by which True and False Revelation in all Eras of the World can be Unerringly Discriminated. By F. W. Evans. New Lebanon, 1853, pp. 128.

63. Public Discourses delivered in Substance at Union Village, Ohio, August, 1823, pp. 36.

64. A Revision and Confirmation of the Social Compact of the United Society called Shakers, at Pleasant Hill, Kentucky. Published by Order of the Church. Harrodsburg, Ky., 1830, pp. 12.

65. A Short Abridgment of the Rules of Music, with Lessons for Exercise, and a few Observations for New Beginners. New Lebanon, 1843; reprinted 1846, pp. 40.

66. Sixteen Years in the Senior Order of Shakers, a Narrative of Facts concerning that singular People. By Hervey Elkins. Hanover, N. H., 1853, pp. 136.

67. The Shaker Society *against* Gass & Banta. (Brief of a case in Kentucky.) No date, pp. 8.

68. Catalogue of Medicinal Plants, Extracts, Essential Oils, etc., prepared and for sale by the United Society of Shakers at Union Village, Ohio.

69. Shakerism Unmasked, or a History of the Shakers. By William J. Haskett. Pittsfield, 1828.

70. Two Years' Experience among the Shakers: A Condensed View of Shakerism as it is. By David R. Lamsen. West Boylston, 1848.

71. The Rise and Progress of the Serpent, from the Garden of Eden to the Present Day, with a Disclosure of Shakerism, etc.; also the Life and Sufferings of the Author, who was Mary Dyer, but now is Mary Marshall. Concord, N. H., 1847.

72. An Account of the People called Shakers—their Faith, Doctrines, and Practice. By Thomas Brown, of Cornwall, Orange County, N. Y. Troy, 1812.

73. History of American Socialisms. By John Humphrey Noyes. Philadelphia, J. B. Lippincott & Co., 1870, pp. 678.

74. Oneida Community Cooking, or a Dinner without Meat. By Harriet H. Skinner. Oneida, N. Y., 1873, pp. 51.

75. Essay on Scientific Propagation. By John Humphrey Noyes, with an Appendix containing a Health Report of the Oneida Community. By Theodore R. Noyes, M.D. Published by the Oneida Community, Oneida, N. Y. (No date—about 1873), pp. 32.

76. Male Continence. By John Humphrey Noyes. Published by the Oneida Community, Office of the *Circular*, Oneida, N. Y., 1872, pp. 24.

77. Hand-book of the Oneida Community, containing a Brief Sketch of its Present Condition, Internal Economy, and Leading Principles. Published by the Oneida Community, N. Y., 1871, pp. 64.

78. Salvation from Sin the End of Christian Faith. By J. H. Noyes. Published by the Oneida Community, Mount Tom Printing-house, Wallingford Community, Conn., 1869, pp. 48.

79. Dixon and his Copyists: A Criticism of the Accounts of the Oneida Community in "New America," "Spiritual Wives," and kindred Publications. By John Humphrey Noyes. Published by the Oneida Community, 1871, pp. 40.

80. Faith Facts; or a Confession of the Kingdom of God and the Age of Miracles. Edited by George Cragin. Oneida Reserve, N. Y., 1850, pp. 40.

81. Favorite Hymns for Community Singing, 1855, pp. 32. (Oneida Communists.)

82. The Way of Holiness; a Series of Papers published in the *Perfectionist*, New Haven. By J. H. Noyes. Printed by J. H. Noyes & Co., 1838.

[The company consisted of himself, his wife, brother, and two sisters.]

83. Paul not Carnal. New Haven, 1834.

84. The Perfectionist. New Haven, 1834.

85. The Way of Holiness. Putney, Vt., 1838.

86. The Witness. Ithaca, N. Y., and Putney, Vt., 1838–43.

87. The Perfectionist. Putney, Vt., 1843–46.

88. The Spiritual Magazine. Oneida, 1848–50.

89. The Free Church Circular. Oneida, 1850–51.

90. The Circular. Oneida, 1854–74.

91. First Annual Report of the Oneida Association. Oneida, 1849.

92. Faith Facts. Oneida, 1850.

93. Second Annual Report of the Oneida Association. Oneida, 1850.

94. Third Annual Report of the Oneida Association. Oneida, 1851.

95. Bible Communism. Brooklyn, 1853.

96. The Trapper's Guide. Wallingford, 1867.

97. Die Wahre Separation, oder die Wiedergeburt, dargestellt in geist-
reichen und erbaulichen Versammlung's Reden und Betrachtungen, besonders auf das gegenwärtige Zeitalter anwendbar. Gehalten an die
Gemeinde in Zoar im Jahre 1830. Gedruckt in Zoar, O., 1856. (The
True Separation, or the Second Birth, presented in Spiritual and Devotional Discourses and Lectures, applicable particularly to the Present
Time. Delivered to the Congregation at Zoar in 1830. Printed at Zoar,
1856.) Three volumes quarto, pp. 2574.

[These are by Bäumeler, the founder of the Zoar Community; and contain a
great many curious theories of life, present and future.]

98. Sammlung Auserlesener geistlicher Lieder, zum Gemeinschaftlichen
Gesäng und eigenen Gebrauch in Christlichen Familien. Zoar, Ohio, 1867.
(Collection of Selected Sacred Hymns, for the use of Churches and Indi-
viduals in Christian Families.) pp. 169.

[Bäumeler's Collection, now in use at Zoar. This is the "second and improved
edition."]

99. Jahrbücher der Wahren Inspiration's Gemeinden, oder Bezeugun-
gen des Geistes des Herrn. Gedruckt zu Eben-Ezer bei Buffalo. (Year-
books of the True Inspiration's Congregations, or Witnesses of the Spirit
of the Lord. Printed at Eben-Ezer, near Buffalo.)

[This is a series of volumes, containing the utterances of the "Inspired Instruments" of the Amana Society. They publish a volume for each year, but are now
in arrears.]

100. Historische Beschreibung der Wahren Inspiration's Gemeinschaft,
wie sie bestanden und sich fortgepflanzt hat, und was von den wichtig-

sten Ereignissen noch ausgefunden werden kann, besonders wie sie in den Jahren 1817 und 1818 und so fort wieder durch den Geist Gottes in neuen Werkzeugen aufgeweckt worden, und was seit der Zeit in und mit dieser Gemeinde und deren herzugekommenen Gliedern wichtiges vorge-fallen. Aufgeschrieben von Christian Metz. (Historical Description of the True Inspiration's Community, etc.) It is written by the Spiritual Head of the Amana Community.

101. J. J. J. Exegetische Reimen-Probe, über die Letzte Rede unsers Herrn Jesu Christi an Seine Wahrhaftige Jünger, etc., begriffen, abge-fasset und mitgetheilet in Einfaltigem Liebes Gehorsam. Neu aufgelegt im Jahr 1860. Eben-Ezer, bei Buffalo, N. Y. (Exegetical Rhymes con-cerning the Last Address of our Lord Jesus Christ to his True Disciples, etc., conceived, written down, and imparted by Simple, Loving Obedience. Newly printed at Eben-Ezer, N. Y., 1860.)

[It is in several volumes, and is a rhymed rendering, with numerous reflections, of several chapters of John, beginning with the 14th. The author was an old Mystic, E. L. Gruber. The first volume, the only one I have, has 437 pages. I do not know why this and other volumes have J. J. J. prefixed to the title.]

102. B. cum D! Die XXXVI. Sammlung, Das ist die Zweite Fortsetz-ung von Br. Johann Friederich Rock's Reise und Besuch im Jahr 1719, etc. Gedruckt im Jahr 1785. (The 36th Collection—that is, the Second Continuation of Brother John Frederick Rock's Journey and Visits in the year 1719. Printed in the year 1785.) pp. 145.

[This is one of the more ancient journals of the Inspirationists, and recounts the visions of Rock, one of their early prophets. I do not know what mystery lies in "B. cum D!"]

103. Das Liebes und Gedächtniszmahl des Leidens und Sterbens unsers Herrn und Heilandes Jesu Christi, etc. (The Supper of Love and Remem-brance of the Sufferings and Death of our Lord and Saviour Jesus Christ; how it was announced, ordered, and celebrated by his Word and Wit-ness in four parts, at Middle and Lower Eben-Ezer, in the year 1855. Eben-Ezer, N. Y., 1859, pp. 284.)

[I have given an account of this book in the description of Amana.]

104. Stimmen aus Zion, zum Lobe des Allmächtigen im Geist gesungen, von Johann Wilhelm Petersen, Dr. (A.D. 1698). (Voices from Zion, sung in the Spirit to the Praise of the Almighty, by John William Petersen, D.D.) Newly printed at Eben-Ezer, N. Y., 1851, pp. 456.

105. Davidisches Psalter Spiel der Kinder Zions, etc. (Psalms after the manner of David, for the Children of Zion : a Collection of old and newly

selected Spiritual Songs, brought together for the Use of all Souls desirous of Healing, and Sucklings of Wisdom ; but particularly for the Congregations of the Lord.) Third Edition, Amana, Iowa, 1871, pp. 1285, of which 111 are music.

[This is the hymn-book at present in use at Amana.]

106. J. J. J. Erster Beytrag zur Fortsetzung der Wahren Inspiration's Gemeinschaft, etc. (First Records of the Continuation of the True Inspiration's Congregations.) Büdingen, 1822.

[This volume contains the earliest utterances of Barbara Heyneman, the present Spiritual Head of Amana, and also "Four-and-twenty Rules of True Godliness," by J. A. Gruber, and "One-and-twenty Rules for the Examination of our Daily Lives," by E. L. Gruber.]

107. Die Schule der Weiszheit, als das Hoch-Teutsche A B C, vor Schüler und Meister in Israel. (The School of Wisdom, and High-German A B C, for Scholars and Masters in Israel.) 1748, pp. 128.

108. J. J. J. Catechetischer Unterricht von der Lehre des Heils, etc. (Catechism.) Printed at Eben-Ezer, 1857, and at Amana, 1872, "for the use and blessing of the Inspiration's Congregations."

[There are two volumes, pp. 96 and 84. The first for youth, the second for members in general.]

109. Der Kleine Kempis, oder Kurze Sprüche und Gebete, etc. (The Little Kempis, or Short Sayings and Prayers, from the Works of Thomas à Kempis, for the Edification of Children. Eben-Ezer, 1856, pp. 382.

110. Seelen Schatz der Gott Begierigen, etc. (Treasure of those who desire God ; showing how a man should die to sin, hate his Adamic life, deny himself, and live in Christ, in order that he may attain to the complete love of God and his neighbor, and achieve a part in Everlasting Salvation.) Eben-Ezer, N. Y., 1851, pp. 243.

111. Lebenserfahrungen von Carl G. Koch, Prediger des Evangeliums. (Experiences of Charles G. Koch, Preacher of the Gospel.) Cleveland, Ohio, 1871, pp. 411.

[This contains curious details of Count Leon's transactions at Economy, and of Keil, the head of the Aurora Community in Oregon.]

112. Hirten-Brief an die Wahren und Ächten Freymäurer Alten Systems. Neue Auflage, 5785. (Episcopal Letter addressed to the True and Faithful Freemasons of the Ancient System. New Edition, 5785.) Printed at Pittsburgh, 1855, pp. 288.

[This is a mystical work much prized by the Harmonists.]

113. The Harmony Society at Economy, Pennsylvania.   Founded by George Rapp, A.D. 1805.   With an Appendix.   By Aaron Williams, D.D., Pittsburgh, 1866, pp. 182.

114. The Bishop Hill Colony Case.   Answer of the Defendants.   Galva, Ill., 1868, pp. 94.

[Contains accounts of the Growth and Decay of the Bishop Hill Community.]

115. The Bishop Hill Colony Case—Statement of the Plaintiffs, Eric U. Norberg and others.

116. Några Sånger, Samt Böner.   Förfatlade af Erik Janson.   Galva, Ill., 1857.

[This is the hymn-book prepared by Eric Janson for the use of the Bishop Hill Commune.]

117. Constitution der Ikarischen Güter Gemeinschaft, etc.   (Constitution of the Icarian Commune, unanimously adopted on the 21st of February, 1850; and, after revision, again adopted 4th of May, 1851.)   Nauvoo, Ill.   Icarian Printing-office, August, 1844, pp. 27.

118. Wenn ich $500,000 hätte!   (If I had Half a Million Dollars!)   By E. Cabet, President of the Icarian Commune.   Nauvoo, Ill., November, 1854.

INDEX.

INDEX.

THE END.